WINE &
BEVERAGE
STANDARDS

WINE & BEVERAGE STANDARDS

DONALD A. BELL

University of Nevada, Las Vegas

VNR *VAN NOSTRAND REINHOLD*
New York

Library of Congress Catalog Card Number 88–31554
ISBN 0–442–22118–5

Printed in the United States of America

Van Nostrand Reinhold
115 Fifth Avenue
New York, New York 10003

Van Nostrand Reinhold (International) Company Limited
11 New Fetter Lane
London EC4P 4EE, England

Van Nostrand Reinhold
480 La Trobe Street
Melbourne, Victoria 3000, Australia

Macmillan of Canada
Division of Canada Publishing Corporation
164 Commander Boulevard
Agincourt, Ontario M1S 3C7, Canada

16 15 14 13 12 11 10 9 8 7 6 5 4 3 2 1

Library of Congress Cataloging in Publication Data

Bell, Donald A.
    Wine and beverage standards / Donald A. Bell.
        p.   cm.
    Bibliography: p.
    Includes index.
    ISBN 0–442–22118–5
    1. Wine and wine making—Standards.   2. Alcoholic beverages—
Standards.   I. Title.
TP548.B3654   1990
641.2'2'0218—dc 19   88–31554
                                                                 CIP

CONTENTS

PREFACE

This book about alcoholic beverages is intended to serve both as a reference work for the hospitality industry and as a text for related courses.

The focus of the book is on the four broad categories of alcoholic beverages: wines, beers, distilled spirits, and cordials, also known as liqueurs. The discussion focuses on establishing quality, processing, storage, service, and sensory standards, differentiating among the four categories and the various types of products within each category.

An overview of the classification of alcoholic beverages and the principles of fermentation and distillation precedes discussion of specific drinks. This introduction to the subject also describes the establishment and use of standards.

Unlike most alcoholic beverages, wine is the product of a single ingredient — grapes — and so its eventual characteristics depend more on a particular ingredient than do other beverages. Thus, the specific grape varieties are of critical importance, and a chapter is devoted to a discussion of the grapes commonly used in the major wine-making countries, as well as their growth and sensory characteristics.

Because alcoholic beverages are subject to government regulations, litigation, and social and cultural influences more than any other product served or used by the hospitality industry, the book also features a section on alcoholic beverages and the law. This deals with federal, state, and local regulations, the types of things that may be regulated, tax structures, dramshop laws and liabilities, public concern with alcohol abuse, and other such matters. Several of the European countries that have wine-making traditions and customs going back centuries also have well-established and specific wine-making regulations, and these are discussed as well.

CHAPTER ONE

INTRODUCTION TO ALCOHOLIC BEVERAGES

WHAT ARE ALCOHOLIC BEVERAGES?

Alcoholic beverages are any potable, or drinkable, liquids containing *ethyl alcohol*, also called *ethanol*. There are four main types of these products: *wines*, *beers*, *distilled spirits*, and *cordials*, also known as *liqueurs*. The amount of alcohol that each type contains varies widely. Beers may contain as little as 2 or 3 percent. Wines typically have an alcoholic strength of 10 to 14 percent, although sherries can go as high as 20 percent. Cordials/liqueurs have alcoholic strengths ranging from the high end of the wine spectrum up to 40 percent or more. Distilled spirits are the highest in alcoholic content, and although the trend today is toward less strength, most spirits still are found in the 40 to 45 percent range, with many examples containing up to 50 percent. There are even several rums commercially available that contain 75 percent alcohol!

According to the federal government's definition of alcoholic beverages, the alcoholic content can range all the way from 0.5 percent to 95 percent. This definition goes back to Prohibition, when the government established what an intoxicating beverage was, and it remains on the books more than a half century later—even though an enormous quantity of a beverage with 0.5 percent alcohol would have to be consumed before anyone actually became intoxicated.

The uses of alcoholic beverages pretty much coincide with the alcoholic

1

content. The low-alcohol products—wines and beers—are normally consumed just as they are. That is, they are drunk straight, or neat. Cordials and liqueurs, usually containing significantly higher percentages of alcohol, may be consumed either straight or mixed, but the amount used in each drink is much smaller than with beer or wine. Distilled spirits are usually consumed mixed with water, soda, fruit juice, or some other liquid. Various flavorings are also widely used with drinks mixed from distilled spirits; this is uncommon with the other types of alcoholic beverages.

CLASSIFICATION OF ALCOHOLIC BEVERAGES

Alcoholic beverages are always created through a conversion process called *alcoholic fermentation*. This produces an end product in the case of wines and beers; distilled spirits and cordials, or liqueurs, must be processed further to extract the alcohol from the fermented beverage.

Depending on the process of creation, alcoholic beverages can be classified into three broad categories: fermented beverages, fermented and distilled drinks, and compounded spirits. There are many examples of each (Table 1–1).

Fermented Beverages

Wine. The fermented juice of a plant product. Wines are typically made from fruits, although it is possible to make them from vegetables, dandelions, and other plants. If a product is identified simply as wine, it must be made from grapes. Wines made from other fruits, such as apples, plums, or peaches, must be identified by the fruit used: apple wine, plum wine, peach wine, and so on. The same regulations apply to wines made from other plants: the plant must be identified.

Beer. A spirituous liquid fermented from a mixture of grains and water.

Mead. A beverage drunk by the ancient Gauls and Anglo-Saxons, fermented from honey and containing about 8 percent alcohol (although one product made in England contains 14.5 percent).

Pulque. A beverage fermented from the milky juice of a species of agave plant, a member of the cactus family. Originating in Mexico, pulque has 4 to 6 percent alcohol by volume and is generally drunk fresh, without aging.

Sake. A fermented beverage originating in Japan. It is made from rice that is cleansed, steamed, and allowed to ferment. Sake contains from 12 to 16 percent alcohol.

Table 1-1   Classification of Alcoholic Beverages

Fermented Beverages	
Wine	The fermented juice of a plant product, typically fruits
Beer	Fermented from a mixture of grains and water
Pulque	Fermented from the milky juice of the agave plant
Sake	A Japanese fermented beverage made from rice
Mead	Fermented honey
Fermented and Distilled Drinks	
Brandy	Distilled wine
Whisky	Distilled from a fermented mash of grains
Vodka	Distilled from a fermented mash of grain, without a whisky's distinctive color, odor, and flavor
Rum	Distilled from fermented surgarcane and/or molasses
Tequila	Distilled from the fermented juice of the mescal variety of the agave plant
Compounded Spirits	
Gin	A grain spirit flavored with juniper berries and other botanicals
Cordials and Liqueurs	Spirits that have been flavored, colored, and sweetened

Fermented and Distilled Drinks

Brandy. A product made by distillation of a wine. If the term *brandy* is used by itself, the product must be distilled from grape wine. Brandy therefore means grape brandy. A brandy can be distilled from any type of fruit wine (typically, only fruit wines are used), but in each case the type of brandy must be identified: plum brandy, cherry brandy, pear brandy, and so forth. The most famous brandy in the world, Cognac, is a grape brandy distilled from wine made in a legally delimited geographical area surrounding the town of Cognac, France. Many other areas, regions, and countries make famous brandies: for example, Armagnac is another famous French grape brandy, *grappa* is an Italian grape brandy, Calvados is a French apple brandy, kirsch is a cherry brandy, and slivowitz is a plum brandy.

Whisky. A beverage distilled from a mash of grains. As brandy is distilled from a wine, whisky is distilled from what is basically a beer. In fact, the fermented liquid is called distillers beer. The types of grains used, the quality and type of water, the method of distillation, the proof (or alcoholic strength) of distillation, the length of maturation, and the type of wood used in aging all contribute to the quality and type of whisky produced. Incidentally, U.S.

regulations spell the word *whisky,* as the Scots and Canadians do, though Americans often spell it *whiskey,* as do the Irish. Similarly, the plural form is commonly spelled either *whiskies,* as in this book, or *whiskeys.*

Vodka. A beverage distilled from a mash made by fermenting a grain mixture. In this it is similar to whiskies, but while a whisky has a distinctive color, odor, and flavor, vodka processing is directed toward elimination of those characteristics. This is done though skillful distillation at high proof and post-distillation processing techniques.

Rum. A distilled beverage from a spirituous liquid made by fermenting sugarcane and/or molasses.

Tequila. The distillate of the fermented juice of the blue variety of the agave plant. As wine is the precursor of brandy, and beer is the precursor of whisky and vodka, pulque is the precursor of tequila.

Neutral Spirits. When alcohol containing liquids are distilled at very high proofs (95 percent alcohol or higher), the resulting distillate is nearly pure alcohol and has little, if any, distinctive character, hence the term *neutral spirits.* Neutral spirits are nearly always produced from a fermented grain mixture. In this case, the correct term is *neutral grain spirits.*

Compounded Spirits

Gin. A juniper-flavored spirit obtained by the distillation and rectification (a further distillation process) of the grain spirits of malted barley and rye, or sometimes corn and maize.

Cordials/Liqueurs. Neutral spirits, brandy, whisky, or other distilled spirits mixed or redistilled with fruits, flavors, plants, or other natural flavoring agents, or extracts derived from such materials. U.S. law states that they must contain a minimum of 2.5 percent sugar (by finished weight).

ALCOHOLIC FERMENTATION

Alcoholic fermentation is the anaerobic (living and producing in the absence of air or free oxygen) conversion of sugar into carbon dioxide and ethyl alcohol in the presence of yeasts. This is also known as *primary fermentation.* When the same chemical reaction is used for specialized products, it is called *secondary fermentation.* Sparkling wines undergo a secondary fermentation in closed containers, thereby retaining the carbon dioxide. Beers may also have a secondary fermentation for the same purpose.

Malolactic fermentation, in which malic acid is converted to weaker lactic acid, is a chemical reaction important to some wines, but it is not an alcoholic fermentation at all. This type of fermentation will be discussed under wine-making standards in Chapter two.

Chemistry of Fermentation

Although alcoholic beverages have been known to humankind for virtually its entire recorded history, it is only relatively recently that we have understood what occurs during the fermentation process. The first attempt at a scientific explanation came from George Ernest Stahl, born in Germany in 1660, in his book *Zymotechnica fundamentalis*. While his theories seem rather bizarre today, they were widely accepted during the eighteenth century.

The eighteenth-century French chemist Antoine Lavoisier was the first to show that by the process of fermentation, sugar is transformed into alcohol and carbon dioxide. Another Frenchman, named Latour, was the first (in 1837) to describe yeast as the organism producing the alcoholic fermentation, although he thought yeast was a vegetable organism. Knetzing and Turpin, in 1838, claimed that yeast consisted of animated organisms, causing fermentation through their own living development. The pair's theory was disregarded by most of their peers, however, and it was left to Louis Pasteur, beginning in 1857, to show that yeast comprised living organisms after all—minute, one-celled fungi—and that fermentation is possible only with live yeast.

In 1810, the French scientist Joseph-Louis Gay-Lussac reported his famous equation describing the overall chemical reaction in fermentation:

$$C_6H_{12}O_6 \rightarrow 2C_2H_5OH + 2CO_2$$

This means that one molecule of sugar yields two molecules of ethyl alcohol, or ethanol, and two of carbon dioxide. Pasteur was able to confirm its overall validity, but he also showed the presence of several unaccounted-for by-products such as glycerol, lactic acid, acetaldehyde, and acetic acid. It is known now that there is a complex series of chain reactions, beginning with glucose and ending with ethanol and carbon dioxide, and that the yeasts themselves do not cause the reactions but instead provide various enzymes that catalyze or speed up the rate of the reactions. The actual conversion takes place in a series of steps, each one controlled by specific enzymes and other necessary materials, such as metal ions.

Because alcoholic fermentation is an anaerobic process, it does not require air. The presence of air, in fact, would slow down or eliminate the production of alcohol. Whatever small amount of air is trapped in the fermenting liquid is consumed during the rapid multiplication of yeast cells in the beginning of fermentation. Escaping carbon dioxide during the latter stages also aids in preventing access to air or free oxygen.

If air or free oxygen were widespread, the fermentation would become aerobic, reducing or eliminating alcohol as an end product. This is due to the very considerable difference in energy released during the two types of fermentation. Both aerobic and anaerobic fermentation are exothermic—that is, they give off heat. During alcoholic—anaerobic—fermentation, consumption of one molecule of sugar results in a change of 56 kilocalories (56,000 calories) of energy. Aerobic fermentation, however, releases 673 kilocalories of energy, about an elevenfold increase. This causes a significant difference in what takes place during the fermentation.

The yeasts require the energy released for their metabolism and reproduction. In anaerobic fermentation, because relatively little of the potential energy is released as sugar is consumed, the yeasts have to work harder at converting sugar into alcohol, instead of reproducing. During aerobic fermentation, however, there is great efficiency in energy production from the consumption of sugar, fueling increased yeast growth at the expense of alcohol production. Most of the sugar, in fact, is consumed to aid yeast cells in their building and reproduction processes. This is why, when wine makers and distillers (or other food producers) want to grow yeasts, as opposed to producing alcohol, they grow them aerobically.

The equation for alcoholic fermentation can be restated as follows:

$$C_6H_{12}O_6 \xrightarrow[\text{Enzymes}]{\text{Yeast}} 2C_2H_5OH + 2CO_2 + 56 \text{ kcal energy}$$

This also can be written out: one molecule of sugar, catalyzed by yeast enzymes, produces two molecules of ethanol, two molecules of carbon dioxide, and fifty-six kilocalories of energy.

Because the primary purpose of fermentation is to produce alcohol, the processor of alcoholic beverages is very interested in how much alcohol can be produced. The theoretical yield is 51.1 percent ethanol and 48.9 percent carbon dioxide, although the actual yields are only about 90 to 95 percent of the theoretical. Among the reasons for this are the amount and kinds of by-products produced, the amount of sugar used by the yeasts, the proportion of sugar used to synthesize new yeasts, the amount of sugar used by other microorganisms, the rate and temperature of fermentation, the air available (there will always be some amount of aerobic fermentation activity), agitation of the fermenting mass, alcohol loss due to volatilization (creation of vapor), and the variety and maturation of the grapes (or similar source). The formula used by most wine makers is one degree Brix = 0.535 percent alcohol by volume; Brix (a scale named for A. F. W. Brix, a nineteenth-century

German inventor) is a measurement of solids in solution and is assumed in practice to be sugar. Thus, a grape mixture with a Brix or sugar content of 20 percent would produce a wine with an alcoholic content of 10.7 percent by volume.

Although ethanol is the primary alcohol produced, it is not the only one. Higher alcohols, known as *fusel oils*, are also products of alcoholic fermentation, and while they are present only in minute amounts, they are very important to the quality and distinctiveness of the final product. These are alcohols with more than the two carbon atoms of ethanol. Some of the more common ones are propanol (three atoms of carbon), butanol (four atoms), and amyl alcohol (five atoms). Methanol, or wood alcohol, has only one carbon atom, and is not considered to be produced by alcoholic fermentation. It can, however, be derived from the hydrolysis of pectin—the decomposition of water-soluble substances that bind cell walls in plant matter—and is normally present in wines in very minute amounts.

Importance and Use of Yeasts

The function of the yeast is to provide suitable enzymes that in turn catalyze the desired series of chain reactions. Because grape skins are populated with wild yeasts, fermentation can proceed naturally; all that has to be done is to gather and crush the grapes. The naturally occurring yeasts will cause a fermentation. This is how wine undoubtedly first was made, and it must have been discovered accidentally.

Leaving the fermentation to nature, however, may not necessarily be the best thing to do. All yeasts are not equal when it comes to alcoholic fermentation; some are much more desirable than others, and some are definitely undesirable. By not specifying particular yeast types, the wine maker sacrifices a great deal of control and risks the success of the wine-making process.

European wine makers make wide use of natural yeast fermentation. Some consider the naturally occurring yeasts to be a critical factor in quality. In comparing this with U.S. wine-making procedures, it must be remembered that vineyard areas in Europe have been established by trial and error over hundreds of years—a thousand or more, in some instances. Europeans produce only a limited range of wine types, often only one, in sometimes large wine-growing areas. Trial and error have shown them which grapes and wine types are best suited for each particular set of geographical and climatological conditions. The presence of specific strains of wild yeasts are most definitely an important part of these conditions. European vineyard areas also tend to be more consistent in climate from one mile to another than do those of California, for instance. An entire European region such as Beaujolais in central France grows basically only one grape and makes only one type of wine, while in the Napa Valley of California a very broad range of wine types is made from an equally broad range of grape varieties. It is not realistic to assume that wild yeast populations would be equally suitable for all these wines.

Another important factor is that California grapes do not have as reliable or as good a source of wild yeast populations as do European grapes. Research has shown the presence in California of many types of yeasts on grapes, not all of which are suitable for wine fermentation. The most desirable yeast is *Saccharomyces cerevisiae*, but it may not even be part of a local population. Even when it does appear, it is outnumbered by unwanted microorganisms. A major problem with wild yeasts is their unpredictability; another is their tendency to multiply and become dominant very quickly. Wild, natural yeast fermentation can result in *stuck*, or unfinished, fermentation and the formation of unpleasant odors. *S. cerevisiae*, of which a great variety of strains exists, has a high reproduction rate, high fermentation efficiency, and tolerance of relatively high alcohol levels (15 to 16 percent). As pointed out, a fermentation efficiency of up to 95 percent is possible (producing 95 percent of the potential alcohol). This is true with *S. cerevisiae;* but some wild yeasts' side reactions can consume much of the sugar, at the expense of alcohol production.

Beer production and the fermentation of alcoholic beverages for distillation purposes require the use of specially prepared yeast cultures; they cannot depend on the presence of wild yeasts. Beer and spirit manufacturers also use strains of *S. cerevisiae* for their fermentation.

The University of California at Davis long ago began the preparation of pure wine yeast cultures for starting fermentation. In the 1960s, the Montrachet strain was the most popular type. In the 1970s there was a great deal of research and experimentation with other strains in order to reduce volatile acidity, eliminate undesirable odors, evaluate the differences in wine aromas, and gain increased control over fermentation. Specific strains have been isolated to perform particular kinds of fermentation. Examples are slow, fast, low-temperature, and high-alcohol, as well as kinds intended to develop distinctive flavors.

Controlling Fermentation

It should be obvious that fermentation is a very complex series of chemical reactions. Much is now known about what happens and why, and the producer of alcoholic beverages can exercise a great deal of control over the process. There are major ways in which the wine maker or distilled beverage producer can control the fermentation process and the type of beverage made.

Yeast Strains. There are countless strains of yeasts that can be used. Each will have its own specific effect on the character of the finished beverage, as well as on the fermentation process itself. It is not as simple as merely mixing some yeast into the liquid to be fermented, be it fruit juice, a grain-water mixture, or whatever. Wine makers strive to produce particular types of wines and will select the yeasts with care. Red wines, white wines, sparkling wines, sauternes or Beerenauslese-type sweet wines, high-alcohol wines, and low-alcohol wines are just a few examples of products calling for different approaches in yeast selection.

Temperature. Fermentation temperature is of critical importance today in wine making, and proper selection of yeasts is necessary for control. Yeasts, like all living organisms, have specific temperature requirements. If the temperature is too high or too low, they will cease to function. In addition, different strains do not react alike to different temperatures. Research has shown, for example, that various strains of *S. cerevisiae* vary considerably in their ability to carry out fermentation, depending on the temperature. Some are highly efficient at low temperatures but will not produce adequate amounts of alcohol at high ones, while with other strains the reverse is true.

In general, wine yeasts ferment effectively over a temperature range of 50 to 90° F (10 to 32° C). If the temperature exceeds 100° F (38° C), the yeasts may die, resulting in stuck, or incomplete, fermentation. It can be very difficult to restart and complete the fermentation when this occurs. Other problems with excessive temperatures include encouragement of microbial spoilage, increased loss of alcohol and other volatiles due to evaporation, and increased formation of undesirable by-products.

In spirit making, the fermentation temperature should not be allowed to exceed 90° F (32° C). If there are adequate means for cooling the fermenting mass, temperatures of 81 to 86° F (27 to 30° C) may be used. If there are no cooling facilities, it is recommended to start the fermentation at no higher than 70° F (21° C).

White wines today are fermented at relatively low temperatures, 50 to 60° F (10 to 16° C), although specific types may vary considerably. These wines are fresher, fruitier, and have greater delicacy. There is also less bacterial and wild yeast activity, higher alcohol yield, and reduced loss of volatile aromatics.

Red wines are fermented at much higher temperatures than are whites, mainly because of the necessity for color extraction from the skins. The temperature range for red wine fermentation is from 70 to about 82° F (21 to 28° C).

During red wine fermentation, carbon dioxide attaches to the skins and other solids and is carried to the surface, where it forms a *cap*, a dense formation of solid material. Temperature increases due to the cap can be as much as 50° F (10° C) and therefore have to be controlled. This is done by physically breaking up the cap with frequent pumping of the *must*, or pulp and skins, from the bottom of the tank over the cap. The traditional European method was to break it up by punching it with hands, boards, or whatever was available. It was not unknown for people to strip and jump in, although it is unlikely this procedure is followed today. Because of this heat buildup and the subsequent punching, red wines were fermented in smaller containers than were whites.

Time. The fermentation time is a factor of the temperature. White wines, fermented at lower temperatures, naturally take longer; how much longer depends on how low the temperature is. An ideal for white wines is said to be when the sugar is converted at the rate of one degree Brix per day, or for a total of from fifteen to twenty-five days. Red wines typically ferment to dryness (no remaining fermentable sugars) in about a week.

Choice of Materials for Fermenters. Fermentation was traditionally done in open wooden containers, and the temperature was whatever the ambient temperature of the environment was. The time depended on the temperature. As a result, the wine maker did not have a lot of control over what was going on, which in turn would lead to great variations in the wines from year to year. Champagne is said to have been discovered accidentally due to unexpected temperature fluctuations. One year, the temperature cooled unusually quickly and stopped the fermentation. Thinking the wine was finished, the wine makers bottled it; in the spring, when it again warmed up, the fermentation began anew. Sparkling wine was born—probably at the expense of many exploding bottles!

In order to ferment white wines at low temperature, it is necessary to have some sort of temperature-controlled fermenting facility. Water-jacketed fermenters made from stainless steel are widely used for this purpose; they can be adjusted for whatever temperature is wanted. Some white wines, notably barrel-fermented Chardonnays, are still fermented in open wooden containers at higher temperatures than is usual for white wines today. In such cases, the wine makers start with musts that have higher solid content, and they typically use Montrachet and Champagne yeast strains. Their objective is to attain the greater complexity that results from the wood contact, increased air contact, and higher temperature. The wine will be less fruity but richer tasting and heavier in body. On the other hand, the process is more difficult to control, it is easier for problems to arise, and it is more demanding of a wine maker's skills.

Residual Sugar. Not all wines are fermented dry. A dry wine is a result of a complete fermentation; that is, all the fermentable sugar has been consumed during the process. Many wines are intended to have varying degrees of sweetness to them, from barely perceptible to very sweet. The sugar remaining in the finished wine is termed residual sugar.

There were two traditional methods of producing these types of wines. With one, the wine maker added sweet, concentrated grape juice to the dry, completely fermented wine. The juice was concentrated by water removal and could have a sugar content of as much as 60 percent. The other method involved the use of a sweet reserve. This is a German technique and calls for sweetening the dry wine with sweet (not concentrated) juice. With today's refrigerated equipment, the process is both simpler and more natural. By lowering the temperature, the fermentation is stopped before all the sugar is consumed. The result is sugar in the finished wine. The yeasts are then removed by filtration, centrifuging, or natural settling. This is now the method most used in California.

This technique is not suitable for all viticultural areas, however, because there must be sufficient sugar in the grapes to provide for adequate alcohol at the time the fermentation is stopped. Many cool growing areas, such as Germany and New York State, simply do not produce grapes regularly with sufficient natural sugar to do this. They may have insufficient alcohol even when the fermentation proceeds to its conclusion.

Sulfur Dioxide. Sulfur dioxide (SO_2) is universally used to control alcoholic fermentation. It inhibits wild, undesirable yeasts without interfering with the activity of *S. cerevisiae.* It also acts as an antioxidant, selectively reacting with oxygen to keep it from causing browning reactions in the must and to promote aerobic fermentation.

Two Special Cases of Fermentation. Carbonic maceration and *thermovinification* are special techniques used in limited areas. The former is an unusual method used in Beaujolais, France, to produce exceptionally fresh and fruity red wines. The grapes are not crushed or stemmed but are placed in the fermenters whole. Intracellular fermentation takes place until the grapes break down. This is called carbonic maceration because when the grapes are not crushed, and the cap is not aerated by punching, the grapes ferment anaerobically surrounded by carbon dioxide.

Thermovinification is a red wine technique developed in France and Germany and used, at present, only experimentally in California. After the grapes are crushed, the must is immediately heated to 156 to 160°F (69 to 71°C). This extracts a great deal of color from the skins. The must is held at this temperature for about a half hour, cooled, and pressed; then the juice is fermented, as with white wines. The result is a softer, less tannic wine that is different from wine made in the traditional manner from the same grapes.

DISTILLATION

Distillation is a separation process; the ethyl alcohol is removed or separated from the fermented beverage. This is done by taking advantage of the different boiling points of the main constituents of fermented beverages, water and alcohol. Water vaporizes (turns from a liquid into a gas) at 212°F while ethyl alcohol changes at 173° F. Therefore, if a spirituous liquid is heated to below the boiling point of water, the alcohol can be selectively vaporized. If this vapor is collected and cooled, it will turn back into a liquid consisting mostly of alcohol. As already noted, the fermentation ingredients determine the classification of the spirit. If alcohol is distilled from wine, the spirit is a brandy; if it is distilled from beer, the product is a whisky; if it is distilled from a beverage fermented from sugarcane, the spirit is rum; and so forth.

Rectification

Technically, if distillation is performed on an already distilled substance, or on one in which all components have the same boiling point, it is termed *rectification*. A rectified spirit is one that has undergone purification by distillation at a licensed rectifier's premises. From a practical standpoint, there is in the United States a rectification tax that is levied on any process that changes the character of the spirit. Examples of such practices are given in Table 1–2.

Alcoholic Proof

The term *proof* is used to describe alcoholic strength, and it has an interesting origin. Prior to the development of alcohol-measuring instruments, the strength of the newly distilled spirit was determined by mixing the spirit equally with gunpowder and lighting it. If it was too strong or too weak, it burned either too fast or not at all. When it was of a proper strength, it burned evenly, with a blue flame, and the spirit was said to have been "proved." This was later found to be about 50 percent alcohol. Thus, the term *100 proof* was used to describe

Table 1–2   Rectification Practices

Blending of two different spirits
Blending of whisky with neutral spirits
Blending of two different whiskies
Redistillation of wood-aged whiskies
Redistillation of neutral spirits for potable products
Addition of anything except water
Compounding spirits, essential oils, or other flavorings and sugar to make
    cordials/liqueurs and gin

a beverage with 50 percent alcohol. A liquid of pure alcohol would therefore be 200 proof. This is the American system of labeling alcoholic content: the proof divided in half equals the percentage of alcohol by volume. The British also use proof, but differently: 100 British proof equals 57.1 percent ethanol by volume. The French use a system called Gay-Lussac, after the scientist, that describes the percentage of alcohol in degrees Gay-Lussac. A spirit with 40 percent alcohol by volume would be 40° GL. Most of the rest of the world uses percentage by volume (Table 1–3).

Three Uses of Proof. Proof can be used to describe the alcoholic content at three different stages in the life of the spirit. One is the proof at the time of distillation, another is the proof of the spirit to be aged, and the third is the bottling proof. The spirit is seldom aged at the same proof at which it comes from the still. For example, it could be cut with water prior to being placed in wood. Following wood aging, the spirit is cut with water again to reach the commercial strength, the bottled alcoholic content.

A spirit could be distilled at 150 proof (75 percent alcohol), cut with water to 120 proof (60 percent alcohol) for wood aging, and four years later cut again with water to 80 proof (40 percent alcohol) prior to bottling. The bottling proof is usually a marketing or economic decision, although there are federal regulations in some cases. The designation Bottled in Bond is one; the requirement is 100 proof. The aging proof may be regulated, either by legal stipulation or by tradition. The distillation proof, however, is of critical importance and is carefully specified by law for virtually all products in all countries.

Relationship between Distillation Proof and Product Character. The differences among spirits are in the portion of the distillate other than the ethyl alcohol. To paraphrase Gertrude Stein: ethyl alcohol is ethyl alcohol is ethyl alcohol. If a spirit were distilled at 200 proof, there would be absolutely no difference among products obtained from a wine distillation, a distillation of grain mash, rice, or sugarcane, or even a distillation performed in a laboratory. Other constituents, however, are also removed along with alcohol during the distillation.

Table 1–3 Comparison of Alcoholic Content Labeling

Country	Label Language	Alcoholic Content
United States	100 proof	50 percent by volume
Great Britain	100 proof	57.1 percent by volume
France	50° GL	50 percent by volume
Most other countries	50 percent	50 percent by volume

If a spirit were distilled at 150 proof, it would contain 75 percent alcohol and 25 percent *congeners*, or secondary products. Such a spirit would have considerably more character in the way of distinctive flavor, aroma, and body than would the 200 proof spirit. It would not, however, have the flavor or aroma potential of a spirit distilled at 120 proof: 60 percent alcohol and 40 percent congeners.

Specific types of alcoholic products must be distilled at particular proofs if they are to be typical examples of that type. Vodka, for example, is not expected to show any distinctive flavor or aromatic characteristics and is expected to be light bodied. It is made from spirits distilled at as high a proof as possible and then further processed to remove whatever congeneric compounds remain. In fact, anything over 190 proof is legally called neutral spirits because it has no distinctive characteristics other than those attributed to alcohol. Bourbon, which is certainly much more flavorful and aromatic and has more body than vodka, cannot be distilled at over 160 proof. Cognac cannot be distilled at over 144 proof; in practice, the average is 140. California brandy, which is typically much lighter than Cognac brandies, has a legal distillation maximum of 170 proof. Light rums are distilled at 160 to 180 proof. Scotch malt (unblended) whisky is distilled at 140 to 142 proof, while the lighter Canadian whisky is distilled out at varying strengths ranging from 140 to 180 proof.

Components of Distilled Spirits

Because most spirits are bottled at less than 100 proof, the primary component is usually water. Whatever water is not provided by the distillation is added when cutting to the aging and bottling strength. Distilled water is used to avoid any flavor or aroma problems. The other major component is, of course, ethanol, or ethyl alcohol.

The congeners, those secondary products produced during alcoholic fermentation, consist of acids, esters, aldehydes, fusel oils, extracts of mineral salts, and solids in minute quantities. Collectively, they do not amount to much in percentage, but they are the factors that determine product character. They come from the fermentation ingredients, and are by-products of the fermentation reactions, as well as from the distillation and aging processes. There are always some congeners, because it is not possible to distill at 200 proof except in a laboratory. Commercial distillation never exceeds 192 proof; but at 96 percent alcohol and up to 4 percent congeners, that product would have little, if any, distinctiveness.

Esters are volatile substances that give aroma to the spirits; their capture during distillation is very important. Aldehydes are produced from alcohol and air reactions and contribute to the character of the spirit. The formidable-sounding fusel oils are actually alcohols containing more than the two carbon atoms of ethyl alcohol. Called higher alcohols, they form complex mixtures that add significantly to spirits. Not all these compounds are desirable, and even those that are should be present in specific amounts. This requires proper equipment and skillful manipulation of that equipment on the part of the distiller.

Pot Stills (Batch Processing)

The original, and still simplest, distillation apparatus is a *pot still* (Fig. 1–1). It is a batch-processing method, not a continuous one. That is, it can process only one load, or batch, of fermented liquid at a time. There are stills that

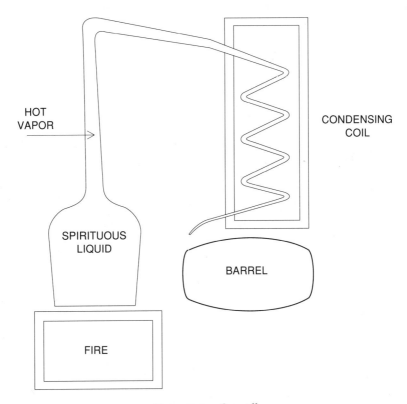

Figure 1–1.   Pot still.

operate continuously; as long as a spirituous liquid is fed in one end, a distilled spirit will come out of the other end. These types of stills will be described in the next section. The pot still, in its most elemental form, consists of a receptacle into which the liquid can be placed and heated. There is some sort of long, tapered neck attached at the top to collect the vapors formed when the liquid is heated. A spiral copper tube is attached to this neck and passes through a cooling medium, usually water. The decrease in temperature condenses the vapor to a liquid again.

The product is a distilled spirit, but it is not necessarily a finished product. Cognac, for instance, is the result of a double distillation, and Irish whiskey (spelled with an *e*) traditionally gets a triple distillation (Fig. 1–2). Highly volatile elements, which vaporize first, can be collected separately, as can the least volatile elements because they vaporize last. In Cognac distillation, the highly volatile fraction is called the *heads* and the least volatile, the *tailings*. The middle distillate is the one that contains the most alcohol, and it is given the second distillation. The heads and tailings are separated again during the second distillation, and the middle portion becomes Cognac.

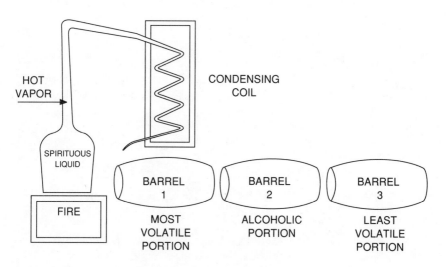

Single distillation: The middle barrel is the end product.

Double distillation: The middle barrel is redistilled and the middle portion of that distillation is the end product.

Triple distillation: The middle barrel is again redistilled and the middle portion of that distillation is the end product.

Figure 1–2. Single distillation, double distillation, and triple distillation.

Pot stills are thought by many to produce a better and more flavorful product and are used for most of the world's finest spirits. Cognac and the better Calvados brandies are all pot-distilled, as are Scotch malt whisky, most Irish whiskey, and some rums and liqueurs. Pot stills generally distill at 65 to 70 percent alcohol (in the second distillation; the first is much lower), and this is close to the optimum for fusel oil extraction. Continuous stills generally draw off the spirits at higher proofs. Thus, fusel oil concentrations are likely to be higher with pot distillation. Esters are concentrated at a level slightly below fusel oils and are drawn off quickly in the heads fraction. The challenge for the distiller is to include enough of them in the middle distillate without including undesirable odorous elements from the heads portion. The least volatile elements, those in the tailings portion, are undesirable because they are low in ethanol and contain heavy, unsuitable flavors and odors. However, they can be redistilled to recover whatever ethanol they do contain.

Coffey Stills (Continuous Processing)

Coffey stills are continuous stills (Fig. 1–3). They produce a distilled spirit continuously as long as they are supplied with a spirituous liquid. First invented by Scotsman Robert Stein in 1826, the design was perfected and patented by Aeneas Coffey, inspector general of excise in Ireland, in 1832. The most common name for the apparatus today is Coffey still, but the terms *patent, tower, column,* and *continuous still* may be used as well. A very important innovation, compared to the pot still, is the ability of the continuous still to separate the many vapor fractions. The removal of ethanol from what is basically a water-alcohol mixture is the basic objective of distillation, but there are many other valuable fractions. The main advantage, of course, is speed and, therefore, increased productivity. The apparatus does not have to be emptied and cleaned between batches, as does a pot still.

Coffey stills are used for most whiskies, as well as American brandy, light-bodied rums, vodka, gin, most cordials/liqueurs, and neutral spirits (Table 1–4).

The apparatus can be described in a simplified way: The alcohol-containing liquid is pumped into the top of a tall column or tower called a *rectifier*. The liquid is carried down to the bottom of the column in twisting pipes. As it descends, hot vapors rising through the column warm the alcoholic liquid. This warm liquid is now pumped to the top of a second column, the *analyzer*. This column is separated from top to bottom by a series of perforated plates. As the hot liquid enters at the top, it drains through the top plate onto the one below, and so on until it reaches the bottom. Steam, entering from the bottom, causes vaporization of the volatile elements of the liquid as it travels down

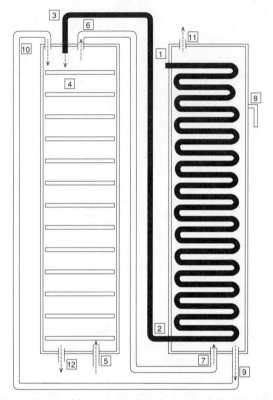

1. The mash enters at the top of the column and travels downward through twisting pipes.

2. At the bottom the liquid, which is now very hot, is pumped to the top of the second column.

3. The hot liquid enters the second column.

4. The liquid seeps down to the bottom via a series of perforated plates.

5. As the mash is descending, it is heated by steam, which enters at the bottom.

6. The steam vaporizes the volatile elements, which rise and pass out as vapor.

7. The hot vapor is brought to the bottom of the first column, where it rises. This hot vapor is what heats the mash in the first step as it travels downward.

8. As the vapor rises, it is cooled by the downward-traveling mash. At the appropriate level, the condensed vapor is drawn off.

9. The least volatile elements condense first and fall to the bottom to be drained away.

10. The condensed least volatile elements are added to the second column, to be redistilled.

11. The most volatile elements remain vaporous and exit at the top.

12. The condensed steam and water from the mash in step number 8 fall to the bottom and are drained away.

Figure 1–3. Coffey still.

Table 1-4 Comparison of Pot- and Coffey-Distilled Spirits

Spirit	Distillation Technique
Whisky	
Bourbon	Coffey
American blended	Coffey
American light	Coffey
Canadian	Coffey
Scotch (malt)	Pot
Scotch (blended)	Coffey
Irish	Pot
Brandy	
American	Coffey
Cognac	Pot
Armagnac	Pot
Calvados (top classification)	Pot
Fruit eaux-de-vie	Pot
Rum (light: Puerto Rico, Virgin Islands, Cuba, Dominican Republic, Venezuela, Mexico)	Coffey
Rum (full bodied: Jamaica, Haiti, Martinique)	Pot
Tequila	Pot
Vodka	Coffey
Gin	Coffey
Neutral spirits	Coffey
Cordials and liqueurs	The base spirit is generally coffey-distilled, but may be made in pot stills

through the column. Only the water and least volatile elements reach the bottom, and they are drained away. The vapors are drawn off at the top and sent back to the first column, the rectifier.

These vapors enter the rectifier at the bottom and rise—in fact, they are the hot vapors that are used to warm the incoming liquid. As the hot vapors warm the liquid, the liquid cools the vapors. The result is that the vapor condenses back into a liquid. Depending on the height at which this occurs, distillates of varying strength can be drawn off. At relatively lower levels, the less volatile elements condense, while at higher levels, the more volatile fractions turn back into a liquid.

In this manner, the distiller can exercise great control over the process and the distilling proof. Because fusel oils are best extracted at alcohol levels of 65 percent, the high-proof spirits distilled at 85 to 95 percent, and the neutral spirits at 95 percent or more, will not have many fusel oils. Bourbon, distilled at 70 to 80 percent, will have a significant fusel oil content. The least volatile elements tend to fall to the lowest part of the column and can easily be avoided.

This more or less describes the original Coffey still and provides an understanding of how continuous distillation works. There are many different distillation processes available. The three most commonly used in the United States are a continuous whisky-separating column, with or without an auxiliary unit for the production of straight whiskies; a continuous multicolumn system used for the production of neutral grain spirits; and a batch-rectifying column and kettle unit, used primarily for the production of neutral spirits that are to be wood aged. The second one, the continuous multicolumn unit, is quite complex. It consists of five columns: one for separation of whisky, one for selective distillation, and one each for product, aldehyde, and fusel oil concentration.

STANDARDS FOR ALCOHOLIC BEVERAGES

A *standard* is defined by the Oxford American Dictionary as "a thing or quality or specification by which something may be tested or measured," and as "the required level of quality." This book will set out what the standards are for alcoholic beverages and, in those cases where there are few required levels of quality, what they ought to be. This will be done with each of the beverages, through an examination of several areas.

Nutritional Standards

All alcoholic beverages provide calories; pure alcohol yields seven kilocalories per gram, and one ounce of 90-proof spirit contains about seventy-three kilocalories. Some beverages, however, also provide nutrients in the form of carbohydrates, minerals, and vitamins. This does not mean that alcoholic beverages should be considered nutritional in and of themselves, but some do serve a supplementary nutritional role.

Federal Standards of Identity

There are long-established federal Standards of Identity for alcoholic beverages. Originally developed after the repeal of Prohibition as part of the strict control over the alcoholic beverage industry, they had two primary purposes. One was to provide a basis for assessing and collecting taxes, and the other was for consumer protection. The standards typically deal with such areas as ingredients, processing methods and techniques, alcoholic content, and aging requirements. The federal Standards of Identity for each of the product types will be defined and discussed.

Raw Materials Used in Processing

As with food processing, the type and quality of the ingredients used for alcoholic fermentation are of critical importance: inferior ingredients produce inferior products. Much of the quality differentiation among beverages is due to this factor, and this book will define the quality standards of the ingredients used for the various types of beverages.

Processing Additives

Alcoholic beverages are not laden with additives as many foods seem to be, but some additives are necessary for microbial control during ingredient growth and fermentation, for clarification, and for enhanced preservation. The accepted industry standards as well as the legal ones will be examined.

Processing Methods and Techniques

With each beverage category, the legal and accepted industry production standards will be established as a frame of reference. Each type of beverage within a category will then be compared to those standards, showing how a variety of unique products can be produced. For example, with whisky, the book will look first at how whisky is made in general. Making bourbon and Scotch, Canadian, Irish, and blended whiskies, however, requires specific alterations during the processing. The standards for these variations will be explained.

Sensory Standards

The most important aspect of food is probably its nutritional value, because obviously people must eat to survive. There is no biological necessity for alcoholic beverages, however. They are consumed for pleasure—for psychological reasons, not physiological ones. Hence, the sensory attributes of these beverages are of paramount importance. As with foods, people take pleasure from a combination of visual, olfactory, taste, and tactile perceptions. There are, in most cases, established standards for how alcoholic beverages ought to look, smell, taste, and feel, and this book will describe them.

SUGGESTED READINGS

Amerine, M. A., H. W. Berg, and W. V. Cruess. *The Technology of Wine Making.* Westport, Conn.: AVI, 1972.

Amerine, M. A., and V. L. Singleton. *Wine: An Introduction.* Berkeley: University of California Press, 1977.

Amerine, M. A., and G. F. Stewart. *Introduction to Food Science and Technology.* New York: Academic Press, 1973.

Barty-King, H., and A. Massel. *Rum, Yesterday and Today.* London: W. Heinemann Ltd., 1983.

Bell, D. A. *The Spirits of Hospitality.* East Lansing, Mich.: The Educational Institute/American Hotel & Motel Association, 1976.

Conn, E. E., and P. K. Stumpf. *Outlines of Biochemistry.* 2d ed. New York: J. Wiley & Sons, 1966.

Grossman, H. J. *Grossman's Guide to Wines, Beers & Spirits.* 6th rev. ed., rev. H. Lembeck. New York: Charles Scribner's Sons, 1977.

Hannum, H., and R. S. Blumberg. *Brandies & Liqueurs of the World.* Garden City, N. Y.: Doubleday & Co., 1976.

Johnson, H. *The World Atlas of Wine.* New York: Simon & Schuster, 1971.

Katsigris, C., and M. Porter. *The Bar & Beverage Book.* New York: J. Wiley & Sons, 1983.

Lichine, A. *Alexis Lichine's New Encyclopedia of Wines & Spirits.* New York: Alfred Knopf, 1982.

Long, Z. *Enological & Technological Developments.* The Book of California Wine. Ed. Amerine, Muscatine, and Thompson. Berkeley and London: University of California Press/Sotheby Publications, 1984.

One Hundred Years of Brewing. Chicago: H. S. Rich & Co., 1903.

Packowski, G. W. *Beverage Spirits, Distilled.* Kirk-Othmer Encyclopedia of Chemical Technology. New York: J. Wiley & Sons, 1978.

Ray, C. *Cognac.* New York: Stein & Day, 1973.

Schug, W. *The Vinification of Fine Wine.* The Book of California Wine. Ed. Amerine, Muscatine, and Thompson. Berkeley and London: University of California Press/Sotheby Publications, 1984.

Vine, R. P. *Commercial Winemaking.* Westport, Conn.: AVI, 1981.

Wagner, P. M. *American Wines & Wine-Making.* 5th ed. New York: Alfred Knopf, 1970.

CHAPTER TWO

WINES

CLASSIFICATION OF WINES

The term *wine* covers several distinct types of fermented beverages; each requires unique production techniques and is typically used for different purposes (Table 2–1).

Table Wines

The category of *table wines* describes ones that are used to accompany foods and are more or less dry. The term *dryness* must be used carefully when de-

Table 2–1   Classification of Wines

Table Wines (14 percent alcohol or less)
  Red wines
  White wines
  Rosé wines
Dessert wines (14 to 24 percent alcohol)
Sparkling wines
Aromatized wines
Specialty wines

scribing wine. More than one marketer has made the statement that "Americans talk dry and drink sweet." What this means is that many American wine drinkers claim to prefer dry wines, wines with little or no perceptible sugar, but in actual practice they consume wines that have distinctly perceptible sweetness. It is a fact that the majority of wines consumed in the United States have easily perceived levels of residual sugar. The top-selling imported wine brand, Riunite, accounts for some 23 percent of all wine brought into the United States and nearly 5 percent of the total amount of wine consumed in this country. Gallo, just with its line of generic wines and its Carlo Rossi brand, accounts for over 15 percent of all wine shipments. All of these wines have residual sugar in varying amounts and are not, technically, dry. They are, however, classified as table wines. The category is subdivided into red, white, and rosé wines. These wines contain 14 percent alcohol or less.

Dessert Wines

As the name implies, *dessert wines* are sweet, and a broad range of wines is included in this category. Some are made by specialized methods and can be said to be naturally sweet; the sugar comes from the grapes. Examples of these types are French Sauternes, German sweet wines, Hungarian Tokaji, and Italian Recioto. Others are made sweet by the addition of sugar. Other examples of dessert wines are the *fortified wines*, such as sherry, porto, Marsala, Madeira, and so forth. A fortified wine is one that has had its alcoholic level increased, generally by the addition of brandy. Not all fortified wines are sweet, however; some sherries and sherry-type wines are bone-dry. Dessert and fortified wines contain from 14 to 24 percent alcohol.

Sparkling Wines

Wines that have retained the carbon dioxide that naturally evolves from alcoholic fermentation are known as *sparkling wines*. The most famous one is Champagne, but there are many other sparkling wines made in France as well as in virtually every other wine-producing country. The alcohol content is the same as with table wines: 14 percent or less.

Aromatized Wines

Vermouth, which can be either red or white and sweet or dry, is the best-known example of *aromatized wines*, fortified wines that are also flavored with herbs and spices. The alcohol content is 15.5 to 20 percent.

Specialty Wines

This includes such diverse products as *wine coolers* and *special natural wines* such as Thunderbird, and Boone's Farm. There are two distinct subcategories, one with more than 14 percent alcohol and one with less.

WINE QUALITY CRITERIA

Wine quality is subjective; what one person likes, another may dislike. A wine one person may pay $500 a bottle for would not be worth anything to another. And a wine's price is not always indicative of its inherent quality. A $500 wine could be very old and extremely rare, which would account for its value; the wine itself could be spoiled and undrinkable. Even casual wine drinkers would agree that there are differences among wines; variations in appearance, odor, taste, flavor, and texture. Discussing criteria for wine quality, therefore, requires focusing on those factors that result in the often substantial sensory differences among wines. They are the grapes, the climate, the soil, and the skill of the wine maker (Table 2-2).

The Grape

The grape is the most important of the criteria determining a wine's quality, and it is the limiting factor. What a skilled wine maker attempts to do is match the grape or grapes, the soil, and the average or typical climatic conditions. If grapes are poorly matched with the soil and climate, they either will not ripen or will ripen improperly and will not attain their maximum potential. If suitable grapes are selected for a given area and the specific weather condi-

Table 2-2 Wine Quality Criteria

Grapes	Climate	Soil	Skill of the Wine Maker
Vitis vinifera *Vitis labrusca,* *Vitis riparia,* *Vitis rotundi-folia* Hybrids	Heat (80 to 90° F best) Rain (ideally about 20 inches, early) Sunshine (about 100 days)	Loose, rocky, gravelly, or pebbly—not rich	Part scientist, part artist Modern wine-making techniques and knowledge

tions are favorable in any given year, the grapes will attain maturity and it will be possible to make fine wine. If the weather is not favorable that particular year, the grapes will not mature properly, and wine of a lesser quality will be made, regardless of the wine maker's skill. Thus, the wine maker, the soil, and the climate are all working together for the benefit of the grapes. The grapes either limit or enhance the potential quality of the wine.

The purpose of proper soil, climate, and wine-making techniques is to maximize the potential of the grapes. To put it another way, it is unlikely that the best Concord or Thompson Seedless grapes, grown anywhere, would produce really fine wine, but grapes such as Chardonnay, Riesling, and Cabernet Sauvignon at least have the potential for producing great wine. The grape species *Vitis vinifera* is responsible for all the great wines of the world (Table 2–3). Although it is a European variety, it is also found in California, Oregon, Washington, Idaho, Chile, South Africa, Australia—virtually everywhere fine wines are made. The native American vines, varieties such as *Vitis*

Table 2–3   Vinifera Grapes and the Major Areas Where They Are Grown[1]

Red	
Barbera	Piedmont, Italy; United States
Cabernet Franc	Bordeaux, France
Cabernet Sauvignon	Bordeaux, France; United States, Italy, and other countries
Corvina	The Veneto, Italy (Bardolino and Valpolicella)
Gamay	Beaujolais, France; United States
Gamay Beaujolais (a clone of the Pinot Noir)	France; United States
Grenache	Rhône, France; United States
Grignolino	Piedmont, Italy
Lambrusco	Emilia-Romagna, Italy (Lambrusco)
Malbec	Bordeaux, France
Merlot	Bordeaux, France; United States
Nebbiolo	Piedmont, Italy (Barolo, Barbaresco)
Petite Sirah (Duriff)	France; United States
Pinot Meunier	Champagne, France
Pinot Noir	Burgundy, France; Champagne, France; United States
Sangiovese	Tuscany, Italy (Chianti); Umbria, Italy (Rubesco)
Syrah	Rhône, France
Zinfandel	United States

[1]The grapes listed are either those that are commonly used for varietal wines in the United States or are used for imported wines that are well known in the United States.

(continued)

Table 2-3 *Continued*

White	
Chardonnay	Burgundy, France; Champagne, France; Chablis, France; United States
Chenin Blanc	Loire, France; United States
Cortese	Piedmont, Italy
French Colombard	France; United States
Furmint	Tokaji, Hungary (Tokaji Aszu)
Garganega	Veneto, Italy (Soave)
Gewürztraminer	Germany; United States
Müller-Thurgau	Germany
Muscat	France; Piedmont, Italy (Asti Spumante); United States
Palomino	Jerez de la Frontera, Spain (sherry)
Pinot Grigio (Rülander), Pinot gris	Italy; Germany; Alsace, France
Pinot Blanc (Pinot Bianco)	France; Italy; United States
Riesling	Germany; Alsace, France; United States
Sauvignon Blanc	Bordeaux, France; Loire, France; United States
Sémillon	Bordeaux, France; United States
Sylvaner (Gray Riesling)	Germany; Alsace, France; United States
Traminer	Germany; Alsace, France
Trebbiano	Italy
Verdicchio	The Marches, Italy

labrusca, *Vitis riparia*, and *Vitis rotundifolia*, are used to make wines, especially in the eastern United States, but the wines are considered to be very different. Many people enjoy them, and it would be incorrect to state that they are not good wines, but they are quite different from wines made from *Vitis vinifera* grapes. For one thing, they have more of a grapey character. Wines made from one of the V. *labrusca* varieties, such as Concord, Catawba, and Delaware, are noted for having a strong odor of methyl and/or ethyl anthranilate. A word commonly used to describe this odor is "foxy"; another description is "Welch's grape juice." Such wines do not seem to have the potential for aging and improving that vinifera wines do. They do not develop the complex flavors and odors associated with fine wines.

Aside from these, there is a third kind of grape grown widely in the United States. This is a hybrid grape, a result of a crossing between a vinifera variety and one of the native ones. These varieties were developed because early Americans considered wines made from native grapes unpleasant, and they could not make wines from vinifera grapes. The combination of climate, soil, pests, and diseases proved to be too much when they attempted to grow vinifera, and centuries passed before vinifera varieties were successfully grown in the eastern United States. The objective of cross-breeding was to develop grapes that could both cope with the environment and produce wine similar to that of vinifera varieties.

The grape variety is of such importance that most countries with long-standing wine traditions carefully regulate it. In fact, most of the quality restrictions and guidelines are grape related. Not only are the grape varieties specified, but so is the minimum alcoholic content, which, because it comes from the grape sugar, is an indication of the maturity of the fruit. The wine yield, or volume of wine permitted from a given vineyard acreage, is often specified, and this is also grape related. Centuries of experience have shown that there is a close relationship between yield and quality. Making excessive amounts of wine seems to dilute the character of the grape, and the wine loses its distinctiveness.

The examples of the importance of grape specificity are nearly endless. Red Burgundy is made from the Pinot Noir grape, white Burgundy and Chablis from the Chardonnay, Barolo from Nebbiolo, Champagne from Pinot Noir and Chardonnay, northern Rhônes such as Côte Rôtie and Hermitage from the Syrah, Sancerre from the Sauvignon Blanc, Tokaji Aszu from the Furmint, and so forth. Even those wines that are blended from two or more grape varieties generally have a dominant one from which they draw their character. Cabernet Sauvignon for Médoc and red Graves, Merlot for Pomerol and Saint-Emilion, Sémillon for Sauternes and Barsac, Sangiovese for Chianti, and Sauvignon Blanc for white Graves are but a few examples.

Climate

Of the four primary factors for quality, the climate is the most variable one. The grape varieties do not change (at least in established vineyard regions), nor does the soil. Either the wine maker or the wine maker's style could change, but typically there will be stability and continuity, at least from one year to the next. With the climate, however, there could be really significant variations from one year to another. A disastrous year could follow a great one, and there is no way to predict what is going to occur. The weather forecast heard in the morning for that day is often inaccurate; it is folly to attempt to look several months ahead. The wine maker cannot gauge the quality of a harvest until the grapes are in and crushed. A growing season could proceed to perfection until an hour before the harvest, but if a tumultuous and persistent rainstorm began at that time, the entire year could be endangered.

The purpose of good weather is to bring the grapes to maturity. The wine maker is interested in two fruit components above all others: sugar and acid. If the sugar level is low (because of immature fruit), insufficient alcohol will be produced during fermentation. If the acid level is low, the resulting wine will also be low in acid and will be said to taste "flat." If the acid is too high, the wine will be tart or sour. The problem is that the two components are at odds with each other. Immature fruit is low in sugar and high in acid. As the fruit matures, the acid level drops; if it becomes overripe, there could be plenty of sugar but too little acid. The wine maker wants to harvest when the two are in balance, neither too much nor too little of one or the other.

The weather obviously plays a critical role. Wine grapes are typically grown in moderate climates. Very hot conditions encourage accumulation of sugar at the expense of acid, while moderate heat allows ripening without the loss of fruit acids. Regions that are too cool hinder ripening, and sugar and acid levels are usually unbalanced: too little sugar and too much acid.

Heat, sunshine, and rain are probably the most important elements of climate. Grapevines will not grow any fruit below 50° F (10° C) or above 113° F (45° C), and temperatures in the 80s (Fahrenheit) are most desirable. At either extreme—hot or cold—sugar-acid balance problems will occur. Sunshine is necessary for the photosynthetic activity of the vines; a rough rule of thumb is that they require some 100 days of sunshine during the growing season. Twenty inches of rainfall are considered ideal, although the vines can cope with about ten inches more or less than that. Extremes in rainfall result in either dehydration or overly watery grapes and microbial problems.

In addition to the total water available, when the rain comes is important. There should be quite a bit during the winter, when the vines are dormant. Too much spring rain can hamper vineyard operations, while daytime rain during the summer results in reduced sunshine. Excessive moisture in the vineyards after the grapes ripen increases the chances of spoilage and microbial activity, and rain during the harvest dilutes the juice and has about the same effect as adding water to the grapes while they are fermenting. All in all, wine grapes are quite particular about growing conditions, and it should come as no surprise that great vintage years are infrequent, even with our advances in science.

Soil

Rich soils, oddly enough, are not especially suited to vineyards. They seem to make growth too easy. The classic varieties have the ability not only to handle stress, but to thrive under it. There is a saying in Burgundy that translates as, "If our soil weren't the best in the world, it would be the worst." What this means is that the soil there is really not suitable for growing much of anything except the Pinot Noir grape. This grape, however, seems to grow better there than anywhere else in the world and, at its best, produces one of the greatest of all red wines.

What is important about soil is that it be loose, rocky, gravelly, or pebbly. This forces the vines to develop deep roots and provides good drainage in the vineyards (Fig. 2–1). In rich soils, the vines do not have to develop extended root systems; nutrients are readily available near the surface. Then any

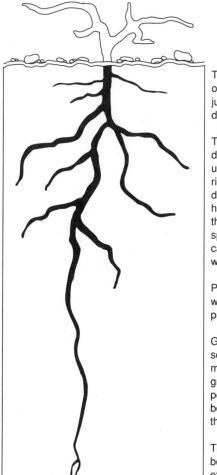

The most suitable soil for grapevines not only provides the necessary nutrients but, just as important, allows the vines to develop deep root structures.

The vine, as illustrated here, is forced to drive deep into the soil and is relatively unaffected by surface conditions. Very rich soils can hamper this kind of root development, because the vines do not have to extend deep into the soil to obtain their nutrients. They will, instead, tend to spread out near the surface. In such a case, they would be affected more by weather and climatic conditions.

Porous, loose soil encourages deep roots, while compact soil with a lot of clay can prevent the desired root growth.

Grapevines also do better in well-drained soils, which do not retain excessive moisture. This explains why so many great vineyard areas are planted in pebbly, gravelly soil. It drains well and both allows and forces the vines to send their roots deep.

The older a vine, the deeper its roots can be expected to be. This is one explanation for the generally increased quality expected from more mature vines.

Figure 2–1. Grapevine roots.

unusual environmental conditions, such as floods or droughts, will easily affect the plants. With deep roots, they are relatively unaffected by surface conditions. The worldwide drought of the late 1970s had a terribly negative effect on most agricultural products, but wine vineyards seemed to survive rather well. Rocky vineyards also absorb and reflect heat from the sun, and this can be important in some locations.

Europeans consider soil to be a critical factor. In this regard, they differ from California wine makers in general, who consider climate (mostly temperature) to be the more important of the two. The explanation of this seeming paradox lies in the climatic differences between California and Europe. It has been said that the California climate is very consistent, and relative to Europe, that is true. Europe does have more variation in temperature from day to day and week to week than does California, but broad regions of Europe tend to have similar temperatures. In California, on the other hand, because of the coastal ranges and fog, there are significant climatic differences within regions. Therefore, California shows climatic variations from mile to mile, while Europe shows them from day to day. A European vintner, explaining the differences between his wines and those of his neighbor, will emphasize the soil, because they both have likely enjoyed the same or similar environmental conditions. His California counterpart can often point out substantial temperature variances between vineyards only hundreds of yards apart.

The Wine Maker and Wine-making Techniques

The wine maker is the final critical factor for quality; a skilled wine maker can salvage a less than successful vintage, while a poor or inexperienced one can ruin a fine vintage. A successful wine maker is part scientist and part artist. The profession demands increasingly sophisticated knowledge of such subjects as chemistry, biochemistry, biology, botany, and microbiology. But as with a concert pianist, a sculptor, or a chef, training, education, and experience alone do not ensure greatness, or even competence. There is in every outstanding wine maker an artist and highly skilled craftsman. This is what sets them apart.

What advances in science have done is to increase the control the wine maker has over the entire process, from beginning to end. Better grapes are available today, grapes that resist disease and other problems and are more productive as well. Grapes are able to be matched more successfully with suitable soil and climatic conditions. Improvements in vineyard management have increased the chances of bringing in a successful harvest, even under less than ideal conditions. The absolutely horrendous vintages, which used to occur with some regularity, seem to be a thing of the past. There were, for example, three such years in France in the 1960s (1963, 1965, and 1968), but none since.

The actual wine-making processes themselves are much more controllable due to greater understanding of fermentation, of the many other reactions that take place, of aging, of the effect of wood and the differences among various woods, and of ways to stabilize and clarify wines. Improvements in equipment and winery design have helped as well. Grapes can be harvested, transported, and crushed much more efficiently than in previous years. Bottling and labeling are still other processes that have become more efficient and productive.

Fine wine, therefore, results from selecting the best grape varieties, matching those grapes to the most suitable climate and soil, and having cooperative weather. If all these conditions are met, skilled and dedicated wine makers can complete the process.

COMPONENTS OF WINES

Wine components can be classified as of either direct or indirect origin. Those of direct origin come from the grape, while those of indirect origin are produced during fermentation and subsequent processing. It is important to recognize that practically all table wines are about 99 percent water, ethanol, sugars, acids, and tannins. The vast differences among wines can thus be attributed to the remaining 1 percent (Table 2–4).

Table 2–4 Wine Components and Origin (Direct or Indirect)

Component	Origin
Water	Direct (unless water is added to correct excess acidity)
Ethanol	Indirect
Sugars	Direct (unless sugar is added to correct inadequate natural sugar)
Fixed acids (tartaric, malic, and citric, mostly tartaric)	Direct
Volatile acids (mostly acetic)	Indirect
Glycerine	Indirect
Phenolics (mostly tannins and color pigments)	Direct
Other components (such as esters and aldehydes)	Indirect

Water

Wine is mostly water, about 83 to 90 percent in most wines, although it can vary with low alcohol and high alcohol wines, and it is of direct origin except in those cases where water is added to reduce excessive acidity.

Ethanol

The ethyl alcohol, resulting from fermentation of sugar, is of indirect origin, and accounts for between 7 and 20 percent of wine. Table wines are typically around 12 percent, although some California wines contain 14 percent or more, and many German wines have as little as 7 to 8 percent. The alcoholic content is important for several reasons. It acts as a preservative and provides stability. It serves as a solvent for color pigments and is primarily responsible for the perception of body. Dilute solutions of alcohol in water have more viscosity than either water or ethanol by itself. One of the problems with low-alcohol wines, the so-called light wines, is that they often have a watery texture. Some of the greatest German wines are as low in alcohol as the light wines of the United States, but the perception of viscosity is enhanced by sugar and generally higher levels of glycerine.

Sugars

When the sugars come from the fruit, they are of direct origin. Sugar can be added, either to the fermenting grape must or to the wine itself. In such cases, any perception of sweetness is entirely or partially of indirect origin. Glucose and fructose are both found in wine, although glucose (dextrose) predominates. The most obvious attribute of sugar is its taste, the sweetness it adds to wines, but it has other important functions. For one, sugar, like alcohol, acts as a preservative. Some of the very sweet white wines can live an astonishingly long time, due in part to the preservative qualities of sugar. Another function of sugar is that it can give wine a syrupy texture and enhance the perception of body. Sugar can also mask undesirable tastes and flavors when present at levels of about 2 percent for whites and 2.5 percent for reds. This is why only the very finest, most delicate, and balanced sherries and Champagnes are allowed to go to market with little or no sugar added. These are the fino sherries and brut or natural Champagnes.

The apparent sweetness of a wine will be affected not only by the amount of sugar present, but also by the acid. Sugar is perceived by most people at about 0.5 percent. At levels below 0.5 percent, the wine will have no perceptible sweetness. The sensory term for this is *dry;* a dry wine is one that is not sweet. Acid appears to alter the threshold for sugar, and wines containing appreciable amounts of sugar generally have to have higher than normal acid levels to be considered successful. Conversely, sugar affects the perception of acid. A totally dry wine with an acid level of 1 percent would be regarded as too sour or tart by most people, but a sweeter wine might need 1 percent acid to be balanced.

Making fresh lemonade is an example of this. When the lemon juice is mixed in water, the solution is very sour and disagreeable to most people. Adding sugar in the proper proportion brings the sweet and sour elements into balance; if excessive sugar were to be added, the acid level would be perceived as too low. One of the things a taster does while evaluating the wine is to check the sweet-sour balance. With a wine having no perceptible sugar, an acid level of about 0.5 to 0.7 percent would be right for most people. With increasing amounts of sugar, however, the acid would have to increase; otherwise the wine would be said to taste "flat," to be deficient in acid.

Even if a wine is fermented dry, it will not be totally sugar-free. There are nonfermentable sugars that will remain, but their level is far below the threshold and they generally have no sweet taste; they would not be detected even by someone with a very low sweetness threshold.

When sugar is increased in wines, it can affect both the visual and the taste characteristics. While the color of red wine is not affected, increasing sugar in white wines can result in more golden tones, and the taste of both red and white wine becomes softer, less harsh, and more mellow. Sugar does not affect the odor of either red or white wine.

Acids

There are two categories of wine acids. The acids in wines that come from the grapes are *fixed acids*, while those arising from fermentation, processing, and aging are called *volatile acids*. The total acidity of a wine is the combination of both fixed and volatile acids. The fixed acids are of direct origin and the volatile acids of indirect origin. Tartaric acid is the most characteristic of the grape and wine acids and generally predominates. Malic acid can be present in significant amounts when grapes are grown in cool climates or when they are not fully ripened. Such wines may have an applelike character. The other commonly found acid in wines, citric, is typically present only in trace amounts.

The acid level is vital to wine quality. In addition to the taste properties of acids, they perform other valuable functions. Acids can counter oily foods, and certain wines enhance seafood in a manner similar to lemon juice. Acids are also important in wine preservation and spoilage retardation. Tartaric acid in particular has excellent preservative properties. Color fixation is yet another area where acids play an important role.

The most common volatile acid is acetic acid, which gives wines a vinegarlike odor and taste. It is caused by bacteria called acetobacters, which can convert ethyl alcohol into acetic acid. These bacteria are presumed to be present in the environment and, if introduced to the wine via air, will eventually result in spoilage of the wine—not spoiled in the sense that the wine is contaminated, for the acetic acid will obviously protect it against pathogenic, or disease-causing, microorganisms, but spoiled in its use as a beverage.

Increasing the level of acids in wines will have no effect on the appearance of either red or white wines. Therefore, a person cannot determine the acid level by looking at a wine. Neither can fixed acids be detected by smelling the wine. Volatile acidity can affect the odor, of course, and a person also may be able to smell unripe fruit. Increasing the acid level affects the taste of the wine—it becomes sharper or more sour—but as we have seen, the sugar level is critical to acid perception.

Glycerine

This is produced naturally as a by-product of alcoholic fermentation; its properties are to increase the viscosity, or body, of the wine and to enhance sweetness. Glycerine is normally present only in small amounts and its effects are often exaggerated. There are, however, certain wines, notably the French Sauternes and German Beerenauslesen and Trockenbeerenauslesen, that may have appreciable glycerine, which would contribute to the oily textures and sweetness of those wines.

Phenolics

Wine phenolic compounds are a complex group that includes color pigments and tannins. Their importance is that they furnish color to wines, supply astringency, are a source of browning substrate, and provide for oxygen reduction.

Anthocyanins are the only significant pigment in red grapes. They are located in the skins and are released during alcoholic fermentation. The various yellowish colors found in white wines are due to flavones, organic compounds found in plant parts. The browning that occurs in both white and red wines is due mainly to oxidation of the color pigments. The rate of browning is dependent on the amount of pigment present, the temperature, and the availability of oxygen. Wine stored at warm temperatures will oxidize faster than at recommended temperatures—55 to 60°F (13 to 16°C)—as will wine that is overexposed to oxygen, either during processing or aging. This is why wines ideally are stored on their sides. The contact between cork and wine should keep the cork moist, while upright storage could cause drying and shrinking of the cork, thus allowing oxygen to enter.

The other major type of phenolic compound, tannin, comes mainly from the skin, stems, and seeds of the grapes, although it may also be extracted from wood during aging. Tannins are natural antioxidants; that is, they will preferentially react with oxygen, thereby avoiding or delaying less desirable oxygen reactions. They can be detected by their astringency and, sometimes, by their bitterness. Often there is confusion between the sensory perception of acids and tannins. Acids have a sour or tart taste, while tannins have a rough or harsh feel. An example would be the difference between the sour taste of lemon juice and the rough feel of strong, oversteeped tea. Red wines, fermented with the skins, the seeds, and sometimes the stems, will have appreciable amounts of tannin; the longer they are fermented on the skins, the higher the tannin content. White wines, which are produced by fermenting only the juice, have little or no tannin. The tannin content of free run grape juice is generally less than 0.02 percent, and this is below the threshold of most people.

Because tannins act as antioxidants, they serve to protect the wine. This is the major reason red wines can age longer than whites. During aging, tannins undergo oxidative reactions with aldehydes and the color pigments, resulting in a precipitate that is insoluble. This is why red wines may have sediment while whites do not. As the tannins oxidize, the harshness and astringency of young red wine is reduced, the color becomes lighter due to loss of color compounds, and the color gradually becomes brown due to oxidation of the color compounds and the tannins.

Other Components

There are many other components in wine in addition to the ones discussed here. The most important of these are the various esters and aldehydes produced during fermentation and subsequent processing and aging. These amount to very little in weight, but make an enormous contribution in flavor and fragrance.

WINE-MAKING STANDARDS

Wine-making practices are, in general, pretty much the same the world over (Fig. 2-2). All wine makers must harvest and crush the fruit, which then

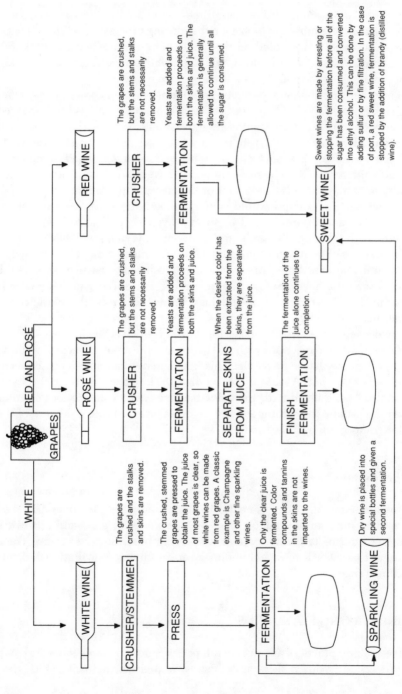

Figure 2-2. Wine-making processes: red, white, and rosé wines.

GRAPES

WHITE

RED AND ROSÉ

WHITE WINE

CRUSHER/STEMMER

The grapes are crushed and the stalks and skins are removed.

PRESS

The crushed, stemmed grapes are pressed to obtain the juice. The juice of most grapes is clear, so white wines can be made from red grapes. A classic example is Champagne and other fine sparkling wines.

FERMENTATION

Only the clear juice is fermented. Color compounds and tannins in the skins are not imparted to the wines.

SPARKLING WINE

Dry wine is placed into special bottles and given a second fermentation.

ROSÉ WINE

CRUSHER

The grapes are crushed, but the stems and stalks are not necessarily removed.

FERMENTATION

Yeasts are added and fermentation proceeds on both the skins and juice.

SEPARATE SKINS FROM JUICE

When the desired color has been extracted from the skins, they are separated from the juice.

FINISH FERMENTATION

The fermentation of the juice alone continues to completion.

RED WINE

CRUSHER

The grapes are crushed, but the stems and stalks are not necessarily removed.

FERMENTATION

Yeasts are added and fermentation proceeds on both the skins and juice. The fermentation is generally allowed to continue until all the sugar is consumed.

SWEET WINE

Sweet wines are made by arresting or stopping the fermentation before all of the sugar has been consumed and converted into ethyl alcohol. This can be done by adding sulfur or by fine filtration. In the case of port, a red sweet wine, fermentation is stopped by the addition of brandy (distilled wine).

undergoes an alcoholic fermentation. The result is technically wine, although few people would recognize it as such in that condition. Malolactic fermentation, changing the acidity, may or may not be allowed to occur; then the wine must be aged for varying periods, clarified, stabilized, bottled, and stored. This is what all wine makers do, although there can be significant differences in how they approach each step. What follows is a discussion of the generally accepted standards of wine making followed by most wine makers today.

Harvesting

The first decision to be made is when to harvest. If the fruit is picked too soon, the acid probably will be too high and the sugar will certainly be too low. If the fruit is allowed to overripen, the sugar will increase or stabilize, but at the expense of acidity. There can also be spoilage and microbial problems. The three factors used to test for fruit maturity are pH, Brix, and total acidity. The pH scale, a measurement of the hydrogen ion concentration, indicates the strength of acidity (or, conversely, alkalinity). Brix is a measurement of the dissolved solids in the grape juice; in practice, this is taken to be sugar. Total acidity is a determination of the amount of fixed acids. Of these, the Brix determination is the easiest because it can be made quickly with an instrument called a refractometer and can be done right in the vineyards.

Because the harvest time is determined by the grapes' ripeness, the harvest date varies from year to year. Harvest date selection is further complicated when several varieties of grapes, each of which has its own maturation pattern, are grown. Some ripen early, some late, and each one varies over time.

Traditionally grapes have been picked by hand, and although this is still the most common method, mechanical harvesters have been used since the 1960s. In the United States mechanical harvesting is increasingly used, and in France it has moved from testing to acceptance in large vineyards. Due to increasing labor costs and decreasing labor availability, manual harvesting today is difficult to justify, especially in the United States. From a quality standpoint, many wine makers feel mechanical harvesting offers an advantage because the grapes can be picked at night when they are cooler, and large vineyard areas can be picked more or less at the same time, while the grapes are at ideal maturity.

Mechanical harvesting is often nearly impossible due to the vineyard's physical characteristics, however, and there are other disadvantages as well. One is the loss of juice that occurs if the grapes break up too much while being removed. Another is the potential for including immature fruit. This is termed the second crop, which with manual picking can be left for later harvesting. Material other than grapes (called MOG) also can be included in mechanical harvesting, and this can cause problems at the winery. There is also an increased possibility of oxidation and phenolic extraction in the crushed grapes. Even the grape variety can create a disadvantage, because some are less suitable than others for mechanical harvesting.

Crushing

Once the grapes reach the winery, they undergo crushing, the purpose of which is to break the skins so that the juices can run freely. There is no shredding or grinding of the grapes, as that could break the seeds, releasing bitter oils and excess tannins. Along with the breaking of the skins, the stems are generally removed, although with some wines it is considered desirable to ferment at least some of the stems. With red wines, the crushed grapes, with or without their stems, constitute the must, and fermentation can then begin. With white wines, the juice is carefully separated from the skins, seeds, and stems and is fermented alone.

Fermentation

The next step, fermentation of the crushed grapes or the juice, has been covered in detail in Chapter One.

Malolactic Fermentation

The malolactic fermentation is a bacterial fermentation, which has nothing to do with sugar or alcohol and is concerned solely with the wine's acidity. Because it also produces some carbon dioxide, however, it can cause confusion and be regarded as a continuation of alcoholic fermentation. What actually happens is that, promoted by certain acid-tolerant species of bacteria known as lactobacillus and leuconostoc, malic acid is converted to lactic acid and carbon dioxide.

The importance of this is twofold: (1) there is less acid, and (2) lactic acid is much weaker than malic. The result is a sharp reduction in total acidity and a softer, less tart or sour taste. There are changes in the odor of the wine as well. The reaction is most pronounced where grapes are likely to have high levels of malic acid, and this is what happens in areas where grapes have difficulty in ripening. With very ripe grapes, acid reduction is not a concern, although insufficient acidity may be. In such cases, the malolactic reaction may be undesirable.

When the reduction of total acidity is not wanted, *racking* and the addition of sulfur dioxide (SO_2) usually prevents or controls the malolactic reaction. Racking, or separation of the wine from the *lees*—the yeast residue that settles to the bottom during fermentation—is helpful because continued contact with the lees promotes the growth of acid-converting bacteria. Early racking reduces the amount of the products of yeast autolysis, or cell breakdown, that the bacteria can utilize for growth. The SO_2 acts by inhibiting the bacterial multiplication.

When malolactic reaction is desirable, it is considered best to have it occur during fermentation, because that provides the proper temperature and the necessary nutrients; but it can, and often does, take place later. At any rate, it must occur prior to bottling because it produces carbon dioxide (CO_2), and the wine would become turgid and gassy.

Malolactic fermentation has long been considered important in Europe, where the organisms involved were cultivated as early as 1897. Austrian, German, and Swiss enologists—scientists concerned with wine—established the importance of biological acid reduction prior to World War I; French enologists followed in Burgundy in the 1920s and in Bordeaux in the 1930s. Wine makers in both Burgundy and Bordeaux believe that the quality of their wines is due, in part, to malolactic fermentation.

Aging

Aging of wine is a continuous process from the time fermentation is completed until the wine is consumed. One of the distinguishing features of wines relative to distilled spirits is that wines age even after they are bottled, while spirits do not. Thus, a wine from the 1970 vintage would be eight years old in 1978, ten in 1980, and fifteen in 1985. A bourbon distilled in 1970 and bottled in 1978 would be eight years old in 1978 and would remain eight years old.

In the winery, prior to bottling, wine can be stored and aged in wood (oak or redwood), concrete (lined or unlined), lined iron or steel, or stainless steel. Although wine develops or ages faster in wood than in the other materials, the type of wood, age of the wood, and size of the container, or cooperage, are extremely important. Oak is considered superior to redwood, which is porous and allows more air into the wine. The age of the wood refers to the length of time it has been used for wine storage. Most of what can be extracted from the wood is removed during the early years, and aging benefits are greatly reduced in used cooperage. If a slower or gentler aging is sought, however, used barrels are desirable. Used barrels can also be *refreshed* by shaving the interior to expose fresh wood. The container size is important because the smaller the barrel, the larger the ratio of wood to wine. A 50-gallon barrel has about twenty times the surface area of a 2,500-gallon cask. Wines therefore age fastest, and show the most dramatic changes, when aged in new, small, oak barrels. The huge wooden storage containers seen in some wineries are more or less permanent and impart little if any wood character; it has long ago been leached out by the wines. In any case, even were the tanks new, the very small wood-to-wine ratio would mitigate against any significant wood character being transferred to the wine.

There are basically two types of changes occurring in wine during wood aging. The principal changes are believed to be due to slow oxidation. Pasteur proved long ago that normal aging of certain red wines cannot take place without oxygen but that the amount required is very small. Excessive exposure to oxygen can result in the development of an oxidized or maderized odor (reminiscent of Madeira). Wine is exposed to some oxygen because the barrels are not airtight. But a wooden barrel can be considered a semipermeable membrane; it allows water and alcohol to escape but does not allow appreciable amounts of air to enter, due to the difference in molecule size between water or alcohol and air or oxygen. This is shown by the fact that a partial vacuum develops in the headspace of a barrel. The wine will also pick up oxygen during the various pumping, racking, and filtering processes. In very large wooden storage tanks, in used cooperage, and in nonwood storage containers, this slow oxidation results in the development of flavor and bouquet, or aroma, in the wine.

In small barrels, particularly new ones, the other type of change takes place: the extraction of certain substances from the wood. There are two types of wood extractives: lignin provides aromatic compounds—vanillin, for example—and these are responsible for the aromatic development of wine during barrel aging; tannins are also dissolved by the wine, and they contribute to a wine's longevity and feel.

The amount of time a wine spends in wood is variable. Some white wines will see no wood at all during their lifetime, going from stainless steel fermenters into stainless steel containers for aging, and then into the bottle. If wood is used it is generally well seasoned and will not impart any wood character. Even some red wines—Beaujolais is an example—receive little wood aging prior to being bottled. Light wines can easily be overpowered by wood, especially new oak, and can lose their freshness, delicacy, and varietal character. There are some white wines, however, that are matured in wooden cooperage. Examples are some of the higher-quality sweet German wines, white Burgundies, and the classic sweet wines from Sauternes and Barsac in Bordeaux.

In general, red wines are aged in wood, but even here it varies from a few months to four or more years. Extended aging in wood can decrease quality, rob the wine of its fruit, and give it an excessively woody character.

The origin and species of oak have a great deal to do with the character of the finished wine. While American white oak is ideal for whiskies, most wine makers prefer European oak for wine. Of the European oaks, the French Nevers, Tronçais, and Limousin oaks seem to be the ones most desired for barrel aging, and German and Yugoslavian oaks are used in America mostly for storage tanks and casks rather than barrels. The American oak is said to have a stronger oak aroma, and the European varieties provide more extractable solids and more phenolics. Each wine maker has his or her preferences, depending on the style of wine sought. Robert Mondavi, for example, ages Pinot Noir and Chardonnay in Limousin oak and most of the rest of its wines in Nevers. The company ranks the species of oak in importance first on the style of wine, followed by the method of coopering, and then the place of origin of the species. The method of coopering refers to how the barrel is made; it is done differently in Europe than in America. Ongoing research at Mondavi has shown variations in the oak character provided by barrels that are coopered differently. When wine is stored in stainless steel, glass-lined steel, concrete, or the bottle, aging will still take place, but it will occur much more slowly and will be the result of slow oxidation. Although there may be little or no exposure to oxygen, it will be present in sufficient amounts from previous processing and handling. In the case of bottle aging, not only is there oxygen dissolved in the wine, but also there is a small amount in the head-space between the wine and the cork, and this is sufficient to continue the slow aging process. If the bottle is stored improperly and the cork dries and shrinks, excessive exposure to oxygen will result and the wine can deteriorate quickly.

Clarification

Newly fermented wine is cloudy, harsh in taste, and yeasty in odor. All wines need some type of *clarification* processing, reds as well as whites, although it is easier with red wines. Whites are more difficult not only because of the obvious difference, but also because colloids, or the unsettled material, tend to remain in suspension following low-temperature fermentation, and white wines today are likely to be fermented at low temperatures. There are several methods, some traditional, some modern, that are used for clarification. They are racking, fining, filtering, and centrifuging.

Racking, as explained earlier, means separating the wine from the lees and other sediment on the bottom of the barrel, by draining or pumping the wine from one barrel into another. This is a process repeated several times during the barrel aging. In Bordeaux, the wines are racked about four times during the first year.

Fining means adding an ingredient that has the property of attracting suspended materials and drawing them to the bottom, where they can be removed by racking or other means. Both organic and inorganic agents can be used. The most common organic ones are tannin, gelatin, isinglass (a proteinaceous fish-based gelatin), and casein (a milk protein). Others include blood, egg white, and skim milk. The most popular one is probably gelatin. The inorganic agents are Spanish clay and bentonite, an absorptive clay. There are also commercial wine-clarifying or fining compounds. One such, called Sparkolloid, produces a gelatinous suspension. Whatever is used, the procedure is to mix or stir the agent with the wine and allow it to settle. One drawback of fining is that it can be time-consuming, not only because of the wait for settling, but also because of the need for further rackings. Another is that fining agents can also remove odor, flavor, and color constituents along with suspended materials. For this reason, it is recommended that fining agents be used as lightly as possible.

Filtering means mechanically removing materials by passing the wine through screens or pads. The advantages are that clarification is immediate because there is no waiting for settling, the results are consistent, it eliminates only insoluble matter, and it can be done at any time.

Wine also can be clarified with a *centrifuge*, which spins out the heavy, insoluble matter; but centrifuging also aerates the wine and, therefore, may not be suitable for fine wines.

Bottling

Wine is placed into bottles for several reasons. One is to protect it against spoilage and quality deterioration by keeping microorganisms and oxygen out. Another is to enable the vintner to ship and sell consistent, dependable wine. At one time consumers took their own containers to a wine merchant and filled them from casks. Even under the best of conditions, the wine quality must have been quite variable. Yet another reason for bottling is that a sealed glass bottle is the ideal container for the wine in which to mature slowly.

Bottles come in various sizes (Table 2–5), shapes, and colors. Prior to January 1, 1975, the United States used English measures, and the most common bottle size for wines was the so-called fifth, which was actually one fifth of a gallon, or 25.6 ounces. Now all wines (and spirits) are required to be bottled in metric sizes, based on the liter (a little more than a quart). Bottles may be as small as 50 milliliters (one-twentieth of a liter) or as large as 4 liters. Bulk wine containers can be as large as 18 liters. The most common bottle size is 750 milliliters, which, at 25.4 ounces, is very close to the old

Table 2–5 Wine Bottle Sizes

Bottle Capacity[1]		Case	Bottles
Metric	Ounces	Capacity	in a Case
100 ml.[2]	3.4	6 L.	60
187 ml.	6.3	9 L.	48
375 ml.	12.7	9 L.	24
750 ml.	25.4	9 L.	12
1.0 L.	33.8	12 L.	12
1.5 L.	50.7	9 L.	6
3.0 L.	101.4	12 L.	4
4.0 L.	135.2	16 L.	4

[1]The Bureau of Alcohol, Tobacco, and Firearms, the regulatory agency of the federal government, has required that wines and spirits be packaged in metric sizes since January 1, 1975.
[2]One liter (L.) equals 1,000 milliliters (ml.)

fifth. Other common sizes are the half bottle (375 milliliters), and the 1.5-liter bottle (50.7 ounces). Liter bottles (33.8 ounces) are common for spirits in the United States but are not widely used for wines. The 50 milliliters size is used only for spirits and cordials and is called a *miniature*.

While some wine bottles may be clear, it is more usual to use colored glass. Greenish brown glass can screen out most of the wavelengths of light that can cause light activated reactions in wine.

Although many European bottlers employ used bottles, they are difficult to sterilize; most American bottlers prefer new ones. They rely on the factory sterility of the bottles and generally only have to rinse them or remove lint by vacuum. Quality control in bottle manufacture is important because the bottle size must be exact and the inside neck must be straight, smooth, and free of defects so the cork can seal itself throughout its length against the glass.

Because the U.S. government requires accurate fill, the exact fill of the bottle is determined by the stated size. If the actual bottle capacity exceeds the stated capacity, an excessive air space will result and the wine will not mature normally. Therefore, standard and consistent bottles are needed. Some large wine producers, such as Gallo and Heublein, have established their own bottle-manufacturing plants so that they can better control this vital aspect of their business.

Once the wine is in the bottle, it has to be protected against the entry of air and leakage or evaporation of wine. Before the discovery of cork, man had to resort to such closures as oil soaked rags, softwood pegs, and wax. Cork comes from the bark of the cork oak tree, mainly from Portugal, although Spain is also an important producer. Cork production is a slow and tedious process, because it takes about 40 years for a tree to produce quality cork from its bark and then ten to thirteen years of regeneration time between harvests. Fortunately, the tree can last 400 or more years, but cork production is obviously a long-term business proposition.

The quality and length of the cork are related to the quality and potential longevity of the wine. Cork is graded, and only the top grades are used for the better wines. Corks 1.5 inches long are about the shortest used in the United States, mostly for wines that are expected to be consumed in one to two years. For wines with longer aging potential, corks of about 2.25 inches are used. Corks may also be agglomerated, or chopped into pieces that are then glued together. Normally, such cork is not used for high-quality wine, but the use for sparkling wines is a significant exception. The traditional cork for Champagne and other quality sparkling wines is made by bonding one to three layers of solid cork onto the bottom of an agglomerated cork.

Plastic bottle stoppers have been developed and are widely used for less expensive wines. They are not as effective as good cork in preventing leakage, but this is probably not very important with wines expected to be consumed relatively quickly. Tests have shown leakage from cork to be about 0.01 milliliters of oxygen per month, compared to 0.16 milliliters per month for polyethylene stoppers, although specially treated polyethylene stoppers can reduce that to between 0.01 and 0.03 milliliters.

Screw cap stoppers can be effective as long as they use an inert material in the cap and it seals the bottle top completely. One problem with cap stoppers is that, compared to a cork, the headspace is increased and so there is greater potential for oxidation. This can be countered by replacing the air in the headspace with an inert gas such as nitrogen. Filling can also be done under a vacuum to reduce oxygen entry.

After the filling and corking, the bottles must be given some time to recover from "bottle sickness." This results from adjustments to and handling of the wine in preparation for bottling and can last for several weeks or even a few months. Therefore, some bottle aging at the winery before release is desirable.

SPECIALIZED WINE-MAKING STANDARDS

The preceding pages describe in general how wines are made, but there are several significant and important wines that are made quite differently. These include Porto from Portugal, sherry from Spain, sparkling wines, and the great sweet wines of Germany and the area around Sauternes in France.

Port

True port, the wine made in the Douro Valley in Portugal, is called porto (or Porto) in the United States, as it is in Portugal, to distinguish it from the port-type wines made in California, New York, other U.S. states, and other countries. In making port, the vintner deviates widely from typical wine-making procedures (Fig. 2–3). For one thing, the wine is sweet, so the fermentation is arrested or stopped before all the sugar has been converted to alcohol and carbon dioxide. The wine is not low in alcohol, however, because brandy (distilled from port) is added. Port is therefore both a fortified wine and a sweet wine.

Port Processing. In producing port or port-style wine, the principal problem is getting enough color from the grapes during the shortened fermentation. The traditional method was to have the vineyard workers tread the grapes intermittently throughout the fermentation, but more efficient and sanitary processes are available today. One is called pumping over, whereby the grape must is continually pumped over the skins; the other is by fermentation in closed concrete tanks. The pressure from the carbon dioxide keeps the juice constantly churning over the skins. Although this agitation increases the color extraction, the free run juice is still not dark enough, so the solid residue, the pomace, is pressed to gain as much color as possible. The fermentation is stopped when about 6 to 7 percent sugar remains, the must and pomace are separated, and the wine is fortified with brandy to bring the alcoholic content up to about 16 to 17 percent. The brandies, distilled from port, are selected by taste and smell. Clean, aromatic, and colorless spirits are preferred. Final clarification of the wine is done by filtering, fining, or refrigerating.

Port Styles. The diversity of port styles can be confusing to many consumers. The primary differentiating factor is whether they are wood aged or bottle aged. Others include the length of wood aging and whether the wine is a blend of several years or the product of one harvest (Table 2–6).

Unless stated otherwise on the label, *wood-aged ports* are blended wines. Like most blended alcoholic beverages — spirits, wines, or whatever — they are blended for consistency in a house style. There will be differences among firms, but the product of any one firm can be followed; that is, it will tend to have the same sensory characteristics over time. Wines that are made entirely from one harvest can vary substantially from year to year. Thus, products that are intended to be consistent are generally blended from wines of two or more years.

As with other wines, with increasing time in wood, port becomes lighter and browner in color, its fruitiness and flavor intensity fades, and the bouquet becomes developed. When bottled young, the wine has a bright ruby color and a fresh, full, and fruity flavor. This is called a *ruby port.* Additional wood

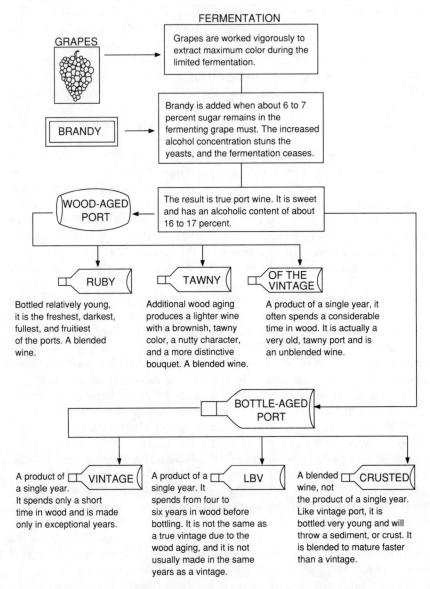

FERMENTATION

GRAPES

Grapes are worked vigorously to extract maximum color during the limited fermentation.

BRANDY

Brandy is added when about 6 to 7 percent sugar remains in the fermenting grape must. The increased alcohol concentration stuns the yeasts, and the fermentation ceases.

WOOD-AGED PORT

The result is true port wine. It is sweet and has an alcoholic content of about 16 to 17 percent.

RUBY

Bottled relatively young, it is the freshest, darkest, fullest, and fruitiest of the ports. A blended wine.

TAWNY

Additional wood aging produces a lighter wine with a brownish, tawny color, a nutty character, and a more distinctive bouquet. A blended wine.

OF THE VINTAGE

A product of a single year, it often spends a considerable time in wood. It is actually a very old, tawny port and is an unblended wine.

BOTTLE-AGED PORT

VINTAGE

A product of a single year. It spends only a short time in wood and is made only in exceptional years.

LBV

A product of a single year. It spends from four to six years in wood before bottling. It is not the same as a true vintage due to the wood aging, and it is not usually made in the same years as a vintage.

CRUSTED

A blended wine, not the product of a single year. Like vintage port, it is bottled very young and will throw a sediment, or crust. It is blended to mature faster than a vintage.

Figure 2-3. Port wine making.

Table 2-6 Port Wine Styles

Wood-Aged Ports

Ruby	The least amount of time in wood. A ruby exhibits the brightest, darkest color, the most fruit, and the most freshness. These wines are blended.
Tawny	Increased wood aging results in lighter colors with a brownish or tawny hue. It loses the freshness of the fruit character and gains a nuttiness and more distinctive bouquet. There are wide ranges in the age of various tawny ports. The wines are blended.
Port of the vintage	Unblended tawny ports, often of considerable age.

Bottle-Aged Ports

Vintage	Unblended; the product of only one vintage. These are produced only in exceptional years and are bottled in the second or third year. They are very long-lived and have a considerable amount of sediment.
Late-bottled vintage (LBV)	These are the product of a single year, but not necessarily an exceptional one. They receive a minimum of four years in wood and do not have the sediment of a true vintage port.
Crusted	Bottled young, as with a vintage wine, but it is a blended wine, not the product of a single year. It has a great deal of sediment, due to the limited amount of wood aging.

aging produces a lighter wine with a brownish, tawny color, a nutty character, and a more distinctive bouquet. These are *tawny ports.*

There are no specific age requirements and, in any case, the age is difficult to determine because they are blended wines. Tawnies are obviously older than rubies, and some tawnies may be much older than others. Some may be made from the finest blends, often quite old, which are refreshed with some high-quality young wine. Other tawnies could be very ordinary blends of no great age, or even blends of red and white wines. In general, the great port houses select young wines with more aggressive character and greater concentration for development into tawnies.

It is important to realize that these wine types are selected and controlled. The wine maker prepares specific blends for specific types and quality levels. The wines are bottled when they reach optimum development and are ready to be consumed at that time. They are typically not improved by additional aging in the bottle.

Another type of wood-aged wine is the *port of the vintage*. This is not a blended wine but the product of a single vintage or harvest. What differentiates one of these from true vintage ports is the quality of the vintage, and the fact that it is wood aged, while vintage port is bottle aged. A port of the vintage, therefore, is an unblended tawny, often of considerable age. It is required to be at least seven years old, and the label must indicate that it was wood-aged and show both the vintage year and the date of bottling.

There are also several *bottle-aged ports*. When growing conditions result in wines that cannot be improved by blending with other harvests, and that show bottle-aging potential, the producers declare a vintage and the wines will be bottled after only a short period in wood. This is *vintage port*. Regulations require that such ports be bottled between July 1 of the second year following the vintage and June 30 of the third year. The vintage is often declared in the spring of the second year, and the wines are available that fall, after bottling.

Vintage ports can age for an astonishingly long time in the bottle, and they develop great character and bouquet. Because they spend a relatively short time in wood, they tend to throw a very heavy sediment and require decanting when served. Very old bottles may even have to be decanted through a strainer or cheesecloth because the sediment is so heavy.

A *late-bottled vintage port*, or LBV, is bottled between July 1 of the fourth year and December 31 of the sixth year. Both the vintage and the year of bottling must be declared on the label. Decanting is generally unnecessary because the wine has spent a minimum of four years in wood. These wines are not equivalent to vintage ports because of the additional wood aging and because the producers typically do not offer an LBV in the same year they offer a true vintage port.

Crusted port is yet another example of bottle-aged wine. Like vintage port it is bottled very young, but unlike vintage port it is blended and is not the product of a single, superior year. It needs to be decanted because of its heavy sediment—hence the term *crusted*—but is blended to ensure earlier maturation in the bottle relative to vintage.

Sherry

Authentic sherry comes from a delimited region on the south coast of Spain called Jerez de la Frontera. In addition to fortification, its production differs from regular wine in several other ways. One is in the handling of the grapes, another in a process known as plastering, another in the encouragement of a yeast film on the barreled wine, and finally, in its unique blending system (Fig. 2–4).

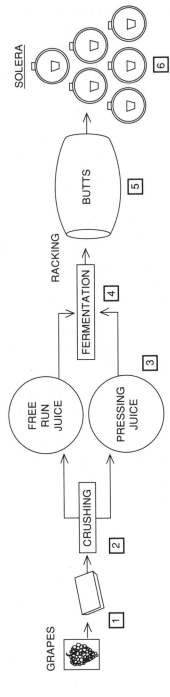

GRAPES

1

CRUSHING 2

FREE RUN JUICE

PRESSING JUICE 3

FERMENTATION 4

RACKING

BUTTS 5

SOLERA

6

1. After the grapes are harvested, they are spread on grass mats for ten to twelve hours to several days prior to crushing.

2. Crushing was traditionally done by men wearing specially designed hobnailed boots, but it is done today by mechanized presses.

3. The free-run juice is mixed with that obtained from a gentle first pressing. Before pressing, the grapes are plastered in order to increase their acidity.

4. Traditionally done in open barrels (wild fermentation), today it is likely to be fermented in temperature-controlled stainless steel.

5. Butts, or barrels, are not completely filled. Air contact is desired to enable development of the *flor*. The wines are lightly fortified with brandy at this point. Because they are fermented dry, they do not need much brandy to bring the alcohol level up to the desired 15 to 16 percent.

6. Sherries are blended and matured in the unique *solera* system (Fig. 2-5).

Figure 2–4. Sherry wine making.

Sherry Processing. Sherry grapes are harvested when fully ripened and spread on grass mats for between ten or twelve hours and several days, before being crushed. The crushing was traditionally done by placing the grapes in troughs where they were worked into a pulp by men wearing specially designed hobnailed shoes. This can no longer be justified economically due to rising labor costs, and today crushing is generally done in modern, mechanized presses. The wine is fermented from the free-run juice plus that from a gentle first pressing. Prior to the pressing, the must is *plastered,* or sprinkled with gypsum (calcium sulfate) to increase the acidity, because grapes grown in very hot climates are likely to have low acid levels. The plastering also decreases the viscosity of the must, which aids pressing.

Traditional barrel fermentation was wild and nearly uncontrollable, so the trend today is to ferment in large fiberglass or stainless steel tanks so that the temperature can be kept down. When fermentation is finished and all the sugar has been consumed, the wines are racked into fresh barrels called *butts.* Unlike other wines, sherry butts are not filled completely to reduce exposure to oxygen. In fact, the reverse occurs; the butts are partially filled to increase contact with air. This is done to encourage development of the *flor,* or "flower," and it is the *flor* that makes sherry unique. The *flor* is a yeast film that covers the surface and affects the wine in two ways: it is responsible for the bouquet, delicacy, and nuttiness of fine sherries, and it protects the wine from exposure to oxygen. Not all the wines will develop the flor, but the ones that do are the most prized, and their development is more closely monitored than that of the others.

Fortification is done following the fermentation. Brandy distilled from sherry wine is used. Compared to port, it is a relatively light fortification. Because sherries are fermented to full dryness, only small amounts of alcohol are needed to bring them up to the 15 percent or higher level. The wines that exhibit the *flor* are fortified the lightest, because an alcohol level of 16 percent or more will inhibit the *flor* growth. The wines without *flor* are expected to develop into richer, heavier sherries and may be fortified up to 17 percent. The wine's alcoholic content increases during aging due to evaporation, and one fortified up to 16 percent may end up with 18 percent alcohol after a few years.

The other deviation from traditional wine-making practices occurs during the aging and blending, when the *solera* system is used (Fig. 2–5). The *solera* system is designed to produce wines that will be consistent in style and character over time. Butts of sherry wine that exhibit similar characteristics are laid down and become the first tier of the *solera.* The next year an equal number of butts of a similar wine are added, the third year the same, and so on. When wine is finally withdrawn, it is generally taken twice yearly—only from the first tier—and never more than half of each butt is removed each

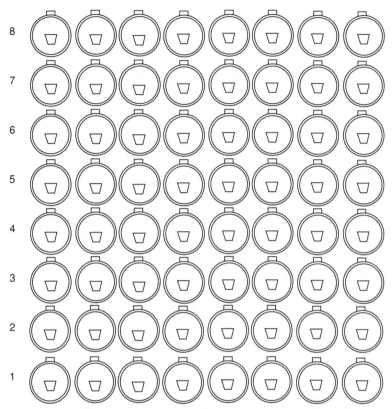

8
7
6
5
4
3
2
1

Sherry wine is withdrawn from the bottom tier and blended for bottling. The wine is replaced by withdrawing an equivalent amount from the tier (*criadera*) above it. An equal portion is taken from each butt, blended, and then added to each butt in the bottom tier. This continues with the *criaderas* above until finally the butt in the top *criadera* is filled with fresh wine.

Figure 2-5.   Sherry solera system.

year. This wine is replaced with wine from the second tier (all tiers above the first are called *criaderas*, or "nurseries"), which in turn is replaced by the third, and so forth until finally the last, or youngest, butts are filled with new wine.

In order to ensure maximum standardization, the wine withdrawn from each butt is divided equally among all of the butts in the lower *criadera*. Thus, sherry is always a blended wine and will not be vintage dated, although it is possible for the wine to bear the date when the *solera* was started.

Sherry Types and Styles. Sherries can range from light, delicate, dry wines to full-bodied, dark, sweet wines (Table 2–7). The classification of sherries into the various types is very complex and begins immediately after fermentation is completed. Basically, all sherries stem from *fino* or *oloroso* types. Those that show development of the *flor* will be called finos, and those without *flor* are expected to mature into the oloroso-type wines. The reasons various butts develop into one type or another are not well understood, and the wine maker does not seem to have much control over the process. Rather, his or her job is to recognize the development and classify and handle the wines accordingly.

Fino sherries retain their dryness, and are delicate and light in color, show a great deal of finesse, and have a characteristic nuttiness. The olorosos are darker and fuller in body and flavor. Many of them will be sweetened as well. Because all sherries are fermented dry, sweetness is obtained by adding varying amounts of a sweetening wine, which is made in a way similar to port, by arresting the fermentation before the sugar is consumed. The result is an intensely sweet wine. Traditionally, the Pedro Ximénez grape was used for this wine, although today the trend is to use the same Palomino grape from which all sherries are made.

A coloring wine, called *vino de color*, is made to give darker, richer colors to the oloroso types. It is made by boiling the grape must prior to fermentation, which results in a dark, heavy, syrupy concentration. Cream sherries are a blend of sweetened olorosos, with or without *vino de color*. Brown sherries,

Table 2–7   Sherry Wine Styles

Fino	
Fino	Fino sherries are fermented dry and show development of the *flor*. They retain their dryness, are delicate and light in color, and have a characteristic nutty taste.
Amontillado	A fino with fuller body, darker color, and a more pronounced nuttiness.
Manzanilla	A fino that is matured in Sanlúcar de Barrameda, a coastal town near the delimited sherry region. It is distinguished by a slight salty taste.
Oloroso	
Oloroso	Sherries that do not show the development of the *flor*. They are darker in color and fuller in flavor and body. They are sweetened with a sweetening wine, and the color may be adjusted with a special coloring wine.
Cream	A blend of olorosos. The color may or may not be adjusted with the coloring wine.
Brown	Sweeter and darker than the creams.

not well known in the United States, are even sweeter and darker than the creams.

Two other sherry types which may be found in the United States are Manzanilla and Amontillado. Manzanilla is a fino matured in Sanlúcar de Barrameda, a coastal town near Jerez de la Frontera, and characterized by a very slight saltiness. Wines made in Sanlúcar de Barrameda, but matured elsewhere, do not develop this characteristic. Amontillado is a fino that has developed a fuller body, darker color, and a more pronounced nuttiness.

Sparkling Wines

Sparkling wines are among the most versatile of all wines. They can be served as an aperitif, before the meal, or accompany the food throughout the meal, or be served with dessert; and, of course, they are the ideal celebration wine. Champagne, the most famous sparkling wine, is probably the most recognized wine in the world. It is also one of the most-copied wine region names. The term *champagne* really should be used only in one of two ways: to describe a sparkling wine from the Champagne region of France, a legally defined geographical area, or to describe a method of making sparkling wine. The French object to others naming their wine Champagne, but not to the use of the champagne process.

Sparkling wines are produced by inducing a second fermentation in a wine that has already been fermented. This is done by introducing additional sugar and yeasts in a closed environment. The carbon dioxide that is produced cannot escape and remains dissolved in the wine; the wine has become "sparkling." The primary factors that differentiate various sparkling wines are the variety and quality of the grapes used, the fermentation container, and the methods used to remove the sediment resulting from the second fermentation.

Champagne is made from the Pinot Noir, Pinot Meunier, and Chardonnay grapes, with the black grapes, the two Pinots, predominating. The Pinot Noir and Chardonnay are the classic grapes of the Burgundy region, but because Champagne is so much farther north, and its soil is so different, the wine made in Champagne does not resemble the red or white wines of Burgundy. The use of black grapes to make a white wine is no longer unusual, at least in the United States, where wine makers are increasingly using their surplus red grapes to satisfy the demand for white wines.

Because Champagne is the reference for most high-quality products, the Pinot Noir and Chardonnay, grown in cool areas, are the preferred grapes for a good many of the world's sparkling wines. There are, however, several notable exceptions. Spain is a major producer of sparkling wines and they are made mostly from native grapes, and the wine makers of the mid-Loire in

France are justly famous for their production of sparkling wines made from the Chenin Blanc grape, the predominant white grape of the region. There are other exceptions and they, like the two cited, are based on either tradition or climatic conditions.

The secondary fermentation must take place in a closed environment, and here the wine maker has a choice of bottles or tanks. The former offers quality (properly done), tradition, and romance, while the latter is more efficient, cost-effective, and productive.

The last of the primary quality factors mentioned, the method of sediment removal, depends on whether the wine is fermented in a bottle or tank, and, if fermented in a bottle, whether it remains in the bottle. Thus, a sparkling wine producer can ferment a wine in a bottle and remove the sediment from that bottle, or transfer the contents of many bottles to a large tank for sediment removal, or do the entire process in a tank. These three techniques are called the *champagne process or method*, the *transfer method*, and the *Charmat method* (Table 2–8).

Champagne Method. The traditional method developed in Champagne, France, is the preferred process for the highest-quality sparkling wines (Fig. 2–6). The wine that is to be used is made in a normal manner and put into special sparkling wine bottles. These bottles are heavy and strong, because they have to withstand considerable internal pressure. The indentation at the

Table 2–8 Sparkling Wine Types and Labeling

Method	Description of Manufacture	Label Terminology
Champagne	The second fermentation and all subsequent processing take place in the same bottle.	Méthode Champenoise, Metodo Champenois, Champagne Method, Fermented in This Bottle
Transfer	The second fermentation takes place in a bottle, but the contents of many bottles are then transferred to large, pressurized tanks, where subsequent processing takes place.	Fermented in The Bottle
Charmat method	All procedures, including the second fermentation, take place in large, pressurized tanks.	Naturally Fermented, Charmat Method, Bulk Fermentation

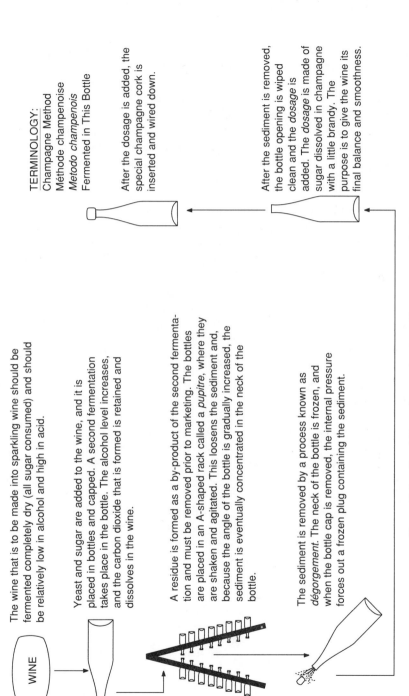

Champagne Method
Méthode champenoise
Metodo champenois
Fermented in This Bottle

After the dosage is added, the special champagne cork is inserted and wired down.

After the sediment is removed, the bottle opening is wiped clean and the *dosage* is added. The *dosage* is made of sugar dissolved in champagne with a little brandy. The purpose is to give the wine its final balance and smoothness.

The wine that is to be made into sparkling wine should be fermented completely dry (all sugar consumed) and should be relatively low in alcohol and high in acid.

Yeast and sugar are added to the wine, and it is placed in bottles and capped. A second fermentation takes place in the bottle. The alcohol level increases, and the carbon dioxide that is formed is retained and dissolves in the wine.

A residue is formed as a by-product of the second fermentation and must be removed prior to marketing. The bottles are placed in an A-shaped rack called a *pupitre*, where they are shaken and agitated. This loosens the sediment and, because the angle of the bottle is gradually increased, the sediment is eventually concentrated in the neck of the bottle.

The sediment is removed by a process known as *dégorgement*. The neck of the bottle is frozen, and when the bottle cap is removed, the internal pressure forces out a frozen plug containing the sediment.

WINE

Figure 2-6. Sparkling wine production: Champagne method.

57

bottom of the bottle, called the *punt*, serves the purpose of spreading the pressure over a larger area of glass, creating a more stable and safer container.

The wine used, called the *base wine*, should be higher in acid and lower in alcohol, compared to most table wines. The need for increased acidity is a sensory one and is related to the presence of carbon dioxide gas. Low alcohol is desired because the second fermentation will produce additional alcohol, enough to bring the total up to a normal level. In Champagne, as in most cool growing areas, it is normal for the wines to be high in acid and low in alcohol. Once the wine is in the bottle, a carefully measured amount of sugar and yeast dissolved in wine is added and the bottle sealed with a cap. Corks are rarely used today to seal the bottle during the secondary fermentation. An alcoholic fermentation proceeds, and when completed, there is a residue, mostly from spent yeast cells. These are not removed immediately, because it is considered desirable to let the wine age "on the yeasts" for a period. In Champagne, a minimum of two years is required, although many will extend this.

The sediment is removed by a complicated procedure whereby the bottles are placed, neck first, in an A-shaped rack called a *pupitre* and shaken at frequent intervals. This is traditionally done by hand, although there are mechanized versions in use today. When done by hand, the *rémueur* grasps the bottle by the base, gives it a shake, and places it back in the rack. Each time this is done, the bottle is twisted slightly and inserted at a higher angle. The objective is to loosen the sediment, concentrate it, and move it down to the neck. When the procedure is completed, the bottle is more or less upright, and the sediment rests on the cap, in the neck of the bottle. In a process known as *dégorgement*, the neck is frozen; when the cap is removed, the internal pressure forces out a frozen plug containing the sediment. The bottle opening is wiped clean, the *dosage* is added, and the cork is inserted and wired down.

The *dosage*, consisting of sugar dissolved in Champagne wine and brandy, is intended to give the wine its final balance and smoothness. When the second fermentation is complete, the wine is fermented totally dry; that is, no fermentable sugars remain. Sparkling wines are seldom marketed in this

Table 2–9   Typical Sparkling Wine Dosage Levels

Style	Dosage
Naturel	0
Brut	less than 1.5 percent
Extra Sec	1.2 to 2.0 percent
Sec	1.7 to 3.5 percent
Demi-Sec	3.3 to 5.0 percent
Doux	more than 5.0 percent

condition; they receive a *dosage* of varying sweetness depending on the characteristics of the wine itself and on the marketing policies of the manufacturer. In general, the higher the quality of the wine, the lower the amount of sugar added. The approximate sweetness level, from driest to sweetest, is designated by the terms *brut*, *extra sec (or extra dry)*, *sec (dry)*, *demi-sec*, and *doux*. These terms are used for most sparkling wines, regardless of their origin, and each producer has its own specific standards. If no dosage is added, the term is naturel or natural. This is an uncommon style, however.

Sparkling wines must be produced by this method in Champagne. If the technique is used anywhere else, the producer can label it in one of several ways: *méthode champenoise, metodo champenois*, champagne method, or Fermented in This Bottle.

Transfer Method. The second fermentation takes place in the bottle, as previously described, but then the contents of many bottles are transferred, under pressure to retain the gas, into tanks (Fig. 2–7). Here the wine is filtered

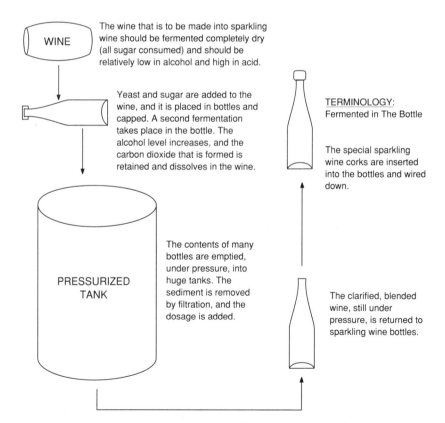

Figure 2–7. Sparkling wine production: transfer method.

and clarified and the *dosage* added prior to its being returned to the bottles. In the United States, this wine can be labeled Fermented in the Bottle. Properly done, this method can produce a fine sparkling wine, but most experts feel that the champagne method is superior.

Charmat Method. Everything, including the second fermentation, takes place in pressurized tanks (Figure 2–8). The method was developed in 1910 by, and named for, a French scientist named Eugène Charmat. Most inexpensive sparkling wines are made with this method; it is the least labor intensive and offers the most control over the various processes. Like the transfer method, however, when it is done well, it can yield very satisfactory results. These wines can be labeled Charmat, Bulk Fermentation, or Naturally Fermented.

Sparkling wines, like port wines, are normally blended from two or more years' harvests. Because of this, wines from a particular firm are more or less

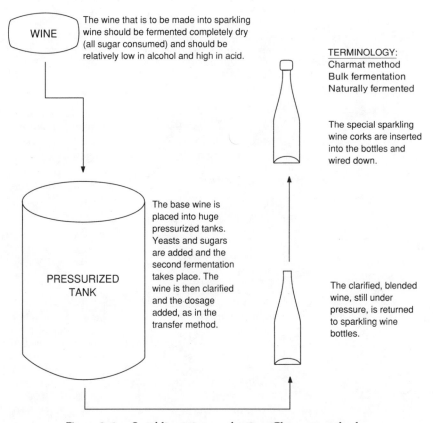

Figure 2–8. Sparkling wine production: Charmat method.

consistent from year to year. In Champagne, when growing conditions produce grapes that cannot be improved by blending, a vintage will be declared and the product will be dated. Sparkling wines from other regions in France and from other countries are sometimes also dated, but nonvintage wines make up the vast majority of what is available in the marketplace. In Champagne, wine makers feel that the vintage wines are improved with bottle age, but not the nonvintage ones. Blended, nonvintage sparkling wines are therefore seldom laid down for bottle maturation and are ready for consumption shortly after bottling—a pleasant thought.

Sparkling wines are bottled in a wide variety of sizes, many of them given unusual names, ranging from a *split*—6.3 ounces, equivalent to one-quarter of a standard 750-milliliter bottle—all the way up to a *nebuchadnezzar*—containing 15 liters, or more than 500 ounces, the equivalent of twenty bottles (Table 2–10).

The Great Sweet Wines

It is a paradox that both some of the least expensive and some of the most expensive wines in the world are sweet. The main difference is the source of sweetness; the sugar can be added from another source or can be provided entirely by the grape. Even with the naturally sweet wines the grape needs some assistance, because no grape, regardless of how ripe it may become, can attain the needed sugar levels. The assistance comes through some form of concentration of the fruit sugars.

In some wines, the grapes are not crushed and fermented when picked, but

Table 2–10   Sparkling Wine Bottle Sizes

Trade Terminology	Bottle Equivalent	Capacity	
		Metric	Ounces
Split	one-quarter	187 ml.	6.3
Half Bottle	one-half	375 ml.	12.7
Bottle	1	750 ml.	25.4
Magnum	2	1.5 L.	50.7
Jeroboam	4	3.0 L.	101.4
Rehoboam	6	4.5 L.	152.2
Methuselah	8	6.0 L.	202.9
Salmanazar	12	9.0 L.	304.3
Balthazar	16	12.0 L.	405.8
Nebuchadnezzar	20	15.0 L.	507.2

are allowed to dry somewhat. During the drying, only water is lost; the grape solids, mostly sugar, remain intact. Such grapes can be fermented into dry, powerful wines or can be used to make sweet dessert wines. Italian Amarone and Recioto are examples of the dry and sweet styles, respectively. The best known of the sweet wines, and probably the most complex and interesting, are the ones produced from grapes affected by *Botrytis cinerea*, the so-called noble rot.

Botrytis cinerea is a mold, and when it appears at the wrong time, it can be a disaster in the vineyard. Under proper conditions, however, it is responsible for some of the most luscious and marvelous wines made.

What happens is that the mold attacks ripe grapes (if the grapes are not ripe, it becomes a vineyard disease) and perforates and breaks down the skin, allowing evaporation of moisture and resulting in shriveling of the grapes. The final sugar content depends on the original degree of ripeness and on how far the process is allowed to proceed.

The fermentation of such grapes generally cannot proceed to dryness. As the sugar is transformed into alcohol, a point is eventually reached at which the alcohol level is toxic to the yeasts and the fermentation ceases. At this point, if all the sugar has not been consumed, the wine is sweet. How sweet depends on how much sugar was originally present; the wines can range from slightly to extremely sweet. Today, the fermentation is generally stopped at whatever ratio of sugar to alcohol is considered most desirable.

The best of these wines are made by repeated pickings of the vineyards, harvesting at any one time only the fully shriveled, nearly raisinlike grapes. These grapes yield very little juice, but have the highest sugar levels. This is why the wines must always be somewhat expensive. The harvesting is expensive and time consuming, and the yield is much lower than with other wines. The wines are not only costly to make, but also scarce, and that also increases their market value.

If all these wines had to offer was sweetness, their appeal would be a good deal more limited than it is. Sweetness must be balanced with acid or it can become tiring and cloying, and the best of these wines have high levels of acid. The acids, like the sugars, increase proportionally as the grape dehydrates. The *cinerea Botrytis* itself creates very complex and distinctive odors and flavors. The texture is also altered, becoming very smooth and oily, in part due to the sugar, and in part from the higher than normal amount of glycerine.

There are several regions in Europe that have long been famous for their production of these types of wines. The Sauternes and Barsac region of Bordeaux in France is probably the best known. *Botrytis cinerea* can be depended on to appear somewhat regularly, and the wines of Sauternes and Barsac are nearly always sweet, although there are variations in sweetness, acidity, and quality from one vintage to another and from one property to another. Sauternes can be used as an example of the low yield from these grapes, for its maximum permitted output in wine per acre is about one-third less than the next lowest in Bordeaux, and the better properties do not even approach the maximum.

In Germany, the highest expression of the wine makers' art are their Auslesen, Beerenauslesen, and Trockenbeerenauslesen. Auslesen means "special selection" of the ripest bunches. These may or may not be infected with *Botrytis cinerea*, although the best of them are. Beerenauslesen means "special berry selection"; the wine maker is selecting only the grapes affected by *Botrytis cinerea*. Trockenbeerenauslesen translates as "special dried berry selection"; only those grapes that are shriveled nearly into raisins are picked. The progression from Auslesen to Trockenbeerenauslesen is a progression in sweetness, richness of color, flavor, and greater development of odor complexity. The *Botrytis cinerea* character also becomes much more pronounced. These wines, especially the latter two, are quite rare and are always expensive.

In Hungary, the sweet wines of the Tokaji area, known to the rest of the world as Tokay, have been made for centuries. They also owe their distinctiveness to the *Botrytis cinerea* but are made somewhat differently than are the ones from France and Germany (Fig. 2–9). The molded grapes are separated during the harvest and placed in containers called *puttonyos*. The sweet Tokaji wines, called Tokaji Aszu, are made by adding varying amounts of the molded grapes to the others.If one *puttonyo* is added to a container of regular grapes, the wine is labeled Tokaji Aszu, one *puttonyo*. Addition of more of the *Botrytis cinerea* grapes results in a label indication of two *puttonyos*, three, and so forth. Five *puttonyos* is the highest normally available in the United States. Unlike Sauternes and the German wines, Tokaji Aszu generally is not served chilled.

SENSORY STANDARDS

Wines are evaluated using the senses of sight, smell, taste, and of touch. It is also believed that thermal perception, the awareness of hot and cold, is important in the sensory evaluation of both foods and beverages. It may even be possible that the perception of pain is used in wine evaluation, because highly acid or tannic wines actually may be triggering pain receptors in the mouth. In evaluating wines, the taster first looks at it, then smells it, and finally tastes and feels it. A special glass is desirable to assist the evaluation (Fig. 2–10).

The abilities of various tasters to identify the many visual, olfactory, taste, and tactile components will vary widely based on their sensory equipment and their experience. Of the two, experience is the more important. Although

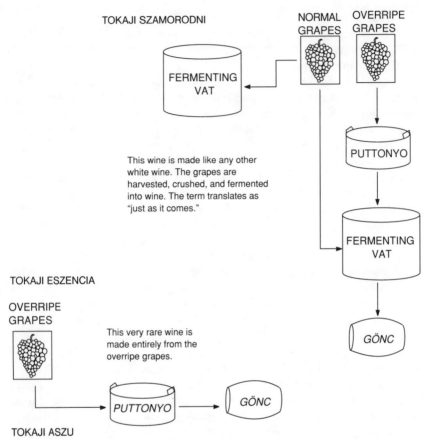

TOKAJI SZAMORODNI

NORMAL GRAPES

OVERRIPE GRAPES

FERMENTING VAT

This wine is made like any other white wine. The grapes are harvested, crushed, and fermented into wine. The term translates as "just as it comes."

PUTTONYO

FERMENTING VAT

GÖNC

TOKAJI ESZENCIA

OVERRIPE GRAPES

This very rare wine is made entirely from the overripe grapes.

PUTTONYO → GÖNC

TOKAJI ASZU

The grapes that have been infected with *Botrytis cinerea* are placed in separate containers called *puttonyos*. Each *puttonyo* has a capacity of about 35 liters. The overripe grapes are made into a paste called *aszu*. This was traditionally done by trodding with the feet, but today is more likely to be mechanized. The *aszu* paste is added in specific proportions to a must made from normally ripened grapes. Fermentation takes place in open vats. The style of the wine is determined by the number of *puttonyos* added to the normal grape must. A wine labeled *three puttonyos* is nearly one-third overripe grapes, while one labeled *four puttonyos* contains about 40 percent of the botrytized grapes. *Five puttonyos*, the highest normally available in the United States, is 50 percent or more.

After a short fermentation period in the open vats, the wines are racked and moved to small wooden casks called *gönci*. The *gönci* have a capacity of about 140 liters. A slow fermentation and oxidation reaction takes place over several years. The *gönci* are not tightly bunged, or sealed, in order to encourage air contact. Over the years a fungus growth is formed on the exposed wine surface, and this reduces the rate of oxidation and makes a significant contribution to the flavor and aroma of the wine.

Figure 2–9. Tokaji Aszu production.

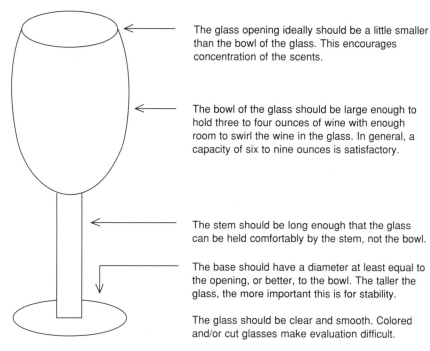

The glass opening ideally should be a little smaller than the bowl of the glass. This encourages concentration of the scents.

The bowl of the glass should be large enough to hold three to four ounces of wine with enough room to swirl the wine in the glass. In general, a capacity of six to nine ounces is satisfactory.

The stem should be long enough that the glass can be held comfortably by the stem, not the bowl.

The base should have a diameter at least equal to the opening, or better, to the bowl. The taller the glass, the more important this is for stability.

The glass should be clear and smooth. Colored and/or cut glasses make evaluation difficult.

Figure 2-10.   Wine evaluation glass.

people differ in their visual, olfactory, and taste capabilities, with most persons the differences are not significant. What inexperienced tasters lack is a frame of reference. They may see, smell, and taste the same things as an expert, but these perceptions have no meaning to them.

Consider this analogy: if a person from another culture who had never seen or tasted broccoli were to eat some, it would not have the same sensory meaning as it would to someone who was familiar with the vegetable. Both tasters would be able to see the green color, it would smell and taste the same to both, and both would have the same aftertaste in their mouths. To the inexperienced taster, however, the appearance, smell, and taste would be new; that person would be able to relate it to little or nothing with which he or she was familiar. The other taster would have a great deal of information stored in his or her memory that would enable that taster to make a rational evaluation. The broccoli is the right color, or it is not. The shape and texture are proper, or they are not. The smell and taste are as they ought to be, or they are not.

This is why some very experienced and expert people can taste a wine and identify not only the grape it is made from, but also the region it is from and, sometimes, even the specific vineyard or property and the year. This is not as mysterious as it may appear. Such a person has probably tasted this particular wine many times, and its sensory characteristics are implanted in the memory. Just as many people could correctly identify strawberry and raspberry ice cream, the wine expert can differentiate between Bordeaux and Burgundy wines, between true Champagne and California sparkling wines, and even among several Bordeaux, Burgundies, or Champagnes.

Therefore, to learn about wines, one must evaluate, and evaluate carefully, as many wines as possible in order to build a library of information in the memory. It is true, of course, that some are better suited for this than others, just as some people can be trained to service an automobile better than others, or to run faster or jump higher. Barring any physical disability, though, and providing there is interest and commitment, anyone can be trained to know something about auto repair, to run faster, to jump higher — and to be more skilled in sensory evaluation.

Visual Examination of Wine

A great deal of information is available to the eye, but the most important things are probably the *color* and the *clarity* of the wine. All wines, even whites, have color, and the color is an indication of the type, the maturity, and the condition of the wine. White wine colors can range from light straw to deep, rich golden tones. Rich golden colors result from very ripe grapes of certain varieties, particularly the Chardonnay. They also can be attributed to the use of wood during maturation, to age in general, and to increased sugar levels. Many white Burgundies and California Chardonnays, for example, have golden tones because they have had contact with wood. These wines are also likely to get more bottle aging than white wines normally would, adding to the golden color. French Sauternes and the German sweet wines are made from very ripe, concentrated grapes, and the finished wines have substantial levels of residual sugar. This also contributes color, as does the long bottle aging many of these wines get prior to being consumed.

Wines made from lighter grapes, or from grapes that have not ripened fully, have lighter colors. It is even possible for a white wine to have a slight greenish tint. The Chardonnay grape, when grown in Chablis, the northernmost and coolest part of Burgundy, does not get nearly as ripe as in the Côte de Beaune region, and the color not only is lighter, but also may show tints of green.

White wines, as they age, not only become darker in color, but also they can lose their brightness and become dull looking. If they are very old, or have been improperly stored at high or widely fluctuating temperatures, or exposed to light, or—especially—if they have been exposed to air, they could develop various shades of brown.

When speaking of color, wine tasters often use the terms *hue, tint,* and *shade;* these are very useful terms, particularly when evaluating red wines. Red wines obtain their color from being fermented with the grape skins; thus, not only are there darker colors present, but also the wines are much more saturated with color compounds. Red wines can range from very light, bright, ruby red colors that are somewhat transparent to heavy, dense, purple-black colors that are nearly impossible to see through. Nearly opaque wines are said to exhibit a great deal of *depth.*

The color comes from the grape variety and the method of wine making. Some grapes produce darker wines than others, and when they are fermented for relatively long periods, they can extract a great deal of very dark pigment. Other grapes naturally produce lighter-colored wines, and the method of wine making can accentuate this. Thus, a French Beaujolais, one of the lightest red wines, has a very bright, light red color that has little density. An Italian Barolo, on the other hand, is not so bright, the color is nearly black, and there is tremendous density of color due to the saturation of pigment. Dark red colors can also come from grapes grown in cool climates.

Rosé wines typically come in varying shades of pink; orange or orange-brown colors are considered undesirable. They have more color pigment than white wines because they have been fermented on the skins; but the skin contact is limited, and the color not only is different from reds, but less intense as well.

Red wines, as explained in the section on wine components (see page 37), gradually lose color saturation as the color pigments react with the tannins and precipitate out. The colors become less dense and the wine becomes lighter in appearance. The pigments that remain oxidize slowly over time and turn brown. Thus, red wines become lighter and browner in color as they age, while white wines become darker and browner as they age. Theoretically, one could have a red and a white wine so old and in such poor condition that the person could not tell which was red and which was white. They would both be a muddy brown color.

The other main criterion of the visual examination is the clarity of the wine. Well-made wine should be very clear and absolutely free of suspended materials. Terms such as *brilliant, clear, cloudy, dull, hazy,* and others are used to describe the clarity. A wine described as brilliant not only is clear, but also has a sparkle to it. Dull is the opposite of brilliant, while hazy indicates that some sort of suspended materials can be seen. These could be due to microbial spoilage, faulty treatment during the wine-making processes, or the normal, natural aging deposit.

The first two factors probably would be accompanied by odor and flavor defects; the latter would not. Many red wines have sediment; it is a result of the normal chemical reactions that take place during aging. If such a wine is not handled and opened properly, this sediment will become dispersed throughout the wine.

It is important to be able to distinguish between sediment that has been stirred up in the wine and suspended materials resulting from spoilage or bad wine making. If the visual examination does not answer the question, smelling and tasting it will. Normal sediment in red wines is harmless but, if stirred up, interferes with both the visual and the taste evaluation. This is why red wines are decanted. The objective is to leave the sediment in the bottle and keep it out of the glass.

White wines do not have any sediment but may have small colorless crystals in the bottle. These are tartrate crystals, which precipitate out of the wine due to cold storage or sudden temperature changes. The wine maker can process the wine so that this is unlikely to occur, but some feel that the procedure involved also strips out many desirable components as well and so will avoid it. At any rate, like red wine sediment, it is harmless and may even be an indication of a fine wine, but it should be left in the bottle when pouring.

Another defect to look for is the presence of bubbles in a still, or nonsparkling, wine. They could be from still-active yeasts or from bacteria that produce carbon dioxide. Good wine-making practices do not allow either *gassy* condition to occur.

Bubbles, of course, are acceptable in sparkling wines. The taster looks for very small bubbles that have excellent persistence — that is, they rise continuously from the bottom of the glass. The larger the bubbles, and the less the persistence, the lower the perceived visual quality of the wine.

Wine tasters often manipulate the glasses in specific ways to aid in the evaluation. The glass is tilted, especially with red wines, to observe how the color changes from the center, where the depth is greatest, to the very shallow edges. A substantial core of color, fading out to the so-called onion skin (a literal description of the color) at the edges can be an indication of a gracefully aging red wine. Young red wines show little if any color change from the center to the edge.

The other thing that is done with the glass is to swirl it in order to evaluate the *legs*, or *tears* (Fig. 2–11). Because a water-alcohol mixture has greater viscosity than water alone, the more alcohol there is in the wine, the greater the tendency for the wine to break up into distinct rivulets and move slowly down the glass. If a glass of water is swirled, the liquid will return quickly in broad sheets rather than rivulets. Alcohol is primarily responsible for the tactile sensation called *body*, the perception of fullness or viscosity of the wine, and so it can be partially evaluated visually.

Another way to check the legs is to pour the wine carefully and observe how the wine rises up the sides of the glass. Alcohol is more volatile than

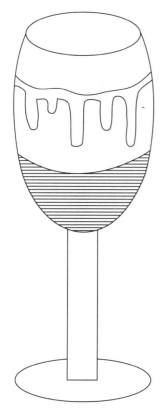

When wine is swirled in the glass, it returns down the sides either in broad sheets of liquid or in distinctive rivulets. Water tends to sheet, while wine, having more body or viscosity (due to the alcohol), breaks off into rivulets that move more slowly down the sides of the glass.

Wine does not necessarily have to be swirled to observe this action. Because of the reduced surface tension resulting from the evaporation of alcohol, the liquid tends to rise up the sides of the glass. The height it attains, the more distinctive the rivulets it forms, and the more slowly it returns, the more alcohol it contains.

Figure 2–11. Wine *tears*, or *legs*.

water and evaporates more quickly. This reduces the surface tension of the liquid and causes the wine to ride up the sides. The greater the tendency to do this, the more apparent the legs or tears and the greater the alcoholic content and body of the wine.

Because alcohol comes from the grape sugar, it is also an indication of riper, more fragrant, and more flavorful grapes. Of course, this is not true when the wine's alcohol has been increased by *chaptalization*, the adding of sugar to the grape must.

Olfactory Examination of Wine

There is probably more information to be obtained from smelling wine than from any other single act—including tasting it. There are only four tastes, sweet, sour, salt, and bitter, and no one can be trained to perceive more than these. Of the four, only sweet and sour are normally present in wines. Salty and bitter tastes are unusual, although some sherries may exhibit saltiness and slight traces of bitterness can be found in certain wines. Consuming the sediment in red wines can lead to bitter tastes, but sediment should remain in the bottle. There are many more odors than tastes, thousands of them, and trained people can detect about 1,000 or more. People can also detect very small differences in concentration, because the odor receptors are several thousand times as sensitive as are the taste receptors. The sense of smell, therefore, is much more advanced than the sense of taste. A typical wine has some 300 compounds, of which about 200 are more or less odorous. Experienced wine tasters, therefore, pay a great deal of attention to olfactory evaluation.

There are two primary types of odors that are noted in wine: the *aroma* and the *bouquet*. The aroma comes from the grape or grapes the wine is made from, while the bouquet is developed during the processing and aging of the wine. In a young wine, made from one grape, the predominant odor should be the smell of that particular grape. This is the aroma, and compared to the bouquet it is neither as complex nor as multidimensional. It is more straightforward and perhaps easier to appreciate.

There are several types of grape odors. Some have a fruity character, some are flowery or floral, while others can be said to be grassy or herbal. For example, Chardonnay and Pinot Noir have a great deal of fruit in their aroma, while Riesling, Gewürztraminer and especially Muscat have a distinctive floral character. The Sauvignon Blanc is said to be somewhat grassy, and the Cabernet Sauvignon grape can remind one of bell peppers. Some grapes have a spicy quality; Gewürztraminer, in fact, translates as "spicy Traminer" (a grape variety). The Syrah of the Rhône region in France often has a distinctive black pepper smell.

Aroma is a characteristic of young wines. The odors that the grape have contributed are still fresh, and the many odorous components produced during slow aging have not yet been developed. When a wine is made from a distinctive grape variety, from ripe grapes, and is skillfully made, the variety can be identified merely by smelling the wine.

The odors that make up the bouquet are of indirect origin; that is, they do not arise from the grape. Fermentation, subsequent processing, and, most important, wood and bottle aging result in the development of many new odorous compounds. Taken together, they are called the bouquet. The great satisfaction and enjoyment wine lovers receive from a well-matured wine is probably due more to the bouquet than to any other single factor. It is broader, less direct, and more ethereal than aroma. It is also much more difficult to describe and categorize than aroma. Just as young wines exhibit distinctive aromas and little, if any, bouquet, mature wines lose their aromatic characteristics and begin to develop bouquet. The condition of youth versus maturity can be detected with both the visual and the olfactory senses.

The sense of smell suffers from adaptation to a greater degree than, for example, the sense of taste. This means that although odors can be more easily detected, there is a temporary loss of the ability to perceive. For this reason, when the wine is smelled, a long deep sniff is taken, and then the taster pulls away. There is no sense in sniffing for a long period of time. This is in contrast to the actual tasting, in which the wine is left in the mouth and moved about for an extended period.

In addition to evaluating the aroma and bouquet, the wine taster looks for undesirable odors. Flaws, defects, or spoilage in the wine can be detected with the nose more easily than with any of the other senses. Acetaldehyde, sulfur dioxide (SO_2), acetic acid, ethyl acetate, and mercaptans are some of the indicators of major problems with the wine.

Acetaldehyde is formed by contact with oxygen. It has a baked, musty odor reminiscent of sherry. As described earlier (see page 52), sherry is deliberately exposed to air while maturing in the butts, and it develops this characteristic odor. When the smell is well advanced in table wines, it is very disagreeable and is a sign of overly long storage, poor storage, exposure to oxygen, or some combination of these factors.

Sulfur dioxide is used throughout the entire wine-making process, from the vineyards to the bottling. White wines are more likely to show excessive SO_2 than reds because it is used more liberally to preserve the wines' freshness and to aid in clarification. A slight odor of SO_2 that dissipates quickly after opening is not uncommon, nor is it cause for alarm. When it is distinct and lingers, however, it is a sign of poor wine making and is a serious flaw. SO_2 can be detected by its characteristic burning matchstick odor.

Acetic acid has been defined as a volatile acid (see page 35); unlike fixed acids, it does not come from the grapes. It is developed naturally by the transformation of ethyl alcohol into acetic acid through the action of acetobacters, or acetic acid bacteria. Because the bacteria are present in the environment, and because wine contains ethyl alcohol, this reaction is inevitable over time. Young, fresh, well-made wines are expected to show very low levels of volatile acid; anything else is an indication of faulty wine making. Well-matured wines, particularly red wines, have higher levels, but it is not a flaw unless the wine takes on the vinegar characteristics of acetic acid. It can be both smelled and tasted and is a reliable indicator of a wine that should be rejected.

Ethyl acetate results from the formation of an ester of acetic acid and ethyl alcohol. It has a paint varnish odor and is both distinctive and disagreeable.

Mercaptans are compounds that have among the most unpleasant of all undesirable odors in wines. Hydrogen sulfide, characterized by a rotten egg smell, can be produced by the reduction of elemental sulfur and can, in reaction with alcohol, produce a mercaptan. Mercaptans are very odorous; they are added to natural gas to make the smell unpleasant and distinctive for safety purposes, and skunk odor contains a mercaptan. Further reduction of mercaptans can result in compounds with an old onion smell.

Wine tasters swirl the wine in the glass prior to smelling it to expose the wine to oxygen and bring it to life. Oxygen is the greatest single enemy of wine during storage, but is beneficial during consumption. If you pour a newly opened bottle carefully into two glasses and swirl one but not the other, the one that has been oxygenated will have a more distinctive and lively odor. Sparkling wines are an obvious exception to this recommendation, because the agitation would encourage the loss of the bubbles.

Taste Evaluation of Wine

Many people use the terms *taste* and *flavor* interchangeably, but they refer to two different kinds of perceptions. Taste should be used only with reference to sweet, sour, salt, and bitter, while flavor is the combination of tastes and odors perceived in the mouth. When food is chewed, or wine swirled about in the mouth, odors are released that rise up the nasal passages and go to the odor receptors in the brain just as if they had been drawn in through the nose. When people claim that they cannot taste anything due to a cold, they are technically incorrect, for the basic tastes can still be perceived. The difference is that they cannot smell anything, either in the mouth or through the nose, and the food or beverage has little or no flavor. Thus the sense of smell is an important part of the sensory evaluation in the mouth.

Although the taste receptors, or taste buds, are located all over the mouth, specific tastes tend to be concentrated in certain areas (Fig. 2–12). Sugar and other sweet tastes are detected on the front of the tongue, salt on the sides of the tongue toward the front, sour or acid also on the sides but farther back, and bitter at the base, or rear, of the tongue. The important tastes for wine evaluation are sweet and sour. Salt is very rare, and bitter tastes are not common. When these latter two are present, they are usually of only slight intensity.

The terms *threshold*, *adaptation*, and *reaction time* are important in sensory perception. Threshold refers to the concentration or strength of a stimulus that must be present in order to be perceived. There is an *absolute threshold*, that concentration at which a stimulus can be detected but not identified. The *recognition threshold* is that at which identification can be made. For example, if sugar is present at below the absolute threshold level, it will not be perceived (tasted). If it is present at the absolute threshold level, the person will be aware of a taste, but will not know what it is. When the concentration is raised to the recognition level, the perception will be identi-

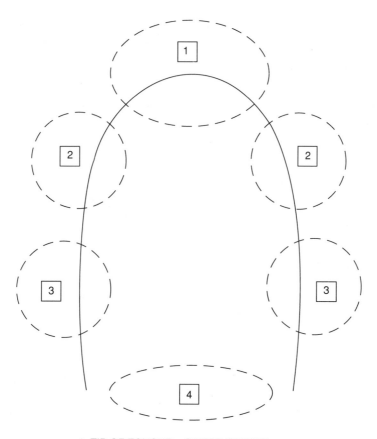

1. TIP OF TONGUE = SWEET (SUGAR)

2. FRONT SIDES OF TONGUE = SALT

3. BACK SIDES OF TONGUE = SOUR (ACID)

4. BASE OF TONGUE = BITTER

Figure 2–12.   Location of taste buds on the tongue.

fied as sugar or sweetness. The recognition threshold for sugar is about one-half of 1 percent, or 0.5 percent, for most people. This is the highest of the taste thresholds; sour, salt, and bitter tastes can be perceived at lower concentrations. When taste stimuli are mixed, the thresholds will change. This is of great importance in the case of sweet and sour tastes.

Adaptation, the temporary loss of the ability to perceive, has been explained with reference to the sense of smell (see page 71). With taste it is less of a problem, because taste deals with compounds of much higher molecular concentrations.

Reaction time, or *sensory lag*, refers to the length of time it takes for the stimulus to produce a reaction. Salt is the fastest, but it will be disregarded here because it is seldom present. In wine evaluation, sugar has the shortest reaction time, followed by sour and then bitter. Therefore, wine is swirled in the mouth for several seconds, to allow time for taste perception, and sugar or sweetness is the initial one.

The interrelationship of the basic tastes is very important; the sweet and acid tastes must be in proper balance. The critical one is acid. If a wine is perceived as low in acid, it will taste flat. Eating an apple can be used as an example of this. If the apple is overripe and acid deficient, it is not very satisfying to eat, even though it could be sweet; it tastes flat. If the apple is perfectly ripe, the increase in acidity gives it a mouth-watering quality and it is much more enjoyable. It is the same with wine; the presence of acid gives the wine a lively, tangy, mouth-watering quality that is absent when the wine tastes flat. A flat-tasting wine just sort of sits in the mouth and is not very interesting.

The perception of acid changes at different sugar levels. A totally dry wine, one with no perceived sweetness, may taste balanced with an acidity of about 0.5 to .07 percent. This wine would taste tart or sour, however, if the acid level were raised to 1.0 percent. A sweet wine with acidity of only 0.5 to 0.7 percent, on the other hand, will taste flat and could require 1.0 percent or more to be in balance.

Sweet wines that have insufficient acid to balance the sugar are often cloying—they are only sweet, not mouth watering, and are tiring to drink. Grapes grown in very warm or hot climates are generally acid deficient and produce flat-tasting wines. Grapes grown in cool climates, or grapes that do not ripen properly for whatever reason, not only have problems due to low sugar levels, but also may have excessive acidity. Properly ripened grapes are those that have attained a desirable sugar-to-acid ratio. Wines made from such grapes taste balanced.

In addition to the balance between sugar and acid, the taster evaluates the many flavors present in wine. Young, or relatively young, wines should show a great deal of fruitiness and freshness. Wines that have matured properly have lost much of these qualities but have made significant gains in flavor complexity. In this regard, it is similar to the difference between aroma and bouquet.

Just as the glasses are swirled to aerate the wine, experienced drinkers will *whistle in* the wine during tasting. This consists of holding the wine in a cupped tongue and inhaling noisily. The effect is the same as swirling a glass: the wine is exposed to additional oxygen and the aroma or bouquet opens up and becomes more distinct.

Once the wine is swallowed—or spit out, as experienced tasters will do when examining many wines at one time—the aftertaste is evaluated. Some wines have a tendency to disappear once swallowed, while others linger on and on.

Tactile Evaluation of Wine

It is important to distinguish between the often confusing perceptions of taste sensations and tactile sensations. Tannins offer particular difficulties in wine tasting. Tannins provide astringency and are felt, not tasted. Inexperienced tasters often mistake the acid taste with the astringent feel of tannins. For example, lemon juice provides acid and is tasted, while strong tea or aspirin produces a rough feel, especially when the tongue is rubbed against the roof of the mouth.

The body, or viscosity, of the wine is another tactile sensation. Wine is more viscous than water because it is a water-alcohol mixture, and the higher the alcoholic level, the greater the perception of body. The taster can gain an early perception of viscosity from examining the tears, or legs, of the wine, but the final decision takes place in the mouth. One of the objections to low-alcohol light wines (wines of less than 10 percent alcohol by volume) is that they have a watery feel compared to wines of normal alcoholic content (10 to 14 percent alcohol by volume).

Sugar in sweet wines can contribute to the perception of viscosity, as can glycerol, but the latter is probably overrated. The normal maximum concentration of glycerol is about 1.5 percent by weight, and tactile sensation at that concentration is minimal. However, it may be a factor in wines such as Sauternes and the sweeter German wines. These wines have a unique and distinctively oily viscosity to them. A term wine tasters use to describe such a sensation is *unctuous*.

Red wines, fermented on the skins, have a greater molecular weight than whites. All other things being equal, they have a weightier, fuller feel in the mouth. Some white wines, notably white Burgundies and California Chardonnays, have a full, creamy fleshiness to them, which is a result of something more than merely the alcoholic content, although these are among the white wines highest in alcohol.

Sparkling wines should have the carbon dioxide dissolved as completely as possible in the wine. A well-made sparkling wine will produce a sensation of creaminess and fullness in the mouth as all the tiny bubbles seem to swell and expand slowly. It is a unique sensation and one of the sources of enjoyment with Champagnes and other sparkling wines.

It is possible that pain can be felt during wine tasting. A wine with an abundance of either tannin or acid actually could result in overstimulation of the sensory receptors.

Sensory Perception Terms

APPEARANCE

Brilliant: Free of suspended material.

Clear: A slight haze from a few suspended particles may be seen.

Cloudy: A definite haze and particular materials can be observed.

Depth: The basic fullness or paleness of the color of a red wine. Some wines may be very dark, almost black, and nearly opaque. The color of such wines would be said to exhibit a great deal of depth.

Dull: There is a definite colloidal haze.

Gassy: The sensation of carbon dioxide gas escaping from the wine. It is best used to describe a tactile perception, but sometimes can be observed as well.

Green tinged, straw, gold, light brown, amber-brown: Progression of colors in white wines.

Hazy: Refers to a definite colloidal haze in the wine. **Dull** is considered a more accurate and specific term.

Hue: The color or tint of the wine.

Legs: An indication of the body, or viscosity, of the wine. A mixture of alcohol and water will rise up the sides of the glass. The more distinctive this process is, the higher the level of alcohol and, probably, the greater the perception of body in the wine. Another way to observe the legs is to swirl the glass and observe the pattern as the wine returns down the sides of the glass. Again, it is possible to make a preliminary judgment as to the viscosity of the wine. Another term with similar meaning is **tears.**

Purple, ruby red, red, red-brown, tawny: Progression of colors in red wines.

Shade: Related to the **hue,** the color. Indicates the gradations of color.

Tears: See **legs.**

Ullage: When bottles leak, they will not be full, and this is termed the *ullage*. It is often accompanied by oxidation.

ODOR

Acetic: The smell of acetic acid (vinegar) and ethyl acetate (smells like fingernail polish remover).

Alcohol: See **hot**.

Alcoholic: See **hot**.

Apricot/Dried apricot: The term often used to describe the odor of wines made from grapes affected by *Botrytis cinerea*. Examples include the French Sauternes and German Auslesen, Beerenauslesen, and Trochenbeerenauslen.

Aroma: The term used to describe the characteristic odor of the grape. A young wine is expected to exhibit aroma, because most of the odors are of direct origin—from the grape(s).

Aromatic: A distinctive odor found in wines made from specific varieties.

Asescence: Same as **acetic**.

Baked: Wines that have been heated have a caramel-like odor.

Blackberry/Raspberry: An odor often found in young red wines. Also the characteristic aroma of a Zinfandel wine.

Bouquet: Odors of indirect origin, produced during the processing and aging of the wine. The opposite of **aroma.**

Burny: A nearly painful perception in the nose. May be found in **hot** wines.

Butterscotch: An odor associated with wines aged in oak. In particular, the term is often used with white Burgundies and Chardonnays matured in French oak.

Caramel: Heated sweet wines. See **baked.**

Complex: A difficult term for tasters to agree about. Technically, it refers to the juxtaposition of several odors. A **bouquet** could be referred to as complex because it is multidimensional, whereas an **aroma,** being more or less one-dimensional, usually would not be.

Corky: The smell of a wine from a bottle with a spoiled or moldy cork.

Fermenting: A yeasty smell.

Flowery: A typical smell in wines from certain varieties. Also many young white wines.

Foxy: The distinctive odor of wines made from the American grape species *Vitis labrusca.* Often called the "Welch's grape juice" smell.

Fresh: The odor of young wines.

Fruity: A distinctive odor in wines. Young wines exhibit this quality, and so do wines form certain grape varieties.

Green: Wines made with unripened fruit.

Green olive: An odor often associated with Cabernet Sauvignon, but found with other wines as well.

Green pepper: Also associated with Cabernet Sauvignon.

Herbaceous: A type of odor attributed to the grape variety. The Sauvignon family is said to have herbaceous odors, whereas other varieties smell **flowery, spicy,** or **fruity.**

Hot: A perception, possibly even painful, due to excessive levels of alcohol. This can be noted both in the nose and the mouth.

Leafy: An objectionable odor that may be found in young wines. See **stemmy.**

Lees: Wines that have been left too long on the lees, or sediment, during fermentation could exhibit this odor. It could be very objectionable, because **mercaptans** may also be present.

Maderized: Similar to **oxidized.**

Mercaptans: Compounds that have very disagreeable odors. Skunk odorant, for example, is a mercaptan. Chemically, they are methyl and ethyl sulfides.

Mildew: A fungus odor from grapes that have been affected with mildew.

Moldy: Wines either made with moldy grapes or stored in moldy containers. Not to be confused with wines made from the "noble" mold, *Botrytis cinerea.* Even this mold, however, requires very specific conditions; otherwise it is a vineyard disease.

Mousy: A bacterial odor. If noted, it could be in wines made from late-picked grapes or from acid-deficient musts.

Oak: The purpose of oak maturation is to develop greater complexity in the taste and odor of wines, most often red wines. When the oak dominates, or the wine smells **woody,** it is considered flawed.

Oxidized: Caused by the presence of a compound called acetaldehyde, the result of chemical reactions between the wine and oxygen. It is also called the "sherry" smell, because sherries are purposely exposed to oxygen during processing. It is considered objectionable in table wines.

Raisin: Found in wines made from semidried or entirely dried grapes. In some wines, a slight raisin character is considered normal, but it is objectionable if too distinctive.

Rancid: A specific term used for old, oxidized, high-alcohol red wines. Usually these wines are also sweet. It is considered an attribute for certain wines.

Resin: The smell of retsina wines. A turpentine odor, which is normal in retsina, could also be due to storage of wine in contaminated containers.

Sauerkraut: From lactic acid. May be found in wines that have undergone excessive malolactic fermentation.

Smooth: A term used to indicate the opposite of **harsh** or **astringent.**

Sophisticated: An aduberated wine. The smell of ingredients or components that normally should not be present.

Spicy: One of the distinctive aromas of certain grape varieties. The classic example is Gewürztraminer (literally, spicy Traminer).

Stemmy/stalky: Could be found in wines fermented from musts containing fresh stems.

Sulfide: Hydrogen sulfide; very offensive.

Sulfur dioxide: The "burning matchstick" odor; always objectionable when detected.

Vanilla: Associated with **butterscotch** in white Burgundies and Chardonnays. Probably due to the species of oak used for maturation.

Vinegary: Acetic acid and ethyl acetate.

Vinous: A term connoting neutrality of aroma. The wine does not have a specific or distinctive odor.

Woody: Wines stored too long in wood or in young, improperly treated cooperage.

Yeasty: A smell arising from fermenting yeasts.

Young: A wine that smells **fresh, fruity,** and **unoxidized.**

TASTE

Acidic: The taste of acid. Similar terms are **sour, tart,** and **acidulous.** These words should not be used to describe the taste of acetic acid.

Acidulous: Taste is overly sour.

Aftertaste: Used to refer to the lingering perceptions of taste, flavor, odor, and feel.

Balanced: The sweet and sour (sugar and acid) perceptions are in equilibrium. An unbalanced wine could exhibit too much sweetness **(cloying)**, or too much acid **(acidulous).** The key point to note is that there are no specific levels of sugar or acid to use for reference. It depends on the balance or ratio of the two, because the presence of each affects the perception of the other.

Bitter: One of the four basic tastes (sweet, sour, salt, bitter). It is perceived mostly on the base of the tongue and the reaction time is slower than the others, hence the term *bitter aftertaste.* Normal in slight amounts for some wines; objectionable when too distinctive.

Cloying: A perception of too much sweetness. Due to excessive sugar and/or too little acid.

Dry: No perception of sweetness.

Finish: Similar to **aftertaste.**

Flat: Insufficient acid. Often found in wines made from grapes grown in hot regions, where the grapes ripen at the expense of acid.

Flavor: The combination of tastes and odors perceived in the mouth.

Fresh: See **fresh** under *ODOR.*

Semisweet: Technically, a slight sweetness but, in practice, wines described as semisweet generally exhibit moderate to distinctive levels of sugar.

Sour: One of the four basic tastes. Not to be confused with acetic. See also **tart.** The opposite of sour is **flat.**

Salty: A rare taste in wine. Some sherries may exhibit it.

Sweet: One of the basic tastes.

Tart: A pleasant sour taste. To go beyond tart would be to reach **acidulous.**

TACTILE

Astringent: Often confused with bitter (or even acid), but astringency is a *feel,* whereas bitterness is a *taste.* Astringency is a puckery type of perception. Associated terms are **harsh, rough,** and **tannic.**

Body: The perception of viscosity due to alcohol. Wines high in sugar can mask or confuse this perception. Wines high in ethanol would be described as **full bodied,** wines low in ethanol as **watery** or **thin.**

Full bodied: See **body.**

Smooth: The opposite of **astringent.** Little, if any, tannin is present.

Syrupy: A wine high in sugar and probably low in alcohol as well.

Thin: The opposite of **full bodied.**

Unctuous: A disagreeable texture found in some overly sweet wines. The taste of such a wine would probably also be described as **cloying.**

Watery: A wine with insufficient **body.**

STORAGE STANDARDS

Wine in the bottle is adversely affected by exposure to air, light, heat, and excessive movement. Ideal wine storage conditions, therefore, are designed to reduce or eliminate these conditions.

Wine should be stored in dark areas and protected from light. The temperature should be cool—55°F (13°C) is considered perfect—but even more important than the specific temperature is the necessity for constant temperature. Fluctuating temperatures are particularly harmful. Warm conditions should be avoided, and hot storage can quickly ruin fine wines.

The storage area should be stable. The wines should not be moved unnecessarily, and they should be stored on their sides. With upright storage, there is a risk of the corks drying and shrinking, which would allow entry of oxygen. When the bottles are on their sides, the continuous contact between wine and cork keeps the corks moist and swollen. A slightly humid atmosphere is also desirable, because it helps guard against drying of the corks.

The traditional underground wine cellar provides all of these conditions. The ground temperature, below the frost line, is just about 55°F it is constant, there is no light, and, unless located on the San Andreas Fault, the cellar is stable and quiet. The humidity is also ideal.

Lacking a cellar, most homes and commercial foodservice operations should try to duplicate the necessary conditions. As long as the temperature can be held constant and cool, and the bottles are stored on their sides, the wines can be held safely for many years. A walk-in refrigerator modified to maintain temperatures of about 55 to 60°F (13 to 16°C) would be quite satisfactory for a restaurant or hotel.

SERVICE STANDARDS
Service Equipment

There is only one really essential piece of wine service equipment—a *corkscrew,* or cork remover—but there are many other very useful implements. There is a variety of successful corkscrew designs, but the most popular is still the 3/1, often called the waiter's corkscrew because it is used by most waiters and can easily be carried in the pocket while working. It consists of a *worm* (the screw itself), a blade for cutting the foil cap, and a lever to assist in pulling the cork. Whatever the design, the best corkscrews have a coiled worm rather than a twisted piece of metal that resembles a drill bit—and often has the same effect on the cork.

An ingenious device that more properly is called a cork remover because it has no worm is the two-pronged Ah-So. It consists of two blades, which are inserted on either side of the cork, between the cork and the bottle neck. The blades are sort of rocked back and forth down the neck, and when they are fully inserted, the cork is removed by pulling and twisting at the same time. This type of remover is especially good for older bottles, which may have corks that can easily crumble or break up. If the cork is a little loose, however, the Ah-So has the disconcerting habit of driving the cork down into the bottle rather than removing it. It has no knife blade for cutting the cap, nor can it be carried as easily as the 3/1, so it is not so good a choice if you can have only one cork remover; but there should be one on the bar as well as in the cellar.

Another interesting design, which should be a standard piece of equipment on any bar, is the *Screwpull.* It consists, of two sections: a device resembling a clothespin which fits over the bottle opening; and the worm, which is inserted through a hole in the top of the other device. The effectiveness of the product is due to its unique worm. It is extremely long and Teflon coated. Therefore, it passes entirely through the cork, even the longest ones, and does so quite easily. The worm is inserted and the cork removed with one continuous twisting motion. It is nearly foolproof and the best choice for any bottles that have difficult or old corks.

Red wines may have sediment—often a considerable amount—and the process of removing it is termed *decanting.* This can be done with just about any container, but a properly equipped dining room or cellar will have wine baskets, decanters, candles or penlights, and funnels.

Pushing the cork down into the bottle is always a potential danger, and there is a clever device called a *cork retriever* that can be used to rescue it. It consists of several wires or thin blades that are slightly hooked on the tips. The entire apparatus is bound together in a handle at the top. The wires are inserted down into the bottle and maneuvered until the cork is upright between them. When the wires are pulled out, they close around the cork, the hooks catch at the bottom, and the cork can be pulled out of the bottle.

For sparkling wines there are *cork pliers* and *bottle sealers*. Champagne pliers are useful in opening bottles with tight corks, and bottle sealers were developed recently to hold opened bottles of sparkling wines safely. They are necessary for the increasing number of operations serving sparkling wines by the glass.

Taking the Order

In a commercial establishment, the wine order should be taken at the same time as the food order. The reason is that the wine should be at the table and opened prior to the service of the food, so that it can be enjoyed with the food. Because white wines may need to be chilled and red wines may require some breathing time, the server should take the wine order as soon as possible.

The order should be taken from whoever is the host. This has traditionally been the male half of a couple or one of the males in a group or party, but this may no longer be the case in many situations. A good server will "read" his or her guests and decide whom to approach for the wine order, or just direct the question to the table in general; for example, asking, "What wine will you be having tonight?"

Regardless of the kind of wine ordered, it should be brought to the table as soon as possible. The wine should be shown to the person ordering it to confirm the brand and vintage. Once the label is confirmed, if it is an unchilled white wine it should be placed in an ice bucket and left on or near the table. A red wine should be opened immediately for the guest to taste and, if approved, left on the table to breathe. Thus, a red wine is ready to be served whenever the food arrives, while a white wine is not. The server should allow time to open and serve the wine before serving the food.

Many wine lists assign bin numbers to each of the wines; this is an excellent idea, because it is useful for inventory control and greatly simplifies service. Employees and guests often have trouble pronouncing wine names, and the use of numbers reduces errors in ordering and serving.

Breathing

The procedure of allowing red wines to breathe is often misunderstood and overemphasized. Breathing is nothing more than allowing the wine to have some contact with air prior to drinking it. Air is the single greatest enemy of wine during storage but is beneficial during consumption. It is the same principle as swirling the wine in the glass prior to sniffing it during evaluation; the oxygen enhances the wine and intensifies the odors and flavors. Many of the great red wines need to breathe before their qualities can be fully appreciated.

Often, someone will comment toward the end of dinner that the wine tastes better than before, and that person may mistakenly assume he or she is feeling the effects of the alcohol and perhaps is not as discriminating. In fact, the wine probably does taste better, especially if it had been opened immediately prior to consumption.

Many ordinary red wines do not especially benefit from breathing, but only very mature, delicate wines should be harmed by it, because they could quickly begin to lose whatever life they have remaining. The general rule of thumb, therefore, is to allow all wines to breathe, fifteen to twenty minutes prior to drinking, except those reds that are suspected of being close to the end. It will not harm them any and will enhance the better ones. Under typical dining room conditions, if the bottle is delivered soon after ordering and opened at that time, there will be adequate breathing time before the food is served.

White wines also can benefit from air contact; this is particularly true of very young, fresh whites. Most guests would not expect them to be opened well before consumption, but it would not be harmful to do so. Again, however, mature wines will not be much enhanced and may even begin to deteriorate. Sparkling wines, of course, should never be opened until the guests are ready for them.

Serving Temperature

The general rule is to serve red wines at room temperature and to chill white, rosé, and sparkling wines, but this is only a superficial generalization. It is true that red wines are served at higher temperatures than the others, and there is a sound reason for this. Red wines have a higher molecular weight and require higher temperatures to volatilize the odor and flavor components. Red wines cannot be fully appreciated at cool or cold temperatures. White wines typically offer freshness and delicacy, and these qualities are enhanced by cool temperatures. Not all wines are the same, however; both reds and whites have a considerable range of weights and flavors, and the serving temperature should be varied accordingly.

White wines normally are not served at temperatures below 40° F (5° C), although very ordinary, inexpensive ones may be better at even lower temperatures, while a full-bodied, complex, and flavorful white such as a good Chardonnay from California or Burgundy should be served at perhaps 50 to 55° F (10 to 13° C). The same reasoning holds for sparkling wines: the inexpensive Charmat method wines are best when very well chilled, while the qualities of a fine Champagne would be muted at very low temperatures. With red wines, room temperature is somewhere between 65 and 70° F (18 to

21° C); some reds, such as the very light and fruity Beaujolais, can be enjoyed best when slightly chilled, down to about 60° F (16° C).

White wines can be chilled by placing them in a refrigerator for an hour or two, or in an ice bucket for fifteen to twenty minutes. When using an ice bucket, be sure to add water to the ice, because the heat transfer will be more efficient than with ice alone. The bottle can be swirled in the bucket from time to time to accelerate the cooling. There are also special wine chillers available that contain cold, moving water. The movement of the water dramatically increases the heat transfer efficiency and they can chill a bottle to the proper drinking temperature in a few minutes. These are more useful to a wine retailer, however, than to a hotel or restaurant dining room. Food and beverage establishments should be storing the wines at cool temperatures, and if they have, an ice bucket will do the job in a very short time.

If wines are held in a refrigerator for service, all the operator has to do is maintain the temperature while at the table. There are several ways to do this. An ice bucket is one, but it requires a lot of handling and the bottles have to be continually wiped free of moisture when pouring. There are also wine coolers available, which partially or completely avoid the use of ice. With one model, there are two circular compartments, one for the bottle and another, smaller one for the ice. It is made of aluminum and quickly becomes ice-cold, and the wine maintains an acceptably cool drinking temperature for a long time. Another type resembles a tall plastic bucket and has a double wall, about one-half inch apart. It contains air and apparently is an efficient insulator, because a chilled bottle placed inside will remain cool throughout the dining period. This type avoids the use of ice altogether; the handling advantages should be obvious. Many models are clear, which allows the wine label to be seen, and most operators consider this valuable from a merchandising standpoint. There are also coolers that have a frozen layer either imbedded or inserted into the container. They are very efficient but require more handling than the air-insulated types.

Opening the Bottle

Wine bottles are generally topped with a foil cap, although some wineries use plastic ones. Whichever is used, the cap has to be removed to expose the cork. This is one reason the 3/1 corkscrew is preferred, because it has a blade to do this. The cap is usually removed by cutting around the top of the bottle, leaving, for aesthetic purposes, most of the cap in place on the neck.

The next step is to wipe the top of the cork. The cap is mostly air free, and there may be a mold growth under it. It is harmless to the wine, but only if it does not come into contact with it. Once this is done, the cork is removed and the bottle lip again is wiped clean. The cork is then presented to the customer — and this often causes confusion. What is the person supposed to do with it? Knowledgeable wine drinkers feel or squeeze the cork to see if it has any resiliency. If it is very hard, it is possible that it has dried; in that case, it may not have provided the airtight seal it was intended for. If it looks swollen and gives a little when pressed, it is likely that it did exactly what it was supposed to do: keep air out. The cork also may be smelled. Although it is rare, the cork could be moldy, and this certainly would have been transmitted to the wine. If the wine has deteriorated for whatever reason, the cork sometimes can provide an early warning system.

Sparkling wines are opened by removing the foil cap and the wire; then, holding the cork firmly in one hand, and the bottom of the bottle in the other, turn the bottle, slowly easing the cork out. Care must be taken when removing the wire, because the pressure in the bottle could cause it to fly out. If that happens, the wine will begin foaming or even spurting from the bottle. One or two fingers should be placed on top of the cork when unwiring the bottle. If the cork shows signs of coming out, try to control it so it does so as slowly as possible. It is recommended to hold the bottle at an angle when opening, to increase the surface area of the wine in the neck. There is considerable pressure difference between the wine and the outside air, and an increased surface area reduces the possibility of foaming or spurting when the cork is removed. In any case, the cork should be removed under control and never be allowed to pop out and fly free. This is not only dangerous, but encourages foaming and loss of wine and carbonation.

Decanting

Only red wines require decanting, because only red wines have sediment. In the home, a very young white wine may be decanted, but the purpose is to aerate it, and the procedure is done more carelessly and quickly than would ever be the case with a fine red.

Decanting of red wines that have no sediment is not necessary, although it may be done as a precaution or simply to aerate the wine, as with whites. A red that needs decanting should be handled with care to avoid agitating the sediment and dispersing it throughout the wine. If the wine has been properly stored, the sediment will be collected on the bottom side of the bottle. Here is where a wine basket is needed. The bottle can be carefully removed from storage and placed in the basket, sediment side down. The basket is carried to the table and the foil and cork are removed, all the while maintaining the same position in the basket and avoiding movement as much as possible. The lip of the bottle is then placed over the decanter, and the wine is slowly poured. A candle or penlight under the bottle neck aids in observing the wine as it flows through. When the sediment appears, the pouring is stopped.

When the wine has been handled carefully, and when the decanting is skillfully done, the bottle will contain all the sediment and nearly no wine, while the decanter will contain clear, sediment-free wine. If there is still some wine left in the bottle, it may be allowed to stand upright and, later in the meal, decanted again. It is possible to recover some of the wine in this manner. Hotels and restaurants do not often know which wines will be ordered, so this is the recommended procedure. At home, where the consumption of a particular wine may be known well ahead of time, the bottle can be stood upright for a few days and then decanted before the meal. This eliminates the need for a basket, although the wine still must be handled very carefully.

Serving and Pouring

A napkin may be used when pouring to wipe the lip and avoid spills, but the bottle should never be wrapped. One exception to this rule is when opening a bottle of sparkling wine. Because of the internal pressure, in past years there had been a danger of the bottle exploding during opening, so it was considered prudent to wrap it. Bottle manufacture has advanced considerably since then, however, and this no longer constitutes a danger, although the bottle may still be wrapped during opening. When pouring, one should expose the label, as with still wines. Of course, anyone who is ashamed of the label may be justified in hiding it during pouring.

It is traditional to offer the person ordering the wine a small amount, an ounce or less, for tasting. There are two reasons for this, one of which still makes sense. At one time, wine was the favored vehicle for political poisoning, and only a very careless person would drink the wine without observing the host drinking it first. This reason should not be very compelling today. The other is that wine is a living substance, subject to continual change throughout its life, and the person ordering it ought to have the opportunity to determine whether it is sound or not.

When the wine is approved and accepted, the other person in a party of two should be served first. If there are three or four people in the group, it is traditionally considered proper to serve the females, then the males, and finally the person ordering the wine. With larger groups, it makes more sense to serve everyone clockwise or counterclockwise, again finishing with the person who ordered and tasted.

When one is pouring, the glass should not be filled to the rim. A one-half or three-quarter fill allows the wine to be swirled in the glass, and this, as already noted, increases the enjoyment. An obvious exception to this rule is when wines are being ordered by the glass. A guest probably would not regard half- or three-quarters-filled glass as a good value. Some operators overcome this problem by providing oversized glasses. Then they can serve an acceptable portion and their guests can swirl to their hearts' delight.

Sparkling wines have to be poured slowly and carefully, because they have a tendency to foam up in the glass. The wine can be poured very slowly in one continuous motion or, more safely, poured in two motions, allowing the foam to subside between pours. Because sparkling wines are not swirled in the glass and the glass looks more attractive when filled, they are generally poured nearly to the rim.

Handling of Rejected Wines

Sooner or later, every dining room operation is going to have a wine rejected for one reason or another. There are three reasons a guest might reject a wine. For one thing, the person may be showing off and trying to indicate his or her supposedly vast knowledge and sensitive tasting abilities. This does happen, but it is infrequent, and it would be a mistake to assume that this is what is going on. The other two reasons account for the majority of instances of rejection: either there is something wrong with the wine, or the guest simply does not care for it.

Wine changes in the bottle. Most wines undergo a steady and continuous decline after being bottled, though a few wines—and nearly all of the great ones—improve for a period lasting from a few years to several decades. In addition, under less than ideal, or even abusive, storage conditions, the wine can deteriorate rapidly. Most wines are sound when shipped to beverage establishments, however, and, if the operation turns the stock at reasonable intervals, quality deterioration should not be a problem even with less than perfect storage. But it is always a possibility. With those restaurants, hotels, and clubs that maintain exceptional cellars and invest in wines in order to store and mature them, the chance of an occasional off bottle naturally increases. Thus, any comment by a guest that the wine may not be in good drinking condition should be taken seriously by service personnel and management.

Even if there is nothing technically wrong with the wine, the guest may not care for it. He or she may think there is something wrong with it and may even say so. In any case, the establishment should want to provide satisfaction, and the wine should be replaced without question. It is important to find out the reason for the rejection. If the wine is truly bad, another bottle of the same wine should be offered in its place. If there is nothing wrong with the wine, the guest should diplomatically be offered another kind of wine, because it is clear that he or she does not like that one.

Here is where a well-trained service staff can pay dividends, because a logical question is, "Why was that particular wine served; why did the waiter, waitress, or sommelier not bother to establish the tastes and preferences of the guests?" With competent and well-trained personnel, this type of rejection will not occur very often. Serving a guest who does not normally drink wine a heavy, full-bodied, bone-dry California Chardonnay makes as little sense as accepting a fish order from a guest who has just stated a dislike for seafood. In both cases, the customer is not likely to be satisfied, and in both cases, the establishment is the loser. Wine types and wine terminology can be very confusing, even to reasonably experienced persons, and it is easy for ordering mistakes to be made. It is the job of the service personnel to guide the guests through both the food and beverage menus in order to maximize their enjoyment and satisfaction.

Wine Glassware

Glassware is a very important aspect of wine service, but foodservice establishments sometimes make it more complicated than it ought to be. It is not uncommon to see hotels, restaurants, and clubs stock many types of specialized wine glassware. There are red wine glasses, white wine glasses, sparkling wine glasses, sherry wine glasses, port and dessert wine glasses—and this is only the beginning.

Within the red wine category, one can choose between the Burgundy style and the Bordeaux style. In the sparkling wine category, the choice is among flute, saucer, and tulip styles. With white wines, in addition to the regular glass, there are the elaborate German or Rhein Wein styles.

Many establishments today, seeking to reduce the potential confusion and lower the inventory investment in glassware, have gone to the all-purpose wine glass concept, whereby one glass is used for both red and white wines. It is still necessary in most cases, however, to stock another style for sparkling wines and perhaps a third for dessert wines and sherries, if there is a significant demand for those products.

A suitable all-purpose wine glass should have a capacity of at least six to nine ounces, have a reasonably long stem, be slightly pinched in at the top, and be clear. The reasons are to allow sufficient room to swirl the wine and let it breathe in the glass, to be able to hold the wine easily and comfortably without touching or holding it by the bowl, to concentrate the aromatic compounds when sniffing the wine, and to be able to see the wine and evaluate the colors, depth, clarity, and other visual characteristics.

The most suitable sparkling wine glass is not the one normally used, which is the saucer glass, also known as a Champagne glass. This style is poor for sparkling wines because its shape encourages the loss of carbonation. Any glass that is taller than it is wide is better for sparkling wines, because it tends to retain the bubbles longer. Such glasses are also more attractive to look at, because the bubbles can be watched as they rise from the bottom of the glass to the top. The ideal shape is either the flute—a tall, narrow glass—or the tulip, also tall but sort of heart shaped. Both of these styles enhance the visual enjoyment of the wine and retain the carbonation as long as possible.

NUTRITIONAL STANDARDS

The primary constituent of wine, other than water, is ethyl alcohol. The only true nutritive value of alcohol is derived from the calories it provides, about ninety-five calories in a four-ounce glass of red wine and ninety calories in four ounces of dry white. Except for iron, the vitamin and mineral content of wine is too low to be of any nutritive value. Studies have shown, however, that wines can enhance the absorption of various minerals and improve the potassium, calcium, magnesium, phosphorus, and zinc levels in the body. Wine, particularly table wine, is an especially effective aperitif because it stimulates gastric secretions and aids the digestion of foods consumed shortly afterward. Wine can also be used in regulating a diet, due to its satiety effect, its ability to make one feel that hunger has been satisfied.

CONSUMPTION PATTERNS AND TRENDS

In evaluating wine consumption, one has to examine the various categories of wines. These are table wines, dessert wines, sparkling wines, wine coolers, vermouth, and special natural wines. Not only have total wine sales changed considerably over the years, but also the market share that each category accounts for has undergone very significant changes.

In the 1950s, dessert wines were the most popular type of wine consumed in the United States, but their share of the market has been shrinking for many years. They were down to 28 percent in 1970, and dropped to under 7 percent by the mid-1980s. Table wines rose from nearly 50 percent in 1970 to 76 percent in 1980, then showed a small decline during the early 1980s. Special natural wines peaked at 15 percent in 1975 and dropped to around the 5 percent level by 1985.

Sparkling wines were strong throughout the 1970s and early 1980s, selling at from 6 percent to nearly 9 percent, but dropped a little in 1985. Vermouth, like dessert wines, has experienced a continuing erosion of its market share for several decades and in the 1980s dropped under 2 percent. The performance of the wine cooler category has been absolutely spectacular. This type of product was not developed until 1983, and in that year it claimed only 1.5 percent of the wine market. By 1985, it was up to almost 15 percent and was responsible for the decrease in market share of what were previously the two strongest wine types: table and sparkling.

The sales story, when expressed in number of cases, is even more dramatic. Total wine sales increased at such a rapid rate that it seemed as though there would be no slowing down until America became one of the major wine-consuming nations, from a per capita standpoint. Wine sales in 1985 rose to 232 million cases, from 112 million cases in 1970. However, the average compound growth rate slowed in the 1980s. In fact, by 1985, the wine cooler category was responsible for whatever growth was being achieved. Without the coolers, wine sales would have flattened out in 1985, something that would have been unthinkable during the booming 1970s.

Table wines increased to nearly 170 million cases in 1984, from 56 million in 1970. Dessert wines declined during the 1950s and 1960s to 31 million in 1970 and less than 15 million by 1985. Vermouth showed a steady decline in total cases shipped, in spite of the rapid increase in overall consumption. Sparkling wines rose to 9.3 million cases in 1970 and were up to 20 million in 1984. Special natural wines peaked at 24 million cases in 1975 but by 1985 were down to around 10 million. Wine coolers first appeared in 1983 and accounted for sales of a little over 3 million cases in that year. In 1984, their sales rose to 15.5 million cases, an increase of 380 percent—and this was exceeded in the first six months of 1985, when sales totaled nearly 16.5 million cases! In 1985, after only some three years on the shelves, wine coolers became the second largest wine category in the United States.

The projections made by the industry newsletter *Impact* show that these trends should continue. By the year 2000, the total wine market is expected to be nearly 350 million cases, with table wines claiming a share of about 68 percent, wine coolers about 15 percent, and sparkling wines about 12 percent. Thus, these three categories are expected to share some 95 percent of the total American wine market, while vermouth, dessert wines, and special natural wines will have become economically unimportant.

SUGGESTED READINGS

Amerine, M. A., H. W., Berg, and W. V. Cruess. *The Technology of Wine Making*. Westport, Conn.: AVI, 1972.

Amerine, M. A., R. M. Pangborn, and E. B. Roessler. *Principles of Sensory Evaluation of Food*. New York: Academic Press, 1965.

Amerine, M. A., and E. B. Roessler. *Wines: Their Sensory Evaluation.* San Francisco: W. H. Freeman and Co., 1976.

Bell, D. A. *The Spirits of Hospitality.* East Lansing, Mich., The Educational Institute/American Hotel & Motel Association, 1976.

Berger, D. *Bottles.* The Book of California Wine. Ed. Amerine, Muscatine, and Thompson. Berkeley and London: University of California Press/Sotheby Publications, 1984*a*.

―――. *Corks.* The Book of California Wine. Ed. Amerine, Muscatine, and Thompson. Berkeley and London: University of California Press/Sotheby Publications, 1984*b*.

Davies, J. L. *Sparkling Wines.* The Book of California Wine. Ed. Amerine, Muscatine, and Thompson. Berkeley and London: University of California Press/Sotheby Publications, 1984.

Fletcher, W. *Port.* André Simon's Wines of the World. 2d ed. S. Sutcliffe. New York: McGraw-Hill, 1981.

Grossman, H. J. *Grossman's Guide to Wines, Beers & Spirits.* 6th rev. ed., rev. H. Lembeck. New York: Charles Scribner's Sons, 1977.

Horn, W., and E. Born. *The Earliest Barrels.* The Book of California Wine. Ed. Amerine, Muscatine, and Thompson. Berkeley and London: University of California Press/Sotheby Publications, 1984.

The Impact American Wine Market Review and Forecast. New York: M. Shanken Communications, Inc., 1985.

Jamieson, I. *The Wines of Germany.* André Simon's Wines of the World. 2d ed. S. Sutcliffe. New York: McGraw-Hill, 1981.

Jeffs, J. *Sherry.* André Simon's Wines of the World. 2d ed. S. Sutcliffe. New York: McGraw-Hill, 1981.

Johnson, H. *Modern Encyclopedia of Wine.* New York: Simon and Schuster, 1983.

―――. *The World Atlas of Wine.* New York: Simon and Schuster, 1971.

Lichine, A. *Alexis Lichine's New Encyclopedia of Wines & Spirits.* New York: Alfred Knopf, 1982.

Long, Z. *Enological & Technological Developments.* The Book of California Wine. Ed. Amerine, Muscatine, and Thompson. Berkeley and London: University of California Press/Sotheby Publications, 1984.

Meinhard, H. *The Wines of Germany.* New York: Stein & Day, 1976.

Mondavi, T. J. *Barrels in Modern Winemaking.* The Book of California Wine. Ed. Amerine, Muscatine, and Thompson. Berkeley and London: University of California Press/Sotheby Publications, 1984.

Osterland, E. *Wine and the Bottom Line.* Washington, D.C.: National Restaurant Association, 1980.

Schug, W. *The Vinification of Fine Wine.* The Book of California Wine. Ed. Amerine, Muscatine, and Thompson. Berkeley and London: University of California Press/Sotheby Publications, 1984.

Sutcliffe, S. *Viticulture, Vinification, and the Care of Wine.* André Simon's Wines of the World. 2d ed. New York: McGraw-Hill, 1981*a*.

————. *The Wines of France.* André Simon's Wines of the World. 2d ed. New York: McGraw-Hill, 1981*b*.

Vine, R. P. *Commercial Winemaking.* Westport, Conn.: AVI, 1981.

Wagner, P. M. *American Wines & Wine-Making.* 5th ed. New York: Alfred Knopf, 1970.

Wasserman, S., and P. Wasserman. *Sparkling Wine.* Piscataway, N.J.: New Century Publishers, Inc., 1984.

CHAPTER THREE
WINE LAWS & REGULATIONS

WINE LAWS AND REGULATIONS OF FRANCE

The initial French attempt to regulate the wine industry came in 1905, in response to the sorry condition the French wine industry found itself in following the devastation of the vineyards by plant lice called phylloxera. Because the relationship between bottle labels and contents had become tenuous, the law was primarily concerned with the elimination of fraud. The core concept of this legislation was that specific location was critical: that certain combinations of soil and climate were superior to others. This place-name approach was unique from a legalistic standpoint and paved the way for all subsequent wine legislation.

The main problem with the 1905 act, and with succeeding amendments, was the failure to recognize the equally important roles of the grape varieties and traditional wine-making practices. Eventually, although the path was tortuous and rocky, the problems were recognized and solved in the early 1930s with the founding of the Institut National des Appellations d'Origine in Paris.

There are now four levels of control covering all the wines of France. The most prestigious, and the one encompassing all the top wines, is the Appellation d'Origine Contrôlée (AOC) or, more simply, Appellation Contrôlée (AC). Appellation d'Origine Contrôlée literally translates as "controlled place of origin." Next is the Vin Délimité de Qualité Supérieure (VDQS), or "delimited wine of superior quality" followed by Vin de Pays, or "country wine," and Vin de Consommation Courante, or "wine for current consumption."

The European Economic Community, (EEC) has two basic categories of wine: Vin de Qualité Produit dans une Région Determinée (VQPRD), or "quality wine produced in a determined region," and *vin de table*, or "table wine." The French system, while more elaborate, fits easily within the EEC framework.

Appellation Contrôlée

These regulations are not intended to guarantee quality; rather, they attempt to ensure authenticity of origin. However, they do control factors that are very much related to quality. These include grape varieties, yield, minimum levels of alcohol, growing areas, vineyard management, vinification, and aging conditions.

The *grape variety* is perhaps the most important of these, because the potential of the wine is ultimately dependent on the grape. As the discussion on wine quality factors in Chapter Two brought out, what a wine maker basically attempts to do is bring the grapes to full maturity and then make wine as skillfully as he or she can. Great wine can be made only from a relatively few grapes, although poor wine also can be made from the same grapes; that is where skill and knowledge become critical.

In some regions—Burgundy is one—a single grape is permitted for the wines, such as Chardonnay for the whites, Pinot Noir for red Burgundy, and Gamay for Beaujolais. Other regions may use several grapes. A good example of the latter is Bordeaux, where the classic red wines are made from Cabernet Sauvignon, Merlot, Cabernet Franc, and related grapes. The wine makers have a great deal of freedom in deciding the ratio or mix of the grapes in their vineyards, but not as to which grapes they may plant. Such a system would be unworkable in the United States, but in Europe they have had centuries of experience by trial and error in determining which grapes or blend of grapes work best in specific areas. It is unlikely that no grapes other than the Pinot Noir were ever grown in the Côte d'Or in Burgundy. It is also unlikely that any of those grapes ever produced as fine a red wine as the Pinot Noir.

There is a negative relationship between *yield* and quality. There are exceptional years, of course, but in general the more wine one makes, the less highly regarded it is. Like most Europeans, the French calculate yield metrically, as hectoliters per hectare. A hectare is approximately equal to two and one-half acres, and a hectoliter is 100 liters, or about 26.4 U.S. gallons. The most usual production limitation is 40 hectoliters per hectare, which works out to 422 gallons of wine per acre of vineyards. This figure can be expected to go up or down depending on the region. Bordeaux has a maximum of 50 while the Médoc's, a more prestigious district within Bordeaux, is 45. Margaux, one of the noted towns in the Médoc, is limited to 40. In Sauternes, where they produce sweet wines from grapes that have lost some of their moisture, the limit is only 25. In Burgundy, a famous village, Gevrey-Chambertin, is limited to 35 hectoliters per hectare, while individual vineyards within the town's delimited region are reduced to 32 or even 30 for the best ones.

Annual reassessment of the vintage is permitted, and an increase is often allowed for that year should conditions warrant it. In past years it was possible for a vintner to make about as much wine as he or she wanted, bottle up to the limit with the best AC, and sell the rest under a lesser classification. This has been disallowed since 1974. Today a grower must select the classification for the entire crop at the time of the declaration of the vintage.

Establishing *minimum levels of alcohol* is important because the alcohol comes from the sugar. The sugar increases as the grapes ripen. Therefore, there is a positive relationship (up to a point) between alcohol and the condition of the grapes at harvest. The objective of wine making is seldom to produce as much alcohol as possible, but wines low in alcohol because they were made from immature fruit obviously will offer less satisfaction than wines of normal strength made from fully matured fruit. Again, as with the yield limitations, as the AC becomes smaller and more specific and designates more highly regarded areas, the regulations become more stringent and require more natural alcohol. In addition, of course, the alcohol level can be, and often is, boosted by chaptalization, or the addition of sugar, during the fermentation. The alcohol minimum is for that which would be produced without chaptalization, regardless of whether it is done or not.

Control of the *growing areas* is the cornerstone of the AC regulations. Each wine in this category will be given a specific AC to place on the label. This AC will depend on where the vineyard is physically located and what types of quality standards it maintains. For example, Château Mouton-Rothschild is certainly one of the legendary wine properties in the world. This vineyard is located in Pauillac, a town in the Médoc, which in turn is a subregion of Bordeaux. The most limited AC that can be awarded in that area is for the town, Pauillac. Therefore, Château Mouton-Rothschild bears on its label the notation Appellation Pauillac Contrôlée. Another vineyard, located in Pauillac but not meeting the standards of Pauillac, would not qualify for that AC. It might qualify as a Médoc, however. In that case, the label would be Appellation Médoc Contrôlée. Failing to qualify as a Médoc, it still might be entitled to the AC of Bordeaux. In other words, one qualifies for a particular AC by being located in a specific location, by growing specific grapes, by meeting minimum alcohol requirements, and by limiting the amount of wine made.

The remaining factors of regulation are not so critical, but they cannot be overlooked, because they have great importance for some of the wines. *Vineyard management* covers such topics as the methods of planting, pruning, and treating the vines; *vinification* deals with wine-making procedures; and *aging conditions* usually involve minimum times. Many regions have traditional wine-making practices that are considered indispensable to the distinctive character of the wines; these are the types of vinification practices that are noted in the regulations. In Champagne, the method of making sparkling wine is very precise and specific, and there is a minimum time for which the wine must be held or aged in the bottle prior to disgorging the sediment and finishing the wine.

The specificity of the AC varies from region to region. In Bordeaux, the smallest unit is a town or village; thus, Mouton-Rothschild carries the Pauillac AC. In Burgundy, however, the AC is extended down to individual vineyards, the Grand Cru vineyards—both red and white. Thus, Romanée-Conti, Chambertin, Montrachet, and the other great Burgundian properties are entitled to their own AC. In Champagne, as mentioned, the regulations are concerned with how the product is made, and there is only one AC for the entire region: Champagne. It also is the one AC wine that does not have to have the phrase Appellation Contrôlée on the label; it merely reads Champagne.

Vin Délimité de Qualité Supérieure (VDQS)

The second level of French wine regulation was instituted following World War II. The VDQS laws are similar in all respects to those of the AC, but are not so strict. They allow higher production, are looser in defining wine-growing zones, may have lower alcohol requirements, and sometimes allow less "noble" grape varieties.

One innovation developed with VDQS wines was the practice of official tasting prior to obtaining labeling rights. Initially, AC wines were not required to be tasted to ensure that they were typical and representative examples of the region, although this is now being done.

It is possible for regions to be "promoted" from VDQS to AC status, and this has taken place several times. The well-known English writer Hugh Johnson refers to VDQS as a sort of "training ground" for AC wines:

Vin de Pays

The phrase Vin de Pays could best be translated as "country wine" and, as a category, dates to 1973. Production and quality standards vary dramatically.

The yield maximum is quite high, ninety hectoliters per hectare, and the approved grape varieties are extensive. The origin must be identified, but here again there is wide latitude, from a village designation to the entire Loire Valley. There is nothing, of course, to prevent a wine maker from making very good Vin de Pays. One way this might happen is if someone wanted to make a nontraditional wine in a particular area, such as growing Chardonnay in Graves. The Chardonnay, regardless of its status in Burgundy and Champagne, is not one of the approved varieties in Graves, so the wine would have to be called a Vin de Pays. While not a widespread practice in France, this type of activity is an important development in Italy.

Vin de Consommation Courante

The phrase Vin de Consommation Courante translates as "wine for current consumption," which pretty well establishes what it is: *vin ordinaire*—the daily drink of the ordinary French people. Its origin need not be identified, and its value to the consumer seems to have a direct relationship to its alcoholic content.

EEC and French Regulations

AC and VDQS wines both qualify for the EEC designation of "Vin de Qualité Produit dans une Région Déterminée" (VQPRD), while Vin de Pays and Vin de Consommation Courante are classified as Vin de Table.

French Wine Terms

Appellation d'Origine Contrôlée (AOC or AC): The law under which all of the fine wines of France are regulated.

Balthazar: A bottle size generally associated with Champagne, containing 12 liters, the equivalent of 16 750-milliliter bottles.

Baumé: A measuring term for sugar content. One degree Baumé equals about 1.8 percent sugar.

Blanc: "White."

Blanc de blancs: "White of whites." Generally used to describe a Champagne or other sparkling wine made entirely from white grapes, rather than the traditional blend of red and white grapes.

Blanc de noirs: "White of blacks." Champagne and other sparkling wines made only from black (or red) grapes.

Botrytis cinerea: The "noble" mold that is responsible for the great sweet wines of Sauternes.

Bouché: A wine bottle sealed with a cork.

Bouchon: Cork.

Bouchonné: A wine spoiled by a bad cork.

Brut: Used for Champagnes and other sparkling wines to indicate a very dry wine.

Bung: The cork for a wine cask or barrel.

Cépage: A grape variety, such as Cabernet Sauvignon, Pinot Noir, and Chardonnay.

Calvados: The famous apple brandy from Normandy.

Carbonic maceration: A wine-making procedure used in Beaujolais whereby grapes are fermented without crushing them, and the carbon dioxide resulting from the fermentation is allowed to blanket the grapes.

Chai: An aboveground storage place where wine is held in casks.

Chambrer: The process of bringing a red wine slowly to drinking temperature.

Chaptalisation: Addition of sugar to the fermenting grape must. Done when natural sugar is insufficient to make a wine of normal alcoholic content. Spelled with a z, not s, in English.

Charmat: A process for making sparkling wines. All the steps take place in large pressurized tanks instead of in the wine bottles.

Château: Used to describe a property. In Bordeaux, the vineyards are legally termed châteaux regardless of whether there is actually a house on the property.

Climat: Used in Burgundy to describe a vineyard.

Collage: The process of fining, which is done to a wine to clarify it before bottling.

Commune: A French parish or township.

Côte: A slope with vineyards.

Crémant: A sparkling wine with reduced pressure: three atmospheres in contrast to the normal six of Champagne.

Cru: Means "growth" in French. It is used to describe a vineyard of high and/or classified quality.

Cuvée: Contents of a wine vat. It may also be used to describe a vineyard parcel or lot, and in Champagne, it is used for the blend of wines made for the second fermentation.

Dégorgement: In Champagne, the removal of the sediment and fermentation residue following the second fermentation.

Demi-Sec: Semidry. In usage, however, it generally indicates a wine that is semisweet. A term commonly used in Champagne.

Dosage: In Champagne, the mixture of wine and sugar added at the end of the process to give the wine its final balance. The difference in sweetness among brut, extra dry, demi-sec, and so forth is due to the *dosage*.

Doux: Sweet.

Grand cru classe: In Bordeaux, the wines that have been officially classified: Médoc, Sauternes, and Barsac in 1855; Graves in 1953 and 1959; and Saint-Émilion in 1955. This term has been legally reserved for the wines of Bordeaux since 1965.

Haut: "High." Used to indicate not the highest quality, but higher geographically. Thus, the Haut Médoc is above Médoc (farther from the Atlantic) on the Gironde River.

Hectare: The metric measurement of area: 10,000 square meters, or 2.471 acres.

Hectoliter: The metric measurement of volume: 100 liters, or 26.4179 gallons.

Institut National des Appellations d'Origine (INAO): See Appellation d'Origine Contrôleé.

Jeroboam: A bottle size used in Champagne and containing 3 liters, or the equivalent of four 750-milliliter bottles.

Liqueur de tirage: The mixture of sugar syrup and yeast added to the base wine to induce a second fermentation in Champagne and other sparkling wines.

Liquoreux: Rich and sweet wines.

Magnum: A bottle size. It contains 1.5 liters, or the equivalent of two 750-milliliter bottles.

Methuselah: A bottle containing 6 liters, or the equivalent of eight 750-milliliter bottles. Particularly associated with Champagne.

Mis en boutilles à la propriété: Estate bottled. See **mis en boutilles au domaine.**

Mis en boutilles au château: Château-bottled designation, which means that the grapes were grown at the named property and that the wine was made and bottled there. This is the terminology used in Bordeaux.

Mis en boutilles au domaine: Estate bottled. This means the same thing as *mis en boutilles au chateâu* but is more apt to be used in Burgundy or other French wine regions.

Mousseux: Sparkling wine. Other than the wines of Champagne, French sparkling wines will use this designation on the label.

Mout: The French term for grape must.

Nebuchadnezzar: An oversized bottle containing 15 liters, or the equivalent of twenty 750-milliliter bottles.

Noble rot: The mold (*Botrytis cinerea*) that is responsible for the sweet wines of Sauternes and Barsac.

Noir: "Black."

Pétillant: Slightly sparkling or crackling. This refers to wines that have a slight pressure due to the presence of a little unfermented sugar when bottled.

Pourriture noble: French for "noble rot." (See **noble rot.**)

Récolte: Wine crop. Differentiated from **vendange,** the wine harvest.

Rehoboam: A large wine bottle with a capacity of 4.5 liters, or the equivalent of six 750-milliliter bottles.

Rémuage: The process of shaking and turning bottles of Champagne to collect the sediment in the neck so that it can be removed.

Rouge: Red wine.

Salmanazar: A 9-liter bottle, equivalent to twelve 750-milliliter bottles, or a standard case in the United States.

Sec: Dry.

Vendange: The wine harvest. See **récolte.**

Vins Délimités de Qualité Supérieure (VDQS): Superior wines from delimited regions. A secondary wine classification to Appellation Contrôlée.

Vin: wine.

Vins de Pays: A controlled class of wines. The third level in the French quality hierarchy, behind Appellation Contrôlée and VDQS.

Vin ordinaire: Ordinary wine; the everyday drink of many French people.

WINE LAWS AND REGULATIONS OF GERMANY
History of German Wine Laws

The wine laws and regulations of Germany, in some instances, are the most rigorous of all the wine-producing countries. They are also unique, differing substantially in philosophy from those of France and Italy. Preceding France and her Appellation Contrôllée regulations by about a half century, the Germans developed their first wine laws in 1879, revising and updating them in 1901, 1909, and 1930. In 1969 sweeping changes were begun, resulting in 1971 in the current German Wine Laws. Since that time, modifications have been made continually, such as when Germany entered the European Economic Community, but the laws remain essentially the same as in 1971.

Differences from Other Countries' Laws

The main difference between the German laws and those from elsewhere is the former's concept of *quality in the glass*. The French, for example, regulate the grape varieties, wine yield, minimum alcohol content, and growing region. They provide detailed quality rankings based on location, including specific regions, subregions, and vineyards. Médoc wines are ranked higher than the wines of Bordeaux; Pauillac and Margaux are considered more prestigious than Médoc; and there are officially classified vineyards within Pauillac and Margaux, such as Châteaux Lafite-Rothschild, Latour, Mouton-Rothschild, and the vineyard of Margaux, that are the most highly regarded of all. Each year, these regions and, especially, the vineyards can make their prestigious, top-rated wines. Even in the case of a poor or even disastrous vintage, the top names are available. In the case of a really poor year, the best properties may choose to bottle no wine under their own label, but the point here is that, should they wish to do so, there is nothing legally to prevent them.

In Germany, on the other hand, the vintner, regardless of the fame of his vineyard or the prestige of his location, must earn the right each year to designate his wine as a top-quality wine. Similarly, it is entirely possible for an unknown vintner, one with an obscure holding, to produce a highly rated wine. There are many other differences between the laws of Germany and those of other countries, but this is the most basic: the concept of quality in the glass, not of quality by inheritance.

Among the other differences is that the Germans allow a much broader use of grape varieties. Due to much of Germany's more northern latitude, there is an unceasing quest for grape varieties that can ripen with predictable regularity, and new hybrids are continuously being developed and brought into use. The Riesling is acknowledged as the king—no question of that—but the Riesling is a late-ripening, low-yielding grape under the best of circumstances and is, moreover, not suitable for all German wine regions.

The Germans also do not attempt to regulate yield. They do not seem to care how much wine anyone makes, and the yields are often startling by French and Italian standards. Minimum alcohol levels, so critical a quality factor in other countries, are also ignored by the German regulations. It is not that they regard the ripeness of the grapes as unimportant, but they do not much care how much alcohol is in the finished wines. Alcohol is not the goal; flavor, delicacy, and balance are.

Instead of directly requiring attainment of minimum alcohol levels, the regulations ensure minimum grape ripeness, in which the Germans are intensely interested. In truth, grape sugar is the most important factor regulated. They do not much care which grapes are used, how much wine is made, or how much alcohol is in the finished wine, but they do care a great deal about how much sugar was in the grapes when harvested. This is the explanation of how a German vintner must earn his or her quality designation yearly. No matter the reputation of the vineyard, if the grapes do not ripen adequately, the top labels are unattainable. In addition, though, as in other countries, delimited geographical growing regions are specified and regulated.

The 1971 laws provide for three levels of quality, and several subdivisions in the top level. The three are Deutscher Tafelwein, Qualitätswein bestimmter Anbaugebiete, and Qualitätswein mit Prädikat. The best illustration of the quality in the glass concept is to point out that the highest-quality category, the Qualitätswein mit Prädikat, can have a variation in the percentage yield of each year's harvest from as little as 10 percent to as high as 90 percent! France always has her Appellation Contrôllée wines, but Germany does not always have her Qualitätswein mit Prädikat wines.

Deutscher Tafelwein (German Tablewine)

At the most basic classification level, there are few regulations or requirements. One is that the wine must be identified as a product of Germany, hence the prefix Deutscher. A label simply proclaiming the wine to be Tafelwein indicates that it is blended from wines of other European countries; generally Italy. For its own table wine, Germany is broadly divided into five regions, which are far less specific than the eleven regions for her two levels of quality wine. The five are usually, but not always, referred to as Rhein, Mosel,

Oberrhein, Neckar, and Main. A Tafelwein that does not have one of these regional designations consists of an interregional blend, to which no single region has contributed as much as 75 percent. When at least 75 percent of the blend does come from one of the five Tafelwein regions, that region can be named on the label. If a district (or Bereich) is identified, a minimum of 75 percent of the wine must have come from that district. Finally, if a village or town is named, the same 75 percent requirement applies. In the case of the latter, however, no interregional blending is allowed; all the wine must come from the named region. With Tafelwein, vineyard or site names are not permitted.

There are also minimum sugar and acidity requirements, and sugaring of the grape must is authorized. In Germany, the terms for what the French call chaptalisation are *verbessern* (bettering) and *Anreichern* (enriching). This consists of adding sugar, either in dry or syrup form, to the fermenting grape must. As in other cool climates (such as Burgundy, Champagne, and New York State), stable wines cannot be made consistently without supplementing the natural grape sugars.

To comply with the EEC regulations, in 1982 Germany created a new category of Tafelwein called Landwein. It is probably most similar to the French Vin de Pays and has requirements a little stricter than other Tafelwein. In the United States, the Tafelwein category is not of any commercial importance, and it would be difficult to find such wines.

Qualitätswein bestimmter Anbaugebiete (Quality Wine from Specified Regions)

Often referred to by the initials QBA, this category is the basic level of quality German wine and has much more rigid requirements than does Tafelwein. There are minimum *must weight* requirements, although they vary slightly according to the region and the grape variety. Must weight is central to German wine quality. Because sugar is heavier than water, weighing the pressed grape juice, or the must, accurately indicates the relative ripeness and sweetness of the grapes. The must weight is a figure depicting the difference between the weights of a liter of water and a liter of must. A liter of distilled water weighs 1,000 grams. A liter of grape must weighing 1,075 grams is said to have a must weight of 75. Tafelwein, for example, must attain a minimum of 44. The Qualitätswein category requires at least 57 to 60, depending on the region. The southern regions have the higher minimum.

There are eleven growth regions, all of them situated either on or near the Rhein and its tributaries. One of these names will always be on the label of a QBA wine, and with the better ones, there will be more specific geographical designations as well. Unlike Tafelwein, QBA wine can indicate an individual vineyard on the label. On this quality level, sugaring is still necessary and permitted, although it is strictly controlled.

A unique requirement of all wines above the Tafelwein level is that they have to be officially tested and given a test number, an *amtliche prüfungsnummer*, which shows up on the label as an A.P. number. The testing consists of a three-part process. The first takes place during the harvest, when the grower must proclaim his or her intention to produce specific wine types. At this point, the appropriate officials will inspect the vineyards and cellars. Following bottling of the wine, the wine maker must submit an analysis obtained from an independent laboratory and three bottles of the wine. The third phase of the testing is the sensory evaluation. Experts open and carefully examine one bottle. Basically, what they attempt to ascertain is whether the wine is typical—typical of the grape named, of the region, of the vintage, and of the town and the vineyard, if the latter appear on the label.

The wines are scored on a twenty-point system, and the judges require a minimum score not only for the total, but also for each sensory category. Thus, a wine could attain the minimum number of required total points, yet be rejected because one of the category scores was below the minimum. The other two bottles are retained by the authorities to be tested should any consumer complaints be received over the next two years.

When the wine is approved, it is given an A.P. number, and this must appear on the label. The digits in the number are read from right to left and indicate the year the application was submitted (not the vintage year), the serial number of the application, and the code numbers of both the producer and the testing office.

Other requirements for Qualitätswein include observing the approved cultivation methods, processing the wine within the boundaries of the region, and following the approved procedures and uses of substances in wine making.

Unlike other wine makers, German vintners are not free to make independent harvesting decisions. This authority is given to the state wine officials, who set the dates for the harvest to begin. These dates vary according to locale, and the harvest in any given region may not begin until approved. Any wine maker, of course, can delay his or her harvest for the purpose of obtaining a special category of wine. Thus, although they cannot pick earlier, wine makers do not have to begin the harvest on the specified date.

Qualitätswein mit Prädikat
(Quality Wine with Special Attributes or Designations)

The highest level of German wines, also called QMP, is reserved strictly for wines that, prior to 1971, were known as Naturrein, or natural wine—wine made without the addition of sugar. The ratio of the two quality designations can vary dramatically. In difficult growing seasons, Qualitätswein will account for the vast majority of the wine produced in Germany, but in a remarkable year such as 1976, some 90 percent of the wine produced in some regions can be Qualitätswein mit Prädikat.

Within this top level, there are specific subcategories. They are, in ascending order of quality, Kabinett, Spätlese, Auslese, Beerenauslese, and Trockenbeerenauslese. As one moves up the ladder of quality, the wines become progressively more rare and expensive. They are also more difficult and risky to make.

Kabinett. A Kabinett is a wine that is made from grapes picked when the harvest is declared and that does not have to be sugared. It has a minimum must weight requirement of from 70 to 73. German laws also refer to alcohol potential, along with the minimum must weight. If fermented to full dryness, a wine could be said to have reached its alcohol potential. If the fermentation is stopped prior to conversion of all the sugar, the wine will fail to attain its alcohol potential and will have one of varying levels of sweetness. This describes most German wines in the Qualitätswein mit Prädikat category. The sweetness increases as one ascends from Kabinett to Trockenbeerenauslesen wines, and the alcohol generally decreases. The alcohol potential of Kabinett wines must be at least 9.1 to 9.5 percent by volume. Kabinett wines must be made entirely from grapes gathered in one district (Bereich), and they are often made from a single vineyard.

The wine maker often has a difficult decision to make when picking at the specified harvest time: to make a Kabinett wine or to sugar the wine and produce a QBA. When the sugar levels are technically adequate for Kabinett, but marginal, it is possible that the wine could be improved, made a little more balanced, by the judicious use of sugar. Marketing considerations also play a role in the decision. There are occasions when a winery may wish to have more or less of a specific wine type to keep its total output in balance.

Spätlese. If a vintner decides to wait and harvest at a later time, the result is a Spätlese, a late-picked wine. The advantage of doing this is that the grapes may continue to ripen and will have more sugar. The danger is that the weather could turn and some of the harvest could be lost. Or, of course, nothing might take place—the grapes might stay more or less as they were for a short period—meaning nothing has been accomplished by waiting. Must weight minimums for Spätlese are from 76 to 85, and the alcohol potential requirements are 10 to 11.4 percent. Like Kabinett wines, Spätlese wines cannot be a blend of more than one Bereich, or district, and it would be normal for them to be from a single vineyard.

Spätlese is probably the best known of the QMP wines and is an attractive wine for the wine maker, because it can be sold for a premium price compared to Kabinett and, especially, QBA. Because the German wines may not always be fermented to full dryness, the sweetness level is expected to increase as one goes from Kabinett to Spätlese and beyond. Even when the musts are fermented totally dry, it is legal to add a certain controlled amount of unfermented grape juice to the wines before bottling. This juice, called Süssreserve, or "sweet reserve," increases the sweetness of the wine. With wines above the Spätlese category, however, the complete fermentation of such high levels of sugar would result in atypically high alcohol levels. Most such wines, therefore, retain natural residual sugar. This is why the wines become progressively sweeter and lower in alcohol; more of the sugar is allowed to remain in the wine.

A Spätlese differs from a Kabinett not only in sweetness; it should be a more balanced and complex wine as well. The grapes are riper and richer; they have more to contribute to the wine. There should be a progression in flavor, color, aroma and bouquet, and texture, as well as in sweetness. If all the higher Prädikats had to offer was increased sweetness, they would not be as valued as they are.

Auslese. The next level up is Auslese, which translates as "special selection." The selected bunches of grapes do not have to be picked at any particular time, as do the Spätlese grapes, and can be gathered during the regular harvest or during the late picking. Because they consist of selected bunches of especially ripe grapes, however, they are usually gathered late in the harvest season.

An Auslese also presents a difficult decision for the wine maker. Removing the ripest bunches from the vineyard could result in reducing the must weight of the remaining grapes. In that case, it is conceivable that a late-picked crop will not qualify as a Spätlese and will drop back to a Kabinett.

The finest Auslesen are not only the product of extraordinarily ripe grapes, but also they are often touched with the mold *Botrytis cinerea*, called the noble rot in France and Edelfäule in Germany. In Germany it is responsible for the most glorious of the Auslesen and other Prädikat wines.

A fine Auslese is an expensive wine to make, because the continued ripening and increase in sugar reduces the water and juice content of the grapes. When affected by *Botrytis cinerea*, the juice content is reduced even further. The wines are also difficult to make from a technical standpoint, because of the high sugar levels. Yet another problem is that, because of the reduced yield, it could well be more profitable to produce a Spätlese, for which there is a larger market. Despite all these difficulties, most German wine makers like to make an Auslese if possible, for there is an old saying that "with an Auslese, honor is satisfied."

The must weight requirements for Auslesen range from 83 to 95, which corresponds to an alcohol potential of 11.1 to 13 percent. As pointed out, however, it is exceedingly unusual to find such alcohol levels; much of the additional grape sugar is retained in the wine rather than converted to alcohol.

Any of the wines described here can be made from grapes other than the Riesling, but none of them can match the range of aromas and flavors offered by the Riesling grape.

Beerenauslese. Beyond the Auslese, there are two other Prädikats, and they are among the rarest of all wines: the great Beerenauslese and Trockenbeerenauslese. The translation of these formidable-sounding words explains exactly what they are. Beerenauslese means "special berry selection"; individual grapes are harvested, rather than entire bunches of grapes. This is extraordinarily expensive and time consuming, for the vineyards must be picked over repeatedly to obtain only the most fully ripened grapes—generally heavily infected with *Botrytis cinerea.* Once the grapes are gathered, it is most difficult even to get a fermentation going, because of the richness of the sugar content. The logical extension of such dedication—some would say madness—is a Trockenbeerenauslese: "special dried berry selection." Not only are the grapes gathered one by one, but only grapes that have dried nearly into raisins are picked. With both these wines, especially the latter, very little juice is obtained, and the Prädikat prohibition against blending between vineyards is relaxed. It would be nearly impossible for one vineyard to produce sufficient juice to make wine making feasible; therefore, the rules permit using grapes from several sites.

At this level, minimum must weights are enormous: 110 to 125 for a Beerenauslese and 150 for a Trockenbeerenauslese. In 1976, sugar levels of over 50 percent were reported in a Rheingau vineyard—the highest ever recorded in the history of German viticulture. The minimum sugar requirement for a Trockenbeerenauslese yields an alcohol potential of 21.5 percent! This is chemically impossible to achieve, but it does illustrate the sweetness of such a wine, because it may be bottled at only 6 to 9 percent alcohol.

Without sufficient acid, wines of such high levels of residual sugar would be impossibly cloying to drink. One would tire of them after only a sip or two. One of the remarkable things about these wines, however, is that they retain their sugar-acid balance. This is why they can age so gracefully; both the sugar and the acid provide adequate protection. The best examples seemingly can go on forever.

One additional subcategory is permitted for Qualitätswein mit Prädikat: Eiswein. This is perhaps the most unusual of all wines, because it is made from frozen grapes. Fully ripened grapes must be picked at temperatures of between 14 and 18° F. The grapes themselves must be frozen when picked and remain frozen while pressing. The pressing expresses only the concentrated sugar juice; most of the water remains behind in the form of ice crystals. Thus, the fermenting grape must has a very high specific gravity—similar to the ones just described—and the resulting wine is capable of great sweetness and complexity.

The name Eiswein (literally, "ice wine") is not used by itself but is attached to one of the other Prädikats, generally a Spätlese or Auslese. A Kabinett or Beerenauslese Eiswein is permitted, but there are difficulties with each. The acidity of a Kabinett is usually too high for an Eiswein, and trying to pick frozen individual grapes (and keep them frozen for pressing) for a Beerenauslese Eiswein presents too formidable an obstacle, although it is possible.

In addition to all the specific legal requirements stated above, there are some general ones that apply to all German wines, regardless of the quality category. They have to do with the minimum percentages of the named grape and vintage. In both cases, the minimum percentage is 85. The varietal requirement of 85 percent is stricter, for example, than the 75 percent requirement in the United States, but looser than in France and Italy, which require at least 95 percent for a varietal designation. This means that up to 15 percent of a Riesling could consist of any of a wide variety of inferior grapes. The same loophole applies to the vintage on the label. In cases of two consecutive harvests of approximately similar quality, it probably does not make any difference, because the blending vintage is nearly always the earlier one; but in the case of widely disparate qualities, a vintner can "stretch" a lesser vintage.

QMP wines, like QBA, have an A.P. number, and the examination process is the same, although the standards are considerably higher, of course.

Geographical Designations

There are four levels of geographical designation in Germany. They are, in descending order, regions, districts, consolidated vineyards, and individual vineyards. The German terms are Anbaugebiet (region), Bereich (district), Grosslage (collection of vineyards), and Einzellage (an individual site or vineyard). There are eleven Anbaugebiete, all located near or on the Rhein River and its tributaries. These regions are divided into thirty one Bereiche, which are subdivided in turn into many Grosslagen and Einzellagen.

The latter two are where a lot of the confusion with German wines occurs. A Grosslage can be thought of as an extended vineyard, or a collection of individual vineyards. The objective was to place together several vineyards into a larger unit. They are large-scale vineyards that show similar climatic and geological characteristics. An Einzellage is a single vineyard. Germany has always had a countless and bewildering array of imposing vineyard names, and one of the many changes made by the 1971 law was to reduce the number of vineyards. There are presently some 2,600 Einzellagen, but it has been estimated that, prior to 1971, there were about 30,000 — no one claims to know exactly how many.

Inevitably, in making such a drastic reduction, there had to be a great deal of consolidation of names and properties. The EEC requires a minimum vineyard size of five hectares (about 12.5 acres), so this was the basic consideration. Several smaller properties, however, were so famous and highly regarded that they were allowed to retain their former borders and names. But many others were combined with surrounding vineyards and given one name—the most famous one, naturally. For example, the famous vineyard of Goldtröpfchen in the town of Piesport is now considerably larger than it was.

The use of town or village names also adds to the confusion, because the Bereiche names are often taken from the best-known towns in the district. Thus, one can have a wine from the Bernkastel Bereich in the Mosel-Saar-Ruwer region as well as any number of wines from the town of Bernkastel itself, a far smaller and more prestigious location. With the latter, the consumer then has to distinguish between single-vineyard wines and consolidated-vineyard wines from Bernkastel. A similar situation occurs in the Rheingau, where there is a single Bereich: Johannisberg. That in itself is an impressive statement of origin, but the most famous town in the Rheingau is Johannisberg—which provides an even more noteworthy pedigree. In the town of Johannisberg, moreover, the best single property is Schloss Johannisberg, and its wines are as sought after as any in Germany. This multiplicity of names, of course is not the exclusive domain of the Germans; the Burgundians in France do approximately the same thing.

To summarize the German laws regarding geographical designation: only names of districts and sites that appear in the official register of vineyards can be used on labels; names of villages and towns can be used (generally with an *er* on the end, as in Johannisberger and Bernkastler); names of the eleven specified quality wine regions and five specified table wine regions also can be used. Finally, to quote the Wine Law, "Governments of wine-growing federal states may pass legislation for further specification, giving more detail of the origin of a typical wine from a certain area, in order to enhance its market value."

There are also legal definitions of origin for certain regional wines of long-standing tradition. For example, Liebfraumilch, according to the decree for the Federal State of the Rhenish Palatinate of December 8, 1971, must "be a white quality wine from the specified wine-growing regions of Rheinhessen, Nahe, Rhenish Palatinate and Rheingau, with a minimum gravity of must of 60 Oechsle, pressed from Riesling, Silvaner, or Müller-Thurgau grapes and being of mild taste. Liebfraumilch, as a Quality Wine, must be furnished with the usual official examination number after having passed the Qualitätsprüfung (quality examination)."

German Wine Terms

Abfüllung: Bottling.

Amtliche Prüfung (A.P.): Refers to the testing procedure that all QBA and QMP wines go through. An A.P. number is assigned to all successful wines.

Anbaugebiet: A wine region. There are eleven such regions for quality wines (QBA and QMP) in Germany.

Anreichern: Literally, "enriching": the process of adding sugar to the fermenting grape must to obtain sufficient or additional alcohol.

Auslese: Wine made from a "special selection" of grapes. This is the third level of QMP wines, and the style is expected to show a progression of natural sweetness and complexity, relative to the first two, **Kabinett** and **Spätlese**.

Beerenauslese: The fourth level of QMP wines. The term translates as "special berry selection"; only overripe grapes infected with the noble mode, *Botrytis cinerea*, are harvested.

Bereich: A wine district. Each **Gebiet** (region) is subdivided into one or more Bereich.

Blau: "Blue" in German, but used with wines to refer to red or black grapes.

Bocksbeutel: A flask-shaped bottle commonly used for the wines of Franken.

Deutsches Weinsiegel: A special label seal that can be earned by producers whose wines score higher than the minimum required for their category.

Diabetiker-Wein: The driest German wine. It cannot exceed four grams per liter of unfermented sugar. Considered safe for diabetics.

Edelfäule: *Botrytis cinerea*, a mold called the noble rot.

Einzellage: An individual vineyard or site; the smallest geographical subdivision. Einzellagen are grouped together with other vineyards sharing similar soil and climatic characteristics and are called **grosslagen**. On German labels, the name of the **Einzellage** or **Grosslage** will follow that of the village **(Gemeinde)**.

Eiswein: Wine made from frozen grapes. The grapes must be frozen both when picked and when pressed, and this concentrates the sugar content of the available juice. The resulting wines are high in residual sugar. Eiswein (literally, "ice wine") is a QMP wine but will be paired with one of the other Prädikats — generally **Spätlese** or **Auslese**.

Erzeugerabfüllung: Estate bottled.

Erzeugergemeinschaft: An association of producers working together for marketing purposes. Wine-making groups or associations are called cooperatives.

Fass: Barrel.

Flasche: Bottle.

Füder: A large oval oak barrel, used in the Mosel. It contains 1,000 liters, or nearly 265 gallons.

Gebiet: Quality wine region. See **Anbaugebiet.**

Gemeinde: Wine village or town; it always precedes the vineyard or Grosslage name on the label. The name has an *er* tagged on at the end, as with Bernkasteler (from Bernkastel) and Piesporter (Piesport).

Grosslage: A collection of Einzellagen, or vineyards. Grosslagen are themselves collected together to form the **Bereiche**—the districts. A German label does not distinguish between a Grosslage or Einzellage; one must know which is which when they are paired with the village name. A Grosslage name is ordinarily considered inferior to the more specific Enizellage, although in the case of a **Trockenbeerenauslesen**, this might not necessarily be true. Such wines often cannot be made from a single vineyard, and the grapes have to be harvested from a broader area.

Halbtrocken: "Half-dry": wines created to counter the claim that German wines are too sweet to match foods properly. Halbtrocken wines are allowed no more than eighteen grams per liter of sugar and are drier than most.

Kabinett: The initial category of Qualitätswein mit Prädikat. A **Naturrein,** a wine made from grapes that have ripened sufficiently so that sugaring is not necessary.

Kellerei: Wine cellar. A term used for those who sell or market wine, as opposed to **Weingut,** a wine-growing estate.

Lage: Site. See **Einzellage.**

Lesegut: Wine crop or harvest.

Must: Grape juice.

Natur, Naturrein: A term made obsolete by the 1971 wine law. It was formerly used to describe wines made without sugaring. The QMP category now legally describes such wines.

Oechsle: The term used to describe specific gravity; the sugar content of the grape juice. Each gram by which a liter of grape must exceeds the weight of distilled water is one degree Oechsle.

Prädikat: See QMP.

Prüfungsnummer: The A.P. number given to a qualifying QBA or QMP wine. See **Amtliche Prüfung.**

QBA: Qualitätswein bestimmter Anbaugebiete, which means "quality wine from specified regions." The middle level of the three-tiered German wine law. The proportion of a particular harvest that falls into this category varies by a considerable margin from year to year. In great years it will be very low, because the grapes ripen to the point where it is not necessary to add sugar to the fermenting must. In less-favored years, however, the vast majority of the grapes require sugaring and are classified as QBA (or even Tafelwein).

QMP: Qualitätswein mit Prädikat, or "quality wine with special attributes." The Prädikats are Kabinett, Spätlese, Auslese, Beerenauslese, and Trockenbeerenauslese, as well as Eiswein.

Rebe: Grape.

Rebsorte: Grape variety.

Restsüsse: The wine's residual sugar.

Roseewein, Roséwein: A pale pink wine made from red grapes only.

Rotling: A pale red wine made from a blend of both red and white grapes.

Rotwein: Red wine.

Säure: Acidity.

Schaumwein: Inexpensive sparkling wine. Better sparkling wines are called **Sekt.**

Schloss: Castle.

Sekt: Quality sparkling wines. Regulated similarly to QBA wines.

Spätlese: Late harvest. Wines picked after the official harvest date. The next QMP level above Kabinett. Such wines are expected to show increased sweetness, character, and complexity befitting the greater ripeness of the grapes.

Stück: The traditional Rhein barrel. It contains 1,200 liters, or about 315 gallons.

Süssreserve: Unfermented grape juice. Naturally sweet, it is blended with a fully fermented wine to give it better balance.

Tafelwein: Table wine. The most basic level of German wine. The name Deutscher Tafelwein indicates German table wine; without the prefix it is not of German origin.

Trocken: Dry. A companion category with **Halbtrocken.** A Trocken cannot contain over nine grams per liter of unfermented sugar.

Trockenbeerenauslese (TBA): "Special dried berry selection." The ultimate in German wine making and one of the rarest and most difficult to make wines in the world. Only the fully molded, dried grapes are harvested, literally grape by grape. The sugar content is so high that the musts resist fermentation, and the alcoholic content of a TBA is usually very low.

Verbessern: To improve, by adding sugar. This has been replaced by **anreichern.**

Weingut: Wine estate. Used only by growers who farm their own grapes.

Weinkellerei: Wine celler. See **Kellerei.**

Winzer: A wine grower.

Winzergenossenschaft, Winzerverein: A growers' cooperative.

WINE LAWS AND REGULATIONS OF ITALY
History of Italian Wine Regulation

Although Italy is and has long been an enormous producer of wine, historically she has been indifferent to rules and regulations, preferring instead to rely on local, or even family, traditions. As a member of the European Economic Community, however, Italy has had to develop governmental standards and regulations to comply with EEC policies. The Italian equivalent to the French AOC is its Denominazione di Origine Controllata, or DOC.

There are four levels in the DOC system, one of which is DOC itself. The others are Denominazione di Origine Controllata e Garantita (DOCG), Vini Tipici, and Vino da Tavola (table wine).

Denominazione di Origine Controllata

Although the system allows for four levels of wines, at present it is strongly dominated by DOC wines. Only recently has one of the others (DOCG) begun implementation; (Vini Tipici) is still attempting to get off the ground; and Vino da Tavola comprises all the rest of the vast number of wines made in Italy.

The DOC legislation was instituted in 1963 and now covers some 200 wines, accounting for about 12 percent of Italy's production. In France, AOC wines total around 20 percent, and the EEC has required Italy to bring the DOC production up to that figure.

The DOC regulates about the same types of things as in France and Germany: grapes, growing zones, alcoholic strength, wine-making processes, and so forth. A description of the requirements for Chianti serves as an illustration of the detail covered by a typical DOC specification. It is a red wine from Tuscany, the provinces of Siena, Florence, Arezzo, Pistoia, and Pisa. As for villages, a huge portion of central Tuscany is subdivided into Classico, Colli Aretini, Colli Fiorentini, Colli Pisane, Colli Senesi, Montalbano, and Rufina. The grapes are a blend of Sangiovese (50 to 80 percent), Canaiolo Nero (10 to 30 percent), Trebbiano Toscano and Malvasia del Chianti (10 to 30 percent), and other grapes up to a maximum of 5 percent. The yield maximum is 87.5 hectoliters per hectare for Chianti and 80.5 hectoliters per hectare for Chianti Classico. The alcohol minimum is 11.5 percent (Chianti) and 12.0 percent (Chianti Classico). A *vecchio* (literally, "old") requires aging for two years, and a *riserva* requires three years in wood.

As the foregoing shows, the Italian DOC is quite specific and comprehensive. As an additional quality control measure, DOC regulations also specify the weight of grapes that may be harvested from each hectare and even the percentage of the weight that may be processed into wine.

Italy is divided into twenty regions, each of which has many DOC wines. Appendix A lists the regions, with the DOC wines in each. DOCG wines and notable Vino da Tavola wines are listed as well.

Denominazione di Origine Controllata e Garantita

DOCG refers to wines of controlled origin that are guaranteed. It is a category that was approved when the DOC was instituted but has taken a long time to be implemented. The philosophy was that such wines would be subject to very strict standards of production and the government would guarantee the quality. Eventually, it was hoped, all the best wines of Italy would be so designated. The first four to be given the status, were Barolo, Barbaresco, Brunello di Montalcino, and Vino Nobile di Montepulciano. These are all red wines, the first two from Piedmont, the others from Tuscany. Chianti, also a red wine from Tuscany, has now been elevated to DOCG status, and other wines are under consideration. The program has been controversial not so much because of the wines classified DOCG to date as for some of the ones being considered—such as the white Albana di Romagna—and for the general apathy of many wine producers toward the concept.

Vini Tipici

This is a category approved by the EEC as the Italian equivalent of the French Vin de Pays and the German Landwein. It is meant to occupy the niche below DOC, and its regulations and controls are less stringent than for DOC, although its wines come from approved areas and grapes. Because such wines will qualify for the EEC's VQPRD category, it is expected that the number of Vini Tipici wines will increase and will include many quality products.

Vino da Tavola

In the absence of full implementation of Vini Tipici, the Tavola category takes in all the rest of the wines of Italy. Unlike the Tafelwein of Germany and *vin ordinaire* of France, however, there are superb Italian wines in this category. The reason is that DOC represents the traditional wines from traditional regions, using the accepted grapes of the regions. The Italian wine scene is comparable to California in that there is a flurry of experimentation going on. New areas are being developed, and new, often non-Italian, grapes are being introduced in established wine-growing areas. Thus, wines are being made that, regardless of their quality, do not qualify as DOC. There is no way to label any of these other than Vino da Tavola.

In this respect, DOC represents the wines that Italy has made for centuries, not the wines she is capable of producing. Another factor that results in some extraordinary wines being classified as Tavola is that some producers, for whatever reasons, choose not to follow the DOC guidelines regarding grape varieties. One such example is Tignanello, a Vino da Tavola made by Antinori in Tuscany. Chianti has historically permitted up to 30 percent white grapes in the blend and required a minimum of 10 percent. Antinori felt the wine could be improved both by eliminating the white grapes and by using a small amount of Cabernet Sauvignon in the blend. The result was a proprietary wine he named Tignanello. It is made in the Chianti region but does not comply with that DOC, hence the Vino da Tavola classification. There are many other examples. Several Tavola wines that are highly regarded are included with the DOC listings in Appendix A. Some of the better wines of Italy, in fact, are not DOC wines.

Italian Wine Terms

Abboccato: Slightly sweet.

Acidita: Acidity.

Acidulo: Acidulous, acidic, or even tart.

Amabile: A little sweeter than **abboccato.**

Amaro: Bitter.

Amarognolo: The almondlike bitter undertones found in many Italian wines.

Ambrato: The amber color or hue found in many dessert wines.

Annata: Vintage year.

Asciutto: Very dry.

Bianco: White.

Botte: Barrel.

Bottiglia: Bottle.

Cantina: Wine cellar.

Cantina sociale: Growers' cooperative cellar.

Casa vinicola: A wine company, generally one that makes wine from grapes it has not grown.

Cerasuolo: Cherry red.

Chiaretto: Literally "claret," it describes many rosé wines.

Classico: The central and best portion of a DOC zone.

Consorzio: A consortium of wine producers who jointly promote a specific wine.

Cooperativa: Growers' cooperative cellar.

Denominazione di origine controllata (DOC): The regulatory system for quality Italian wines.

Denominazione di origine controllata e garantita (DOCG): The highest echelon of Italian wines; wines that are not only controlled regarding production and origin, but "guaranteed" as well.

Dolce: Sweet wine; generally meant for wines that have from 5 to 10 percent residual sugar.

Enoteca: A wine library.

Etichetta: A wine label.

Fattoria: A wine estate; Tuscan terminology.

Fiasco: Flask; traditionally used to describe the straw-covered Chianti bottle.

Frizzante: Half sparkling; less pressure than normally found in a sparkling wine. Also can be translated as "fizzy."

Frizzantino: Wine with a barely perceptible sparkle or prickle.

Gradazione alcoolica: Alcoholic content; expressed in percentage by volume.

Imbottigliato (or *messo in bottiglia) nel 'origine* (or *del produttore all'origine)* : Estate bottled.

Liquoroso: Strong, generally fortified wine. May or may not be sweet.

Litro: Liter.

Marchio depositato: A registered brand name or trademark.

Metodo champenois: Sparkling wine made by the traditional Champagne method.

Nero: Very dark red or black.

Passito: High-alcohol wine, often sweet, made from grapes that have been dried to concentrate the sugar.

Produttore: Producer.

Riserva: DOC and DOCG wines that have been given additional aging.

Riserva speciale: Wines that have been aged even longer than **riserva.**

Rosato: Rosé or pink wine.

Rosso: Red.

Secco: Dry.

Semisecco: Literally, "semidry," but it actually means medium sweet.

Spumante: Sparkling.

Stravecchio: Very old. The term has legal meaning only with DOC wines.

Superiore: A wine designated as superior under DOC rules. Generally taken to mean an increased alcohol requirement.

Tenementi: An estate.

Tenuta: An estate.

Uva: Grape.

Vecchio: Old. There are specific DOC regulations that govern the use of this term.

Vendemmia: Year of the vintage. Synonymous with **annata.**

Vigna, vigneto: Vineyard.

Vignaiolo, viticoltore: Grape grower.

Vino da arrosto: A roast wine; full flavored and bodied.

Vino da pasto: Everyday wine.

Vino da tavola: The officially regulated term for non-DOC wines.

Vino santo: Wine made from grapes dried indoors over the fall and winter.

Vite: Vine.

Vitigno: Grape variety.

SUGGESTED READINGS

Amerine, M. A., and E. B. Roessler. *Wines: Their Sensory Evaluation.* San Francisco: W. H. Freeman and Co., 1976.

Anderson, B. *Pocket Guide to Italian Wines.* New York: Simon and Schuster, 1982.

———. *Vino.* Boston and Toronto: Little, Brown and Company, 1980.

German Wine Atlas and Vineyard Register. Trans. Fowler. 4th rev. ed. London: Mitchell Beazley Ltd., 1980.

Jamieson, I. *The Wines of Germany.* André Simon's Wines of the World. 2d ed. S. Sutcliffe. New York: McGraw-Hill, 1981.

Johnson, H. *Modern Encyclopedia of Wine.* New York: Simon and Schuster, 1983.

Lichine, A. *Alexis Lichine's New Encyclopedia of Wines & Spirits.* New York: Alfred Knopf, 1982.

Meinhard, H. *The Wines of Germany.* New York: Stein & Day, 1976.

Sutcliffe, S. *The Wines of France.* André Simon's Wines of the World. 2d ed. New York: McGraw-Hill, 1981.

CHAPTER FOUR

WINE GRAPE STANDARDS

Because the grape is the primary differentiating factor among various wines, and because each grape should have recognizable and consistent sensory characteristics, regardless of where it is grown, it is vital to examine the major grapes used in wine production around the world. Wines made from one grape species in different countries and regions will differ and show regional characteristics, of course, but there should also be similarities based on the specific grape or grapes used. The wines should be more or less consistent in appearance, odor, flavor and taste, and texture. There are exceptions, but most wines will reflect the characteristics of the specific grapes they were made from, when grown successfully and handled skillfully.

The format for the discussion of each grape is first to name the grape (with synonyms, if appropriate), then to identify the countries and regions where it is grown. The list will not include every region in the world where a particular grape may be grown but will concentrate on those areas that are generally considered to produce representative wines.

Wines are grown differently in California from most of the traditional wine-growing regions. It is typical within a specific European region to grow certain grapes and make a finite number of wine types. In fact, most of the established European vineyard areas have legal requirements as to which grapes may be grown. These requirements are based on long years, often centuries, of trial and error to determine the variety or varieties best suited for the soil and climatic conditions.

In California, within a particular region such as Napa Valley, for example, dozens of varieties are grown and even more wine types made. As wine making in California matures, however, the matching of regions with grapes has become very sophisticated, and the range of varieties grown in particular microclimates is diminishing. Still, there is a very broad range of grapes grown in California and seldom a fixed relationship between a viticultural area and the grape varieties. Therefore, a particular grape will be identified as being grown in California but, in most cases, specific regions there will not be noted.

Along with the areas of growth, this chapter will examine growing conditions and any unique wine-making techniques for each grape. In addition, the types of wines made from each grape (table wines, dessert wines, fortified wines, and sparkling wines) will be identified, along with the regions that specialize in one type or another. Finally, the sensory attributes of wines made from each grape will be discussed.

RED GRAPES
Aglianico

Major Wine Regions: Aglianico is an ancient vine, originally brought into Italy by the Greeks. Today its growth is mainly confined to a few regions in southern Italy. The major one is Campania, where Antonio Mastroberardino produces one of Italy's great reds, Taurasi, entirely from the Aglianico vine. Another noted Aglianico wine from Campania is Falerno (in Latium, wine makers also produce a wine called Falerno, or Falernum, although that one is blended with Barbera). Basilicata has several areas dependent on the Aglianico vine, including Aglianico dei Colli Lucani, grown in Basilicata but produced and bottled in Apulia, as well as Aglianico del Vulture and Aglianico del Matera.

Grape Growth and Wine-Making Techniques: In Taurasi, where it is acknowledged to produce the finest wines, the Aglianico is grown at high elevations (one to two thousand feet), where the climate is cooler and the vine ripens a little later than in the other areas.

Types of Wine Produced: Red table wine.

Sensory Characteristics: Full bodied, with a deep ruby color. It has a full aroma and maintains its aromatic and color strength through many years. A robust wine with elegance.

Barbera

Major Wine Regions: Barbera is probably the most widely grown red grape in Italy, producing DOC wines in Piedmont, Lombardy, and Emilia-Romagna as well as being used for blending in nearly every other region. It is most associated with Piedmont, however, where it is estimated to grow at least half of the red wine.

It is also heavily, but not widely, planted in California. In the mid 1980s, there were over eighteen thousand acres grown in the state, mostly in the Central Valley.

Grape Growth and Wine-Making Techniques: The grape is highly valued in California, because its excellent acidity allows it to be grown in the hot Central Valley. It is grown sparingly in the cooler North Bay counties, and although those wines are considered to be superior to those from the Central Valley, the vines yield only about half as much wine. If the climate is too cool, the grape has difficulty in ripening; if too hot, it may not have sufficient acidity when ripe to produce balanced wines. The wines made in the coastal counties are longer lived than those from the Central Valley and are closer in character to the wines of Piedmont.

Types of Wine Produced: Red table wine, used as a varietal and in blends, both in Italy and California. In Italy, it may occasionally be vinified as a semisweet, a sweet, even a *frizzante*—lightly sparkling—or a sparkling wine.

Sensory Characteristics: Quite variable. The color may range from a light garnet to a deep, rich red to an inky purple. It generally has good to high acidity, and may be somewhat tannic when young. In Piedmont, it is often produced in a lighter style, ready to drink earlier and exhibiting more fruit. The styles are probably too broad to make any definitive comments as to specific sensory characteristics. The California coastal versions are typically high in acid, dark, and tannic, and require a few years of bottle age.

Brachetto

Major Wine Regions: Piedmont, Italy.

Types of Wine Produced: A pale red, a semisweet sparkling, or a *frizzante*.

Sensory Characteristics: Brachetto has an attractive light red color, an aromatic, fruity odor, and a fresh taste with a slight sweetness. It is not as sweet as most Asti Spumante and can be used as an aperitif wine or to accompany pastries and fruits.

Cabernet Franc (Bouchet, Gros Vidure)

Major Wine Regions: This grape is closely related to the Cabernet Sauvignon and is used in Bordeaux as a *support*, or blending, grape. It is especially important in Saint-Émilion and is probably the second choice in Pomerol. In general, it can be found wherever Cabernet Sauvignon is grown, and it serves the same purpose as in Bordeaux, although occasionally it may be used as the primary varietal in a blend (see Cabernet Sauvignon).

Wine makers in northeastern Italy have long grown Cabernet Franc, although the current preference is moving toward Cabernet Sauvignon.

In the Loire Valley in France, Cabernet Franc is used to make red wines that range from fresh and light to very fine wines that have the ability to age for many years. The best red wine made in the Loire is from Chinon and is produced from Cabernet Franc. It is also used for producing rosé wines in the Loire.

Grape Growth and Wine-Making Techniques: Similar to Cabernet Sauvignon.

Types of Wine Produced: Table wines; red and rosé. The Loire rosés are often slightly sweet to sweet.

Sensory Characteristics: The aroma is considered to be less distinctive than Cabernet Sauvignon, but clearly in the Cabernet group (see Cabernet Sauvignon).

Cabernet Sauvignon (Petit Vidure)

Cabernet Sauvignon, probably the most well known wine grape in the world, is grown in many regions and countries and has an astonishing record for success. It likely produces more fine wine, in more areas, than any other grape variety.

Major Wine Regions: Bordeaux is the area associated most closely with Cabernet Sauvignon, especially the classic red wines of Bordeaux. These may be the most famous wines in the world, and many of them are made primarily from Cabernet Sauvignon. In Bordeaux, Cabernet is blended with several other grapes, most notably the Merlot and Cabernet Franc, while in other regions it tends to be unblended, at least initially.

Many other regions, as they mature in their wine-making practices, begin to experiment with blending the Cabernet in order to obtain the type of balanced and complex wines the Bordelais are noted for. California is an example. The fame of the great California Cabernets was built mostly on 100 percent Cabernet Sauvignon wine, but recent years have seen a significant increase in blended wines. Even so, Cabernet Sauvignon still accounts for the major portion of the blend. In the United States, a wine must contain a minimum of 75 percent of a specific grape in order to be labeled identifying that grape. California Cabernets, even when blended, typically contain more than the minimum requirement. Cabernet acreage in California increased from 6,600 in 1977 to some 26,000 five years later, an indication not only of the quality potential of the grape, but of its marketability as well.

In Bordeaux, the Médoc is the region most associated with Cabernet Sauvignon, although even there, it accounts for only about 50 percent of the acreage. The soil appears to be the factor deciding which vines to plant, and the mixture of varieties in each vineyard depends on the soil composition unique to a vineyard. Thus, the eventual style of wine is dictated by the soil. In this respect, the wine makers of the Médoc differ from their counterparts in California, who plant specific varieties with a particular type of wine in mind.

Included with the Médoc as the most prestigious red wine regions in Bordeaux are the Graves, Pomerol, and Saint-Émilion. The best Graves reds are made in the northern sector, next to Médoc, and are similar in that the Cabernet Sauvignon is the primary grape in the blend. In Saint-Émilion the Merlot is king, while the Cabernet assumes the role of the support grape in the blends. The wines of Pomerol are strongly based on Merlot, and the Cabernet is less important.

The Italians, particularly the Tuscan wine makers, have had significant success in blending Cabernet Sauvignon with traditional Italian red varieties. In most of those cases, the Cabernet is not the *informing*, or primary, grape but instead is used as the support, or blending, grape. An example is Tignanello from Antinori, which is essentially a *riserva*-style Chianti using about 10 percent Cabernet Sauvignon in the blend. In Umbria, Lungarotti produces a wine made entirely from Cabernet. At Bolgheri, along the Tuscan coast, the Marchesi Incisa della Rocchetta produces Sassicaia mostly from Cabernet Sauvignon, with a little Cabernet Franc blended in the Bordeaux style.

In Spain, Cabernet has been planted and is being used in small amounts in several well-known wines, such as the Gran Coronas of Torres, the wines of Riscal in Rioja, and in Vega Sicilia, reputedly the most expensive red wine from Spain. In an unusual twist, a Los Angeles restaurateur, Jean Léon, produces a varietal Cabernet in Catalonia, some 16,000 cases from 250 acres of Cabernet.

The wine makers of Australia have made a major commitment to Cabernet Sauvignon and are producing highly regarded wines from it. Among the best growing regions are the Hunter Valley, the Barossa Valley, Coonawarra, and Victoria.

South Africa is a country that is trying to develop an international reputation and market for her wines, and her best reds have long been made from Cabernet Sauvignon, although wine makers there, too, are increasingly experimenting with blending in other Bordeaux red grapes, such as Merlot and Cabernet Franc.

The best wines of Chile are also the reds made from Cabernet Sauvignon. There, as in Bordeaux, they blend with other grapes, principally Malbec and Merlot.

Grape Growth and Wine-Making Techniques: The Cabernet, judging by its international success, does not seem to be overly demanding as to growing conditions. It should be grown in a moderate climate, because it is rather late ripening. It also buds late and is an advantageous grape to grow in areas subject to spring frosts. Because both the Napa Valley floor and the Médoc are prone to frosts, it makes sense that the Cabernet is well suited there.

Hot climates rob it of its character and intensity; in California, for example, it is at its best in the cooler coastal counties. Napa and Sonoma are the best known, but fine Cabernet is grown in all the central and northern coastal counties. However, warm soils are necessary. In Bordeaux, the best soils are the gravelly ones found in the Médoc, whereas in Pomerol, the soil has a lot of cool clay, making it unsatisfactory for Cabernet. Hence the predominance of Merlot in that region.

Types of Wine Produced: Cabernet Sauvignon is used almost exclusively for table wines, mostly red, although it is increasingly being used for *blush* wines in California, white wines made from red grapes. Such wines became very popular in the United States during the 1980s and proved to be a valuable outlet for red grapes during a period when the consumption of white wines soared dramatically, compared to reds. In the Loire Valley in France, a fine rosé is made from the Cabernet.

One Napa winery, Beringer, makes a port-style wine from Cabernet Sauvignon, but this is not a typical use of the grape.

Sensory Characteristics: Cabernet Sauvignon grapes are small and dark and yield a wine with an intense color variously described as dark, ruby, or garnet. In addition to the darkness of the color, it is deep and dense, because so many color components are drawn from the grapes during fermentation.

Many terms have been used to describe the aroma, the grape smell, of Cabernet Sauvignon. The ones that seem to be most agreed upon are herbaceous, black currant, aromatic-spicy, green olive, and green bell pepper. In some California Cabernets, mint and/or eucalyptus odor can be easily noted. Cabernet Sauvignon is one of the grapes that will transmit a distinctive and recognizable aroma to its wine.

The bouquet of a matured Cabernet Sauvignon is what makes it one of the most—if not the most—honored and respected of all wines. It is generally matured at least partly in oak and produces complex odors reminiscent of wildflowers, violets, cassis, chocolate, and cedar, with other overtones.

The tastes should be consistent with the odors: intense Cabernet fruit flavors when young, and a host of complex flavors blended harmoniously when mature. In texture, good Cabernets are fairly full bodied, the typical California examples more so due to the higher levels of alcohol. Due to high concentrations of tannin, they are also harsh when young, but this contributes to their longevity. Few natural (unfortified) wines have the maturing potential of top Bordeaux reds.

Carignan (Carignane, Carignano, Cariñena)

Major Wine Regions: Originally from Spain, for hundreds of years the Carignan has been the mainstay of the Midi region on the Mediterranean coast in southern France. In California, it has been grown since Prohibition, mostly in the San Joaquin Valley, although in recent years the acreage has declined. In Italy, it is grown on the island of Sardinia and is used in several wines.

Grape Growth and Wine-Making Techniques: As evidenced by its principal location, the Midi in southern France, this is a hot-climate grape. In California, the majority of the plantings are in the San Joaquin Valley. Its main claim to fame is its vigor and productivity, averaging eight to ten tons per acre in the warm valley and up to six in cooler coastal areas. If the yield is allowed to get too high, however, low acidity can be a problem. Other growing hazards include bunch rot in warm regions and mildew in cool ones.

Types of Wine Produced: Red table wine. The bulk wines of the Midi are based on the Carignan. In California, it is used mostly for blending in generic reds, but some varietal bottlings are produced.

Sensory Characteristics: The best California varietal Carignans, from the warmer parts of Sonoma and Mendocino, are said to be faintly reminiscent of Cabernet Sauvignon. The acidity is moderate to low, but color is excellent, one of its positive attributes as a blending wine. In France it is considered, to quote Hugh Johnson, as a "harmless but dull" grape.

Cinsaut (Hermitage, Oeillade)

Major Wine Regions: Cinsaut is an important grape in the southern Rhône, particularly in Châteauneuf-du-Pape. In South Africa (where it is sometimes referred to as Hermitage), it is the most popular grape for red table wines. The Australians, using the name Oeillade, grow it widely in the Barossa Valley.

Grape Growth and Wine-Making Techniques: A high-yield grape.

Types of Wine Produced: Generally used for blending in red table wines.

Sensory Characteristics: Regarded as lacking in character but useful in blending for its ability to lighten the blend.

Corvina Veronese

Major Wine Regions: Corvina Veronese is the primary grape of the red wines of Verona, Italy. (The other grapes used in the blends are Rondinella, Molinara, and Negrara.) These wines include Bardolino, Valpolicella, Recioto della Valpolicella, and Recioto della Valpolicella Amarone (or, more simply, Amarone).

Grape Growth and Wine-Making Techniques: Recioto indicates a specialized wine-making technique. The upper portions of the grape clusters, the ones that receive the most sun during growth, are semidried to concentrate the sugars and solids. When these sugar-laden musts are fermented to total dryness, an alcoholic, powerful wine, Amarone, is the result. When some of the sugar is allowed to remain in the wine, a sweet wine, Recioto, is the end product.

Types of Wine Produced: Bardolino and Valpolicella are red table wines, rather on the light side and best consumed fairly young. Recioto della Valpolicella is a sweet dessert wine. Amarone is a powerful, high-alcohol wine. A sparkling Recioto is sometimes made as well.

Sensory Characteristics: The distinguishing characteristic of both Bardolino and Valpolicella is a slight almond bitterness in the finish. They are both ruby hued, with the Valpolicella the deeper colored and fuller bodied of the two. Both exhibit an attractive grapey scent. Amarone is very dark, dry, and strong. It is also full bodied, smooth, and velvety. The slight bitterness in the aftertaste of Bardolino and Valpolicella is more pronounced in Amarone. The name, in fact, comes from the Italian word *amaro*, meaning bitter.

Dolcetto

Major Wine Regions: Dolcetto is responsible for seven DOC wines in southern Piedmont in Italy (Dolcetto d'Acqui, d'Alba, d'Asti, delle Langhe Monregalesi, di Diano d'Alba, di Dogliani, and di Ovada). There are also many non-DOC (unclassified) wines named Dolcetto made in this region.

Types of Wine Produced: Red table, sometimes *frizzante*, or slightly sparkling.

Sensory Characteristics: Several styles of wine are made from this grape, from fairly full-bodied and tannic to light and fruity wines. The color can range from deep purple to bright ruby. It is fermented to full dryness and has a slight bitter almond finish. It is generally best when consumed within a year or so. The ones with the reputation for being the biggest and sturdiest are the Dolcetto di Diano d'Alba, the Dolcetto di Dogliani, and the Dolcetto di Ovada.

Freisa

Major Wine Regions: Piedmont, Italy. Non-DOC and DOC Freisa (Freisa d'Asti and Freisa di Chieri) are produced. The non-DOC wines from the better producers are considered to be superior.

Types of Wine Produced: Dry red table, *frizzante*, and *spumante*, or sparkling.

Sensory Characteristics: The color is bright cherry-ruby, it has good acid, and the aroma has been described as raspberry or berrylike.

Gamay (Napa Gamay)

Major Wine Regions: Gamay is the grape responsible for one of the most famous and appreciated wines in the world: Beaujolais. Beaujolais is part of Burgundy, comprising the major portion of the southern part of that region. The only grape permitted in Beaujolais is the Gamay.

It is also widely grown in California, as is its cousin, the Gamay Beaujolais. The latter grape is actually a clone of the Pinot Noir and legally can be named either Gamay Beaujolais or Pinot Noir. As handled in California, the two grapes make similar wine, although the Gamay is the later ripening, more productive of the two, and is successful in a wider range of climates. It is also more difficult to handle and more easily abused, because it is thin-skinned. Virtually all of both types are planted in coastal counties, with Gamay or Napa Gamay, accounting for a little over half of the total. The largest single area is Napa, which contains 25 percent. Gamay Beaujolais is more or less equally distributed among the coastal counties.

Grape Growth and Wine-Making Techniques: In Beaujolais, the soil is granitic, much different from the rest of Burgundy and ideal for the Gamay. The making of Beaujolais is unique, like the wine. To enhance the fresh grape fruitiness of the Gamay, carbonic maceration is used. Entire bunches of grapes are placed in the fermenting vats: stems, stalks, and all. The weight of the grapes causes the lower layers to break, and a natural fermentation ensues. The carbon dioxide produced pushes up the air and blankets the uncrushed upper layers. The fermentation continues under anaerobic conditions surrounded by carbon dioxide, and many of the uncrushed grapes begin splitting, further contributing to the process. After about a week, the liquid is separated, and the remainder of the grapes are pressed to extract as much juice as possible. The juices are mixed and fermentation continued until all the sugar has been consumed.

Types of Wine Produced: Red table wine.

Sensory Characteristics: The style of wine produced in Beaujolais seems to be the model for California as well. Beaujolais is not a balanced wine. All good wines should exhibit fruit and freshness when young; Beaujolais concentrates on these characteristics nearly to the exclusion of body, substance, weight, and longevity. It has a bright cherry color, but little color density; it is light bodied and has a fresh, fruity aroma and a grapey flavor. It is best served slightly chilled and is thirst quenching and delicious. Beaujolais is sometimes referred to as a "gulping" wine: a wine to drink and enjoy, not to reflect upon.

Grenache (Alicante, Garnacha Tinta)

Major Wine Regions: Originally from northern Spain (Garnacha Tinta), the grape is best known as the Grenache of the southern Rhône, especially in the regions of Tavel, Gigondas, and Châteauneuf-du-Pape. It is also a significant grape in California, accounting for about 17,000 acres, of which 75 percent or more is in the San Joaquin Valley.

Grape Growth and Wine-Making Techniques: The Grenache offers alcohol and high yield in the warmer areas. It does not produce strongly colored wines, and this is why it is used mostly in California (and Tavel) as a rosé wine and blended in Châteauneuf-du-Pape with other grapes that can provide a maximum of color extract. Many more grapes (up to thirteen varieties, some of them white) are permitted in Châteauneuf-du-Pape than in most French wine regions, where three or four would be considered a lot. Grown in cooler areas in California, it is recommended by University of California at Davis researchers for rosé wines; when grown in warm regions, it is recommended only for dessert wines.

Types of Wine Produced: Rosé in Tavel and California, dry red table in Châteauneuf-du-Pape, Gigondas, and other southern Rhône Valley regions.

Sensory Characteristics: Châteauneuf-du-Pape is a big, strong wine, dark colored, full bodied and with a lot of flavor. It is not considered to have the finesse or character of the best wines from Burgundy or Bordeaux, but can be a very fine wine needing a few years to round out. Tavel rosé is one of the more popular French rosé wines in the United States, and it is generally drier than most wines of this type. The color is an orange-pink, a characteristic of the Grenache grape. California rosés made from the Grenache also exhibit an orange hue, but usually are somewhat sweet, or at least semisweet.

Grignolino

Major Wine Regions: The Grignolino is native to Piedmont in northern Italy, where it is still an important grape, although not as much as in former years. It now produces two DOC wines (Grignolino d'Asti and Grignolino del Monferrato Casalese) and many non-DOC, or unclassified, wines. It is planted in California, but there are only about sixty acres.

Types of Wine Produced: Dry red table wines, sometimes rosé.

Sensory Characteristics: In Italy, it makes a red wine with a light color, sometimes with an orange-red hue. It is quite dry and has a hint of bitterness in the finish. Because of clonal variation in California, it is difficult to describe. The color can range from an orange tint to light red, the taste is fruity and tart, and there may be a fair amount of tannin. Most of the acreage is in Santa Clara County, with the remainder in Napa.

Lambrusco

Major Wine Regions: Emilia-Romagna in Italy, where the grape makes Lambrusco wine, which was responsible for Italy's dominance of the American wine market in the 1970s.

Types of Wine Produced: Light, red, slightly *frizzante* wines. The carbonation is kept low to avoid the high taxes on sparkling wines.

Sensory Characteristics: All kinds of wines are made, from red to rosé and even white. In the United States, they are generally semisweet to sweet, slightly fizzy *(frizzante)*, light bodied, and very fruity.

Malbec (Auxerrois)

Major Wine Regions: In Bordeaux it is an important blending grape, and in Cahors, a region east of Bordeaux, it is the primary grape. Italian growers in Apulia and the Veneto often use it as a support grape for red wines.

Types of Wine Produced: Dry, red table wine.

Sensory Characteristics: In Cahors, where the grape is known as Auxerrois, the traditional style was for so-called black wines. In the unique rocky limestone soil above the Lot River, the grape is thick skinned and, coupled with the traditional method of lengthy fermentation, produced much darker-colored wines than did Bordeaux. This style is not much in evidence today, and the wine now is somewhat light and ready to drink far sooner, after only a couple of years.

Merlot

Major Wine Regions: After the Cabernet Sauvignon, Merlot is the most important red grape in Bordeaux. In some viticultural regions in Bordeaux, such as Pomerol, it is the primary grape. Château Pétrus, both the most famous Pomerol estate and often the most expensive of Bordeaux reds, is composed nearly entirely of Merlot. Northeast Italy is also an important home for Merlot. It is widely grown there both for varietals and for blending. In California, it was pretty much unknown following Prohibition, but during the 1960s and 1970s, growers became increasingly interested in it as a blending grape to use with Cabernet Sauvignon, as is the custom in Bordeaux. Plantings in California went from nearly none prior to 1960 to over twenty-two hundred acres by 1980. During the 1980s it continued to gain favor, and some growers were even using it as a varietal—sometimes, in an interesting reversal, using Cabernet as a blending grape.

Grape Growth and Wine-Making Techniques: The soil in Pomerol is composed of cool clay; because the Merlot ripens earlier than the Cabernet, it does better in such soil. In most of the top Pomerol vineyards, in fact, the Cabernet Sauvignon either is not planted, or is present in only minor amounts. Of the Cabernets, the Cabernet Franc is more widely used. Compared to Cabernet Sauvignon, Merlot not only ripens earlier and provides similar color and flavor characteristics, but also has less tannin. This is what makes it such a valuable counterpoint to Cabernet Sauvignon; it has the capacity to soften the blend and bring it to maturity sooner. Interestingly, the use of Cabernet with varietal Merlot is just the opposite: to stiffen or beef up the wine. It is the general custom to wood-age Merlot; the most common choice in the United States is European wood, although some American oak also is used.

Types of Wine Produced: Dry red table wine.

Sensory Characteristics: Similar to Cabernet Sauvignon, with the exceptions noted above. It is also said to be a little fuller and "fatter."

Meunier (Pinot Meunier)

Major Wine Regions: Champagne, France. Champagne is a white sparkling wine made principally from black grapes. The grapes regarded as the most important for quality in Champagne are the Chardonnay and Pinot Noir, but the Pinot Meunier actually exceeds them in acreage, accounting for nearly 45 percent of the vines, compared to about 24 percent for Pinot Noir and 31 percent for Chardonnay.

Grape Growth and Wine-Making Techniques: The Pinot Meunier is more successful than Pinot Noir in chalk-deficient soils, and it is more frost resistant. This accounts for the size and location of the plantings. Champagnes are normally blended wines, except for the Blanc de Blancs (made entirely from Chardonnay), and the Pinot Meunier contributes robustness and fruit to the blend. Such wines develop neither the refinement nor the bouquet of Pinot Noir wines.

Types of Wine Produced: Sparkling wine—the most famous sparkling wine and perhaps the best-known wine in the world.

Sensory Characteristics: See the discussion of Champagne and other sparkling wines in Chapter Two.

Nebbiolo (Spanna)

Major Wine Regions: The great grape of Piedmont, Italy, Nebbiolo is responsible for Barolo, Barbaresco, Gattinara, and many other wines in Piedmont
and its neighboring regions. In the area near the towns of Novara and Vercelli,
the local term for the grape is Spanna, and wines are made based on that
name. Nebbiolo is also widely planted in the Valle d'Aosta and Lombardy.
The name comes from the fog, the *nebbia* of the Piedmontese autumn. Some
is also grown in California, but surprisingly little interest has been shown
to date, considering the Italian heritage of many of the wineries and wine
makers and the unquestioned greatness of the Nebbiolo.

Types of Wine Produced: Dry red table wine.

Sensory Characteristics: The quintessential wines made from the Nebbiolo
are Barolo and Barbaresco. Barolo is referred to by the Piedmontese as "the
king of wines and the wine of kings," and it has long had the reputation as one
of the best red wines in Italy, if not the best, and one of the great wines of
the world.

Barolo is a powerful wine with dense color and tannic hardness when
young. Its color gradually evolves to a brick red, it softens, though it remains a
big wine, and it develops a scent some have described as tarlike, others as
reminiscent of truffles. Like all great wines, it is difficult to describe because of
its complexity. Barbaresco is similar to Barolo, but on a slightly smaller scale.
Its power is less, but it is regarded as perhaps more refined and probably more
consistent from vintage to vintage.

Gattinara is another fine wine made in Piedmont from the Nebbiolo,
although, unlike Barolo and Barbaresco, it can be blended. Up to 10 percent
of Bonarda can be used to produce Gattinara. There are soil differences as
well. At its best, it can approximate Barolo, but its recent history is one of
inconsistency. Like Barolo and Barbaresco, Gattinara is a town that lends its
name to the local wine.

There are also wines named Spanna, a local name for the Nebbiolo and
wines given the varietal name along with the area of production, such as
Nebbiolo d'Alba. A wine called Nebbiolo delle Langhe has been suggested for
less than top-quality Barolo and Barbaresco grapes. It would have to meet the
DOC criteria but would be ready to consume earlier and, of course, less
expensive. Nebbiolo del Piemonte is a generic term for wines made from the
Nebbiolo grape in Piedmont. When made by well-regarded producers and
with specific place names, they can be fine wines.

Petite Sirah (Petite Syrah, Duriff)

Major Wine Regions: In California, this grape was assumed in the past to be the same variety as the Syrah in the Rhône. It is now widely believed that it is really a grape called the Duriff. The confusion resulted not only from the similarity in names but also from the wines themselves. It is grown in Australia using the Duriff name.

Types of Wine Produced: Dry red table wine.

Sensory Characteristics: The typical Petite Sirah is very dark—as close to black as wine gets—and has considerable tannin. The tannin both makes it necessary to age the wine and provides aging protection. The wine sometimes exhibits a black pepper character in the aroma. This is not a widely accepted wine, due to the general consumer reluctance to drink red wines and the necessity for aging. The result is a slow decline in the number of wineries making varietal wines.

The primary red grape of Australia is the Shiraz (Rhône Syrah), and the resemblance of the Duriff to Syrah gives it occasional use in that country for the making of very dark wines.

Pinot Noir (Pinot Nero, Spätburgunder)

Major Wine Regions: The grape of red Burgundy, the Pinot Noir is, along with the Cabernet Sauvignon, one of the two greatest red wine grapes. There may be arguments among wine lovers as to which is the best wine, Burgundy or Bordeaux, but most knowledgeable wine consumers would not argue about the dual supremacy of Pinot Noir and Cabernet Sauvignon.

In Burgundy, it is grown in the Côte d'Or (the Slope of Gold) and is the only grape permitted for the red wines there. Unlike Bordeaux and many of the regions discussed up to now, Burgundy makes wines from a single grape variety. The reds are made from either the Pinot Noir or the Gamay (in Beaujolais), and the whites are made from the Chardonnay.

The Côte d'Or is divided into a northern and a southern sector, called the Côte de Nuits and Côte de Beaune, respectively. Red wines are made in both areas, but virtually all the top-rated vineyards are located in the Côte de Nuits. The Côte de Beaune, unlike its northern neighbor, produces both red and white Burgundies.

Germany is best known for her white wines; only a little red is made, but the best is from the Pinot Noir (Spätburgunder in German). Grown in such a northern latitude, the wine is totally different from that found in Burgundy. It is a much lighter and more delicate wine, best consumed young.

The vine is also widely grown in northeastern Italy, mostly for blending, and a little is grown in Spain. Because of the greatness of the grape in Burgundy, it is also grown in such diverse wine regions as Austria, Australia, South Africa, Chile, and elsewhere. The results generally have been inconsistent and mixed, for the Pinot Noir is perhaps the most difficult of red grapes to manage.

The greatest of sparkling wines, Champagne, uses Pinot Noir as the critical red component of the blend. As was pointed out with Pinot Meunier, Pinot Noir accounts for the smallest acreage among the three Champagne grapes, but it is considered the most important of the three. Champagne is normally made from a cuvée, or blend, consisting of about two-thirds black grapes, and the better producers prefer the Pinot Noir. An important use of the grape in Italy is for the *brut spumanti*, or dry sparkling wines.

California is an important producer of Pinot Noir; there are about 10,000 acres in the state, grown in all the major coastal counties. It has proved to be one of the most difficult of vines to handle in California, and it is only in recent years that wine makers felt they were beginning to understand the grape, its growing requirements, and the wine-making techniques best suited to the variety. One of the more exciting developments in American wine-making has been the success of Pinot Noir in the Pacific Northwest, particularly in Oregon. There are those who feel that these wines have come closer to the Burgundian originals than have their American predecessors.

Grape Growth and Wine-Making Techniques: Unlike Cabernet Sauvignon, Pinot Noir has resisted planting outside its traditional French home. The two reasons wine makers feel are the most compelling are the climate and the wine-making techniques, although many regard the soil and clonal selection to be critically important as well.

Burgundy is a cool region; for evidence we need look no further than the common practice of chaptalizing, or adding sugar to, the grape musts during fermentation in Burgundy. Chaptalization is done when the grapes do not attain sufficient sugar levels on their own. This is a fact of life in cool regions. In Germany and New York State, for example, the wines are routinely chaptalized. It is not permitted in Italy and California, but that is only because it is not necessary. Where it is permitted, it is done because good wines could not be made consistently without it. Little attention was paid in California to climate in early Pinot Noir plantings, but recently the trend has been to replace vines in warmer regions and plant in cooler areas. Because of the diversity of microclimates in California, suitable areas have been identified in a variety of locations. One that has shown promise is the Carneros section of Sonoma and Napa, the southern end of both valleys, adjacent to the cool and foggy San Francisco Bay.

Burgundian wine-making techniques have been much studied and emulated in recent years. Specifically, what has been found is that in Burgundy, the grapes are often fermented with their stems, quite a different procedure from the normal process of de-stemming the grapes after picking. Another difference is that Burgundian wine makers work, or agitate, the fermenting musts, frequently breaking the cap, or mass of solids at the top, to increase extraction of color and flavor components. Both practices have been replicated with encouraging results in California. Some wine makers even have formulas or recipes for the percentage of stems that will be retained for fermentation.

The ideal soil in Burgundy is loose, sparse, and alkaline. Like Champagne, it is also permeated with limestone. One of the problems in California is finding similar soils. All too often the soils are too rich and deep, lack limestone, and are acidic. The tendency of the Pinot Noir to develop many different clones has also been cited as a problem in matching the Burgundian potential. Some feel that the quality of the top reds from the Côte d'Or is at least partially due to the diversity of Pinot clones grown in the vineyards. In California, by way of contrast, they tend to take great effort to keep the Pinot clones both pure and consistent.

There are those who feel that criticism of American Pinot Noirs is neither fair nor realistic, because red Burgundy wines have proven to be inconsistent and have their detractors as well. At any rate, it is obvious that American wine makers have turned the corner on this difficult varietal and that its best days in this country are ahead of it.

One of the factors that accelerated the growth of Pinot understanding has been the tremendous increase in the number of wineries producing sparkling wines. The best of these are based on Pinot Noir, as in Champagne, and a great deal of research and experimentation has accompanied the development of the sparkling wine business in America.

One additional comment on the Pinot Noir is that it is seldom blended. Other red grapes, Cabernet Sauvignon in particular, may be, but the unique Pinot Noir character seems to be lost when blended with other grapes.

Types of Wine Produced: Dry red table wines and sparkling wines.

Sensory Characteristics: Compared to Bordeaux reds, Burgundies are softer, warmer, and fuller bodied, have more fruit in their scent, and possess a kind of meaty texture. Although they are as dry, they do not taste as dry or austere; they may even strike one as somewhat sweet, because of the opulence of the fruit. The bouquet is very complex and perhaps more ethereal and evanescent. The color is both lighter in hue and less dense than that obtained from the Cabernet Sauvignon. Tannin is not as predominant an influence as with many red grapes, and while Pinot Noirs may not last as long as top Cabernets, they can be enjoyed sooner, while the fruit that is one of their attributes is still prominent. Enjoyable when young, they still have the capacity for graceful maturation. Wines made from Pinot Noir probably do not have the aging potential of Cabernet Sauvignon, but then, few if any grapes do.

Primitivo

Major Wine Regions: Apulia, Italy. Grape scientists feel that Primitivo is the grape from which the American Zinfandel is descended (see Zinfandel).

Types of Wine Produced: Dry red and slightly sweet table wine, and a sweet, port-style wine.

Sensory Characteristics: Dark, dense colors, with a hint of blackberries in the aroma and flavor. Good aging potential with the natural wines, while the sweeter, fortified ones may last for years and years.

Ruby Cabernet

Major Wine Regions: Ruby Cabernet was the first of the California hybrids, grapes bred specifically to meet warm climate requirements. It is a cross between Cabernet Sauvignon and Carignan and was developed to produce a Cabernet-like wine when grown in hot regions, such as the San Joaquin Valley. This it does, because it has definite Cabernet character, although it is a simpler wine, without the nuances or complexity of good Cabernet.

Grape Growth and Wine-Making Techniques: Grown in the warm valleys, it is a generous producer and yields wines with a good acid balance. There are some 15,000 acres in California, the majority in the warmest regions. Grown in cooler regions or in cool years, it can make wines with too much tannin.

Types of Wine Produced: Dry red table wine, sometimes with a little residual sugar to balance the fruit.

Sensory Characteristics: See Cabernet Sauvignon (except not so intense or refined).

Sangiovese (Brunello, Sangiovese Grosso, Prugnolo Gentile, Sangiovese di Romagna)

Major Wine Regions: Sangiovese is the classic grape of Tuscany, Italy, where it is used to make Chianti, Brunello di Montalcino, and Vino Nobile di Montepulciano, three of the five highest classified wines in Italy. (The others are Barolo and Barbaresco.) Under various names, and representing different strains, it is one of the most widely distributed vines in Italy. Considering its broad success in Italy, it is perhaps surprising that it is not grown in California, with its rich Italian heritage and eclectic approach to wine making.

Grape Growth and Wine-Making Techniques: Chianti is the largest DOC region in Italy, and produces the most DOC wine. Chianti is a blend prepared from a formula established in the nineteenth century by Barone Bettino Ricasoli, the second prime minister of Italy and an enthusiastic maker of wines at his castle in Brolio. According to the baron, Chianti is to be blended from Sangiovese (50 to 80 percent), red Canaiolo (10 to 30 percent), and Trebbiano and Malvasia (10 to 30 percent combined).

The two latter grapes are white, and this led to a long-standing controversy as to whether Chianti is improved by the addition of white grapes. Many wine makers felt that the wines would be better without the white grapes, or less than the minimum 10 percent required. Others had strong feelings about the use of other, nontraditional grapes. Antinori was one of the latter, and that wine maker has championed the use of Cabernet Sauvignon. One of the finest wines in Italy is Tignanello from Antinori: essentially a Chianti with no white grapes and about 10 percent Cabernet Sauvignon. Because it does not meet the DOC requirements, it is marketed as a Vino da Tavola, or table wine.

Many very fine — even some great — wines in Italy are non-DOC due to the nature of the modern Italian wine industry: a restless urge to experiment and make better wines. This is in marked contrast to France and Germany, whose carefully defined viticultural regulations cover all the fine wines. With Chianti's recent elevation to DOCG status, the rules on grape ratios were relaxed, allowing smaller percentages of white grapes and small amounts of grapes not previously allowed. Other wine-making requirements, of course, were made more stringent, befitting the elevation to DOCG status. Not all Chianti will qualify for DOCG, if for no other reason than the wine maker will see no compelling reason to change.

Although there are many styles of Chianti, it can be divided into two basic types: the young, fruity, and fresh wine often bottled in the traditional *fiasco*, the fat, straw-covered flask; and the wine bottled in a Bordeaux-style container, a more serious wine meant for aging and development in the bottle.

A local production technique called *governo* refers to the addition of very sweet grape must to a recently fermented wine. A second fermentation ensues, resulting in more color, higher alcohol, increased smoothness, and sometimes a little fizz, or carbonation. The technique is considered to be detrimental for wines intended to mature for several years, and it is not as widespread as in the days when most Chianti was sold in *fiaschi*, or flasks.

From the town of Montalcino, near Siena, comes what is probably Italy's most expensive red wine: Brunello di Montalcino. The name means wine that is made from Brunello grapes at Montalcino; Brunello is the local name for a strain of Sangiovese Grosso. Brunello is a big wine with a lot of structure and color. It is austere and needs many years to mature fully. The most famous producer is Biondi-Santi, to whom credit is due for having developed Brunello into the highly regarded wine it is today. There are many firms that produce Brunello, but the consensus seems to be that they are not all equally successful. At its best, though, this is a great wine.

Aside from the prices, a point of controversy concerning Brunello is the necessity for long wood aging. The regulations require a minimum of three and one-half years in the barrel—five for Brunello *riserva*. Some producers make a more youthful version, Rosso del Vigneti di Brunello, in light vintage years or from younger vines. Villa Banfi has its Centine Rosso di Montalcino, essentially a Brunello di Montalcino with only one year in wood. The wine master, Enzo Rivella, makes it from wines he feels would not benefit from the longer time in wood. Such wines show some of the promise of Brunello, but they are structured on a smaller scale, ready to drink far sooner, and much less expensive.

In the town of Montepulciano, in the southeast of Tuscany, is made yet another DOCG wine, the inclusion of which was controversial. Vino Nobile di Montepulciano is essentially a Chianti, made from a similar grape mixture and heavily based on the Sangiovese, here called Prugnolo Gentile. The criticism of Vino Nobile is directed toward its inconsistency, not its quality potential.

Another highly regarded Sangiovese-based wine in Tuscany is Carmignano, one of the world's first place-names, dating back to 1716 and now made with a little Cabernet Sauvignon in the blend.

Located next to Tuscany is Umbria where, in Torgiano, a small town near Perugia, Lungarotti makes a Sangiovese-blend wine called Rubesco. It is highly admired, and the *riserva* is one of the best red wines of Italy.

Types of Wine Produced: Dry red table wine.

Sensory Characteristics: See discussion above.

Syrah (Shiraz, Hermitage, Sérine)

Major Wine Regions: The Syrah is the grape of the northern Rhône. Unlike the south, where in an area such as Châteauneuf-du-Pape many varieties are permitted, the wines of Hermitage, Crozes-Hermitage, Saint-Joseph, and Cornas are made from this single variety. Côte Rôtie, ranked with Hermitage as the greatest of the northern Rhône reds, is a blend of Syrah (80 percent or more) and Viognier, a white grape.

In the southern Rhône valley, Syrah is one of the many grapes allowed in the blends, not the most important—that would be the Grenache—but still regarded as a valuable grape, especially for adding color, one of the drawbacks of the Grenache.

Known as the Shiraz in Australia, traditionally it has been considered the best red grape, and it maintains this position today in spite of the current interest in Cabernet Sauvignon. It also has been found to blend very well with the Cabernet.

A little Syrah, or Sirah, is grown in California, but most of what is grown there is really a different grape called the Petite Sirah. In the early 1980s, there were only about 100 acres of Rhône Syrah in the state, compared to some 8,500 for Petite Sirah. This latter figure is dropping somewhat, and plantings of the true Syrah can be expected to increase in coming years.

Types of Wine Produced: Dry red table wine and, in Australia, port.

Sensory Characteristics: The Syrah makes very dark wines with a concentrated fruity flavor and a smoky aroma. It is very tannic, which explains the occasional use of some white grapes for blending. With maturity, the bouquet develops a scented floral character. The best Rhône vineyards are those in Côte Rôtie, the northernmost viticultural area, and Hermitage. Crozes-Hermitage is regarded as making uneven wines, the best of which can rival Hermitage in quality.

Zinfandel

Major Wine Regions: California. This is the one fine wine grape that has been regarded as California's own. Long thought to be of Hungarian origin, it is now felt to be descended from the Italian Primitivo, the grape of Apulia, Italy. Although it produces its best in the coastal counties, it is grown everywhere in California and currently accounts for about 30,000 acres. Historically, Zinfandel had been the most important red grape in California, but most of it went into generic reds, and it was not identified as a varietal. In the years following the repeal of Prohibition, Zinfandel was the most widely planted red wine grape in the state, with over 50,000 acres. The problem it faces today in competition with Cabernet as a quality wine is that most Cabernet is grown in suitably cool climates. It is difficult to find varietal Cabernet from warm areas; this is not necessarily true with Zinfandel, because there are still over 10,000 acres in the San Joaquin Valley. On the other hand, the historical dominance of Zinfandel means that there are a lot of old vineyards in existence, and older vines have higher quality potential. Compared to Zinfandel, most Cabernet plantings are relatively young.

Grape Growth and Wine-Making Techniques: Zinfandel is perhaps the most versatile of wine grapes, producing a wide variety of styles. It is widely used today for the popular blush wines, white wines made with red grapes, which typically retain a faint reddish or pink hue. It also is used for making rosés and a *nouveau*-style wine similar to French Beaujolais in that it uses the carbonic maceration technique described for the Gamay.

For the sake of simplicity, red table wines made from Zinfandel can be divided into two main styles, one younger and fresher and the other the claret or Cabernet style. The former is handled so that it emphasizes freshness, the berrylike fruity character, and early maturity. The fuller style is developed to show increased body and complexity, more color, and more tannin. It not only is fermented differently but also is more likely to receive oak aging in a small barrel. Because it does not provide tannin as liberally as Cabernet Sauvignon, small amounts of Petite Sirah may be added to increase the aging potential.

Yet another style is the late picked or late harvest, which can be either dry or sweet. These wines are high in alcohol, often exceeding the 14 percent limit for table wines, and can suffer from a so-called jammy or raisiny quality obtained from overripe grapes and are extremely full bodied and heavy. Many such wines have been made, but the style seems to be losing favor. Among other drawbacks, they are quite difficult to match with food, and they have not been able to carve out a niche in the marketplace.

The very versatility of the grape probably works against it in the attempt to compete with the Cabernet, because it is difficult for consumers to determine exactly what they are getting when they purchase a Zinfandel. The Cabernet has a well-defined style due to the general desire to emulate the wines of Bordeaux; there is no such unanimity with Zinfandel.

Types of Wine Produced: See above.

Sensory Characteristics: As pointed out, the sensory characteristics vary as widely as the styles produced. The outstanding characteristic is probably the raspberry or blackberry aroma.

WHITE GRAPES
Aligoté

Major Wine Regions: Burgundy, France, where it is the secondary grape to Chardonnay. Labeled, with or without the addition of Chardonnay, with the *appellation* Bourgogne Aligoté.

Types of Wine Produced: Dry white table wine.

Sensory Characteristics: Aligoté tends to be rather high in acid and is best consumed young, when its acidity and freshness can make it enjoyable and refreshing.

Chardonnay (Beaunois, Gamay Blanc, Morillon, Petite Sainte Marie)

Major Wine Regions: The greatest grape for white table wines, Chardonnay can be compared to the Cabernet Sauvignon in that it has proven its greatness in many viticultural areas beyond its traditional home. This is the grape that in Burgundy makes such wines as Chablis, Meursault, Puligny-Montrachet, Chassagne-Montrachet, Le Montrachet, Pouilly-Fuissé, and Mâcon Blanc.

In California, the Chardonnay has proven to be the most successful white wine grape. It generally brings the highest prices to growers, and its acreage has increased dramatically. The grape evidently has no significant history in California; prior to 1959, there were only about 200 acres in the entire state. By 1982, however, there were nearly 20,000 acres, almost one-third of which were nonbearing due to having been recently planted.

Italian vintners in Trentino–Alto Adige, the Veneto, and Friuli have extensive plantings, and it is showing up in other regions as well. Villa Banfi has planted it at its Montalcino vineyards in Tuscany and is making varietal wine there. The use of Chardonnay as a varietal grape, as opposed to blending it, is a fairly recent but promising development.

Torres, a leader in Spain in experimenting with French and German grapes, is growing Chardonnay and using it in its Gran Viña Sol. Jean Léon, the Californian mentioned in connection with Cabernet Sauvignon, also makes Chardonnay in Catalonia, although on a smaller scale. As with the Cabernet, his primary market is the United States.

In Australia, the home of a vibrant and exciting wine industry, the Chardonnay has been added only recently, but it looks to have great promise. South Africa similarly has begun to turn to Chardonnay with some enthusiasm. It is not yet of much significance in South America, however.

Grape Growth and Wine-Making Techniques: In general, although there are exceptions, white grapes do not blend as well as reds. There are more examples of great single-grape white wines than of reds. This is very true of Chardonnay; to show at its best, it has been found that it must be a 100 percent Chardonnay. U.S. regulations permit a wine to be given a varietal name if 75 percent of the grapes came from the named grape. As seen with Cabernet and some other red grapes (a major exception is Pinot Noir), this can often be advantageous to the wine maker, but not with white grapes in general and Chardonnay in particular. It loses its characteristic aroma and flavor.

In making the wine, producers must guard against the tendency of Chardonnay to oxidize easily. For this reason, if mechanical harvesting is used, it is often accompanied by field crushing, because fermentation begins and carbon dioxide blankets the grapes, shielding them from oxygen.

When fermentation is completed—in temperature-controlled stainless steel for wines intended to be fresher and fruitier, and barrel fermentation for more full-bodied and complex wines—the wine maker has to make an aging choice. The wines can be given some wood aging, as is traditional in Burgundy, or matured basically in stainless steel or large, neutral wood casks. Oak adds complexity and nuances of odor and flavor. It also gives the wine a smooth, buttery texture. Without the wood influence, the wine will be lighter and fresher and have more of the Chardonnay fruit character. It all depends on what style the wine maker is looking for. In Europe, styles tend to be well developed, because they have had long experience with the grapes and the regions. In California, there is still an atmosphere of experimentation, and styles vary considerably, not only from winery to winery, but even within the same winery from year to year.

Not only is the use of oak important; equally significant are the variety of oak and the size and age of the barrel. At one tasting of four Chardonnays, each aged six months in a different oak—German, French Nevers, Yugoslavian, and American—the one aged in American oak had a freshly sharpened pencil smell; the Yugoslavian, a spicy aroma; the German, a distinctive odor of walnuts; and the Nevers, commonly used in Burgundy, gave the wine the vanilla-butterscotch character so familiar in its wines. The size of the barrel is important because of the ratio of wood to wine. The smaller the barrel, the higher the ratio. The classic size is fifty to sixty gallons. Very large casks impart little, if any, wood character. Over time, with continued use, the tannins and other wood components would be gradually withdrawn, and the effect of wood aging would be proportionally less. Eventually, there would be no wood character transferred to the wine. Considering the high cost of French oak barrels—about $300 each—many wineries choose to mature the wine in used cooperage, or to vary the time between new and used barrels.

Cool growing conditions are best for Chardonnay. Burgundy, for example, is cooler than Bordeaux, Chablis is by far the coolest portion of Burgundy, and Champagne is, except for some areas of the Rhine in Germany, the northernmost of all the fine wine regions in the world. Scientists at the University of California at Davis recommend it for cool regions; the success in a broad variety of locations seems to suggest that climate is more important than soil. In Champagne, the Chardonnay is used to balance the fruit and power of the Pinot Noir and provide elegance and bouquet. It accounts for about one-third of the vines planted in the Champagne District, and it is the only white variety used. In both Italy and California, the Chardonnay is also an integral part of the cuvée, or blend, of the better, champagne method sparkling wines. The best growing locations in California, as in Champagne, have been cool. The Carneros region, the southern portion of the Napa and Sonoma valleys, is the region of choice for several sparkling wine vintners.

Types of Wine Produced: Dry white table wines, Champagne and other quality sparkling wines.

Sensory Characteristics: Chardonnay gives the impression right from the beginning of being a rich, substantial wine. It has more color than most whites and, with wood and bottle aging, can acquire a deep golden hue. Young Chardonnay has a distinctive ripe grape aroma and has been extensively (and poetically) described by various adjectives, depending on the degree of ripeness of the grapes, including green apple, ripe apple, fig, melon, lemon, citrus, and pineapple; when given skillful wood maturation, the vocabulary expands to include vanilla, butterscotch, caramel, toast, and butter. Suffice it to say that Chardonnay has the most entrancing odors of any white grape. In the mouth, it is a big, full-flavored wine, possessing a unique, buttery texture and a long, lingering finish.

Chasselas (Gutedel, Fendant)

Major Wine Regions: In France, it is grown in Pouilly, in the upper Loire, and in Alsace. The Sauvignon Blanc is the grape of importance in Pouilly, but the Chasselas also is traditionally grown there. However, it cannot be sold as Pouilly-Fumé, the region's famous wine; the regulated labeling is Pouilly-sur-Loire. Germany grows it as the Gutedel, and in Switzerland it is known as the Fendant.

Types of Wine Produced: White table wines.

Sensory Characteristics: It is a neutral wine that can be refreshing when very young.

Chenin Blanc (Pineau de la Loire)

Major Wine Regions: Chenin Blanc is the ubiquitous grape of the middle Loire, where it is known as Pineau de la Loire, although it is not a member of the Pinot family (Pinot Noir, Pinot Blanc, Pinot Gris). In Touraine, Anjou, and Vouvray, it is the dominant grape, and at Saumur, it produces some of the best French sparkling wines outside of Champagne.

California is a major producer of Chenin Blanc, and had 37,500 acres in 1981, up from 8,700 ten years earlier. It is now second only to Thompson Seedless in plantings in the state, the majority of which are in the central counties. Monterey has the largest acreage among the coastal counties, 2,300, with Napa second at 1,700.

Grape Growth and Wine-Making Techniques: Most California Chenin Blanc wines are bottled with some residual sugar, from a little less than 1 to about 2.5 percent. Oak flavors are not desired, so the wine is held either in stainless steel or in very large or used cooperage. The standard currently sought after is for a slightly sweet to sweet light wine with a fruity appeal, meant to be consumed young, when it is fresh. A very few producers take another approach and ferment all the sugar, sometimes in oak barrels, then give the wine a short aging in wood. This is more reminiscent of the Chardonnay approach and, when well done, can produce a nice wine, albeit completely different from what most consumers expect from Chenin Blanc. Considering the substantial range of sweetness, it can be confusing to purchase California Chenin Blanc wines. Some are dry, some have barely perceptible sweetness, some are a little sweet, and some are quite sweet. It must be pointed out, however, that the range of possibilities makes it an attractive grape to wineries.

The Loire wine made from the Chenin Blanc most likely to be found in the United States is that of Vouvray. Usually it will be in the lightly sweet, fruity style, and it is best consumed young. The best wines of Vouvray are the sweet ones, although they are more difficult to find in the United States and are very dependent on the vintage. In the best years, the grapes ripen with extremely high sugar levels, and outstanding, luscious sweet wines can be made.

Its success in the Loire as a sparkling wine grape (Saumur and Vouvray) is due to the ability of the grape to retain acids during maturation. The best sparkling wines are made from cuvées of good acidity. When the Chenin Blanc does not ripen properly, such as in cool years, the wine can be thin and tart, but this is ideal for processing into sparkling wine. The champagne method is used, and some of the producers have been at it for a very long while. Ackerman-Laurance dates back to 1811, for instance, and Bouvet-Ladubay was founded in 1851.

Types of Wine Produced: White table wines, which can be dry, but most have some residual sugar; also, sweet dessert wines and *méthode champenoise* sparkling wine.

Sensory Characteristics: The flavor of Chenin Blanc is fairly neutral, but it can taste good because of its fine sugar-acid balance. Its aroma is less distinctly recognizable than some other varieties' and could be characterized as mildly floral. It develops bouquet with maturity, but with the exception of the French dessert versions, Chenin Blanc should be consumed young. Many, despite their residual sugars, are nice food companions because of the acidity.

Cortese

Major Wine Regions: Piedmont, Italy, especially at the town of Gavi, as in Cortese di Gavi. Piedmont, home of Barolo and Barbaresco, is not generally known for white table wines, but the Cortese is highly respected and considered one of the better whites of Italy. One with a high reputation is Gavi dei Gavi, a Cortese di Gavi made by La Scolca.

Types of Wine Produced: Dry white table wine.

Sensory Characteristics: Very dry with distinctive acidity, it has a fresh vitality and is considered excellent with fish. It is not deeply colored, more of a pale or straw shade. The Gavi dei Gavi of La Scolca is noted for a richer texture, more distinctive aroma, and a longer finish.

Emerald Riesling

Major Wine Regions: California. A cross between Riesling and Muscat, developed to produce a grape that would provide Riesling characteristics when grown in a warm or hot climate. Technically, the grape has been considered very successful, but acreage has dropped since the 1960s. There are plantings in the southern, or warm, end of the Salinas Valley in Monterey, and Madera and Lodi in the San Joaquin Valley.

Grape Growth and Wine-Making Techniques: It was specifically bred to grow under the warm conditions that Riesling will not tolerate, being a grape that requires a cool growing season. A huge producer, it crops up to twelve tons per acre in interior regions. This factor, combined with its relatively good quality, makes its current lack of popularity puzzling. Its weakness as a vine has been identified as a vulnerability to bunch rot and a tendency of the grapes to oxidize readily while being processed.

Types of Wine Produced: White table wine.

Sensory Characteristics: Similar to the Riesling, but not so complex nor so interesting. Unlike many wines grown in the warm regions, it is fairly well balanced.

Folle Blanche (Gros Plant, Picpoul)

Major Wine Regions: At one time this was the primary vine of Cognac, France, used to make the wines that were distilled into the region's famous brandy. It is still grown there but is no longer the major grape, having been supplanted by the hardier and more productive Saint-Émilion. In Armagnac, France, where the other famous French brandy is produced, the Folle Blanche retains more importance, although the Saint-Émilion has made inroads there as well.

There is a small amount of the grape in California, where it is used mainly in sparkling wine cuvées. The wine it makes is quite tart, and that is valuable to the cuvée.

Grape Growth and Wine-Making Techniques: In the two regions of importance, Cognac and Armagnac, typical wine-making regulations and procedures are not important. The growers are not concerned about the yield, the thinness of the wine, the ripeness of the grapes, the tartness of the wine, or other such factors. Low-alcohol, high-acid wines, while unsuitable for drinking, are perfect for distillation into brandy.

Types of Wine Produced: Strictly speaking, the vine is not used much for wines; traditionally it has been a source of brandies.

Sensory Characteristics: See above.

Furmint

Major Wine Regions: Tokaji, Hungary, where it is used to make the *aszu*, or sweet, wines of Tokaji.

Grape Growth and Wine-Making Techniques: See Tokaji winemaking procedures in Chapter Two.

Types of Wine Produced: Sweet dessert wine.

Sensory Characteristics: Aszu, the most celebrated of the Tokaji wines, is amber-colored and has a full-bodied, creamy texture. The flavor, particularly the four and five puttonyo styles, has the distinctive Botrytis character. Unlike the wines of the Sauternes or the German Beerenauslesen and Trockenbeerenauslesen, Tokaji Aszu is served at room temperature.

Garganega

Major Wine Regions: The Veneto, Italy, where the Garganega is the primary grape of Soave, certainly the best-known Italian white wine. It is second only to Chianti among DOC wines in volume produced and the leading DOC in volume exported to the United States. There is a Classico region in Soave that is considered the best growing section, and a *superiore* is permitted if the alcoholic content is 11.5 percent (1 percent higher than standard Soave) and the wine is aged nine months. Although unlikely to be found in this country, a little spumonte is made as well.

Types of Wine Produced: Dry white table wine.

Sensory Characteristics: According to Burton Anderson, Soave is "straw-yellow, sometimes with green glints, lightly fragrant, dry, of medium body, and delicately fruity—ideally with an acidic bite and a hint of almond at the finish." It must be admitted, however, that much of the Soave that appears in the United States is not up to this standard.

Gewürztraminer

Major Wine Regions: Alsace in France, Germany, and California. In both Alsace and Germany, the Gewürztraminer is highly esteemed, second only to the Riesling as a quality grape. California enjoyed a spurt of optimism over Gewürztraminer and plantings were increased to 4,700 acres by 1981, but this is expected to decline due to difficulties in growing the grapes, making the wines, and marketing. The wines of Sonoma, the oldest and most planted in California, have received the most critical acclaim.

Grape Growth and Wine-Making Techniques: Gewürztraminer grows best in cool areas, such as Region I in California, the Rhine and its tributaries in Germany, and Alsace in France. The growing difficulties identified in California deal with the rapid transition from fully ripe to overripe grapes. The character of the wine is deficient unless the grapes are fully ripe, but if they ripen beyond that, the wine becomes somewhat flabby, losing its crisp and definitive character. This apparently can occur within a time span of only a few hours. Unwanted reddish color is another problem. The lightly red-skinned grapes impart pink tinges to the wine if the wine maker is not careful. Beyond that, there could also be oxidation problems. One characteristic of the grape is its slight bitter aftertones, and in California this element can become obtrusive.

In Alsace, the Gewürztraminer is vinified dry, all the sugar is fermented out, and the wines are considered ideally suited for classic Alsatian foods such as sausage and choucroute. Much of what is made in California follows the German model in retention of sugar (often addition of sugar in Germany), albeit with higher levels of alcohol. As in Germany, the grape can also be made into a late-harvest sweet dessert wine, similar in style to a Spätlese, Auslese, or even Beerenauslese.

Types of Wine Produced: In Alsace, dry white table wines; in California, some dry, mostly slightly sweet, but a few very sweet, wines; in Germany, the full range of wines, all the way up to the quite rare Trockenbeerenauslesen.

Sensory Characteristics: The dominant character of Gewürztraminer is its spiciness. The name translates as "spicy Traminer"; the original vine was known as the Traminer, some production of which exhibited the spicy quality. This was deemed both interesting and pleasant, and attempts were made to produce a strain that would consistently emphasize it. The result is what is now termed Gewürztraminer. The Traminer has been left by the viticultural wayside.

When made in the lightly sweet style in California, its spiciness is somewhat muted, and the perfume or floral scent is more forward. The Gewürztraminer is in the Muscat family, all of which contain the compound linalool, which is responsible for the distinctive floral aroma of the grapes and wine.

The dry Alsatian style emphasizes the spice; these wines are fuller bodied and more flavorful. Among the most distinctive and recognizable of wines, they are fine matches for hearty and flavorful foods.

Greco

Major Wine Regions: Greco was probably introduced into Italy from ancient Greece, and its wines have been praised since Roman times. The major growing areas today are in Campania, where Antonio Mastroberardino makes Greco di Tufo, and in Calabria, where it is used for a sweet dessert wine called Greco di Bianco or Greco di Gerace.

Types of Wine Produced: Dry white table wine and sweet dessert wine.

Sensory Characteristics: Greco di Tufo is pale-straw to medium gold in color, fairly full bodied, with a faint almond flavor and bouquet. As made by Mastroberardino of Taurasi fame (see page 121), it is one of the best white wines of Italy. Greco di Bianco, or Greco di Gerace, despite its extremely high alcohol, has been described by Burton Anderson as "delicate, flowery, and perfumed."

Malvasia (Malmsey)

Major Wine Regions: Grown all over Italy, it is a specialty in Latium, where it is used to produce the two best-known wines of that region, Frascati and Est! Est!! Est!!! With both these wines, as well as with others in Latium, it is blended with the Trebbiano. Also paired with the Trebbiano, it is used in Chianti for the white portion of the traditional blend.

It is also widely grown in Spain and Portugal, being used in both red and white blends. On the famous island of Madeira, it is one of the four grapes used to produce the legendary wines. Following the devastation of the vineyards by phylloxera in the last century, the Malmsey, as Malvasia is called in Madeira, and the other classic varieties (Bual, Verdelho, and Sercial) came to constitute only a very small portion of the grape crop, having been replaced by the more prolific, but inferior, Tinta Negra Mole. The Tinta was used to make all the traditional varietal styles of Madeira, but with Portugal's entry into the European Economic Community, wines identified as Malmsey, Bual, and so forth are required to contain a minimum of 85 percent of the named grape. Consequently, there is a flurry of activity in replacing current vines with the classic varieties.

Grape Growth and Wine-Making Techniques: Madeira is probably the most long-lived of all wines. Today one can drink vintages from the early nineteenth century that are still in perfect condition. The supply of such wines is understandably very limited, and they are quite expensive. Madeira is fortified with highly rectified alcohol, heated by a process called *estufa*, or "stove," up to 113 to 131° F and held for three to six months.

Types of Wine Produced: Madeira and, in Italy, dry white table wines.

Sensory Characteristics: Est! Est!! Est!!! is a dry, crisp wine with a clean, lightly fruity flavor. Frascati, famous since Roman times, is similar, perhaps a little softer and with a little more color. Vintage Madeira is sweet, full bodied, medium-dark to dark in color, rich tasting, and fragrant.

Marsanne

Major Wine Regions: Northern Rhône in France; in Hermitage, Crozes-Hermitage, and Saint-Joseph, it is used with Roussanne to make distinctive white wine. White Hermitage of the last century was felt to be the best white wine of France and one that would age nearly indefinitely. Even today, ten years is given as a good age for it, a long time by most modern white wine standards.

Types of Wine Produced: Dry white table wine.

Sensory Characteristics: Hugh Johnson describes white Hermitage as having a "haunting combination of foursquare breadth and depth with some delicate, intriguing, lemony zest."

Müller-Thurgau

Major Wine Regions: The most broadly planted grape in Germany, although not the best; that honor easily goes to the Riesling. The Müller-Thurgau is the dominant vine in five of the eleven German wine regions and accounts for 61,000 of some 232,000 acres, or 26 percent. The Riesling is second but, at 19 percent, is well behind. Although the Riesling is the preferred grape for the best wines, it is a very late ripener, making every autumn in this cool climate an adventure—but not necessarily an adventure wine makers anticipate with any pleasure. Thus, more than any other country, the German viticulturists have experimented with cross-breeding varieties in order to come up with grapes that will exhibit the sensory characteristics and the hardiness of the Riesling but will be easier to grow, will produce a greater yield, and, most important, will ripen earlier. The Müller-Thurgau, developed in 1882, was the first and the most successful, and it not only has survived a century but also has come to dominate German vineyards. Historically it has been accepted as a cross between the Riesling and Silvaner grapes (technically noted as Riesling × Silvaner, with the maternal parent always given first, the male parent second), but some ampelographers, or students of vines, question the Silvaner's involvement and suspect that the Müller-Thurgau represents a crossing and recrossing between Rieslings of different regions. It is probable that its exact origin will remain a mystery.

Many hybrids now are grown in Germany, several being of fairly recent origin. Among them are Bacchus (Silvaner × Riesling), Ehrenfelser (Riesling × Silvaner), Faber (Weissburgunder/Pinot Blanc × Müller-Thurgau), Huxelrebe (Gutedel × Courtillier musque), Morio-Muscat (Silvaner × Weissburgunder/Pinot Blanc), Optima (Silvaner × Riesling × Müller-Thurgau), Ortega (Müller-Thurgau × Siegerrebe), Perle (Gewürztraminer × Müller-Thurgau), and Scheurebe (Riesling × Silvaner). The most successful of the recent crosses is the Kerner, developed from the Riesling and, interestingly, a red grape, the Trollinger.

Grape Growth and Wine-Making Techniques: The advantages offered by the Müller-Thurgau are early ripening (generally the first white grape to be harvested), lack of strong soil preferences, resistance both to winter cold and spring frosts, and heavy crops.

Types of Wine Produced: White table and dessert wines of varying degrees of sweetness.

Sensory Characteristics: Light in color and acid, it is mild and fresh tasting. The aroma is distinctly floral and Muscat-like.

Muscadet (Melon de Bourgogne)

Major Wine Regions: Muscadet, the westernmost region of the Loire, in France. One of the least complicated wines in the world; the grape, the wine, and the region are all the same: Muscadet. The grape was originally from Burgundy, where it still can be found as Melon de Bourgogne.

Grape Growth and Wine-Making Techniques: Because it has low acidity, it is particularly susceptible to oxidation, and the traditional wine-making procedure was to leave it in the barrel until bottling, thereby reducing contact with air. Modern wine-making techniques and equipment have rendered this unnecessary, but the objective of protecting the wine from air contact remains valid. It does well in the thin, stony soil of Muscadet and ripens early, an advantage in the rainy and windy autumn of Muscadet.

Types of Wine Produced: Dry white table wines.

Sensory Characteristics: Typically, it is light and fruity, low in acid, and best consumed young. Because it is a coastal region, the foods of Muscadet naturally revolve around what the French refer to as *fruits de mer,* or fruits of the sea. The wine is a natural and familiar companion to such foods.

Muscat (de Frontignan, Muscat Blanc, Moscato Canelli)

Major Wine Regions: In Languedoc, a region along the central-south Mediterranean coast of France, there are three zones that grow the Muscat and make a sweet brown wine: Frontignan (the best known), Mireval, and Montpellier. One of the few locations where dry Muscat is made is Alsace, France. Because of its opulent and floral fragrance, it seems natural to make a sweet wine from the Muscat. In Piedmont, Italy, at the town of Asti, the grape is used to produce Asti Spumante, the delightful Italian sweet sparkling wine. In Sicily, it is used to produce a sweet wine, called a Moscato.

A small amount is grown in California, about 1,400 acres, which generally is vinified into a wine of either moderate or high sweetness. The feeling is that sugar complements the perfumed quality of the aroma and can also mask the slight bitterness that is characteristic of the variety.

Types of Wine Produced: Sweet dessert wines, sweet sparkling wine, dry to sweet white table wines.

Sensory Characteristics: The Muscat aroma is the most immediately recognizable of vinifera varieties, in the grapes as well as the wine. It is intensely floral and perfumed and is best consumed young, while its fruit is intense and forward.

Palomino

Major Wine Regions: Jerez de la Frontera, Spain, where it makes Spain's most famous wine, sherry.

Grape Growth and Wine-Making Techniques: See the discussion of sherry wine-making procedures in Chapter Two.

Types of Wine Produced: Fortified wines ranging from dry (fino, Amontillado, Manzanilla) to rich (oloroso) to sweet (cream).

Sensory Characteristics: See Chapter Two.

Pedro Ximénez

Major Wine Regions: Jerez de la Frontera, Spain. The Pedro Ximénez was the traditional grape used for the sweet wines needed to prepare cream sherries. It has largely been supplanted by the Palomino, although it is still used for very sweet, heavy wines.

Pinot Blanc (Pinot Bianco, Weissburgunder)

Major Wine Regions: A member of the Pinot family, this grape is the white Pinot and is grown in France, in Burgundy and Alsace. In Burgundy it serves to support the Chardonnay, while in Alsace it stands on its own as a varietal. It is also used in the making of Crémant d'Alsace, the fine sparkling wine of Alsace.

Under the name Pinot Bianco, it is grown all over northern Italy, generally for blending, but it is also bottled as a varietal. As in Alsace, it is often used for the production of sparkling wines. In the Alto Adige region of Italy, the grape is called the Weissburgunder, the name by which the grape goes in Germany, where it is grown in Baden.

California has about 2,000 acres, most of which appear destined for sparkling wines, although a few wineries do make a fine varietal wine.

Grape Growth and Wine-Making Techniques: The Pinot Blanc is often confused with the Chardonnay, possibly related to the fact that the Chardonnay used to be, and sometimes still is, incorrectly called Pinot Chardonnay. Its use in European vineyards to back up Chardonnay undoubtedly adds to the confusion. Compared to Chardonnay, its varietal character is less distinctive and specific, and it has higher acid totals. These factors are what makes it desirable in California and other areas as part of a sparkling wine cuvée. When produced in California as a varietal wine, it is often handled as a Chardonnay by the use of barrel fermentation and wood aging. It can become a rather substantial and distinctive wine when handled carefully and skillfully.

Types of Wine Produced: Dry white table wines, white sparkling wines.

Sensory Characteristics: When made in the Chardonnay style, rather like a wood-aged Chardonnay; otherwise they are more neutral, fresh, and uncomplicated wines.

Pinot Gris (Pinot Grigio, Tokay d'Alsace, Beurot, Ruländer)

Major Wine Regions: The third member of the Pinot family, this is a mutation of the Pinot Noir. Under the name Tokay d'Alsace, it is ranked behind only Riesling and Gewürztraminer as a quality grape in Alsace.

Called the Pinot Grigio in Italy, it has become increasingly popular, not only for blending, but also as a varietal wine. The Italian region Alto Adige, with its German heritage, refers to the grape as Ruländer, the name by which it is known in Germany.

There is little, if any, in California, but it is grown in Oregon, and several outstanding varietals have been made in recent years.

Types of Wine Produced: Dry white table wine.

Sensory Characteristics: Alexis Lichine describes Tokay d'Alsace as a "full, golden wine with a marked bouquet and lingering aftertaste on the palate." Hugh Johnson describes the smell as "dense, stiff and intriguing." Both agree that the wine ages well. The Oregon wines, difficult to find outside the state, have met with critical success and are considered by some as the ideal accompaniment to Columbia River salmon. They are fresh tasting, with good acidity, and are loaded with flavor.

Riesling (Johannisberg Riesling, Rhine Riesling, White Riesling, Riesling Renano)

Major Wine Regions: Along with Chardonnay, the Riesling is the greatest of the white wine grapes. Also like Chardonnay and Cabernet Sauvignon, it has been planted around the world with notable results. Its historical greatness began in Germany, where it still reaches heights not matched anywhere else. Planted in just under 20 percent of the German vineyards, it is second to the Müller-Thurgau, but it is the most extensively planted grape in the two finest regions, the Rheingau and Mosel-Saar-Ruwer. The fame and quality of the grape can be illustrated by the frequency with which the name has been applied to other, inferior grapes. In fact, the name Riesling is not a guarantee that it is the true Riesling.

In the United States, White Riesling and Johannisberg Riesling are legally correct; a wine identified simply as a Riesling is something else, usually a Sylvaner (which also may be given a geographic designation, such as Franken Riesling, Sonoma Riesling, Monterey Riesling, and so forth). In California, the technical achievements of the wine makers have exceeded the sales. Very fine wines are being made, but they have not had commensurate success with the consumer. The wines of the Pacific Northwest have been highly praised, none more so than the White Riesling. Washington, in particular, has developed a reputation for the quality of this varietal.

The grape has long been grown in Italy and is gaining favor in the northern regions. The Riesling Italico, or Italian Riesling, is not the Riesling of the Rhine, that term being reserved for Riesling Renano. The two varieties are often used together. Complicating matters even further, Müller-Thurgau also may be identified as Riesling.

White Riesling wines also can be found in Australia, South Africa (Rhine or

Weisser Riesling only, but it has been the custom in South Africa to call many white wines Riesling), Austria, and many of the Eastern European countries. Austria, in particular, has produced magnificent examples of Auslesen, Beerenauslesen, and Trockenbeerenauslesen from Riesling.

Grape Growth and Wine-Making Techniques: The White Riesling is a very late-ripening grape, ideally suited to the Rhine with its long, sunny autumns. Of course, the Rhine also offers unpredictable weather, and the Germans have concerned themselves for over a century with developing Riesling crosses that will mature earlier and more predictably.

California wine-making equipment and techniques have made a marked improvement where the White Riesling is concerned. By picking earlier than had been the custom, using cold-fermentation procedures, and leaving a little residual sugar in the wine, the heavy, clumsy, and dry examples of the past quickly have become just an unpleasant memory. California wine makers also have proved themselves equal to the challenge of coaxing the ultimate from the grape: the great sweet botrytised wines, similar to the Auslesen, Beeren-auslesen, and even, in a few remarkable instances, Trockenbeerenauslesen of Germany. Several locations have been identified where the *Botrytis cinerea* occurs with controllable regularity, the best probably being near the Salinas River in Monterey.

Types of Wine Produced: Light, off-dry to slightly sweet white table wines; sweet dessert wines.

Sensory Characteristics: The aroma of the White Riesling is fruity-floral, with some Muscat character. The compound most responsible for the aromatic distinctiveness of the Muscat, linalool, also has been found in White Riesling. The wines have a crisp, fruity acidity and clean, refreshing flavors. Colors can range from a pale green, such as is found in the wines of the Mosel in Germany, the most delicate of all Rieslings, to richer and deeper golden tones. Sweet White Rieslings have a range of golden colors progressing to the dark, burnished gold hues of the Beerenauslesen and Trockenbeerenauslesen styles. The smell is redolent of dried apricots, and the flavors are full, intense, and lingering. The texture is smooth and buttery. Of necessity, such wines are very expensive, but not to be missed as a sensory experience.

Roussanne

Major Wine Regions: Northern Rhône; in Hermitage, Crozes-Hermitage, and Saint-Joseph, it teams with the Marsanne to produce some of the most highly regarded white wines in France. The Roussanne is considered the more important of the two grapes.

Sauvignon Blanc (Fumé Blanc)

Major Wine Regions: Bordeaux, France, where, in the Graves district, it teams with Sémillon to make the white wines of the district; also in France, Sancerre and Pouilly-Fumé in the Loire. It is considered very promising in northern Italy, and it is used to produce DOC varietals in Alto Adige, Emilia-Romagna, and Friuli–Venezia Giulia.

The Sauvignon Blanc in California has been a great success, ranked second as a white wine grape only to Chardonnay. In fact, several producers have handled it and marketed it similarly to Chardonnay, making full-bodied, rich wines with a touch of wood.

The alternative name, Fumé Blanc, came about because of marketing difficulties in the late 1960s, when there was more of the variety available than could be sold. Robert Mondavi came up with the name Fumé Blanc, based on the fact that the wine made in the Loire at Pouilly-Fumé and Sancerre was produced from the Sauvignon Blanc, which was sometimes identified as Blanc Fumé. With its new name, it quickly became much more acceptable to the consumer, and many producers began using Fumé Blanc to identify the wine.

Grape Growth and Wine-Making Techniques: Three basic styles of wine are produced from Sauvignon Blanc. They could be compared to the wines of the Loire and Bordeaux. One style emphasizes freshness and fruit; this could be said to be the Loire style. Another, the Graves style, accents fullness of body and flinty or earthy flavors. In Sauternes, luscious, oily-textured sweet wines are made, and this style, too, has come to the forefront in California. Sweet Sauvignon Blancs have been made in California for decades, but not with the aid of *Botrytis cinerea*, as is the case in Sauternes. The initial enthusiasm for *Botrytis*-affected wines was limited to the White Riesling, but in time, the Sauvignon Blanc received such treatment also, often blended with Sémillon as is done in Sauternes.

To produce the Loire style, the grapes are picked a little early, when they have higher acids, and cold-fermented to accentuate their fruit and varietal character. These wines are not given any wood aging—seldom much bottle aging either—and are best when consumed young.

What has been referred to as the Graves style (and these are only broad generalizations) are produced from riper grapes, with less acid but more sugar and other compounds that can be extracted from the grapes. The grape juice may even be allowed to remain in contact with the skins for a time prior to fermentation, to increase the extract. Fermentation probably takes place at higher temperatures, possibly even barrel fermentation, and it is customary to give the wine some wood maturing prior to bottling. These wines benefit from bottle age.

The sweet style is made similarly to procedures described in Chapter Two (see page 61), with the addition of the possibility of induced *Botrytis* under controlled conditions.

Types of Wine Produced: Dry white table wines, sweet dessert wines.

Sensory Characteristics: The Sauvignon Blanc, or Fumé Blanc, is one of the most distinctive and easily recognized varietals. The University of California at Davis associative flavor description of the Sauvignon Blanc is "fruity, green olive, faintly herbaceous." Another term often used is "grassy," and "earthy" is common as well. As explained above, the colors, textures, and bouquets are spread over a broad spectrum, due to the diversity of styles.

Sémillon (Chevrier)

Major Wine Regions: One of the two primary white grapes of Bordeaux, the Sémillon is grown in Graves as the second, or blending, grape and in Sauternes as the primary grape. In Australia, it is the most important white grape but is often mislabeled as Riesling, as in Hunter Riesling or Clare Riesling. Hunter Riesling is especially well regarded.

In California, it is respected by both the wine makers and the scientists— but, unfortunately, not the people who buy wine. In 1981, the plantings in California totaled 2,900 acres, small by comparison with several other noble white grapes.

Grape Growth and Wine-Making Techniques: It is prized in Sauternes not only for its sensory characteristics, but also for its thin skin, which allows it to be more easily acted upon by *Botrytis*.

Types of Wine Produced: Dry or off-dry white table wines; sweet dessert wines.

Sensory Characteristics: Tends to be much fruitier in flavor than Sauvignon Blanc and is especially successful when blended with it.

Silvaner (Franken Riesling)

Major Wine Regions: Germany, where it once was the most popular grape. In the early 1960s, Silvaner accounted for 35 percent of the vineyards in Germany; twenty years later, it was down to about 11 percent. It has been replaced by the Müller-Thurgau as the workhorse of the German wine industry. It is also no longer an important grape in California, where the fate of the Silvaner has been more honorable: it has been supplanted by the Riesling. Silvaner was commonly used to produce wines called Riesling, with or without a geographic designation (such as Monterey Riesling, Sonoma

Riesling). The more sophisticated consumer of today seeks a White Riesling. There are only about 1,400 acres in the state, mostly in Monterey County.

Grape Growth and Wine-Making Techniques: Like White Riesling, the Silvaner is a late ripener, thus sharing that vine's primary disadvantage but without the compensation of its superb wines. Silvaner does well on a variety of soils and has good yield, but compared to Riesling, it is more sensitive to winter cold and spring frost and is not as reliable as a late-harvest grape. Unless the grapes are grown in a suitably cool climate such as the recommended Regions I and II, the wines tend to be low in acid.

Types of Wine Produced: Off-dry to somewhat sweet white table wines; sweet dessert wines.

Sensory Characteristics: The wines are pale in color and have a mellow, fruity-floral aroma. They are not in the class of good White Rieslings, but at their best they can give an approximation of those wines.

Trebbiano (Saint-Émilion, Ugni Blanc, Frontignan)

Major Wine Regions: This is an interesting grape—although the wine often is not. In Italy, known as the Trebbiano, it is the white grape that is found nearly everywhere, in all sorts of wines, red as well as white: the workhorse of Italian white wines.

In France, it is named Saint-Emilion, and it is the main grape of Cognac and is nearly as important in Armagnac. Therefore, it is used essentially to make wines that are then distilled into brandy. Although these are probably the two finest brandies in the world, the fact remains that good wine for distillation is pretty poor wine for drinking. The distiller wants wines that are high in acid and low in alcohol. The Saint-Emilion, in chalky soil in these areas, delivers.

In the Mediterranean and in California, the grape is known as the Ugni Blanc, a marketing person's worst nightmare come true. Are names important? Sauvignon Blanc never had much popularity until Robert Mondavi coined the name Fumé Blanc. Wente Brothers once produced a varietal Ugni Blanc, but consumers referred to it as that "ugly blank" wine, and they seldom bought any. Wente blended it with Chenin Blanc, called it Blancs de Blanc— and it became a successful product. The alternative name for Sémillon, Chevrier, may do the same thing for that underappreciated variety in California.

Types of Wine Produced: Light white table wines, distilling wines for brandies.

Sensory Characteristics: Its most widespread use is as a blending grape for Italian white wines, although there are several Trebbiano wines made. It is light in body, best consumed young, and possesses no distinctive flavor or aroma.

Verdicchio

Major Wine Regions: The Marches, Italy, a coastal region in central Italy, east of Tuscany. Several DOC and non-DOC wines are made from the variety, often blended with Trebbiano and Malvasia. Verdicchio is the name of both the grape and a wine district in the Marches.

Types of Wine Produced: Light, dry white table wines; some *spumonte* is also made.

Sensory Characteristics: Burton Anderson describes Verdicchio dei Castelli di Jesi, from the best-known zone, as "pale-straw with green tints, a fine scent and, at best, taut dryness and good fruit-acid balance underlined by a hint of bitter almond." Like most Italian whites, it has been improved in recent years by better wine-making equipment and procedures.

Viognier

Major Wine Regions: This is the grape of Condrieu and Château Grillet in the northern Rhône. It also accounts for about 20 percent of the plantings in Côte Rôtie. It had become biologically degenerate in Condrieu, so that by the 1960s, its total acreage there plus in Château Grillet had declined to less than twenty-five. Modern technology has revived the vine, and the acreage in Condrieu has doubled. The wine is very rare and is priced accordingly.

Type of Wine Produced: White, fruity wine, best consumed young.

Sensory Characteristics: According to Hugh Johnson, "its scent and flavor have no parallel." He also feels that it is especially good as a *premeur* and consumed nearly before it completes fermentation.

SUGGESTED READINGS

Anderson, B. *Pocket Guide to Italian Wines.* New York: Simon and Schuster, 1982.

———. *Vino.* Boston and Toronto: Little, Brown and Company, 1980.

Fletcher, W. *Port.* André Simon's Wines of the World. 2d ed. S. Sutcliffe. New York: McGraw-Hill, 1981.

German Wine Atlas and Vineyard Register. Trans. Nadia Fowler. 4th rev. ed. London: Mitchell Beazley Ltd., 1980.

Jamieson, I. *The Wines of Germany.* André Simon's Wines of the World. 2d ed. S. Sutcliffe. New York: McGraw-Hill, 1981.

Jeffs, J. *Sherry.* André Simon's Wines of the World. 2d ed. S. Sutcliffe. New York: McGraw-Hill, 1981.

Johnson, H. *Modern Encyclopedia of Wine.* New York: Simon and Schuster, 1983.

Lichine, A. *Alexis Lichine's New Encyclopedia of Wines & Spirits.* New York: Alfred Knopf, 1982.

Meinhard, H. *The Wines of Germany.* New York: Stein & Day, 1976.

Sutcliffe, S. *The Wines of France.* André Simon's Wines of the World. 2d ed. New York: McGraw-Hill, 1981.

Wasserman, S., and P. Wasserman. *Sparkling Wine.* Piscataway, N.J.: New Century Publishers, Inc., 1984.

CHAPTER FIVE

BEERS

Beer is a generic term for an alcoholic beverage that is fermented from malted barley and other cereals and flavored with *hops*, the flowers from a particular vine. Beer is also the name of one of the two major types of brewed and fermented beverages; the other is *ale*, which is fermented and stored differently.

BEER QUALITY: FACTORS AND STANDARDS

The quality of beer depends on the quality of its ingredients. This is important with all alcoholic beverages, but perhaps even more so with beer. The ingredients from which beer is made are water, barley malt, other starchy cereals such as rice and corn, hops, yeast, and sometimes sugars.

Water

Because water constitutes from 85 to 90 percent of beer, its importance is obvious. Early breweries were necessarily located where suitable water was available. Some examples are Pilsen, in what is now Czechoslovakia; Munich and Dortmund, both now in West Germany; Milwaukee, Wisconsin; and Golden, Colorado. The water has to be pure and must have a known and consistent mineral content. When a Bavarian type of beer was first attempted in Pilsen in 1842, the far lower mineral content of the local water produced a much different and pleasing style of beer, a light but strongly flavored beer still referred to as a *pilsner* (sometimes spelled *pilsener*). Water that is suitable for a *lager* type of beer would not be satisfactory for a good ale, and the differences among many beers can be attributed to the water quality.

Nevertheless, the quality of water is probably overemphasized today, because any modern brewery has the capability to correct or adjust water from any source. Impurities, even pollutants, can be removed, and any necessary salts and minerals can be added. Thus, it can be assumed that all breweries today have access to whatever water quality is considered suitable and essential to the type of beer they are making. Of course, if suitable water is naturally available, the brewing process becomes less expensive and more efficient. But while undeniably still important, water no longer should be a limiting factor in the brewing industry.

Barley Malt

Barley and other cereal grains contain starch that can be converted into the sugar required for alcoholic fermentation. An enzyme called *amylase* (or *diastase;* the terms are used interchangeably) has the capability, when in a solution with starch in water, of breaking down the starch and forming *maltose* sugar molecules. This enzyme is produced as a by-product of *sprouting*, or grain germination. The process is called *malting;* thus, germinated barley is called *malted barley*, or *barley malt*. Malted barley is necessary not only for brewing but also in the production of all grain-based distilled spirits. Without it, there would be no conversion of starch to sugar, and no alcoholic fermentation.

Breweries typically do not do their own malting, though some do, but they carefully specify how it is to be done. The germination is stopped by heat-drying or even roasting, which produces a darker color and a more distinctive malt character in the beer, the types of things with which the brewer is concerned.

Brewers also specify the type of barley to be used. The best is considered to be two-row barley, which has two rows of fertile flowers on the plant. Four-row and six-row barley are also used, but they are not so highly regarded, though they are less expensive.

Adjuncts

Barley is the traditional grain for beers, and many of the world's fine beers are made mostly, some even exclusively, from it. According to the Bavarian

Purity Order of 1516, beer could be made only from barley malt, water, and hops, and this is still the only way in which beer can be brewed in Germany, Switzerland, and Norway, although even in those countries there are exceptions allowed for specialty brews made from wheat.

The term used for any grains other than barley is *adjuncts;* the most common are refined corn grits and brewer's rice. The use of adjuncts lowers the brewing cost, but this is not the only reason they are used. In the United States, there is a relative abundance of corn compared to barley. Because barley is already more expensive than corn, its relative scarcity further increases the cost. Barley is also more difficult to handle. The grains are very hard and must be soaked until they become soft, then allowed to malt. All this is time consuming and expensive. On the other hand, corn can be prepared for brewing by cooking it quickly and inexpensively in water to convert the starch to sugar. Another reason for the use of adjuncts is that they produce a lighter product—lighter in color, body, and flavor—and this is the style overwhelmingly preferred by the American consumer. Light, clear, and crisp beers can be made without the use of adjuncts, but it is easier with them.

Hops

Hops, the primary flavoring ingredient in beers, are the flowers of a vine in the mulberry family, *Humulus lupulus.* Only the flowers of the female plant are used; they resemble little pine cones with very small petals. Their resins and essential oils are responsible for the zesty bitterness in beers, and they also contribute significantly to the overall character and provide a pleasantly pungent aroma. They are a natural preservative, too, and aid in resisting contamination by preventing the development of wild bacteria. One hops component, however, can react with sunlight to produce a skunky smell, so brewers often remove it.

Although the most highly regarded hops are probably those from Czechoslovakia, Germany produces excellent ones as well. In the United States, the plants from California, Oregon, Washington, and Idaho are considered the best. Most brewers use a mixture of hops, and many provide more than one *hopping* during the brewing process to add character and complexity to their products.

Yeasts

The primary responsibility of yeast is to convert sugar into ethyl alcohol, but its importance goes well beyond that. The strain of yeast used is of critical importance not just to the specific style of beer, but even to its type. Alcoholic fermentation produces many by-products that influence the character of the finished product. Beers made from the same recipe, but using different yeasts, can taste and smell very different. This is a challenge for one brewer in one plant, and it can be a tremendous problem for a national brewer trying to produce uniform beers in several plants. Thus, breweries take great pains to guarantee the purity of the yeast strains they use.

Sugars

Although cane sugar is not a standard brewing ingredient for regular beers, it may be used to increase the percentage of alcohol in some of the stronger malt liquors.

BEER BREWING: PROCEDURES AND STANDARDS

The first step in creating beer is the malting, described above: the germination of barley in order to produce the enzymes that convert unfermentable grain starch to fermentable grain sugar. This begins the process (Fig. 5–1).

Mashing

The next step is the *mashing*, done in a *mash tun*, or *mash tub*. This consists of mixing the malt and adjuncts, if any are used, with hot water and cooking them at up to 154° F for one to six hours. The purpose is to convert the starch to sugar and extract the maximum soluble materials from the ingredients. When this has been accomplished, the resulting liquid, now called *wort*, is separated from the insoluble solids and sent to the brewing kettle.

Brewing

Hops are added to the wort and the mixture is boiled for an hour or two in order to extract flavors and aromatics. This also sterilizes the wort by killing undesirable yeasts and bacteria and, through *caramelization*, darkens the liquid. Due to the high heat, some of the insolubles may be made soluble, a process called the *hot break*. The wort is then strained, cooled, and sent to the fermenter.

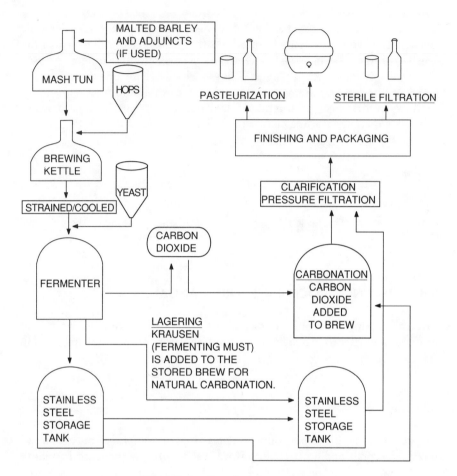

Figure 5–1.   Beer-brewing process.

Fermenting

The fermentation temperature depends on whether a beer or an ale is being produced. Beers are fermented at from 37 to 49° F, ales at 50 to 70° F. There are several other differences between the two types that begin to show up in this stage. For example, the yeasts are considerably different. Beer yeasts sink to the bottom of the fermenting tank and carry out their responsibilities from there, while ale yeasts have a tendency to stick together, increasing their surface area, and rise. The higher temperatures used in fermenting ales also encourage the yeasts to rise. Thus, beers are classified as *bottom fermentation brews* and ales as *top fermentation brews*.

Because of the difference in temperature, it takes longer to ferment beer than it does ale. Beers typically receive eight to eleven days of fermentation, while ales need only five to six days. The carbon dioxide that is produced along with alcohol is retained and stored, to be added back later in the brewing process.

Lagering

The brew is essentially completed at this point, but it needs to be matured prior to being packaged and shipped. *Lagering*, from the German word *lagern*, meaning "to store," is the term used to describe the maturation process. This aging period varies; it can last from several weeks to several months. Lagering temperatures are very cold—near freezing, in fact. Over time, impurities precipitate out, the brew becomes more mellow, and it develops flavor and aroma. This generally takes place in stainless steel or glass-lined tanks, because wood is considered harmful to most beers. The use of beechwood chips has nothing to do with wood aging; they are used to clarify the beer, which they do by attracting impurities.

Carbonation

The carbon dioxide retained from fermentation is added now to the matured beer to provide its effervescence. Another, more natural way of providing carbonation is known as *krausening*. Small amounts, about 15 percent, of the fermenting wort, called krausen, are added to the stored beer. The carbon dioxide that is produced dissolves in the beer and is retained there, similar to what happens with sparkling wines.

Clarification

Prior to packaging, the beer is pressure-filtered to give it a sparkling brilliance.

Brewing Summary

A useful way to summarize the quality factors and brewing processes and their effects on the products is to differentiate between two familiar American beers: Budweiser and Michelob. Both are made by Anheuser-Busch; one is its premium product, while the other is positioned as the super-premium. Budweiser is made from a grain ratio of 70 percent barley (two row and six row) and 30 percent rice. Anheuser-Busch feels that rice is superior to corn, and it is the company's adjunct of choice. Budweiser gets three hoppings with a mixture of eight to nine domestic and imported hops, and it is lagered for at least twenty-one days. Michelob is produced from a grain mixture containing 80 percent barley (all two-row) and 20 percent rice, gets three hoppings, all with imported hops, and is lagered for at least thirty-two days. Michelob is considered to be the better product. Not coincidentally, its ingredients are superior and more costly, and the maturing is longer, which is also more expensive. Quality beer results from quality ingredients and careful, time-consuming, and expensive processing.

BEER STRENGTH: STANDARDS

The alcoholic content of beer and its relationship to quality is not always well understood by the consumer (Table 5–1). Beer strength is frequently over-stated and overemphasized. A lot depends on the occasion and the purpose for which the beer is being consumed. Just as there are occasions when a light

Table 5–1   Beer Strength Chart

Alcohol Percentage		Beer
By Volume	By Weight	
3.0	2.4	Lights (Lite); sweet stouts
3.5	2.8	
4.0	3.2	Dry stouts; Munich beers; regular U.S. beers
4.5	3.6	U.S. premium beers; Pilsners
5.0	4.0	
		U.S. ales, super-premium beers, malt liquors; English pale ales; Dortmunder beers
5.5	4.4	English old ales
6.0	4.8	German bocks
6.5	5.2	
7.0	5.6	German doppelbocks
7.5	6.0	
8.0	6.4	U.S. malt liquors (upper limit)
		There are a few products made that are higher in alcohol, but they are scarce and very difficult to find. Examples include Thomas Hardy's Ale, some barley wines, and some German doublebocks.

Riesling is preferable to a full-bodied and mature Chardonnay, or a Beaujolais to a Rhône or Burgundy, there are times when a lower-alcohol and lighter beer is more suitable than a full-bodied, stronger one.

It is also important to note whether the alcoholic strength is stated by weight or volume. In the United States, federal regulations do not permit alcoholic labeling unless it is required by state laws, and when alcoholic content is referred to, it is by weight. The strength of American beers cannot be compared fairly to beers of other countries if, as in Canada, they use alcohol by volume. A beer that has 3.2 percent alcohol by weight has 4.0 percent by volume, a significant difference. Since the repeal of Prohibition, the individual states have had the right to regulate the alcoholic content of malt beverages, and the requirements and limitations vary from state to state. This is why some imported beers are not equally available across the United States and why national brewers have to make different products for certain states. For example, a highly regarded regional beer made in Minnesota, Cold Spring Strong, cannot be sold there because it contains over 4 percent alcohol, and Minnesota law limits beer to 3.2 percent.

For these reasons, it is not possible to make definitive statements about beer strengths in the United States, but some generalizations can be made. The U.S. light beers are the lowest, 3.2 percent by weight or lower; regular U.S. beers average about 3.5 percent by weight (4.4 percent by volume); premium beers just short of 4.0 percent by weight (about 4.9 percent by volume); and super-premiums 4.2 percent by weight (5.25 percent by volume). Ales are generally stronger than beers, and U.S. ales average some 4.0 percent by weight (5.0 percent by volume), while some British ales are even stronger. Thomas Hardy's Ale, for example, actually contains 10 percent alcohol by weight (12.5 percent by volume). The strongest products made in the United States are the malt liquors, some of which go as high as 6.4 percent by weight (8.0 percent by volume).

Thus, alcohol per se is not a quality factor. Some malt beverages are stronger than others, but this has little if anything to do with their quality. That is determined by the quality of the ingredients and the skill and patience of the brewer.

BEER TYPES AND STANDARDS

Based on the way the yeasts operate during fermentation, beers are classified into one of two types: top fermentation and bottom fermentation brews (Table 5–2). Beers were traditionally produced by top fermentation until Bavarian brewers discovered that, during cold storage, the yeasts sank to the bottom and the beer became more stable. Bottom fermentation techniques were developed and later perfected by brewers in Pilsen and Vienna. The German

Table 5–2   Beer Classification Chart

Bottom Fermentation Beers (Lagers)	Top Fermentation Beers
Pilsner, or pilsener	Ale
Münchner or Bavarian	Cream ale
Dortmunder	Porter
Bock	Stout
Doppelbock (doublebock)	Alt
Malt liquor	Weisse and wheat beer
Light beers (Lite beers)	

term for ale, the basic top fermentation brew, is *alt*, which translates as "old," referring to the old brewing technique.

Bottom fermentation brews are generically called lagers. These beers are typically stored for a period while they mature. The storage is carried out at very cold temperatures, and the beers are generally best when served chilled. There is no generic term for the top fermentation beers, although most of them are known as ales of one style or another. They are fermented and frequently stored at higher temperatures than lagers and often are served only slightly chilled, if at all. Although not always, they are generally higher in alcoholic content, darker in color, and more distinctively flavored and hopped. A beer expert named Michael Jackson has characterized them as the red wines of the beer world, as opposed to the whites obtained from bottom fermentation, and this seems to be an appropriate way to characterize the two types.

Bottom Fermentation Beers, or Lagers

Pilsner, or Pilsener. A beer made in the style of Pilsen, Czechoslovakia, it has a pronounced hops character, is light in color (but not necessarily in body), and is dry and crisp on the palate. Most American beers are made in the pilsner style, although the hops character is not as assertive.

Münchner or Bavarian. As the pilsners emphasize hops, the Müncher beers are distinctive for their malt aroma and character. They are darker than pilsners, ranging from deep amber to dark brown. In Munich, they use the terms *dunkel*, or dark, and *helles*, or light, to distinguish the beers, but both are characterized by a maltiness that overshadows the hops.

Dortmunder. This style, taken from the German city of Dortmund, strikes a balance between the Pilsen and Munich beers. It is darker and fuller bodied than a pilsner but not as much so as a Münchner. The character is also more balanced between hops and malt, neither emphasized to the extent of the other two.

Bock. A dark-colored and heavy-bodied beer, bock is richer and sweeter than regular lagers. At one time, bock was considered a seasonal specialty, appearing in the spring, but this no longer seems to be the case. There are no clearly defined standards for bock, and different brands vary.

Doppelbock (Doublebock). In Germany, Doppelbock is a separate style of beer. It is very strong, ranging from 6.0 percent by weight (7.5 percent by volume) all the way up to 10.5 percent by weight (13.2 percent by volume). The latter beer is made in Bavaria and is appropriately named Kulminator.

Malt Liquor. A lager beer type, malt liquor has more alcohol than is typically found in the pilsner styles. Extra enzymes are sometimes used during fermentation to boost the alcohol level, which starts at about 3.2 percent by weight and extends to as high as 8 percent. There is a great variety of alcohol levels due to various state regulations. In some countries, a malt beverage of over 5 percent by weight is required to be labeled a malt liquor. In the United States, some malt liquors can be a mixture of beer and malt wine.

Light Beers, or Lite Beers. An American specialty, this refers to calorie-reduced beers rather than to the color. They are low in alcohol, generally about 3.2 percent by weight (4.0 percent by volume), although some products, known as extra lights, may be as low as 2.3 percent by weight (2.8 percent by volume). To compensate for the problem of lack of flavor resulting from brewing at such a low alcohol level, they can be generously hopped or, more commonly, made by diluting a special high-extract beer that has been fermented dry. There are presently no legal standards, but the term is most often understood to mean fewer than 100 calories per twelve ounces of beer. This compares to a range of about 135 to 170 calories for other beers.

Top Fermentation Beers

Ale. There are several sensory characteristics that distinguish ales. The taste, derived from top-fermenting yeasts, is one. Another is the distinctive hoppiness, which affects the aroma and gives them their typical bitterness in the aftertaste. They are usually, but not always, higher in alcohol, bigger bodied, and darker than lager beers. The British are the great lovers of ales, and this type of beer is favored in England, Ireland, and Scotland, as well as Canada, to a lesser degree.

Cream Ale. This is not a true ale; it is often a mixture of some ale with a lot of lager.

Porter. Once the most popular style of beer in England, it was supplanted by the paler ale style and, in the 1970s, ceased being made altogether. It is now being produced in England again, but it is difficult to find. The style is made in other countries, generally as a specialty. Porter is brewed partially from roasted unmalted barley. The caramelization that results from the roasting gives the beer its dark brown color. It has a distinctive bitterness, derived from both the roasted barley and a high level of hops.

Stout. The logical extension of the porter style, stout remains highly popular in the British Isles. It, too, uses roasted unmalted barley; it is differentiated from porter by being richer in flavor, darker (nearly black), fuller bodied, and stronger. There are two styles of stout: the dry, bitter style, as made in Ireland by Guinness and others, and the sweet type as made by many English breweries. A classic drink called the black velvet is made from bitter stout; it is a mixture of equal parts of Champagne and stout.

Alt. The German term for ale; literally, "old." This style is produced in several cities in northwestern Germany.

Weissbier and Weizenbier. Weissbier means "white beer," and Weizenbier is "wheat beer." They are mostly German specialties but are also made in Belgium. In Germany, their production is exempted from the requirement that the only grain used be barley, and wheat is mixed with the barley in varying proportions, from one-third wheat to as much as two-thirds.

SENSORY STANDARDS

Beers are evaluated much like any other food or beverage. The appearance, smell, taste, flavor, and texture are all examined. Beers vary considerably, and careful sensory examination can prove as interesting and useful as with wines.

Appearance

As with wine, the two factors of interest concerning a beer's appearance are the color, or hue, and its clarity, or freedom from suspended materials. Colors range from very pale gold to rich amber, copper, dark brown, even black. There is quite a broad range, and often this is indicative of the style or type of beer.

Virtually all commercial beers, even the dark ones, are extremely clear with a sparkle, called brilliant. Unlike wines, a light haze in a beer might not necessarily be an indication that something is wrong. It could be the result of using high malt levels, which, having more protein, could make hazing more likely. It could also improve the depth of flavor.

Another important appearance factor is the *head.* A well-made beer will exhibit a dense, creamy head composed of small bubbles. Just as sparkling wines are at least partly judged by the persistence and size of the bubbles as they rise in the glass, the quality of the beer making can be evaluated in this way. To the extent that the beer is carbonated artificially, the head will lack persistence and have large and short-lived bubbles. A good, naturally carbonated (krausened) beer will show small bubbles that rise and continue to build the head. The foam will also be more stable and will tend to stick to the glass and form rings as the beer is consumed. One word of warning, however: unless the glass is perfectly clean, the head and carbonation in a fine beer can be ruined.

Smell

The two most prominent odors in beer are those derived from hops and malt. Hops are always boiled with the wort in the brewing kettle, and this provides the bitterness characteristic to some degree in all beers. Many brewers also add *finishing hops* at the end of the boiling process and even during the maturation stage, a process called *dry-hopping*. Both of these additional hoppings intensify the hops aroma. The types of odors that come from the hops depend in large part on the origin of the hops. Some have a clean, head-clearing pungency, sometimes described as reminiscent of a pine forest, while others can be spicy, geraniol, or minty.

The malt smell is also very distinctive, whether the malts are the normal pale ones or the more heavily roasted dark malts. In the latter case, the beer will exhibit toast, espresso, perhaps even chocolate smells.

Esters, by-products of fermentation, are compounds that have complex fruity odors. Esters are responsible for many of the more desirable odors developed in wines. Some of the types of smells encountered in a muted form in beers are apple, pear, citrus, butterscotch, peach, sweet corn. When such odors become overly distinctive it is considered a serious flaw, but they are an essential part of the complexity in a beer's aroma and bouquet.

For several reasons, beer can also exhibit undesirable odors. One of the components of hops can cause a skunky smell when catalyzed by light. Skunky smells can also be the result of mercaptans formed by exposure of malt proteins to sunlight. Oxidation results from exposure to oxygen and can cause odors reminiscent of damp paper or cardboard. Even if the package is sealed properly, there is still some oxygen in the air space, and high storage temperatures can accelerate the oxidation reactions. Some other signs of beer deterioration include nail polish smells, from acetone, probably a result of a bacterial fermentation of corn mash; and rancid butter, the smell of butyric acid, probably a result of the oxidation of butyl alcohol or butyl aldehyde, or a reaction between anaerobic bacteria and lactic acid. Lactic acid itself can be produced during brewing and is responsible for a sour-milk character in the odor.

In smelling beer, therefore, one looks for hops and malt odors and evaluates the balance between them as well as their intensity and character. Next, the presence of fruity odors should be established. Finally, the taster should check carefully for any off odors that would indicate either faulty brewing, poor storage conditions, or both.

Taste and Flavor

In the taste of beer, as in the odors, the two most prominent characteristics are due to malt and hops. Malt is inherently sweet, but a good all-malt beer is never cloying. Depending on the style of the brewery, the percentage of malt in the grain mixture, the degree to which the malt is kilned or roasted, and the quality of the barley used, the malt character will be lighter or heavier, sweeter or barely sweet, restrained or assertive.

Balancing the sweetness of the malt is the bitterness of the hops. The degree to which the beer is hopped is partly a matter of the type and style of the beer and partly due to consumer preference. In general, ales are expected to be more bitter than lager beers, and pilsner lagers typically are more hopped and more bitter than the Bavarian or Munich style. The English prefer their malt beverages well hopped and bitter, while the Americans do not. Hops also contribute to the apparent dryness of the beer.

Texture

This is the feel of the beer in the mouth, and it is composed of carbonation, body, and astringency. In addition to their effects on taste, hops provide an astringency—which is a feel, a tactile sensation, not a taste. With wines, the body is due mainly to the alcoholic content, while with beers, the opposite may be true. The higher the alcohol level, the greater the proportion of fermentable materials that have been converted. These are the grain sugars, and their elimination reduces the body, or fullness, and the weight of the beer in the mouth. With the light beers, however, this is not the case. The opposite of fullness in body is characterized by a watery texture; the light beers, with their very low alcohol levels, are thin and watery compared to more robust malt beverages. In this instance, the low alcohol level is only one of the texture factors because, to reduce calories, all fermentable sugars have been eliminated as well.

STANDARDS FOR SOME BEER-PRODUCING COUNTRIES
United States

Americans tend to consume malt beverages as they do soft drinks: as cold as possible, and to quench thirst. The overwhelming preference is for beers that are light bodied, light colored, muted in terms of hops bitterness, and not particularly assertive in terms of the malt. Thus, the national brewers, by necessity, must produce beers of this nature. American beers are not characterized by great diversity; there is not the broad range of types and styles that are found, for example, in Europe. Most of the beer produced in the United States is lager beer, closer to the pilsner style than any other, but without its distinctive hoppiness. Anheuser-Busch uses rice as its adjunct of choice, rather than corn; it does so because the company feels that rice enhances the crispness of the brew, and this is a quality in line with what the consumer demands in America.

It makes no sense to criticize the American brewing industry for its beers, because the brewers are obviously making products that satisfy the market; the United States, after all, is the largest brewing nation in the world. It makes equally little sense to criticize American consumers either, because clearly they can differentiate quality. One needs only to be reminded of the disastrous experience of Schlitz, when that company changed its brewing formulas and standards, to realize that quality within a particular style is not only appreciated, but demanded.

Of course, there are distinctive beers made in the United States, but they are considered regional specialties and, although they are growing in popularity and interest, at present they have little impact on national sales statistics. The growth of the import beer market in the United States is also evidence of an increasing interest in more distinctive malt beverages.

Canada

Canada is second only to the Netherlands as an exporter of beer to the United States, and its products are well known and appreciated here. In style, the Canadian beers reflect their British heritage, but they are definitely made for the North American market. Canadian ales are both popular and well regarded, and compared to the British ones, they are paler, fruitier, and somewhat toned down. The three largest producers in Canada are Carling, Labatt, and Molson. Moosehead, although not one of the giants in Canada, has become the second-largest and fastest-growing Canadian beer brand in America.

Mexico

Mexico currently ranks fourth as a country of origin for imported beers in the United States, and it is one of the fastest growing as well. Three brands, Dos Equis, Corona Extra, and Tecate, are listed among the ten top-selling imports. The Mexican brewing industry, interestingly, has a Viennese background, dating from the era when Mexico was a part of the Hapsburg empire, and the German influence is shown by the production of relatively full-bodied lagers with some character.

England, Ireland, Scotland

Top fermentation brews—ales in England and Scotland, stouts in Ireland—characterize the production and consumption of beer in the British Isles. English ales are made in two basic styles, mild and bitter; of the two, the bitter is much more popular. Scottish ales tend to have more body than their English counterparts and more of a malt character, less derived from hops. The Irish like their stout dry and bitter, well hopped, and it is their preferred malt beverage, while the English style is sweet and consumed as more of a specialty beverage, compared to the ales.

Germany

While the British prefer top-fermented beers, the majority of the beers consumed in the world are made by the bottom fermentation lager technique, and that is of German origin. Although Germany is not the leading beer-producing country in the world (that distinction goes to the United States), West Germany has over 1,300 breweries, far more than any other country, and Germans consume more beer as well. Of the three top beer-consuming countries in the world, in per capita consumption, two are German: West and East Germany.

Germany produces a wide variety of styles of beer. Düsseldorf is the home of the German *alts*, or old-style beers, already referred to, the German top-fermented ales. The northern areas, particularly Hamburg and Bremen, specialize in beers that emphasize the hops character. Bavaria, and its most famous city, Munich, produces the malty type of lagers, which is interesting because Bavaria has long been famous for its cultivation of hops. Dortmund beers are generally considered to be more balanced between hops and malt. The original Dortmund export beer was developed to be drier than the Munich and Bavarian beers, but not as hoppy as the Pilsen style. The term *export* in German beers was first used as an indication that the beers were shipped to other cities in Germany; it did not necessarily indicate that they were exported to other countries.

In Cologne, a unique style of beer is produced. Cologne in German is Köln, and beer from there is called Kolschbier, or simply, Kolsch. Kolsch is top-fermented but is lighter in color and body than ales, and has a restrained hop character.

France

The best known of the French beer-producing areas, appropriately enough, is Alsace, with its Germanic location and traditions. The beers are lagers, and compared to the nearby German beers, they are not so malty and have a somewhat fruity character, which is probably due to the use of French malting barley.

Switzerland

The beers of Switzerland, like those of Germany, are protected by beer purity laws and can be produced only from water, yeast, hops, and barley malt. Most of the breweries are in the German-speaking region, primarily Zurich, but breweries can be found in the French and Italian regions as well. One author has described their styles as similar to the wines produced in those areas: the German beers are perhaps the sweetest and maltiest, the French the driest, and the Italian the most assertive.

The Netherlands

The leading country for beer imported by the United States, the Netherlands also boasts the number one import brand: Heineken. Other popular beers from the Netherlands are Amstel and Grolsch, the beer in the unique pot-stoppered bottle. All are made in the pilsner style.

Czechoslovakia

Although Czechoslovakia is not an important exporting nation to the United States, it is noteworthy for being the parent of the most popular beer style in the world, and for having named both the world's best-selling brand and the top super-premium brand in the United States. Pilsen, Czechoslovakia, is where the pilsner style originated. Budweiser, the best-selling beer in the world, is named after the town of Budweis (now known as Čeşké Budêjovice), and Michelob, the top super-premium beer, was inspired by the town of Michelovce. The one Czech beer that can readily be found in the United States is Pilsner Urquell, which translates as "original pilsner" and is still made today in the town of Pilsen. As with all imports, the condition of the beer can be a problem because of time and shipping distances, but when in top condition, Pilsner Urquell is considered to be one of the very finest beers in the world.

PRESERVATION, PACKAGING, AND STORAGE STANDARDS

Beer that is to be packaged in cans or bottles is generally *pasteurized* for product safety and stability. Pasteurization is a heat treatment, the purpose of which is to ensure that there are no viable bacteria or yeast cells in the packaged product. The normal procedure is to heat the beer up to 140 to 145° F for about twenty minutes, followed by rapid cooling.

Another method, known as *flash pasteurization*, calls for much higher temperatures, 180 to 185° F, combined with a shorter exposure time, about one minute. There are three primary reasons beer is pasteurized. Bottles and cans are often shipped considerable distances; partially due to the shipping distances, they are expected to have a longer storage life; finally, cans and bottles cannot withstand the increased pressures that result from any continued yeast activity in the beer.

Many beer drinkers prefer unpasteurized beer, because the heat treatment is considered to reduce the freshness of the taste and flavor. A process known as *sterile filtration*, which is capable of filtering out yeast cells and other impurities, can be used on canned and bottled beer. The advantages are that the beer retains a fresh, draftlike taste, yet has an adequately long shelf life. The disadvantage is that, like barrel beer, it must be kept under constant refrigeration.

Pasteurized beer packaged in bottles and cans has a shelf life of about three or four months. Even though it does not have to be refrigerated, quality deterioration—loss of flavor and aroma—can be slowed by storage at cool temperatures; 40 to 70° F is recommended, and temperatures above 70° F should be avoided. Another storage condition that absolutely must be avoided is exposure of the beer to direct sunlight. The result is quick and unpleasant: the formation of skunky odors. Canned beers are protected from this, and dark bottles help, but in both cases, even if the sunlight did no harm, the sun's heat most likely would.

Draft beer is packaged in metal barrels, called *kegs*, and is not pasteurized. As a result, it retains maximum freshness, but at the cost of a greatly reduced shelf life and the need for constant refrigeration. Were anything to go wrong, or if there were any continuing fermentation, the container would be sufficiently strong to ensure safety, but the result would be irreversible quality deterioration. The only way to prevent it is to hold the kegs at a temperature of from 36 to 38° F and to use them as quickly as possible. Beer packaged in untapped, or unopened, barrels has a shelf life of about a month to a month and a half. If stored at 45° F or over, it can turn cloudy or even sour; at temperatures of 70° F or over, serious deterioration would take place very quickly. Freezing of draft beer also must be avoided; that would result in the precipitation of insoluble solids, in the form of flakes. Holding the beer at too cold a temperature for a long time also can cause gushing when tapped or opened.

Bottles and cans that have been pasteurized cannot be labeled as draft beer, although terms such as *draft brewed*, *draft flavor*, and similar ones can be used, as long as the label clearly states that it has been pasteurized. Unpasteurized bottles or cans, or ones that have been sterile-filtered, can be labeled draft. Beer that is drawn from containers of one gallon or more through a tap or spigot can be called draft at point of service, even if pasteurized. Otherwise, only unpasteurized beer in barrels can be called draft beer.

SERVICE STANDARDS
Glassware

One of the most important aspects of beer service, and often one of the most overlooked, is the cleanliness of the glassware. The glass must be *beer clean*, which means that it is free of grease, film, lint, or any other foreign substance. The latter includes any detergent residue. The use of special fat-free washing agents, specifically formulated for bar use, is necessary to obtain properly cleaned glassware. Unclean glassware can ruin the head on the beer, causing it to deflate and break up, leaving large, unattractive bubbles. Carbonation is then lost, and off odors and off flavors could be introduced as well. When the glass is clean, the head will remain dense and will be deposited in foamy rings as the beer is consumed.

Draft Beer Service

With the service of draft, or unpasteurized, beer from kegs, the beverage operator wants to pay careful attention to the cleanliness of equipment, dispensing pressure, and beer temperature. The equipment includes the spigot, the tapping apparatus, and the lines. It is especially important to keep the lines as clean as possible, and most authorities recommend both a daily flushing with water and a more thorough cleaning every other week. The latter may be done by the beer distributor, but if not, the operator will have to assume responsibility for it. The daily flushing is a simple matter of disconnecting the line from the keg and hooking it up to a water faucet. Water is run through the line and spigot until there is no remaining beer residue. Beer lines should never be allowed to stand dry for very long, so the water will be left in the lines overnight. When the line is attached again to the keg, the pressure will force the water out and the operator can draw beer again from the spigot.

Pressure for the draft system is provided by tanks of carbon dioxide. The gas is introduced, or tapped, into the keg via one line, and the beer is sent out to the serving spigot by another line. The operator should pay close attention to the pressure gauge at all times to ensure proper pressure. Too much or too little pressure will cause problems when drawing the beer.

Americans strongly prefer most beverages to be served as cold as possible—it is suspected that this is at least partially responsible for the white wine boom in the United States—and beer is no exception. However, draft beer held and served at too cold a temperature may become flat and cloudy. But if it is not cold enough, it could become gassy, a condition known as *wild beer*.

Serving Temperature

Europeans drink beer somewhat warmer than do Americans, and the English consume it considerably warmer, often at room temperature. English products, therefore, are carbonated at a lower level than ours are. In the United States, lager beers are generally served at between 40 and 45° F, ales and imported beers at 45 to 50° F. As always, the consumers' personal preferences will prevail, but temperatures below 40° F should be avoided. In addition to the storage conditions, the type of glassware used affect the serving temperature. If the glassware is at room temperature—that is, not chilled—the thicker and heavier the glass, the more it will increase the beer temperature. A thick mug can increase the temperature about five degrees. Some operators frost their glasses in the freezer or a special frosting device, but sometimes this can make the beer too cold. Refrigerating the glassware may be the best solution—the temperature will be about the same as the beer—but space considerations can make this difficult, if not impossible, in many bars and restaurants.

Pouring

Beer should be poured so that a dense, creamy head of from one-half to one inch is produced. Beer poured into a glass without producing a head is not attractive and retains too much carbon dioxide. This fills up the customer, discourages repeat sales, and reduces the perception of flavor. Try pouring a bottle of beer into two glasses. With one, carefully pour down the side of the glass while tilting it, and avoid creating any head at all. With the other, pour the beer vigorously into the center of the glass, creating a healthy head. Carefully and objectively taste the two. Most people prefer the one with a head; it tastes better, more alive. Of course, too large a head can create marketing problems with customers, because the higher the head, the less beer there is in the glass. Consistently pouring draft beer with a higher than specified head can also significantly increase the number of glasses in a keg, something an unscrupulous bartender can work to his or her financial advantage —unless customers start going elsewhere!

NUTRITIONAL STANDARDS

Unlike most other alcoholic beverages, beer has food value beyond the mere provision of calories. Beer contains both carbohydrates and protein. It would be misleading, and an exaggeration, to state that beer is a healthful and nutritious beverage, but it does have value as a food. Its alcoholic content is the lowest of the major types of alcoholic beverages—beers, spirits, cordials, and wines—and, consumed in moderation, it certainly is not out of place in a balanced diet.

CONSUMPTION PATTERNS AND TRENDS

Beer is far and away the most popular of all the alcoholic beverages, based on consumption. Wine sales passed that of distilled spirits in 1980 and has steadily increased its lead since then, but beer consumption—over 5.5 billion gallons—is more than ten times that of wine. Like all alcoholic beverages, however, beer consumption has been adversely affected by the political and social climate of the 1980s. The annual per capita consumption of the 21-plus population peaked at 36.97 gallons in 1979, and it has declined continuously since then. Total consumption figures tell the same story. The average annual compound growth rate, which averaged nearly 3.5 percent in the late 1970s, flattened out in the early 1980s, and actually went into a decline in 1984.

The most significant aspects of beer consumption over the past twenty-five years have been the dramatic increases in consumption of imported beers and the emergence of the light and domestic super-premium categories. Imported beers increased from less than 1 million barrels—at thirty-one gallons per barrel—in 1970 to over 7 million by the mid-eighties.

Light beers, which were not known in 1970, accounted for over 19 percent of the beer market in 1984, 35.3 million barrels. The super-premium category went from slightly over 1 million barrels in 1970 to around 10 million in the early 1980s. Another category that has performed better than the market as a whole is malt liquor, although its total market share is small—about 3.5 percent.

Impact, a biweekly newsletter directed toward the alcoholic beverage industry, anticipates a continuing decline in malt beverage consumption through the year 2000. Import beers should continue to grow, while light beers and low-alcohol beers could maintain their current positions. The sales weaknesses and declines of the other segments are expected to continue.

SUGGESTED READINGS

Bell, D. A. *The Spirits of Hospitality.* East Lansing, Mich.: The Educational Institute/American Hotel & Motel Association, 1976.

The Friends of Wine. Bimonthly and annual beer issues: Silver Spring, Md.: Les Amis du Vin, Inc., 1981–86.

Grossman, H. J. *Grossman's Guide to Wines, Beers & Spirits.* 6th rev. ed., rev. H. Lembeck. New York: Charles Scribner's Sons, 1977.

The Impact American Beer Market Review and Forecast. New York: M. Shanken Communications, Inc., 1985.

Jackson, M. *The Pocket Guide to Beer.* New York: Perigee Books/G. Putnam's Sons, 1982.

Katsigris, C., and M. Porter. *The Bar & Beverage Book.* New York: J. Wiley & Sons, 1983.

Knowing Alcoholic Beverages. Liquor Store Magazine. New York: Jobson Publishing Corp., 1978.

One Hundred Years of Brewing. H. S. Rich & Co., Chicago: 1903.

CHAPTER SIX

DISTILLED SPIRITS

QUALITY CRITERIA FOR DISTILLED SPIRITS

There are significant differences in quality among whiskies, brandies, and other types of distilled spirits. There are also significant differences in price, and by and large, the prices reflect these quality variations. Like wines and beers, distilled spirits ultimately reflect the quality of their ingredients. Whether one is making a whisky from grain, brandy from fruit, or rum from sugarcane, a great deal of attention is paid to the starting materials. However, the distilled spirit manufacturer has greater control over the production processes than a wine maker does and can more successfully overcome year-to-year ingredient variations.

Another factor affecting quality is the method of distillation. Most spirits are distilled in a Coffey, or continuous, still (Fig. 6–1, and see Fig. 1–3). However, pot stills are used for some of the most famous beverages; for example, straight malt Scotches are pot-distilled, as are Cognacs and certain rums.

Proof of distillation is a critically important quality factor and is regulated for nearly all spirits, although the distiller of some spirits has a range of proofs that can be used. Bourbon, for example, cannot be distilled at over 160 proof, but the manufacturer can elect to go lower. Two bourbons, one distilled at 160 proof and the other at perhaps 130, would be entirely different.

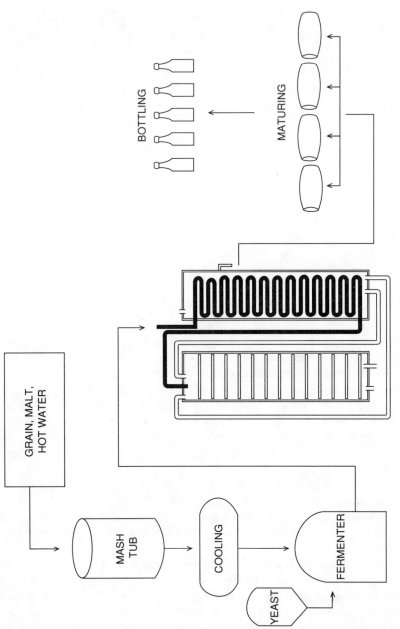

Figure 6-1. Whisky processing.

Following distillation, there are many processes that enable the distiller to alter or enhance the spirit. Charcoal filtering, practiced by some whisky manufacturers, is one example. Another is wood aging. The type of wood is generally regulated, but some spirit makers have options to experiment, and nearly all can determine how long the spirit will remain in contact with the wood. Wood aging is expensive, because the product cannot be sold right away and the volume is gradually reduced over the years due to evaporation. This is an example of the relationship between quality and price. Although increased wood aging will improve many spirits, they must be sold at a higher price, because their production costs also increase.

Blending, a process important to only a few wines, is another critical factor in the quality of distilled spirits (Fig. 6–2). Spirits must maintain brand consistency, and it is the blending that ensures this. Whether a person is drinking a Hennessy VSOP Cognac, a Jack Daniels whisky, a Bacardi rum, or whatever, the brand must always remain the same, whereas vintage-dated wines are expected to be different. Because the distiller begins with plants and fruits that vary from year to year, spirits cannot be made with a strict recipe. Skillful blending is required to maintain odor, taste, and flavor consistency.

GENERAL PRODUCTION STANDARDS

Whisky will serve here as an example of how distilled spirits in general are made. The next section will examine how these procedures are altered when making various types of whiskies and other spirits.

Mashing

In wine making, the natural fruit sugar is fermented into ethyl alcohol; but in the manufacture of whisky and some other spirits, grains are used—and they contain starch, not sugar. Hence, as with beer, the first steps involve malting and mashing. Malting refers to the process of allowing grain to germinate, or sprout, and barley is the grain most typically used. The germinated malt contains an enzyme, called amylase or diastase, that has the unique ability to convert grain starch to maltose, or grain sugar. Ground-up grain undergoes *cooking*, which makes the starches gelatinous, and then *saccharification*, or conversion of the starches to grain sugar, thanks to the barley malt enzyme.

Fermentation

Because the mash now contains fermentable sugars, the addition of yeast initiates the production of ethyl alcohol. During fermentation, perhaps 5 to 6

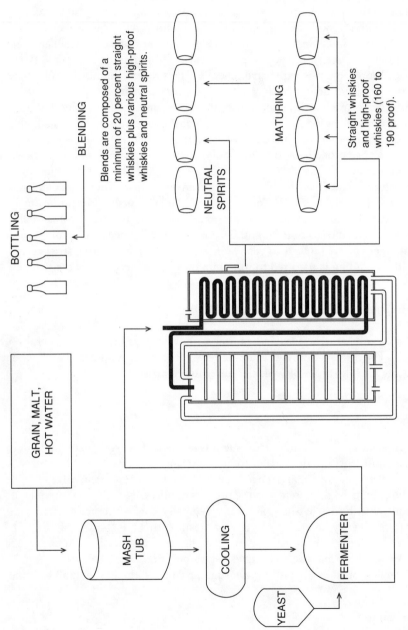

BOTTLING

BLENDING

Blends are composed of a
minimum of 20 percent straight
whiskies plus various high-proof
whiskies and neutral spirits.

MATURING

NEUTRAL
SPIRITS

Straight whiskies
and high-proof
whiskies (160 to
190 proof).

GRAIN, MALT,
HOT WATER

MASH
TUB

COOLING

FERMENTER

YEAST

Figure 6-2. Blended whisky processing.

percent of the available sugar is consumed in side reactions, and the secondary products formed largely determine the characteristics and sensory qualities of the final product. These are the products known as congeners, and in whisky making they are retained during the subsequent operations, unless the objective is to produce grain neutral spirits. They include aldehydes, esters, higher alcohols called fusel oils, some fatty acids, phenolics, and many unidentified trace substances.

The term *sour mash* is frequently misunderstood. Sweet mash whisky is produced by using selected yeasts to begin the fermentation; with sour mash, it is started by using the residue of a previous fermentation. This results in a slightly sweeter and heavier-bodied whisky; it is not at all sour, as the term suggests. It also encourages yeast growth and inhibits bacterial contamination. Most bourbons are made using the sour mash yeasting method, although this will not always be stated on the label.

Distillation

Up to this point, the process for making whisky is similar to that used for beer, and the product, in fact, is called distillers beer. The two critical factors in the distillation process are the type of still utilized and the proof of distillation. U.S. law stipulates that a product labeled as whisky must be distilled at less than 190 proof, or 95 percent alcohol. Above 190 proof, the spirit loses the congeneric substances characteristic of the grains used and legally becomes a neutral grain spirit.

Maturation

A newly distilled spirit is colorless, pungent in taste, and harsh, and it must be matured to acquire smoothness and mellowness. Most spirits are matured in wood, which provides color as well. Colorless spirits, such as gin and vodka, cannot be placed in wood; they must be processed differently to reduce the harshness. In the United States, for example, vodka must be charcoal-filtered.

After distillation, whiskies are diluted with distilled water, aged in wood, diluted again, then bottled. Thus, the proof of distillation has no relationship to bottling proof. Bottling proof has more to do with marketing needs than anything else. One spirit could be distilled at 190 proof and bottled at 100 proof, while another could be distilled at 125 proof and bottled at 80 proof. The former, although stronger, would be lighter and have no distinctive character, while the latter would be heavier in body and have a more distinctive flavor and odor.

The changes in the spirit during wood aging are caused by three types of reactions occurring simultaneously and continuously in the barrel: (1) complex wood constituents are extracted by the liquid; (2) there is oxidation of components originally present in the liquid, as well as of materials extracted from the wood; and (3) there are reactions among various organic substances present in the liquid, leading to the formation of more and new congeners.

As with wine, the type of wood is very important, and most of the major spirits are aged under strict requirements. Some whiskies, such as bourbon, require that the barrels be new and that the insides be charred. This is done by setting the inside of the barrel on fire until a layer of char is developed. Charring improves and softens the taste of the spirit and provides both body and color. Some whiskies and other spirits do not have to be aged in new, unused wood, however, nor do the barrels have to be charred.

Length of aging is a complex matter that depends on the character of the whisky. A light-bodied whisky does not need as much wood as a heavy-bodied one. Some whiskies may be fully matured after only four years in wood, while others could require eight years or even more. The decision on how long to mature is actually made when distilling. The manufacturer decides what specific type of spirit to make, and there is a close relationship between distilling and aging strategies. In a Coffey still, the distiller can pull the spirit off at whatever proof is wanted and can control the eventual body and character of the product.

Table 6-1 Summary of Distilled Spirits

Spirit	Main Ingredients	Type of Still
Whiskies		
Bourbon	Corn, with rye and barley malt	Coffey
Rye	Rye, with corn and barley malt	Coffey
Corn	Corn	Coffey

[1]U.S. law requires a minimum of two years for all whiskies regardless of their origin and the regulations where they are produced.

DISTILLED SPIRIT TYPES AND STANDARDS

This section will examine the major types of distilled spirits available in the United States and how their specific production standards deviate from the general methods just described, as well as their federal Standards of Identity and their sensory standards (Table 6-1).

Whiskies

Whiskies traditionally have dominated the American spirits market, but this is no longer the case. In 1960 whiskies accounted for some 74 percent of the American market, while the so-called white goods (gin, vodka, rum, and tequila) could claim a market share of only 19 percent. The remainder was in specialties, mostly brandies. In 1984 the whisky share dropped to 41.5 percent while that of white goods increased to 41.8 percent and the specialties to 15.7 percent. Nevertheless, whisky still claims a significant share of the American distilled spirit market.

The spelling of the various whiskies is worth noting. The Scots and Canadians use the word *whisky*, the Irish spell it *whiskey*, and the Americans use both spellings. However, U.S. regulations use the spelling *whisky*, and this book follows that usage, except for the Irish kind.

Distillation Proof	Type of Wood Used	Aging Time[1]
Maximum of 160	New white oak, charred	Minimum of two years. Bonded must be aged four years. Most bourbon is aged well beyond the minimum.
Maximum of 160	New white oak, charred	Minimum of two years. Bonded must be aged four years. Like bourbon, most is aged longer.
Maximum of 160	Used or uncharred new oak	Minimum of two years.

(continued)

Table 6-1 *(Continued)*

Spirit	Main Ingredients	Type of Still
Whiskies (cont.)		
American blended	Corn, with rye and barley malt	Coffey
American light	Corn, with rye and barley malt	Coffey
Canadian	Corn, with rye and barley malt	Coffey
Scotch:		
Malt	Barley malt	Pot
Blended		Coffey
Irish	Mostly barley, with other small grains; not all the barley is malted	Pot
Brandies		
American	Grapes	Coffey
Cognac	Grapes	Pot
Armagnac	Grapes	Semicontinuous
Calvados		
Pays d'Auge	Apples	Pot
Calvados	Apples	Semicontinuous

Distillation Proof	Type of Wood Used	Aging Time[1]
Straight whisky portion equals a maximum of 160; the balance is neutral spirits at a minimum of 190	New white oak or used charred oak	Minimum of two years.
160 to 190	Used or uncharred new oak	Minimum of two years.
From mid-bourbon range to about 190	No requirements; most is matured in used cooperage	Minimum of two years (three years under Canadian laws).
About 140 to 160	Used cooperage; some distillers prefer used sherry barrels	Minimum of two years (three years under Scottish laws).
	Used oak	Minimum of two years.
About 170	Used cooperage. As with scotch, used sherry barrels are preferred	Minimum of two years (three years under Irish laws).
Up to 170	Used oak	Minimum of two years.
Maximum is 144, but most is done at 140	Limousin or Tronçais oak	Minimum of two years, although it is often aged much longer. Age statements are not permitted, because it is always blended.
As low as 104	Black oak of Gascony	Minimum of two years, but much is aged longer. Age statements are permitted.
About 140	Limousin oak	Minimum of two years in the United States. French law permits sale after a year, but it generally gets much more.
About 140	Limousin oak	Minimum of two years in the United States. French law stipulates only one year. It is usually bottled fairly young, about two to three years.

Table 6–1 *(Continued)*

Spirit	Main Ingredients	Type of Still
Brandies (cont.)		
Fruit eaux-de-vie:		
Kirsch	Cherry	Pot
Poire Williams	Bartlett pear	Pot
Framboise, Himbeergeist	Raspberry	Pot
Mirabelle	Yellow plum	Pot
Quetsch	Violet plum	Pot
Slivowitz	Violet plum	Pot
Rums		
Light	Sugarcane, molasses	Coffey
Full bodied	Sugarcane, molasses	Pot
Tequila	Blue agave	Pot
Vodka	Grain	Coffey
Gin	Grain	Coffey

Distillation Proof	Type of Wood Used	Aging Time[1]
About 100	None; glass- and enamel-lined containers are used when aging is done	One to four years.
About 100	None	None.
About 100	None	None.
About 100	None; glass- and enamel-lined containers are used when aging is done	One to four years.
About 100	None; glass- and enamel-lined containers are used when aging is done	One to four years.
About 100	Generally used	Variable.
160 to 180	Used oak, which may or may not have been charred	Puerto Rican law requires a minimum of one year, but it may be aged longer.
140 to 160	Used oak, which may or may not have been charred	Longer than the light rums, but there are no specific requirements. Some may be matured for ten to fifteen years, and an age statement on the label is permitted.
104 to 106	Not necessarily aged; if it is, it is done in used whisky barrels	One to four years.
Minimum of 190	None	None.
Minimum of 190	None	None.

Bourbon Whisky. The preceding description of whisky making more or less follows that of bourbon, and it will be used for our frame of reference. Many grains are allowed in bourbon, but the mixture must contain a minimum of 51 percent corn; the remaining ingredients are generally divided between rye and barley malt. A common mixture is 60 percent corn, 28 percent rye, and 12 percent barley malt, known as a mixture of 60 percent corn and 40 percent *small grains.* Other popular proportions of the three ingredients include 70–18–12, or 30 percent small grains, and 75–13–12, or 25 percent small grains. Here is where the manufacturer can begin to control the character and type of product made. The formula with the greater proportion of small grains produces a heavier and fuller product, because rye and barley malt produce more intensive flavors than corn.

The distillation proof cannot exceed 160, and many are distilled at 110 to 130 proof. Although bourbons are heavier bodied and more distinctively flavored than many other whiskies, the range of distilling proofs used clearly shows how there can be significant differences among bourbons.

The federal Standards of Identity for bourbon also require that it be stored at not more than 125 proof in charred new oak barrels for not less than two years. Bourbons distilled at over 125 proof must then be diluted with distilled water befor maturing; those distilled at or below 125 proof do not necessarily have to be diluted.

Other whiskies similar to bourbon are rye, wheat, malt, and rye malt. With each, the Standards of Identity are the same as with bourbon, except that the 51 percent minimum applies not to corn, but to rye, wheat, malt, and rye malt, respectively. The proof of distillation and storage requirements are the same: no higher than 160 proof and storage in new, charred oak for at least two years.

A product labeled corn whisky has the same distillation proof limitation (160), but it must be made from a fermented mash containing at least 80 percent corn and stored in uncharred or reused charred oak. Therefore, it will be lighter and less distinctive than bourbon, due both to the higher proportion of corn and to the use of either reused or uncharred barrels.

There are two well-known distilleries in Tennessee—Jack Daniels and George Dickel—that produce products that are consumed as bourbon and meet the legal requirements for bourbon. The production of both is identical to bourbon except that they filter the distillate through maple charcoal prior to aging.

Bourbon originated in Kentucky, and is in fact named for Bourbon County, where it was first distilled in 1789. Although bourbon is still commonly associated with Kentucky, it can be made anywhere in the United States as long as it meets the Standards of Identity. However, it is legally defined as a distinctive product of the United States and must be produced in this country. Whisky made elsewhere, even by this method, may not legally be labeled bourbon.

The whiskies described here are straight or unblended whiskies. A product labeled simply as straight whisky is made from a miscellaneous grain mixture. Blended straight whisky is a mixture of the same type of straight whiskies. Examples include blended straight bourbon or blended straight rye.

The term *Bottled in Bond* means that the spirit is straight, or unblended, and has been distilled at no more than 160 proof at one plant by one distiller. It must also be aged at least four years and bottled at 100 proof. A further requirement is that it be bottled in a bonded warehouse, but because all spirits now are bottled in bonded warehouses, the stipulation no longer has meaning.

American Blended Whiskies. Blended whisky contains at least 20 percent by volume of 100 proof straight whisky, mixed with other whiskies or neutral spirits. Straight whisky must be distilled at no more than 160 proof, while the blending whiskies can be withdrawn from the still at up to 190 proof. In the United States it is legally whisky if below 190 proof, and neutral spirits if above. If the blend contains at least 51 percent of a straight whisky, such as bourbon or rye, it may be called blended bourbon, blended rye whisky, or bourbon/rye whisky—a blend.

Blended whiskies may also use a blending agent to aid in the final "marrying" of the various spirits. Sherry is the most common one used, and it is permitted up to 2.5 percent, although it is unusual to use as much as even this small amount.

Blended whiskies can be very complex products, containing many different types of straight whiskies, other whiskies, and neutral spirits. In addition, all of the blend components, including the neutral spirits, may be aged for various periods. The manufacturer has nearly total control over the character of the finished product and can more or less "build" any type of spirit desired. In practice, the challenge is not to create new types of products, but to duplicate exactly the products that have been marketed over the years. Such brands as 7 Crown, Imperial, Four Roses, and others are counted on by the consumer to be the same over time.

American Light Whisky. In recent years, the American market has turned toward lighter alcoholic beverages. This is evidenced by the drop in market share of whiskies and the increase of the white goods. They are colorless, lighter in body—though not necessarily in alcohol—and significantly less distinctive in flavor and aroma compared to the whiskies—the so-called brown goods. Within the brown goods market, there has also been a shift from the heavier American products, bourbon and blended whiskies, to the lighter imported Canadian and Scotch whiskies. These latter whiskies are lighter because they are distilled at higher proofs than are allowed in the United States, and American distillers have felt themselves at a competitive disadvantage.

The result has been a new class of American whisky: American light whisky. The first such products were distilled in 1968 and were available for sale four years later, on July 1, 1972. The regulations provided for the distilling of whiskies at above 160 proof but below 190 proof, and storage was permitted at proofs above 125. To enhance the development of their lighter characteristics further, they were allowed to be matured in used or uncharred new cooperage. If mixed with less than 20 percent by volume of 100 proof straight whisky, the mixture was labeled blended light whisky.

The distillers were not very successful, however; not only did they not slow the shift to white goods but also they did little to alter the swing toward imported whiskies. In fact, light whisky was so unsuccessful that much of it had to be redistilled into neutral spirits.

Canadian Whisky. The U.S. Standards of Identity provide that Canadian whisky is a distinctive product of Canada, manufactured there in compliance with Canadian laws regulating its manufacture for consumption in that country. Canadian whiskies can contain no spirits less than three years of age and are generally bottled at six or more years.

The distinctive characteristics of Canadian whisky are its lightness of body and delicacy of flavor. This is accomplished in several ways. One is in the quality and choice of grains used. Although Canadian whisky is often thought of as a rye whisky, the major grains used are corn, rye, and barley malt, with corn predominating. The Canadian government imposes no limitations as the United States does on grain formulas, distilling proofs, or types of cooperage for maturation. As a result, much of what goes on in the manufacture of Canadian whisky remains a distiller's trade secret (Fig. 6–3).

The major reason for its lightness of body is that, because the distillers do not have to cope with restrictions on distillation proof, they are free to draw the spirits off at a variety of proofs that are optimal for the separation and selection of desirable congeners, or secondary products. All the spirits used in Canadian blends are legally whisky, because they are distilled at below 190 proof. American blended whiskies are mixtures of heavy straight whiskies with a low distillation proof and very high-proof, characterless spirits. The Canadian product is skillfully blended from spirits distilled from the middle of the bourbon range to about 185 proof. Because Canadian whiskies are blended products, they are labeled blended Canadian whisky or Canadian whisky—a blend.

The final factor contributing to the distinctive Canadian character is the cooperage. Oak is employed, but there are no restrictions requiring the use of new wood, and a substantial amount is aged in matured barrels. This seems to

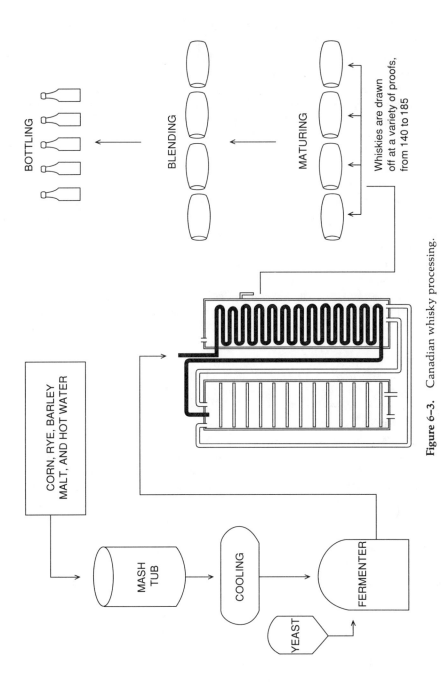

Figure 6-3. Canadian whisky processing.

be especially compatible for the whiskies produced and contributes to the flavor's delicacy. As with the grain proportions, the specific mix of new and used cooperage is each distiller's trade secret.

The similarity between the standards for Canadian whisky and American light whisky is not coincidental. The light whisky regulations were established with the intention of producing a similar product. Note that both allow a broad range of high-proof whiskies to be used in the blends, and neither requires the exclusive use of new cooperage.

Scotch Whisky. It is a matter of conjecture as to who were the first to distill whisky, the Scots or the Irish; both claim the honor. The Scots, however, may have been the first to practice aging, and it was their discovery and use of blending spirits that transformed Scotch whisky from a somewhat earthy, highly distinctive product to the lighter product known today as blended Scotch whisky or, more simply, Scotch whisky.

The British description of Scotch does not offer many clues as to why it is the distinctive and highly regarded product it is: "Spirits described as Scotch Whisky shall not be deemed to correspond to that description unless they have been obtained by distillation in Scotland from a mash of cereal grain saccharified by the diastase of malt and have been matured in warehouse in cask for a period of at least three years." Nor does the U.S. Standards of Identity, which require only that it be a distinctive product of Scotland, manufactured in Scotland in compliance with the laws of Great Britain regulating the manufacture of Scotch whisky for consumption in Great Britain and containing no distilled spirits less than three years old. In addition, if it is a mixture of whiskies, it must be labeled blended Scotch whisky or Scotch whisky—a blend.

Scotch is unique because its processing is quite different from the whiskies previously described (Fig. 6-4). To begin with, it is a blend of two types of whisky: one type is made entirely from malted barley, the other from mixtures of grain similar to American and Canadian whiskies. With Scotch, it is the malt whiskies that provide its distinctive characteristics, and an understanding of how the malts are produced is necessary to fully appreciate Scotch whisky.

The only grain used is barley, and it is saturated with water and steeped in large vats, then spread on broad cement floors and allowed to sprout, or germinate. At this point, the barley is said to be malted. The next step is the key one, and the one responsible for producing the outstanding taste characteristic of scotch; its subtle smoky flavor. The malted barley is dried on huge screens, below which peat fires are lighted. The barley takes up the smoky aroma of the burning peat, which is partially carbonized vegetable matter, heather, fern, and evergreen that has been aged and compressed over the centuries.

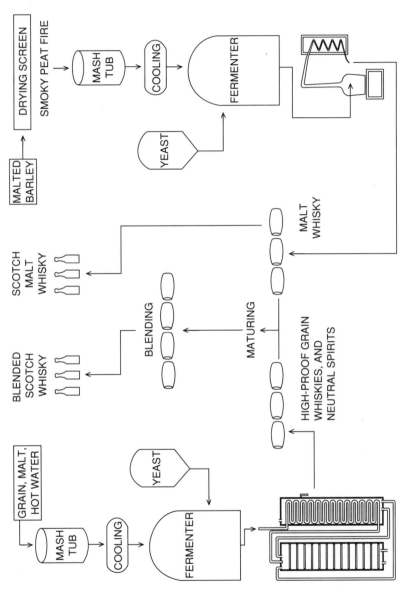

Figure 6–4. Scotch whisky processing.

The next step is familiar: the dried barley is ground up, mixed with water, heated, gelatinized, and converted to sugar. Following this, the liquid portion is drained off, cooled, and fermented, as with other alcoholic beverages.

Distillation of the fermented beverage takes place not in Coffey stills, but in pot stills. This is a second key step differentiating Scotch from other whiskies. The stills are made of copper and, while the reasons are not fully understood, the size and shape of the still has a definite influence on the spirit. Two distillation cycles are used, and the distillate is separated into three portions. The first and third are called *foreshots* and *feints* (heads and tailings in the United States). The middle portion is given a second distillation, and the product from that becomes malt whisky. Proof of distillation is in the 140 to 160 range, and the whisky is diluted to maturation proof, about 111 proof, for storage in oak.

There are some 100 distilleries producing malt whiskies in four major areas of Scotland, and their products vary according to the region. Most of the distilleries are located in the Scottish Highlands, and they are considered the best of the malts: full flavored, yet lighter and more delicate than the other types. Whiskies known as Islay malts are from Islay in the Inner Hebrides and Cambeltown on the promontory of Kintyre. They are usually stronger flavored and heavier bodied, with a more pronounced smokiness. The other type, Lowland malts, are from the comparatively few distilleries in the south and are used mostly for blending.

Aging is done in used cooperage, and some distillers prefer used sherry casks, because the spirit can extract color; otherwise, caramel or burnt sugar is used for coloring. Used oak does not have the same coloring effect on the spirit as will new, charred oak, such as that required for bourbon. Although the aging requirement is for a minimum of three years, most malts get more, and twelve or even fifteen to twenty years are not uncommon. Not only does used cooperage impart less color compared to new charred oak, but also the spirits mature more slowly. It may seem that Scotch is aged longer than bourbon, but this is not necessarily the case; the ages are not equivalent.

This process produces unblended single-malt whiskies, and although they are bottled and have been developing a growing following in the United States, it is the blended types that are responsible for the fame of Scotch whisky. The making of grain whiskies for blending follows the procedures described for American and Canadian whiskies. Corn, rye, and barley are the grains used, and they are distilled in Coffey stills. Unlike the neutral grain spirits used in American blends, however, they have some flavor, body, and character, because they are distilled at legal whisky proofs, about 180 to 186, and are aged in matured oak casks.

The final step is the blending. It is the blender whose complex artistry is responsible for the production, year after year, of consistent and distinctive brands. It is the blending that can produce a nearly infinite number of whiskies. As many as twenty to forty or even fifty different malt and grain whiskies are used to produce a brand. The best blends are believed to be composed of about 50 percent Highland and Lowland malts and a small amount of Islay malts, with the remainder made up of various unmalted grain whiskies. Following the blending, the whisky is allowed a "marrying" period and is reduced to bottling strength by the addition of soft water from the Scottish lochs (lakes or sea inlets).

An increasing amount of Scotch (and Canadian) whisky is being imported in the barrel for tax and marketing purposes. Because the U.S. tax is on 100-proof spirits, but is based on the volume, regardless of the proof, the tax on bottled whisky is higher than on barreled spirits. This is because Scotch is bottled at less than 100 proof, while barrels are shipped at the finished aging proof, which is in excess of 100 proof. The importer also pays less in shipping costs, because the reduction to bottling proof is done in the United States. The result is lower prices to the consumer.

Irish whiskey. The Standards of Identity for Irish whiskey—spelled with an *e*—is that it be manufactured in either the Republic of Ireland or Northern Ireland, in compliance with their laws regulating the manufacture of Irish whiskey for home consumption, and contain no distilled spirits less than three years old. If such a product is a mixture of whiskeys, it is labeled blended Irish whiskey or Irish whiskey—a blend.

Irish whiskey is most similar to Scotch, but it differs in several significant ways. The grains used are not exclusively barley—for other small grains are used—and not all the barley is malted. The barley malt is also not dried over peat fires; thus, Irish whiskey does not have the characteristic smoky taste that Scotch has. The spirit is pot-distilled in stills having a much larger capacity than those used in Scotland, and it is triple-distilled, making it unique among the world's great spirits. Only the middle portion of the third distillation is used, and it is estimated that a mere 10 percent of the fermented mash becomes Irish whiskey.

Distillation is generally carried out at a higher proof than Scotch malt; as a result, the spirit is flavorful but lighter than the straight malts, and more flavorful and heavier bodied than blended Scotch whiskies. Aging is lengthy and takes place in used sherry casks for a long period. The Irish have a saying that to make whiskey, "it takes seven days of a man's time and seven years of the whiskey's time."

This procedure describes how the traditional Irish whiskey, straight whiskey, is made, although blended whiskeys now are also available. Like Scotch, they are blends of straight with high-proof grain whiskeys, and they have been developed in response to the trend toward lighter products. The repositioning of Irish whiskey as a premium blended one has resulted in some sales gains, but the category is not of much commercial importance in the United States. All Irish whiskey accounts for only 0.2 percent of the American distilled spirits market, and no Irish whiskeys, straight or blended, appear in the top 100 brands.

Brandy

According to the Standards of Identity, brandy is essentially a distillate or mixture of distillates obtained solely from the fermented juice, mash, or wine of fruit, or from the residue thereof, distilled at less than 190 proof in such manner as to produce the taste, aroma, and characteristics generally attributed to the product, and bottled at not less than 80 proof (Fig. 6–5).

There is one exception to the bottling proof requirement for spirits, and it is unique to brandy. As spirits mature in wood, the alcoholic content is gradually reduced; thus, a brandy aged in wood for fifty years may have reduced to below 80 proof. In such a case, it could be bottled as low as 72 proof. This exception is unique to brandy, because only brandies—and only a few brandies at that—normally receive such lengthy wood aging.

Although brandy is permitted to be distilled at up to 190 proof, beverage brandies are distilled at about 140 to 170 proof. Distillation at above 170 proof defines it as *neutral brandy*, a product widely used in this country for the production of dessert wines.

There are two principal types of brandy produced in the United States: *straight brandy* and *rectified brandy*. Straight brandy is similar to straight whisky, a spirit that is simply bottled after being withdrawn from the aging casks. A rectified brandy is one that has received some sort of processing treatment, such as blending together brandies of different ages or adjusting the color to a standard with caramel. There is nothing inferior about rectified brandy; nearly all imported products, including Cognac, can be classified as rectified, because they are blends and contain small amounts of caramel.

The name brandy, by itself, indicates that the spirit has been obtained from grapes. Brandy can be produced from any fermented fruit, but then must be identified by the name of the fruit. Fine brandies do not have to be made from grapes; there are many magnificent examples made from cherries, apples, pears, and other fruits.

Brandies are produced with both pot stills and continuous stills. In France and much of Europe, pot or batch distillation is the only kind allowed; in the United States, both systems are employed. Most American brandy, however, is distilled continuously. In general, a pot still produces a brandy with more flavor, while that from a continuous still is lighter and more delicate.

Products identified as flavored brandies—blackberry-flavored brandy, cherry-

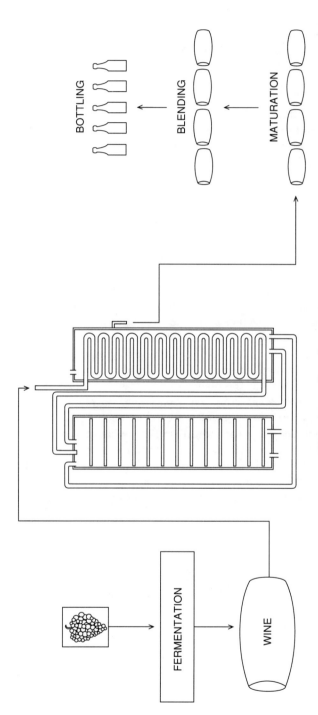

Figure 6-5. Brandy processing.

flavored brandy, and so forth—are not true brandies at all, but cordials. They are flavored, colored, and supplemented with added sugar. The spirit base is generally neutral brandy.

Many brandies are not aged in wood because they are intended to remain colorless and, in the case of many of the nongrape brandies, the fresh, delicate aroma of the fruit must be retained. These brandies usually are stored in glass or stainless steel until bottled.

Some regions, such as the French areas of Cognac, Armagnac, and Calvados, specialize in brandies, but brandy is actually produced nearly everywhere that wine is made. In places such as the Douro Valley in Portugal and Jerez de la Frontera in Spain, brandies must be produced in order to fortify the wines, but in others, it just appears to be an inevitable adjunct to the wine business.

American Brandies. The two top-selling brandies in the United States are American. E. & J. Brandy (Gallo Winery) and Christian Brothers Brandy each sell 1.5 million or more cases per year and rank in the top 100 brands. Their sales are each more than double that of the two top-selling imported brandies: Hennessy Cognac and Courvoisier Cognac. American brandies are generally distilled in a Coffey still at up to 170 proof, aged in used oak for two or more years, blended, and sweetened with up to 2.5 percent sugar. Less important commercially but also available are American straight brandies with no additives except a little caramel for coloring, and premium brandies that may contain some pot-distilled spirits. One California sparkling wine producer, Schramsberg (located in the Napa Valley), has developed an entirely pot-distilled brandy for marketing like Cognac, as an after-dinner brandy. In general, though, American brandies are lighter and more delicate than European types and are well suited for mixing in a wide variety of drinks.

Cognac. Surely the most famous brandy of all is Cognac, but many consumers do not understand the relationship between Cognac and brandy. Put as simply as possible: Cognac is a brandy, but only one brandy is Cognac. To qualify, the brandy must be made from grapes that have been grown in a legally delimited region in France: the Cognac region. It is located on the Atlantic coast, just north of the Bordeaux wine region. The grapes have to be fermented into wine there and the distillation must also be done there, using traditional methods and equipment.

Within the Cognac region of France there are six zones, classified according to the calcium carbonate content in the soil. The higher the calcium content, the better the ranking. The ranking of these zones, from top to bottom is Grande Champagne, Petite Champagne, Borderies, Fine Bois, Bons Bois, and Bois Ordinaires. A Cognac made entirely from Grande Champagne grapes is labeled Grande Champagne or Grande Fine Champagne. Fine Champagne means that at least 50 percent of the brandy is from Grande Champagne, with the remainder from the bordering Petite Champagne district. These are the finest and most expensive Cognacs.

The differences among the districts show in the flavor, body, and bouquet, as well as the aging time and potential. Brandies from the Grande Champagne have the finest and most delicate flavor; those from the Bon Bois and Bois Ordinaires are much coarser in flavor. Grande Champagne brandies have the lightest body; those from the lowest classifications are heavy and clumsy. The Champagne brandies develop a refined and elegant bouquet; the others do not. Brandies made from Grande Champagne grapes have far more potential for aging, but they age much more slowly and take longer to mature. Because of these differences, most Cognacs are blends of brandies from different regions, mostly from the first three. Little, if any, of the three Bois zones' grapes goes into the better Cognacs. Blending is done to balance the quality characteristics of the regions. Borderies blended with a Champagne brandy, for example, accelerates the aging and provides a little more body.

Although Cognac is dominated by a relatively few, large, and world-famous firms, most of the distilling is done by small producers, often the farmers who grew the grapes. These brandies are then purchased by the shippers, who blend and mature them. Courvoisier, for example, owns neither vineyards nor distilleries, and Hennessy purchases about 90 percent of the brandies it needs. The consistency one finds in Cognac brands is a result of purchasing consistency and skillful blending on the part of the shippers.

Cognac is distilled from wine made mostly from the Saint-Émilion grape, known in other parts of the world as the Ugni Blanc or Trebbiano. It produces a wine ideal for distilling, one low in alcohol with good acidity. The acid helps to preserve the wine prior to distillation and enhances aging. Low-alcohol levels are desirable simply because it means that more wine must be distilled for each gallon of brandy produced. It would be less expensive and more efficient to distill wines with a higher alcohol content, but they would not produce brandies with the depth of flavor and complexity of Cognac.

One of the many distinctive aspects of Cognac production is that it is distilled exclusively in pot stills made of copper (Fig. 6–6). The product is distilled twice, and only the middle portion of the second distillation becomes Cognac. The maximum distillation proof permitted is 144, and most Cognac is distilled at about 140 proof.

Following distillation, the spirit is aged in oak obtained either from the local Limousin Forest or from the Tronçais Forest in mid-France. There are no legal requirements about the type of wood, but traditionally only Limousin oak was used. With an increasing need for oak casks and with easier transportation, many Cognac shippers began to use wood from the more distant Tronçais. Both are in general use now, and although some shippers do

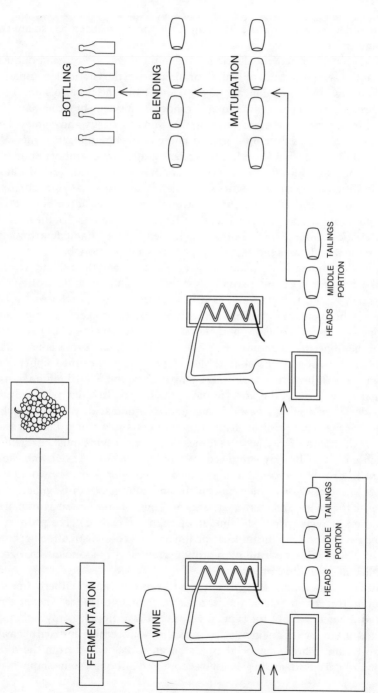

Figure 6–6. Cognac processing.

FERMENTATION

WINE

HEADS   MIDDLE   TAILINGS
         PORTION

HEADS   MIDDLE   TAILINGS
         PORTION

MATURATION

BLENDING

BOTTLING

204

have a preference, there do not seem to be easily detectable differences between the two.

Cognac is aged in both new and used cooperage. Generally, newly distilled brandies are placed in new oak, then transferred to older wood as it matures, but each shipper has personal preferences and practices. For example, Delamain, a shipper specializing in light, delicate brandies, insists that its distillers use only mature, used wood, even for newly distilled spirits. Because of the pattern of wood usage, and because Cognac is a blend of spirits aged for different periods, it is not accurate to speak of a specific age as is done with bourbon and Scotch, for example. Therefore, age statements are prohibited with Cognac.

Three basic types of Cognac are made. One, accounting for some 80 to 90 percent of the production, is usually labeled three-star, VS (for Very Superior), or simply Cognac. It is the youngest blend of each shipper, primarily composed of brandies that have spent about three to five years in wood, with a small portion of more mature brandy added to increase the smoothness and complexity. The actual age of a Cognac is always a matter of conjecture, but because the total aging stocks in Cognac are between three and four times the annual sales, it would be difficult for the average blend to be older than four years.

The next level is that commonly designated as VSOP (or Very Superior Old Pale). Note that the letters used by the Cognac trade are English in origin. VSOP is an unusual phrase, because unlike wines, spirits become darker as they mature in wood, not paler. Some of the other frequently used labels are F (fine) and X (extra). A VSOP (also known as VO or Very Old, and Réserve) Cognac generally has an average age of from seven to ten years. Its flavor is fuller and smoother than a three-star, and it has a more complex bouquet. VSOP Cognacs are fine premium brandies and are meant to be sipped, as opposed to being mixed. They are also relative bargains, because the difference in quality is usually greater than the price difference.

The third basic level consists of more mature, scarce, and expensive brandies. Some examples are Napoleon (made by Courvoisier), Cordon Bleu (Martell), Bras d'Or (Hennessy), Anniversaire (Monnet), and Réserve Prince Hubert (Polignac). Their average age is probably from fifteen to twenty-five years, and they have developed considerable complexity in both flavor and bouquet from the long period in wood. They also have higher tannin levels and more oak character than younger brandies. In Cognac it is legal to use sugar to round out the flavors and reduce the harshness of younger brandies, but on this quality level it should not be necessary.

There are other Cognac brandies beyond the ones described, but they are not available in commercial qualities and are fabulously expensive. They are designated as Extra Vieille, Extra, XO, Grande Réserve, and Cordon Argent, among other names. They contain brandies of considerable age, often fifty years or more, and show not only great complexity and subtlety, but substantial tannin and wood character as well.

Armagnac. After Cognac, Armagnac is probably the most famous brandy. The Armagnac region is part of the ancient province of Gascony and is located in southwest France, south of Bordeaux. There are three subregions that are important for brandy production: Haut Armagnac, Ténarèze, and Bas Armagnac. The Haut Armagnac, the upper Armagnac, is named not for its elevation or brandy quality, but because it is the most distant of the three from the ocean. Its soil is the chalkiest of the three, most similar to the best Cognac soil, but in Armagnac, surprisingly, this soil results in the least desirable brandies. In fact, very little of the Haut Armagnac brandy is used in the blends today. The central section of Armagnac is Ténarèze; its brandies, while seldom bottled straight, are considered to be of high quality and essential to a well-balanced blend. The third subregion, Bas Armagnac, is ranked first for both quality and quantity. Its soil is composed of a mixture of sand, slate, and clay and produces a brandy that is more refined and elegant than the others. Unblended Bas Armagnac is available; to qualify, it must be 100 percent Bas Armagnac and must be blended in a separate warehouse if the merchant handles any other types. Most Bas Armagnac, however, is blended with brandy from the other regions, mostly Ténarèze, and sold as Armagnac.

The grapes grown in Armagnac are similar to those from Cognac. The differences are that in Armagnac, Folle Blanche and Baco 22A grapes are widely planted in addition to the Saint-Émilion. The Folle Blanche was the traditional Cognac grape, but it fell into disfavor because of its susceptibility to molds and other plant diseases. The Baco 22A, a hybrid, is a cross between the Folle Blanche and an American grape called the Noah. It seems particularly well suited to the sandy soil of the Bas Armagnac and Ténarèze, and it makes a wine similar to the Folle Blanche.

Although there are soil and grape differences between the regions of Armagnac and Cognac, the primary difference between their brandies lies in the method of distillation and the wood used for aging. Armagnac is distilled in a sort of semicontinuous still and receives only one distillation, compared to Cognac's double distillation. It is also distilled at a considerably lower proof, as low as 104. This is the traditional way to distill Armagnac, and it results in a spirit that has a higher congeneric and fusel oil content, compared to Cognac, and is fuller bodied and drier on the palate, because no sugar is used to reduce the harshness and make the brandy smoother. A change in the regulations has allowed Armagnac producers to build slightly taller stills and distill at up to a maximum of 144 proof. These practices allow for the production of a lighter distillate. Some distillers in Armagnac have experimented with Cognac-style pot stills, which have been permitted since 1972, but the long-range effect of this is still uncertain.

Following distillation, the spirit is aged in the local black oak of Gascony. Most other spirits, including Cognac, are matured in white oak; the black oak of Armagnac, which has much more sap, adds its distinctive character faster. Therefore, an Armagnac will be more mature than a Cognac of the same age. Unlike Cognac, Armagnac is bottled by vintage and may be labeled either with a specific age statement, such as "10 years old," or with the actual vintage date. At ten years Armagnac is well aged, due to the black oak. The general practice is to mature the freshly distilled Armagnac in new wood for a year or two, then transfer it to used cooperage. This slows the extraction of tannin and reduces the woody character inherent with long maturation in oak.

There are three types of quality and age marketed. The youngest averages about three years. The VSOP types get between five and ten years. Brandies labeled as Hors d'Age or Vieille Réserve may have fifteen to twenty-five years of aging.

A fine, mature Armagnac is one of the world's great brandies and should be enjoyed like a fine Cognac: sipped neat, or unmixed, in a snifter after a meal.

Apple Brandy. Apple brandy is made by distilling *hard cider,* or fermented apple juice. In the United States this is called applejack, which was an important beverage in the early days of our country. There was another — and, it is hoped, no longer used — method of making applejack. If hard cider is frozen, only the water portion freezes; the alcohol does not. Therefore, if the ice portion is removed, what remains is nearly pure alcohol. This must have been a rather rough and fiery spirit.

The federal Standards of Identity allow for the designation of either apple brandy or applejack if the product is entirely derived from apples. Blended applejack or applejack — a blend is a spirit composed of at least 20 percent apple brandy, stored in oak containers for a minimum of two years, plus not more than 80 percent neutral spirits, and bottled at not less than 80 proof. Blended applejack is the type most likely to be found in the United States, because it is lighter than straight apple brandy and is more in line with current taste preferences. It is not sold in any significant quantities, however.

Calvados. Normandy, France, site of the Allied landings during World War II, is apple country. As a result, producers make cider there, not wine as in so many of the other regions of France. From cider it is a short step to brandy, and Normandy is famed for its apple brandy, Calvados. The production of Calvados is controlled by the French Institut National des Appellations d'Origine, the same agency that regulates the production of France's finest wines. Three categories of brandy are recognized and regulated: Calvados du Pays d'Auge, Calvados, and *eau-de-vie de cidre.*

The most prestigious, Calvados du Pays d'Auge produces the most distinctive brandies. It comes from a small area in central Normandy. The name Calvados is used for brandies produced in ten other regions surrounding the Pays d'Auge and is classified as *appellation réglementée,* not the more limited and higher regarded *appellation contrôlée;* the distinction is intended to be the same as with the finest French wines. *Eau-de-vie de cidre* is a more general classification, also *appellation réglementée,* covering most of the rest of the traditional cider-producing regions in western France.

Calvados du Pays d'Auge must be produced nearly exactly like Cognac. It is double-distilled in pot stills at about 140 proof. It is required to have a minimum of one year of aging in wood, today generally from the Limousin Forest, but it typically receives much more. The aging casks are quite large, often holding 2,500 gallons or more. The optimal maximum age is said to be from twenty-five to thirty years, although it may be aged beyond this.

Brandy labeled simply as Calvados does not have to be pot-distilled; it is prepared in small, semicontinuous stills similar to those used in Armagnac. Bottling is done at a relatively young age, two to three years, although some older brandies are usually used in the blend. A good younger Calvados has a fresh apple aroma but lacks the complexity and smoothness of the older examples. *Eau-de-vie de cidre* generally is not found on the American market, being consumed mostly in France.

Fruit Eaux-de-Vie. Distilled fruit spirits are called fruit eaux-de-vie, true fruit brandies, white spirits, or white alcohol. This is because, not having wood aging, they retain the colorless, sparkling clear appearance of all freshly distilled spirits. The objective of the distiller is to capture the unique essence of the fruit being used, and to avoid altering or diluting it in any way, such as by aging it in wood or by adding sugar or other adulterants.

These products are pretty much a European specialty; most Americans are not very familiar with them, and little is produced by American firms. Production of these eaux-de-vie is centered primarily in three areas in central Europe: Switzerland, the Black Forest (Schwarzwald) of Germany, and Alsace in France. In these areas, especially in Alsace, producers distill virtually all fruits, and some flowers, into spirits, but there are only a few that are made in commercially important quantities. These are cherries, pears, raspberries, and plums.

There are two basic production methods. One is to ferment a fruit into a wine and then distill it into a brandy of about 100 proof. Distillation is generally done in pot stills, and the middle portion of the second distillation becomes the eaux-de-vie (Fig. 6-7). This is nearly identical to Cognac distillation, and copper pots stills similar to those for Cognac are used. This method is followed for the stone fruits, such as cherries and plums, and for pears.

The other method is used for the soft fruits, such as raspberries. These fruits contain insufficient sugar to follow the normal routine of fermentation and distillation. The fruits are first macerated in a high-proof spirit, and the highly flavored infusion is distilled (Fig. 6-8). In Germany and Switzerland, neutral, high-proof alcohol is used for the maceration, and the product is known as a

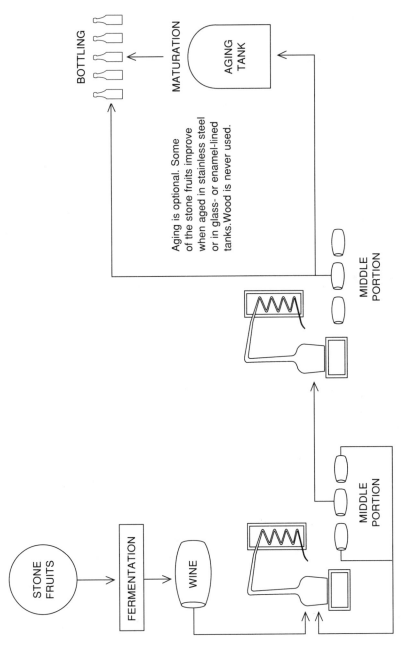

Aging is optional. Some of the stone fruits improve when aged in stainless steel or in glass- or enamel-lined tanks. Wood is never used.

Figure 6-7. Eaux-de-vie processing: Distillation.

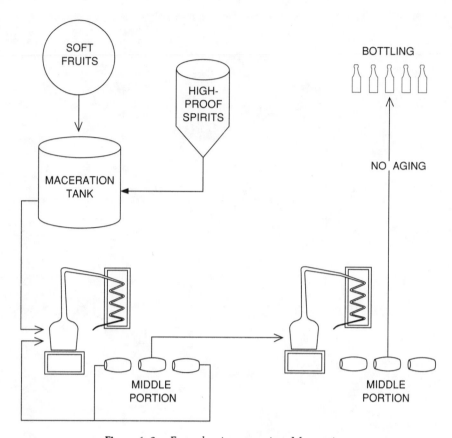

Figure 6–8. Eaux-de-vie processing: Maceration.

Geist (German for a "ghost" or spirit). Thus, a raspberry brandy becomes Himbeergeist, or, literally, "spirit of raspberry." In France, producers retain the name eaux-de-vie but are required to use fruit spirits to prepare the infusion. The best firms use unaged Cognac brandy.

Compared to grapes, none of the fruits used contains appreciable amounts of sugar. As a result, the fermented wine is quite low in alcohol, about 4 to 8 percent, and a great deal of fruit is needed. A one-liter bottle of pear or strawberry brandy could require fifty pounds or more of fruit; for this reason, the good fruit eaux-de-vie necessarily must be expensive.

Cherry (Kirsch, Kirschwasser). Kirsch is made in all three major production areas, but the most famous is the one from the German Black Forest, the Schwarzwalder kirsch. It is said to be the most complex and the fullest bodied.

The French kirsch, like most French eaux-de-vie, tend to be lighter and more delicate than those from Switzerland and Germany. In Germany, and in the German-speaking part of Switzerland, producers use the word Wasser (water) to distinguish a fermented and distilled beverage from a macerated and distilled one, a Geist. Cherry eaux-de-vie (like those made from the other stone fruits) appears to improve with aging, and the better ones are matured prior to bottling, but never in wood. Glass- and enamel-lined containers are common, and stainless steel is used as well.

Pear (Poire Williams, Williams Birnenbrand). A good pear brandy has an intense and delightful aroma of fresh pears, but the taste is seldom as distinctive. The Bartlett pear, called the Williams pear in Europe, is the variety used, and its aroma makes it probably the most easily identified of the white brandies.

Raspberry (Framboise, Himbeergeist). Raspberry brandy, like the other soft-fruit brandies, does not improve with aging; typically it is bottled soon after distillation. It has a character distinctly evocative of ripe raspberries and is very popular in the United States. The Alsatian products, which must be macerated with fruit brandies rather than neutral spirits, are very highly regarded. The German and Swiss Himbeergeists are felt to be a little lighter and perhaps less complex. In the French-speaking section of Switzerland the brandy is called a framboise, but it does not have to be macerated with fruit eaux-de-vie.

Yellow Plum (Mirabelle, Mirabellenwasser). This is generally considered to be a French specialty, although there are also yellow plum brandies made in Germany and Switzerland. Some consumers and many producers feel that these are the finest of all the fruit eaux-de-vie. Mirabelle does not have as distinctive an aroma as the pear and raspberry brandies, but it is more perfumed and flowery. The flavors are round and fruity with some complexity and a lingering aftertaste. Like kirsch, mirabelle is improved with aging, and one to four years is suggested.

Violet Plum (Quetsch, Zwetschgenwasser, Slivowitz). Produced in Alsace, in Germany, and in Switzerland, the violet plum produces a brandy that has a spicy plum character and is more full than the mirabelle, but probably not as complex.

In Yugoslavia and other Eastern European countries, a specialty is slivowitz, a yellow plum eaux-de-vie that obtains its distinctive character from wood aging, sometimes for as long as eight to twelve years. It has a straw to medium yellow color but is not at all similar to the wood-aged grape and apple brandies discussed earlier.

These are the most popular and widely produced white fruit brandies, but there are as many others as there are fruits (and flowers) from which to make them. Eaux-de-vie are also produced from apricots, peaches, acacia flowers, currants, strawberries, blackberries, elderberries, and even holly. The latter is probably the most expensive of all; the berries must be hand-harvested, and the cost of the berries alone could be twenty dollars per liter of brandy.

Rum

The federal Standards of Identity for rum are fairly simple and straightforward. Rum is an alcoholic distillate from the fermented juice of sugarcane, sugarcane syrup, sugarcane molasses, or other sugarcane by-products, produced at less than 190 proof in such manner that the distillate possesses the taste, aroma, and characteristics generally attributed to rum, and bottled at not less than 80 proof; it also includes mixtures solely of such distillates.

The quality factors for rum are the same as for the other distilled beverages examined. As the Standards of Identity state, there are several types of sugarcane products that may be used, and this is a critical factor. Others include the yeasts used for fermentation, the distillation system, the aging time and materials, and the skill of blending.

Sugarcane Juice. This is simply the juice extracted by milling the sugarcane. It is not in widespread use in large scale commercial rum making.

Sugarcane Syrup. The syrup is obtained by evaporating water from the cane juice to produce a brown, viscous liquid, which has a higher sugar content than does the juice.

Molasses. Also called blackstrap molasses, it is a residue of sugar production and the most commonly used fermentation material. The sugar in the syrup is crystallized and separated from the other solids by centrifuging it at high speed. A typical composition of Puerto Rican blackstrap molasses shows about 60 percent sugar, but this can vary depending on the quality of the sugarcane, the degree of evaporation, and the efficiency of the processing.

Other By-Products. Skimmings and *dunder* are also used as fermentable materials. Skimmings are the froth that is removed from the heating pans following lime treatment of the cane juice to remove impurities. Dunder is a residue from previous distillations, which is allowed to undergo a bacterial fermentation. In a technique similar to that used to make sour mash bourbon, the dunder is used to begin new alcoholic fermentations. Like sour mash, it helps control the pH and buffers the fermentation as well as aids in flavor development.

Choice of Yeasts. Some rums are made using only natural fermentation— that is, the yeasts available in the environment are the only ones used to begin the fermentation. This is often termed a *wild* or *spontaneous* fermentation and can last from five to ten or more days, depending on the availability of free yeast spores and temperature conditions. Other rums are fermented using selected and cultured strains of yeast, and the fermentation lasts from two to four days. The longer, slower natural fermentation permits development of more congeners, and this affects the character of the distilled product.

Distillation Systems. Both pot stills and multicolumn continuous distillation systems, such as the Coffey still, are used for rum production (Fig. 6–9). With pot stills, the familiar double-distillation technique is used, and only the middle portion of the second distillation becomes rum. As with other products, the continuous distillation systems result in higher proofs and lighter spirits.

Rum is produced throughout the Caribbean Islands, and while there are many types, they can be characterized simply as either light bodied or full bodied. The differences between the two types have to do mostly with the method of fermentation and the system of distillation used.

Light Rums. The best known of the light rums are the ones from Puerto Rico. Light rums are also made in the Virgin Islands, Cuba, the Dominican

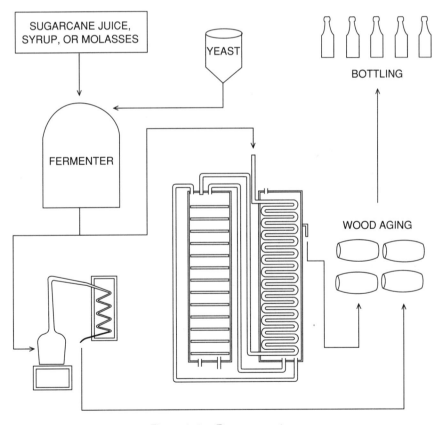

Figure 6–9. Rum processing.

Republic, Venezuela, and Mexico. In fact, Cuba was the original home of Bacardi, which is now, by a wide margin, the largest-selling spirit brand in the world and in the United States. A light-bodied rum is made by fermenting molasses with specially selected strains of yeast and distilling in continuous stills over a range of 160 to 180 proof.

Maturing is done in previously used cooperage, which may or may not have been charred. Puerto Rican law requires a minimum of one year in wood, and it may be aged longer. An age statement is permitted on the label but is not required. The less time spent in wood, the lighter and more neutral the product. Fuller and more distinctive rums result from increased wood aging.

The younger rums, those with the lightest taste and body, are marketed as white or silver. Rums that are deeper colored and more highly flavored are aged a minimum of three years and are called gold or amber. Caramel is used to adjust the color and make it uniform.

Rums are characteristically dry tasting, with a slight molasses flavor. The gold style is more mellow and distinctively flavored, compared to the white, but it too is considered a light alcoholic beverage—in body, not calories.

Full-Bodied Rums. The best-known examples of the full-bodied style are the Jamaican rums. They are fermented from molasses augmented by the addition of dunder, and natural yeast spores are used. The fermented liquor is double-distilled in pot stills at from 140 to 160 proof. Maturation is done in large oak casks called *puncheons*. These rums require more aging than the light styles, because of their full body and greater congener content. The typical dark color is not due to wood, however, but is controlled by the amount of caramel added.

A traditional Jamaican rum is very dark, full bodied and pungent tasting, and it has a buttery molasses aroma and flavor. It is more popular in Great Britain than in the United States, where the trend for several years has been toward the lighter beverages.

Other Styles. In between the extremes of the Puerto Rican light style and the Jamaican heavy style are the rums from Haiti, Martinique, Guyana in South America, and Batavia, or Djakarta, on the island of Java in Indonesia. In Haiti and Martinique, fermentation is carried out with sugarcane juice, not molasses, and the resulting liquor is pot-distilled. They are medium to full bodied, the best are full of flavor, and they can develop a fine, mellow bouquet.

In Guyana, along the Demerara River, molasses is distilled using Coffey stills. Demeraran rum is much darker than even Jamaican, but it is lighter bodied and not so pungent tasting. It is famous, or perhaps infamous, for bottling at up to 151 proof, a practice that has been adopted by rum producers in other countries.

Arak, or arrack, is a rum distilled from molasses in the Indonesian capital, aged there for some three to four years, and then sent to the Netherlands for an additional four to six years' aging. Although it has some brandy characteristics, it is used much like any other rum.

New England rum as a type is obsolete and, since 1968, no longer listed in the federal Standards of Identity, but it has a long history in the United States. Distilling of imported molasses into rum was the largest manufacturing industry in the American colonies prior to the Revolution. New England rum was also one point of an unsavory trading triangle. The rum was used to purchase slaves in Africa, the slaves were exchanged for molasses in the West Indies, and the molasses then underwent distillation into more rum in New England.

There is also a product, produced both in Puerto Rico and Jamaica, called liqueur rum. This is aged in wood for long periods, up to fifteen years, and has some of the characteristics of fine brandies.

Tequila

Tequila is a distinct product of Mexico. According to the federal Standards of Identity, Tequila is an alcoholic distillate from a fermented mash derived principally from the *Agave tequilana Weber* ("blue" variety), with or without additional fermentable substances, distilled in such manner that the distillate possesses the taste, aroma, and characteristics generally attributed to tequila and bottled at not less than 80 proof; it also includes mixtures solely of such distillates (Fig. 6–10).

When the blue agave plant reaches maturity, at about ten to twelve years old, the *pineapple*, or base, is removed. This pineapple may weigh up to 150 pounds, and it contains a sweet sap that is suitable for fermentation. The pineapple is first steamed for several hours in masonry ovens to extract the juice. Additional juice is obtained by shredding and rolling the mescal heads. Fermentation is started by adding some must from a previous fermentation. Following fermentation, which takes about two and one-half days, the alcoholic liquor is double-distilled in copper pot stills at 104 to 106 proof.

Tequila is not necessarily aged; often it is bottled when it leaves the still. In such a case it is labeled white tequila. If any wood aging is done, it is in used whisky casks, imported from the United States, and the spirit takes up a little gold in the color and becomes somewhat more mellow. This is designated as gold tequila. The aging of gold tequila is not regulated by the Mexican government, but it does recognize an *anejo*, aged one year, and a *muy anejo*, aged as much as four years.

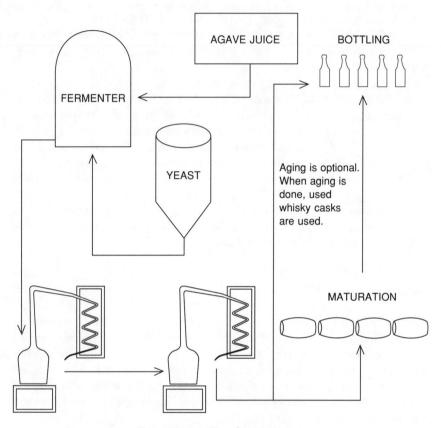

Figure 6–10. Tequila processing.

Tequila consumption in the United States increased rapidly during the 1970s but slowed in the 1980s. It accounts for a little over 2 percent of the U.S. market, ahead of only Irish whiskey and cocktails, or mixed drinks. Only two brands, José Cuervo and Montezuma, are listed among the 100 top-selling spirit brands in the United States.

Vodka

Vodka is defined as neutral spirits that are so distilled, or so treated after distillation with charcoal or other materials, as to be without distinctive character, aroma, taste, or color. Neutral spirits are distilled spirits produced from any material at or above 190 proof. In the United States, neutral spirits are generally distilled from a mash of grain and are called neutral grain spirits. Vodka is not aged, and it is bottled at proofs ranging from 80 to 100 (Fig. 6–11).

The objective with vodka processing is to remove as many of the congeners as possible so as to render the finished product free from any taste, aroma, or flavor. Neutral spirits, by definition, have little character because they are distilled at very high proofs and contain only minute traces of fusel oils, aldehydes, esters, acids, or solids. Vodka processing is intended to remove these remaining compounds.

Charcoal has been found to be an effective purifying agent and is used in two ways. With one, the newly distilled spirit is filtered through charcoal. A minimum of 1.5 pounds of charcoal per gallon of spirits is required, and contact time must be at least eight hours. The other method calls for mixing the charcoal and spirits and agitating them for eight hours or more. A minimum of 6 pounds of charcoal per 100 gallons of spirits must be used. Because the distilling industry is capable of devising other, equally effective methods, the government also permits vodka to be made with any other method that results in a product without distinctive character, taste, or aroma.

Vodka and gin are similar in that both are produced from neutral spirits. The difference between the two is that gin is processed to add specific flavors and aromas, while vodka is processed to remove any elements that might provide flavor or aroma.

Although vodka is produced in the United States entirely from grains, it is possible to make it from any fermentable material, because the objective is to produce a neutral product. The common belief is that vodka traditionally was made from potatoes. Some probably was, but Russia and Poland, where it originated, are mostly grain countries, and it is likely that most Russian and Polish vodkas were—and continue to be—grain based.

Eastern Europeans, especially the Poles and Russians, have always been fond of vodkas that are additionally flavored. A Polish specialty is Zubrówka, a vodka flavored with a grass found only in the forests of eastern Poland. Because these grasslands are inhabited by a particular species of bison, the beverage is referred to as buffalo grass vodka. The Soviet Union produces a pepper vodka called Pertsovka, which is flavored with an infusion of cayenne and other ingredients. It has a spicy aroma and a fiery hot, lingering taste.

Vodka has had an amazing success in the United States since World War II. It was not until the early 1950s that vodka sales were even reported separately in the trade statistics, but by 1975 they made up the single largest sales category. By the mid-1980s, vodka accounted for nearly 23 percent of all distilled spirits sales in the United States, nearly as much as the combined total of bourbon and Canadian whiskies, the next two highest categories.

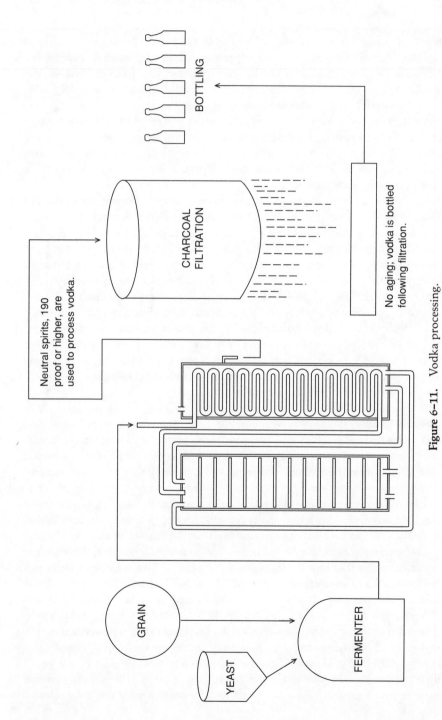

Figure 6-11. Vodka processing.

Neutral spirits, 190 proof or higher, are used to process vodka.

CHARCOAL FILTRATION

BOTTLING

No aging; vodka is bottled following filtration.

GRAIN

YEAST

FERMENTER

The reasons for this are vodka's neutrality, hence its mixability, and the consumer trend toward lighter beverages. Americans, by a wide margin, top the world in consumption of fruit juices and soft drinks, and vodka mixes exceptionally well with these beverages, without obscuring their basic character as other spirits do.

Gin

Gin is a product obtained by original distillation from mash, or by redistillation of distilled spirits, or by mixing neutral spirits, with or over juniper berries and other aromatics, or with or over extracts derived from infusions, percolations, or maceration of such materials, and it includes mixtures of gin and neutral spirits. It derives its main characteristic flavor from juniper berries and is bottled at not less than 80 proof. Gin produced exclusively by original distillation or by redistillation may be designated further as distilled. Dry gin (London Dry gin), Jenever gin (Hollands), and Old Tom Gin (Tom gin) are types of gin known under such designations.

As the Standards of Identity make clear, gin is a complex product and more of a manufactured product than other alcoholic beverages. There are two basic types produced: Dutch (or Hollands, Jenever, Schiedam) gin and Dry (English or American) gin.

Dutch Gin, or Hollands. Dutch gin is made by fermenting a grain mixture (barley malt, corn, and rye) into a beer and then distilling and redistilling it in a pot still. The product of this process, called *malt wine*, is drawn off at a very low proof: 100 to 110. The malt wine is then pot-distilled with juniper berries and other botanicals at less than 100 proof. The primary flavoring agent is juniper berries; there is less reliance on the use of other botanicals than in the United States or England. The resulting beverage, because of the low distillation proofs, is much more full bodied and distinctive than the dry gins, and they have a malt character in both the aroma and the flavor. Because of this, they do not lend themselves to mixing and are best consumed neat, or straight.

Dutch gin is not aged, although there are no regulations prohibiting it. Any coloration in Dutch gin is the result of slight additions of caramel coloring, not of wood.

Dry Gin (English and American). The use of the term *dry* simply means that the gin is not sweet; there is no difference in this regard among products labeled London dry, very dry, extra dry, and so forth. The name London dry has lost its original geographical significance and is now used by manufacturers in many countries, including the United States.

American gin is allowed to be made either by distillation or by compounding (Fig. 6–12). Compounded gin is produced by mixing distilled neutral spirits

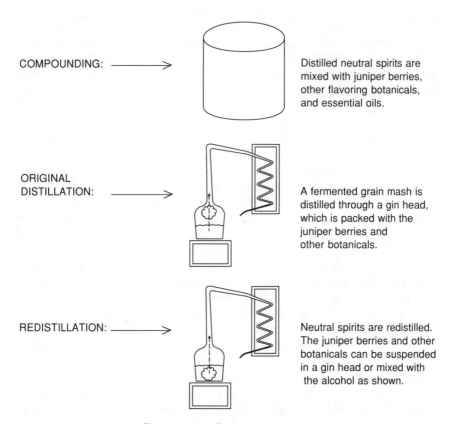

COMPOUNDING: ⟶   Distilled neutral spirits are mixed with juniper berries, other flavoring botanicals, and essential oils.

ORIGINAL DISTILLATION: ⟶   A fermented grain mash is distilled through a gin head, which is packed with the juniper berries and other botanicals.

REDISTILLATION: ⟶   Neutral spirits are redistilled. The juniper berries and other botanicals can be suspended in a gin head or mixed with the alcohol as shown.

Figure 6–12. Dry gin processing.

with essential oils or extracts of the various botanicals, primarily juniper berries. The objective is to add distinctive aromatic and flavor character to the essentially characterless spirit. This method does not have to be identified on the label; it is labeled simply as dry gin (or extra dry, or very dry).

Gins labeled as distilled can be produced by one of two methods: original distillation or redistillation. In original distillation, a fermented mash is distilled and the vapors pass through an apparatus called a *gin head*, which is packed with the botanicals. Flavors and aromas are picked up by the vapors and remain when condensed back into a liquid. Redistilled gin is made by redistilling neutral spirits. In this method, the botanicals may be suspended in a gin head or mixed in with the alcohol to be redistilled.

Gin quality depends on the neutrality of the spirits (freedom from flavors and odors) and on the quality of the botanicals. In addition to juniper berries, the botanicals used are angelica root, anise, coriander, caraway seeds, licorice, cardamom, cassia bark, orris root, bitter almonds, and lime, lemon, and orange peels. Each producer has his or her own character and quality standards and is free to vary the use and proportion of the botanicals in any way desired. Because the nature of the ingredients varies from season to season, sophisticated producers prepare their formulas on the basis of the essential oil content of the raw materials.

English gin is produced by distilling a grain mash at from 180 to 188 proof, slightly lower than with American gins. As with the American gins, the botanicals are either suspended above the spirit in the still or mixed with the spirits during distillation. It is possible to conduct the distillation under reduced pressure and, with the lower temperatures, avoid thermal decomposition of the flavors. Because of the slightly lower distillation proof, English gins may have a little more character compared to the American ones.

When it comes from the gin still and has had its proof reduced to bottling strength, gin is ready to drink and does not require aging. Storage until bottling is accomplished in stainless steel or glass-lined tanks. Although producers in the United States are permitted to age in wood if they desire, they are prohibited from placing any age statements on the label. Gin that has been stored in wood for a short period acquires a pale, golden color and can be labeled golden gin.

Flavored gins may be made by adding specific flavors such as lemon, pineapple, orange, and mint, but the flavor has to be identified on the label. Such products are sweet, as are gins labeled Old Tom. Another product with the name gin on it is *sloe gin*, which is not a gin at all; it is a cordial, and it will be discussed in the chapter on cordials and liqueurs.

STORAGE STANDARDS

Storage requirements for distilled spirits are rather simple: in most establishments the only requirement is that the products be secured from theft and pilferage. With other types of products stored in foodservice and beverage operations, protection from quality deterioration and contamination or spoilage is at least as important as security, often more so. However, distilled spirits are basically inert products; the alcoholic content ensures that they cannot become contaminated, nor will they deteriorate in quality over time or if stored improperly. There are a few exceptions to this, but they apply mostly to products that have been opened. Very mature brandies, Cognac and Armagnac, for example, are necessarily more delicate than most spirits and tend to lose their unique character after being opened. Until they are opened, however, they are as stable as any of the other types of products.

Because of their high levels of alcohol, distilled spirits should be stored upright, unlike wines, which are stored on their sides so that the corks can remain moist, preventing the entry of air. Some spirits are also corked, and lengthy exposure to liquids containing high percentages of alcohol can result in deterioration of the cork. Spirits that are sealed with a screw-type closure can be stored upright or on their sides, but upright storage is also far more efficient in terms of space requirements, shelving design, and ease of access.

Other than ensuring that the storage area is secure, the normal rules of storage do not apply. Time and temperature considerations are not important. Spirits change and mature only in wood, not in the bottle. A wine made in 1975 is eleven years old in 1986, while an eight-year-old bourbon bottled in 1975 will still be eight years old in 1986. Temperatures do not matter either, as long as they are reasonable. Even in an area such as Las Vegas, where the summertime temperatures can get as high as 115° F, spirits would not be harmed in an uncooled storage area. This is not true of most other alcoholic beverages, particularly wines and beers. Spirits also do not have any specific ventilation requirements; there is no need to have any particular number of air changes per hour in the storage room.

However, spirits must be held in a secure area. Other than cash, distilled beverages are probably more desirable to thieves than anything else in a food and beverage operation, and it must be assumed that if they are readily accessible, they will disappear, probably sooner rather than later. A secure area is one that cannot be easily entered by unauthorized individuals and that has access limited to as few persons as possible. It is also recommended that the number of times authorized personnel have to use it be limited. In a well-run beverage operation, it is possible to reduce these occasions to a few deliveries per week and the daily issue to the bar or bars.

It is also quite feasible to maintain a *perpetual inventory* over the liquor storeroom. This is a running account that shows the stock on hand at any given time (Fig. 6–13). Once the beginning inventory is known, the procedure is to post all deliveries to the perpetual form. The delivery invoices are used for this purpose. The only authorization for removing any bottles from the storeroom should be written requisitions generated by the bar, and these are also posted to the perpetual. If these postings are done properly, the perpetual will show accurately how many bottles of each of the various brands should be present at any time. It is then a simple matter to spot-check the actual counts whenever a delivery is being stored or an issue made. An accurate perpetual inventory also simplifies ordering, because a physical inventory may then be unnecessary.

SERVICE STANDARDS

Distilled spirits are the most versatile of all alcoholic beverages in terms of service. Spirits can be taken neat, without being mixed with anything else, but

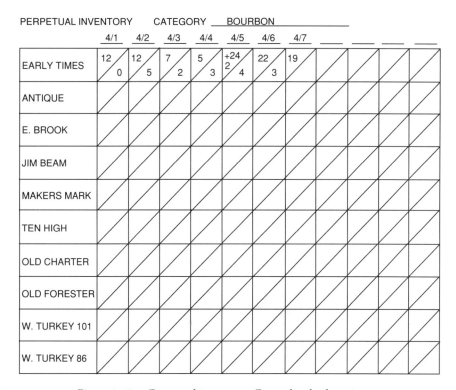

PERPETUAL INVENTORY   CATEGORY ___BOURBON_____

	4/1	4/2	4/3	4/4	4/5	4/6	4/7				
EARLY TIMES	12 / 0	12 / 5	7 / 2	5 / 3	+24 2 / 4	22 / 3	19				
ANTIQUE											
E. BROOK											
JIM BEAM											
MAKERS MARK											
TEN HIGH											
OLD CHARTER											
OLD FORESTER											
W. TURKEY 101											
W. TURKEY 86											

Figure 6–13.   Perpetual inventory: Example of a form in use.

they are typically used with one or more additional ingredients. They are mixed, combined, shaken, and blended with a range of ingredients that is limited only by the imagination. Just a few examples are water, ice, fruit juices, vegetable juices, milk, cream, ice cream, soft drinks, cordials, wines, fruits, eggs, and condiments such as tabasco sauce, bitters, and Worcester-shire sauce. Spirits are also frequently mixed with other spirits. The potential drink combinations are vast, and new ones are constantly being developed.

Drinks made with distilled spirits also rely a great deal on food garnishes. Flowers, fruits, herbs, vegetables, and condiments such as olives and pickled onions are several examples of the foods used. Spirits are unique in the variety of ways in which they are served; wines, beers, and, to a large extent, cordials and liqueurs are used mostly by themselves.

Spirits and drinks prepared with spirits are not generally thought of as beverages to be used to accompany meals, as are wines and beers. One of their traditional uses was as an aperitif, a before-dinner drink, but during the 1970s, they lost a considerable amount of this business to wines.

When mixed, distilled spirits are most likely to be used as social beverages, but even this usage has been eroded by increasing wine consumption during periods other than mealtimes. One area that seems not to be affected by the switch to wines and lighter beverages is the after-dinner drink market. Spirits that lend themselves best to being used in this manner are the brandies: both the wood-aged Cognacs and Armagnacs and the fruit brandies such as kirsch and framboise. A fine, well-aged, single-malt Scotch is also suitable for after dinner, as are some of the more mature wood-aged rums. There are dessert wines, but they have been steadily losing their once-impressive share of the wine market. Cordials and liqueurs, on the other hand, do very well as after-dinner drinks.

Because spirits are used in a greater variety of ways than other types of alcoholic beverages, it follows that they would be served in a greater variety of glassware. The better Cognacs and Armagnacs are best served in snifters, while the small, stemmed pony or cordial glass is suitable for lighter brandies and the unaged fruit brandies. There are also rocks glasses, cocktail glasses, old-fashioned glasses, highball glasses, collins glasses, zombie glasses, hurricane glasses, sour glasses, margarita glasses, and, of course, shot glasses. These are only the traditional glass styles; the companies that manufacture glassware are constantly developing new styles for specialty drinks. All of these, particularly the traditional styles, are available in a wide range of sizes, which further complicates glassware selection, purchasing, storage, handling, and use.

NUTRITIONAL STANDARDS

The process of distillation removes any nutrients that may have been present in the base ingredients. All that remains are the congeners, ethyl alcohol, and water. Due to the high levels of alcohol, there is energy value in the form of calories, but no food value beyond that. Although spirits are not regarded as nutritious, many medical authorities believe they have some physiological and psychological benefits when consumed in moderation. There have been studies that indicate moderate consumption of alcohol can actually be beneficial to people with heart disease and can, in general, reduce the risk of heart attacks.

CONSUMPTION PATTERNS AND TRENDS

Distilled spirits consumption in the United States, after many years of continuous increases, slowed in the late 1970s and began declining in the 1980s. The period from 1960 to 1970 showed an average annual compound growth rate of 4.9 percent. From 1970 to 1980, the statistics still indicated an increase in consumption, but the rate of increase dropped to 2.8 percent. Beginning in the early 1980s, total consumption actually began to drop from year to year. *Impact*, the alcoholic beverage industry newsletter, expects this trend to continue through the end of the century.

Although this outlook is rather bleak, the picture looks quite a bit better—or, in some cases—within the individual spirit categories. The whisky category is suffering in general. Sales peaked in 1970 and have declined ever since. Whisky sales in 2000 are projected to be only a little over half of what they were in 1960. This loss of popularity is due mostly to the American whiskies: bourbon and American blended whisky. Scotch and Canadian whiskies performed strongly, and by 1984 Canadian whisky had the largest share of the market in the whisky category. Canadian whiskies are expected to maintain their market dominance, and Scotch is projected to attain parity with bourbon in the 1990s.

The picture for white goods—vodka, gin, tequila, and rum—is much brighter. Overall consumption rose rapidly through the 1960s, 1970s, and early 1980s, and although it leveled off in the mid-1980s, predictions are that sales will remain steady through the end of the century. No growth is expected, but in the battered spirits industry, sales stability is very welcome. Among the white goods, gin is a remarkably consistent performer. Its share of market, actual and projected from 1960 to 2000, is in the 8 to 10 percent range.

Tequila has maintained a small but steady share of the market since its rise to prominence in the 1970s. Both sales and market share are expected to increase slightly in the future.

Vodka and rum are the stars of the distilled spirits market. By the mid-1970s, vodka was the highest-selling single-spirit category, and it is expected to maintain this position easily. By the year 2000, its market share is projected to be two and one-third times that of the next highest spirits categories, Canadian whiskies and rums. Rum literally came from nowhere in the 1970s to post dramatic gains until the mid-1980s. Although sales performance flattened at that time, the prediction for rum consumption is that it will probably increase slightly over the next fifteen to twenty years. In the face of declining overall consumption, this is considered a strong performance.

Another winner in the spirits market is the brandy category. Brandies accounted for only 3 million cases in 1960 but by 1985 were pushing 10 million. Brandies are projected not only to maintain sales in the coming years, but actually to increase a little, thereby gaining an improved share of a declining market.

The other two categories that, for statistical purposes, are considered part of the distilled spirits market are cordials and liqueurs, and cocktails, or mixed drinks. The cordials market is discussed in Chapter Seven. The cocktails or mixed drink category has been a small but consistent part of the spirits industry since the late 1970s. Case sales rose to some 4 million by 1980, and the expectation is that they will rise a little above that level and gain a slightly increased share of the market, perhaps 4 percent, by the year 2000. Even so, this would tie them with tequila as the second-lowest category, only marginally ahead of blended whisky at 3 percent.

SUGGESTED READINGS

Barty-King, H. and A. Massel. *Rum, Yesterday and Today*. London: W. Heinemann Ltd., 1983.

Bell, D. A. *The Spirits of Hospitality*. East Lansing, Mich.: The Educational Institute/American Hotel & Motel Association, 1976.

Grossman, H. J., *Grossman's Guide to Wines, Beers & Spirits*. 6th rev. ed., H. Lembeck. New York: Charles Scribner's Sons, 1977.

Hannum, H., R. S. Blumberg. *Brandies & Liqueurs of the World*. Garden City, N.Y.: Doubleday & Co., 1976.

The Impact American Distilled Spirits Market Review and Forecast. New York: M. Shanken Communications, Inc., 1985.

Johnson, H. *The World Atlas of Wine*. New York: Simon & Schuster, 1971.

Katsigris, C. and M. Porter. *The Bar & Beverage Book*. New York: J. Wiley & Sons, 1983.

Knowing Alcoholic Beverages. Liquor Store Magazine. New York: Jobson Publishing Corp., 1978.

Lichine, A. *Alexis Lichine's New Encyclopedia of Wines & Spirits*. New York: Alfred Knopf, 1982.

Packowski, G. W. *Beverage Spirits, Distilled*. Kirk-Othmer Encyclopedia of Chemical Technology. New York: J. Wiley & Sons, 1978.

Ray, C. *Cognac*. New York: Stein & Day, 1973.

CHAPTER SEVEN

CORDIALS & LIQUEURS

DEFINITION OF CORDIALS AND LIQUEURS

The terms *cordial* and *liqueur* can be used interchangeably, because both refer to the same type of product. There is no legal difference between them, but in practice, cordial is often used with American products and liqueur with European ones. For the most part, liqueur will be used here, except when referring specifically to an American brand or product line.

The federal Standards of Identity define cordials and liqueurs as products obtained by mixing or redistilling distilled spirits with or over fruits, plants, or pure juices therefrom, or other natural flavoring materials, or with extracts derived from infusions, percolation, or maceration of such materials, and containing sugar, dextrose, or levulose, or a combination thereof, in an amount not less than 2.5 percent by weight of the finished product. The Standards of Identity prohibit use of the terms *distilled* or *compound* when describing or labeling the product.

The production of liqueurs is superficially simple and straightforward, but the difficulty in skillfully extracting flavors, odors, and colors from vegetable materials should not be underestimated. They can be very complex products, because of the incredible diversity of ingredients that are often used.

PRODUCTION STANDARDS

There are three methods of flavor, odor, and color extraction: *percolation*, *maceration*, and *distillation*. The choice of method depends mostly on the nature of the ingredients used. Two of the extraction techniques proceed at cold (or cooler) temperatures; the third method involves heat. The cold methods take much longer to complete but generally must be used with ingredients whose flavoring components are delicate and subject to damage by heat. Soft fruits (such as strawberries and raspberries), stone fruits (such as cherries and apricots), and foods such as coffee and vanilla beans typically undergo cold extraction, while most plants, herbs, peels, and seeds are extracted under heat. Percolation and maceration do not involve heat; distillation does.

Percolation and maceration can be likened to the making of coffee and tea, respectively. With percolation, as in coffee making, the materials from which the flavors are to be extracted are suspended above the liquid, in this case a spirit (Fig. 7–1). The spirit is pumped up and sprayed over the flavoring

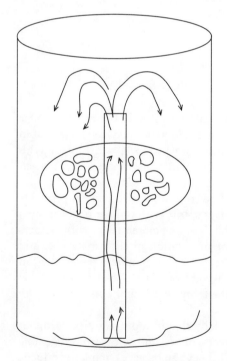

The flavoring ingredients are suspended above the spirit. The spirit is pumped up and sprayed over the flavoring ingredients, then allowed to seep down through them.

Figure 7–1.   Cordial processing: Percolation.

ingredients, then allowed to seep down through them. This procedure is repeated continuously until all or most of the desired constituents are removed, a process that can take several months.

Maceration, on the other hand, is similar to the technique used in the preparation of tea (Fig. 7–2). The materials to be extracted are placed in the liquid and allowed to steep, or soak, for a considerable time. When the stone fruits, such as peaches, apricots, and cherries, are treated in this way, oils may be extracted from the pits, or seeds, of the fruit. This accounts for the slight bitter almond character that is sometimes perceived in these liqueurs. The steeping liquid in maceration is normally alcohol, but water may be used, in which case the process is called *infusion*.

With both percolation and maceration, following the separation of the spirit from the ingredients, the spirit-soaked ingredients may be distilled to obtain whatever flavor and odor components remain. This distillate is added to the macerated or percolated spirit before the finishing process.

The hot extraction method is distillation, or redistillation in the case of an already distilled spirit (Fig. 7–3). Some very delicate ingredients, such as mint, may be distilled in water, perhaps even under a vacuum to reduce the distillation temperature. Normally, though, the ingredients are infused in a spirit, and the spirit is redistilled. Pot stills are used, and only the middle distillate is retained; the heads and tailings are either discarded or, as in Cognac, redistilled.

Materials to be extracted are placed in high-proof alcohol and allowed to steep for a considerable period.

Figure 7–2.   Cordial processing: Maceration.

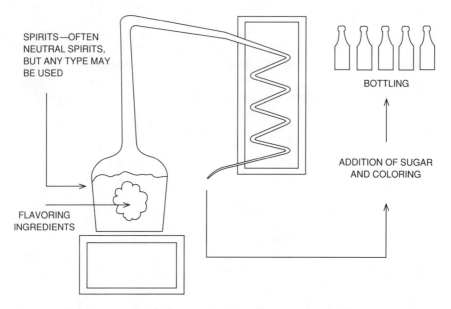

SPIRITS—OFTEN
NEUTRAL SPIRITS,
BUT ANY TYPE MAY
BE USED

BOTTLING

ADDITION OF SUGAR
AND COLORING

FLAVORING
INGREDIENTS

Figure 7–3.   Cordial processing: Distillation and redistillation.

COMPONENTS OF CORDIALS AND LIQUEURS
Sugars

One factor that differentiates liqueurs from other spirits is that legally they must contain sugar, and they often have appreciable amounts of it. French liqueurs must contain at least 20 percent. U.S. law requires a minimum of 2.5 percent, but most contain substantially more than that, up to as much as 35 percent. The Standards of Identity permit products that contain less than 10 percent by weight to be designated as dry. With wines, this range is perceived as fairly to very sweet, but with cordials and liqueurs, the perception of sweetness at that level is not so pronounced.

The sweetening agents permitted are sugar, dextrose, and levulose, enabling the manufacturer to use a wide variety of products. Sugar, either beet or cane, in the form of a simple syrup is the most common sweetening material, although honey, maple syrup, and corn syrup are also used.

The liqueurs designated as creme generally have the highest sugar content. The term *creme*, which is French for "cream," denotes the smooth creamy or syrupy texture that results from the sugar. In France, a liqueur labeled creme must contain at least 40 percent sugar. The sugar content of cremes can be illustrated by the after-dinner drink called pousse-café. This is made by pouring several cordials of varying colors in a glass so that they *layer,* or float on one another. A chart showing each cordial's specific gravity, a measurement of weight, is necessary to prepare this specialty drink, and the cremes are usually at the top of these charts. Having the most sugar, they are the heaviest.

Flavorings

A vast array of ingredients are used to flavor liqueurs and provide them with a nearly limitless range of sensory characteristics. Few products rely on only one ingredient, or even a few, and some are so complex that they require fifty or more. Some of the more common ingredients are apricots, apricot stones (for the almond flavor in amaretto), anise, blackberries, cherries, coffee beans, cacao beans, black currants, mint, vanilla beans, oranges and orange peels, caraway seeds, mandarins (tangerines), licorice, strawberries, peaches, almonds, and raspberries. These are also the ingredients that are most likely to provide the dominant tastes.

It would not be easy to provide a complete list of all the other ingredients that can be used, but the following ones also deserve mention: angelica roots and flowers, cloves, cinnamon, coriander, saffron, thyme, rose hips and petals, tea, nutmeg, juniper berries, lemon peels, honey (used for flavoring as well as sweetening), cumin, ginger roots, sage, rosemary, honeydew melons, sloe berries, plums, hazelnuts, macadamia nuts, allspice, cranberries, blueberries, bananas, pineapples, and passion fruit.

Spirit Base

The most common spirit base used in liqueurs is neutral spirits, but several products, many of them world famous, use specific distilled products. In the whisky category, bourbon, rye, and Irish, Canadian, and Scotch whiskies all find their way into certain products and provide a distinctiveness characteristic of that whisky. Brandies are widely used, and a few manufacturers even use Cognac as the spirit base. Of the other spirit categories, rum seems to be the only one used to provide the spirit base for true cordials and liqueurs. There is also a product category called *spirit liqueurs,* which are not really liqueurs in the sense that they have been described here. They are simply sweetened spirits, and they are called Scotch liqueur, gin liqueur, and so forth. Vodka and gin are sometimes also flavored with citrus, grape, cherry, or mint and sweetened enough to qualify for the cordial category.

Another liqueur component that has proved to be very popular in recent years is cream. Introduced in America through Bailey's Irish Cream, this drink is based on a technological breakthrough—that of developing a method of stabilizing mixtures of fresh cream and spirits. There are many such liqueurs on the market now, and their variety seems to be limited only by the spirits and liqueurs already available. Irish whiskey, Scotch whisky, Grand Marnier liqueur, amaretto liqueur, Myers Jamaican Rum, and many other drinks have been used as the spirit base for this new category. These liqueurs should not be confused with the crèmes, the very sweet liqueurs and cordials whose name refers to the sugar content. The designation of cream, on the other hand, indicates the use of fresh cream in the formulation.

PROOF STANDARDS

There are no proof requirements in the federal Standards of Identity, although France requires a minimum alcoholic content of 15 percent, or 30 proof. There is quite a broad range of proofs in cordials and liqueurs available in the United States, from 30 to 110 proof; the creams are the lowest. In general, cordials and liqueurs are bottled at lower alcoholic strengths than are distilled spirits.

CLASSIFICATION OF CORDIALS AND LIQUEURS

There are several ways to classify this category; one is according to the major types of flavoring ingredients. These are herbs and spices, seeds and plants, and fruits.

Herb and Spice Cordials and Liqueurs

Benedictine. The recipe for Benedictine, perhaps the best known of the French herbal liqueurs, is thought to date back to the early 1500s. Lost during the French Revolution, it was not rediscovered until 1863. The specific recipe is a carefully guarded secret, and only three people reportedly ever know the complete details. In fact, the distillery maintains a Hall of Counterfeits, displaying hundreds of failed imitations.

Benedictine is made from twenty-seven different herbs, plants, spices, and peels, which are either distilled or macerated with neutral spirits. Bottling is at 86 proof. In response to the consumer trend of mixing Benedictine with brandy, the firm brought out its own mixture, called B&B, which today accounts for the majority of Benedictine's sales in the United States. B&B is made by blending Benedictine with Cognac brandy and is bottled at the same proof: 86.

Chartreuse. Chartreuse is made from a secret blend of some 130 plants. It was originally developed by the Carthusian religious order but has been in secular hands since World War I, although both the formula and production remain under control of three Carthusian brothers. There are two Chartreuse liqueurs produced: green and yellow. Both have a spicy herb flavor that is difficult to describe because of the complexity of the ingredients. The yellow is bottled at 80 proof, the green at 110. Brandy and neutral spirits provide the spirit base.

Drambuie. This is one of the best known and appreciated liqueurs in the world. Like so many of the others, it has an ancient and interesting history. Drambuie is produced by the Mackinnon firm near Edinburgh from a recipe that dates back to 1746, when it was given to a Mackinnon ancestor by Prince Charles Edward Stuart—Bonnie Prince Charlie—in gratitude for hiding and protecting the prince after defeat in battle. The liqueur has been made commercially only since 1906, but it was made by the Mackinnon family for personal use prior to that. It is prepared from a secret blend of herbs, malt and grain whiskies, both well aged, and honey for sweetening. Drambuie is bottled at 80 proof.

Fior d'Alpi. Made in northern Italy, this is packaged with a twig in the bottle, upon which excess sugar crystallizes. Traditionally a real twig was used, but today it is likely to be made of plastic. The liqueur is fairly sweet and features herbal and mint flavors. Bottling proof is high, up to 92.

Galliano. Galliano dates from the late nineteenth century; it was named for Major Giuseppe Galliano, a hero of the Italo-Abyssinian war in what is now Ethiopia. It is made by preparing several different distillations of herbs and spices, which are then aged in stainless steel for a few months. These distinctively flavored and aromatic spirits are blended together with water and sugar and then colored. The character is that of anise and vanilla blended with various herbs. The color is bright gold, and it is bottled at 80 proof.

Glayva. Made in Scotland with a spirit base of straight grain whisky, Glayva is flavored with an essence of herbs and sweetened with honey. It is considered to be lighter than Drambuie and has some anise character.

Irish Mist. Irish whiskey provides the spirit base. The whiskey is aged about seven years and blended with honey and herbal extracts. It has the flavors of Irish whiskey, honey, and herbs, is not overly sweet, and is bottled at 80 proof.

Izarra. A Basque liqueur made in the style of Chartreuse, Izarra is bottled in two forms: green and yellow. It is flavored by distillates and macerations of local flowers from the Pyrenees, augmented by many other plant ingredients. The spirit base is composed of both neutral spirits and Armagnac. Green Izarra is bottled at 100 proof, yellow at 86 proof.

Jeremiah Weed. This is a gold-colored cordial that is made from bourbon and has a distinct bourbon flavor. It is bottled at 100 proof.

Lochan Ora. A Scotch whisky liqueur produced by the makers of the well-known premium Scotch, Chivas Regal, this drink, like Drambuie, has a Scotch, honey, and herb flavor and is gold colored. It is perhaps a little lighter, and it is bottled at 70 proof.

Strega. An Italian herbal liqueur, Strega has a more noticeable anise-vanilla character than do the French products. It is gold colored and bottled at 80 proof. Neutral spirits form the spirit base.

Yukon Jack. Made from Canadian whisky, this liqueur is light gold in color and has the characteristically light flavor of Canadian whisky. It is bottled both at 80 and 100 proof.

Seed and Plant Cordials and Liqueurs

Amaretto. An almond-flavored liqueur, amaretto is made by distilling apricot stones. Amaretto di Saranno is probably the best-known brand, but amaretto has become a generic liqueur produced by a wide variety of cordial firms. It is amber in color and is bottled at proofs ranging from 48 to 56.

Anisette. The flavor of anisette comes from aniseed, and the liquor has an anise-licorice character. Made from neutral spirits, it is usually bottled in a colorless form. The Marie Brizard firm of Bordeaux, France, has the best reputation for anisette, but it is now a generic liqueur and many brands are on the market. Bottling is done at from 40 to 60 proof.

Bailey's Irish Cream. The first of the cream liqueurs to hit the American market, it was one of the great marketing successes in distilled spirit and cordial history. There has been an enormous number of cream products introduced since then, but none has managed even to come close to displacing Bailey's dominant position in this category. Made from a blend of Irish whiskey and cream, it has a whiskey-chocolate flavor. The color can be described as coffee with milk. The bottling proof, like most of the creams, is quite low, 34 proof.

Cheri-Suisse. This liqueur is made in Switzerland and has a chocolate-cherry flavor. The spirit base is neutral alcohol, and the color is reddish-pink. Cheri-Suisse is bottled at 60 proof.

Chocolate Cordials. There are several cordials on the market that combine the flavor of chocolate with another primary flavor. Examples include mint, almond, cherry, orange, and raspberry. Both the Hiram Walker and Leroux companies have a variety of such products.

Crème de Cacao. Made by distilling cocoa beans with neutral alcohol, then blending the distillate with a maceration prepared from vanilla pods and neutral alcohol, this drink has a chocolate and vanilla character and is produced in both clear and brown colors. As with other crèmes, these are typically quite sweet. The most common use for crème de cacao is as a mixer;

its flavors blend well with a variety of products. This is one of the most basic generic liqueurs and is widely produced. Bottling proof ranges from 50 to 60.

Crème de Menthe. Possibly the most widely produced of the generic cordials, crème de menthe has a distinctive mint flavor, which is generally not blended with other flavors as is common in liqueur production. The color is either deep green or clear; there is no difference between the taste and aroma of the two. The clear is the natural color; the green is made by adding a coloring agent. Neutral spirits form the spirit base, and it is bottled at 60 proof.

Crème de Noyaux. This drink has an almond flavor, which is obtained from macerations and/or distillations of apricot or peach stones. It is a generic liqueur and is made by many firms in several ways: red, clear, and cream. The spirit base is neutral spirits, and bottling proof is from 50 to 60.

Creme de Vanille. This liqueur is flavored by vanilla beans; the beans from Mexico are regarded as the best. Vanilla is used more commonly as a complementary flavor in liqueurs, rather than as the primary or only one, as in this case. This product can be made in America with imitation vanillin flavor, without identifying it as such. It is bottled at 60 proof.

Kahlúa. A Mexican coffee liqueur, by a wide margin this is the largest-selling brand of liqueur in the United States. Produced from neutral spirits, it has a roasted coffee bean aroma and a very sweet coffee flavor. The bottling proof is 53.

Kümmel. Liqueurs prepared from caraway and cumin seeds have been made commercially since the end of the sixteenth century. Kümmel is prepared from neutral spirits and has a distinctive caraway flavor, sometimes with undertones of anise. It is clear and is bottled at 70 to 100 proof.

Ouzo. A Greek, anisette-type product made from brandy, it is clear and bottled at high proofs: 90 to 98.

Pasha. A coffee liqueur made in Turkey, this is bottled at 53 proof.

Peppermint Schnapps. A mint liqueur produced by many firms, it most closely resembles clear crème de menthe but is lighter and less sweet. A recent development in the American market has been the introduction of other schnapps flavors. Peach and apple schnapps have shown the most remarkable sales gains, but strawberry and others also have done well. Peppermint schnapps is prepared from neutral spirits and bottled at from 40 to 60 proof.

Pernod. A French liqueur, yellow-green in color, it has an intense anise-licorice flavor. It is made from neutral spirits and bottled at a fairly high proof: 90.

Sabra. A liqueur made in Israel from Jaffa oranges, chocolate, and neutral spirits, it is bottled at 60 proof.

Sambuca. Made from the elder bush, *Sambucus nigra*, its flavor is very much like that of aniseed, and the liqueur has a distinct licorice character. Neutral spirits are used, and it is clear in color and bottled at 40 to 84 proof.

Tia Maria. A coffee-flavored liqueur from Jamaica, it is made from rum and Jamaican coffee beans. Tia Maria is a little lighter and drier—less sweet—than Kahlua and, at 63 proof, is somewhat higher in alcohol.

Tuaca. Made in Italy from brandy, Tuaca has an eggnog-cocoa character, which comes from the small amount of milk used in the formulation. It is yellow-brown in color and bottled at 84 proof.

Vandermint. This is one of the most popular chocolate-mint liqueurs. It is made in the Netherlands from neutral spirits and has a predominant mint character. The color is that of dark brown chocolate, and it is bottled at 52 proof.

Fruit Cordials and Liqueurs

Apricot Liqueur. Both a generic and a branded liqueur, it may be called apricot cordial or liqueur, or known by a specific brand name such as Abricotine or Apry. Its flavor comes mainly from apricots, the color is orange-amber, and it is made from neutral spirits. The range is from 60 to 70 proof.

Blackberry Liqueur. Also referred to as blackberry cordial, its flavor comes primarily from blackberries but occasionally may have some raspberries or even wine blended in. The spirit base is usually neutral spirits, but when made as a flavored brandy, neutral brandy is used. Blackberry-flavored brandy is the most popular of the flavored brandies in the United States. It is bottled at 60 proof.

Cherry Liqueur. The flavor comes from black cherries, with neutral spirits or brandy used for the spirit base. It, too, is marketed either as a cordial, a liqueur, or a flavored brandy. The bottling is at 30 to 60 proof.

Cointreau. A triple sec liqueur, this is probably the most popular orange liqueur in the world. It is distinctively packaged in a square bottle and, like all triple secs, is clear in color. It is made from the peels of bitter and sweet oranges, along with other supporting ingredients. These are double-distilled with neutral alcohol in pot stills. Cointreau is bottled at 80 proof.

Cordial Médoc. This is produced in Bordeaux, France, and is unusual in that its spirit base is composed not only of neutral spirits, but of Cognac and Armagnac as well. It is dark amber in color, and the flavors are derived from the brandies and a blend of fruits. Bottling is at 80 proof.

Crème de Bananes (Banana Cordial). The banana flavor is an easy one to imitate, and many banana cordials may contain artificial flavoring, although its use must be stated on the label. Neutral spirits form the spirit base, and the cordial is given a yellow color. The intense aroma is of banana oil rather than fresh bananas. Bottling proof is from 50 to 60.

Crème de Cassis. A liqueur with a black currant flavor, it is bottled at low proofs: 30 to 50. Neutral spirits are used, and the color is red-black. Although normally classified with cordials and liqueurs, Crème de cassis does not qualify according to its method of manufacture. It is actually more of an alcoholic fruit juice, somewhat like a fortified fruit wine.

Cassis, or black currants, contain more vitamin C than any other fruit, and they have had medicinal properties ascribed to them for centuries. The formula for crème de cassis was developed in the mid-nineteenth century by a producer of liqueurs in Dijon, France, site of the famous vineyards of Burgundy. The liqueur became well known and production spread rapidly, until by 1873 there were some 750 acres planted on the high slopes of the Côte d'Or. Dijon became the most famous and important, although not the only, cassis-producing region in France.

The fruit is harvested in late June and July, crushed, and placed in oak vats with neutral spirits to macerate for several months. Because the fruit and its juice are delicate, the final blending in of sugar and water is not done until just before bottling. The alcoholic content must be at least 15 percent (30 proof), and it is typically bottled at 16 to 18 percent (32 to 36 proof). In some cases it may even be as high as 50 proof. Because of the relatively low alcohol level and the delicacy of the fruit, crème de cassis is more perishable than other liqueurs and should be consumed reasonably quickly. After it is opened, it should be finished within a few weeks.

This drink is very sweet, with an intense black currant flavor. The body is quite full, and this, along with the flavor intensity, should provide for a well-balanced beverage and reduce the perception of sweetness. The color is a very dark red-black.

The classic use of crème de cassis is in a drink called Kir, in which it is mixed with white wine in a glass. The traditional proportion is four parts wine to one part crème de cassis, the latter poured first, but it really depends on personal tastes. A popular variation is Kir Royale, the same drink made with a sparkling wine. In Burgundy, Kir goes by the unlikely name of *rince cochon,* which translates as "pig rinse."

Curaçao. The flavor of this drink comes primarily from the peel of the bitter orange. The most famous ones are grown on the island of Curaçao, in the southern Caribbean just off Venezuela. It is marketed in three ways: orange, clear, and blue. The latter, one of the more unusual cordial colors, is used to make the drink called a blue-tailed fly. It is bottled at 54 to 80 proof.

Forbidden Fruit. This is a grapefruit-flavored liqueur, which uses brandy as the spirit base, is red-brown in color, and is bottled at 64 proof.

Goldwasser. Originally made in Danzig, Germany, near the end of the sixteenth century and still considered a German specialty, Goldwasser is unusual in that it contains tiny particles of gold leaf. Its flavor is derived primarily from orange peel, with other ingredients—coriander is an important one—used to add complexity. Goldwasser is clear and bottled at 80 proof.

Grand Marnier. Along with Cointreau, the most famous of the orange liqueur brands. It is prepared with orange peels, using Cognac brandy as a base. The oranges used are the bitter variety from Haiti; no sweet oranges are used in the formula. The firm that makes Grand Marnier, Marnier-Lapostolle, also produces a limited amount of Cognac under its own name. Grand Marnier is light amber in color and is marketed at 80 proof.

Mandarin. A mandarin is a tangerine, and the liqueurs are brandy based, tangerine flavored, colored bright orange and bottled at 80 proof.

Maraschino. This drink is made from Dalmatian marasca cherries. The cherry stones, used in the distillation processes, give the liqueur a cherry-almond flavor. It is clear and made from neutral spirits. Proofs range from 60 to 80.

Midori. A Japanese liqueur made from the honeydew melon, it uses neutral spirits for a base. It is ice green in color and bottled at 46 proof.

Peach Liqueur. See apricot and cherry liqueurs.

Peter Heering. Probably the best known of the cherry liqueurs, it is made in Denmark and was formerly known in the United States as Cherry Heering. It is fairly low in alcohol—49 proof—and has an intense ripe cherry flavor. Neutral spirits and brandy are used, and the color is dark red.

Raspberry Liqueur. See apricot and cherry liqueurs.

Rock and Rye. An American cordial made from rye whisky and neutral spirits and flavored by fruit and whisky. It is gold-brown in color and made by a number of producers, at 60 to 70 proof.

Sloe Gin. As previously mentioned, this is a cordial, not a gin. The flavor comes from the sloe berry, a wild plum. Neutral spirits are the spirit base, and the cordial is red colored and bottled at 42 to 60 proof.

Southern Comfort. The most famous American whisky cordial, it is made from bourbon and flavored with fruits, primarily peaches. The color is gold, and it is made at two proof strengths: 80 and 100.

Strawberry Liqueur. See apricot and cherry liqueurs.

Triple Sec. Triple secs are basically white Curaçaos. They are made by nearly all cordial and liqueur manufacturers and come in proofs ranging from 60 to 80.

STORAGE STANDARDS

Most cordials and liqueurs, like distilled spirits, are basically inert products, and storage does not present many problems. Exceptions include products such as crème de cassis either from Burgundy or made in the Burgundian style. Due to the low alcoholic content and delicacy of the fruit, it is more perishable than other liqueurs and should not be stored too long. It is not necessary to hold it under refrigeration when unopened, but it should be stored in a cool area. After opening, it should be consumed fairly quickly, within a few weeks, and probably should be stored refrigerated.

Another exception consists of the creams. Due to the use of fresh cream in the formulas and the fairly low alcoholic content, about 34 proof, they are less stable than other cordials, and the storage time should be reduced. The manufacturers of such products claim a shelf life of over a year, so the beverage operator does not have to take extreme storage measures; they simply should watch the turnover of these products a little more carefully than the others'.

Other than these exceptions, cordials and liqueurs are quite stable. In general, they do not have as much alcohol as distilled spirits, but they have sugar in moderate to very high levels, and this acts as a preservative. Beyond the aspects of security and convenience, storage location is not important, nor is the storage time. Length of storage is dictated by the financial consideration of inventory turnover, not by constraints of the products themselves.

SERVICE STANDARDS

Cordials and liqueurs, like brandies, are usually served in specialized glassware. The most common is the cordial or pony glass, a small glass holding from one to one and one-half ounces, with or without a service line etched on it. Small brandy snifters, of from four to five ounces, are also appropriate for many cordials.

The spectacular pousse café, made of several layers of different colored and flavored cordials, is served in a tall, slender glass that is usually flared open at the top. The traditional way to prepare this drink is to add the cordials in reverse order of their specific gravity, laying each lighter one carefully on top of the next heavier one. If the specific gravity, a measure of the solids or sugar content, of two cordials is at least 0.1 percent apart, the liqueurs will layer without mixing—at least in theory, for this is a difficult drink to prepare. Bartenders assemble the succeeding layers by pouring the cordial slowly over the back of a small spoon or over a cork held in place at the end of an ice pick. The idea is to diffuse the liqueur as it is poured, so that it can gently layer itself on the previous one.

An ingenious device developed by the Bols Company reverses the order in which the liqueurs are poured. The lightest one is added first, through a small, funnel-like apparatus with an extensible tube. As the succeeding heavier cordials are added, they push up the lighter layer on the bottom. This process is continued until the drink is completed. A pousse café may be finished with a thin layer of warmed brandy on the top, which is then flamed. The companies that produce complete lines of cordials can supply a list of the specific gravities of their products. Armed with this, and a little imagination, a skilled bartender can prepare an interesting variety of drinks.

Cordials are typically used as after-dinner drinks, but they also have great value in the preparation of many mixed drinks, and their use in the kitchen should not be overlooked. Because of their sweetness, they are widely used in dessert preparations, in particular the fruit-based products. Crème de menthe parfaits, Grand Marnier soufflés, and fruitcakes are just a few examples of the literally limitless ways in which cordials can be used by creative cooks and chefs.

NUTRITIONAL STANDARDS

Cordials and liqueurs have long had a reputation for their medicinal properties, but in truth, they probably only supply energy in the form of calories. The caloric food value comes from the alcohol and sugar and is thus quite variable, because the alcohol ranges from about 15 to 55 percent and the sugar from the minimum legal requirement of 2.5 percent up to 30 percent or more. A specialized product such as the crème de cassis made in Burgundy may have additional food value due to the high vitamin C content of black currants and the unusual manufacturing process used. Due to the use of fresh cream in the cream cordial formulations, these drinks also may have some food value in the form of vitamins and minerals.

CONSUMPTION PATTERNS AND TRENDS

Cordials and liqueurs, traditionally an economically unimportant and nearly nonexistent sector of the total distilled spirits market, have become its brightest growth star. Through 1970, the category had such low sales that it was not even listed in the distilled spirit market tabulations. By 1975, however, it had grown to 13 million cases, and by the mid-1980s it was up to 18 million cases, or nearly 43 million gallons. The share of market performances show a similar trend. From nothing at all, it went to 7 percent in 1975 and was about 10 percent by the mid-1980s.

The growth in the 1984–85 period was particularly spectacular. One company, Dekuyper Cordials, on the strength of its innovative line of schnapps, increased its sales by 37.8 percent in 1984 and by a nearly unbelievable 94 percent in 1985. In 1984 it became the leading producer of cordials in the United States and moved into the twenty-first position on the list of the top 100 distilled spirit brands. The next year, it vaulted to the ninth position. In that year, two of its products, Original Peachtree Schnapps and Original Apple Barrel Schnapps, accounted for almost the entire sales increase of the top brands of distilled spirits.

The increase in sales is only part of the story. As evidence of the confidence the spirits producers have in the continued growth of the category, one only has to look at advertising expenditures and introductions of new products. According to *The Impact American Distilled Spirits Market Review and Forecast*, advertising expenditures for the category increased from $13 million in 1975 to over $60 million by the early 1980s. The same publication in 1985 listed sixty-five new products, and thirty-nine were cordials and liqueurs.

SUGGESTED READINGS

Bell, D. A. *The Spirits of Hospitality.* East Lansing, Mich.: The Educational Institute/American Hotel & Motel Association, 1976.

Grossman, H. J. *Grossman's Guide to Wines, Beers & Spirits.* 6th rev. ed., H. Lembeck. New York: Charles Scribner's Sons, 1977.

Hannum, H., and R. S. Blumberg. *Brandies & Liqueurs of the World.* Garden City, New York: Doubleday & Co, 1976.

The Impact American Distilled Spirits Market Review and Forecast. New York: M. Shanken Communications, 1985.

Katsigris, C., and M. Porter. *The Bar & Beverage Book.* New York: J. Wiley & Sons, 1983.

Knowing Alcoholic Beverages. Liquor Store Magazine. New York: Jobson Publishing Corp., 1978.

Lichine, A. *Alexis Lichine's New Encyclopedia of Wines & Spirits.* New York: Alfred Knopf, 1982.

CHAPTER EIGHT
ALCOHOLIC BEVERAGES & THE LAW

REGULATIONS
Federal

The alcoholic beverage industry may be the most regulated business in the United States. This applies to all aspects of the business: manufacture, importation, advertising, distribution, retail sale, and consumption of all alcoholic beverages. Because of its importance in the generation of revenues, taxing and tax collection are an especially important sector of alcohol regulation.

The federal agency in the United States that has jurisdiction over the alcoholic beverage industry and its practices is the Bureau of Alcohol, Tobacco, and Firearms (BATF), a division of the Department of the Treasury. The types of things the agency is responsible for include trade practices, revenue collection, and protection of the public.

State

Each of the states must meet federal standards, as a minimum, but they have the authority to go beyond federal requirements and regulations. For example, the BATF requirement for labeling a wine with the name of a state is that at least 75 percent of the wine must be from the named state, but California requires 100 percent of the wine to be from California before it can be so labeled. This is similar to many food regulations, in that federal standards must be met but any state may legislate more stringent requirements.

Alcoholic beverage regulations are very confusing and not at all consistent across the country. This is because most regulations are state and local; the federal government is primarily interested in the imposition and collection of taxes. The most basic way to look at state regulations is to divide them into *control states* and *licensed, or open,* states (Table 8–1). In a control state, the state itself is the source of alcoholic beverages; it is the sole purchaser of such products from the wineries, breweries, distillers, and importers. Some control states are also the sole source for retailers and consumers alike; both groups must purchase from state stores. In other control states, off-premise sellers, such as supermarkets and other retailers, are licensed to sell to consumers but must purchase their merchandise from the state.

Control states are monopolies; they have no competition and act accordingly. There are uniform prices within each of the control states, but the prices can vary widely from state to state, due to differing tax structures, markup, and discount policies. In Oregon, for example, the state taxes and the markup equal 94 percent of the product cost; in Mississippi, they total 33.9 percent.

The availability of products in control states is generally less than in licensed states. The state has nearly complete control over what products to stock and tends to stock only those alcoholic beverages with the highest demand. This is a profitable and safe decision for the state but does not necessarily provide a wide range of products for consumers.

There can even be restrictions on how much each buyer may purchase. An example might be a minimum order of three bottles and multiples of three. In this case, buyers could not order one or two bottles; they would have to take three, regardless of how slowly the product turned over. They also could not order four or five bottles, or eight, but would be limited to orders of three, six, nine, twelve, and so forth.

Other practices and policies typically found in control states include a lack of credit or delivery. The on-premise operators must pay for the goods at the time of pick-up and have to arrange for their own delivery. In some cases, they actually have to pick up the order themselves; in others, they can get together with other establishments and hire common carriers. In both cases, however, the state avoids the expense of delivery.

In licensed, or open, states, on- and off-premise retailers must purchase from authorized wholesalers and distributors who have to possess a variety of federal, state, and local permits and licenses. The prices and markups typically are not regulated, so there are differing prices within each state and some price competition among the distributors is normal. The prices that the suppliers charge the wholesalers, however, must be standard.

Credit and delivery are generally the same as with any other products. That

Table 8–1   Control and Open States

Licensed, or Open States	Control States
Alaska	Alabama
Arizona	Idaho
Arkansas	Iowa
California	Maine
Colorado	Michigan
Connecticut	Mississippi (wholesale only)
Delaware	Montana
Florida	New Hampshire
Georgia	North Carolina
Hawaii	Ohio
Illinois	Oregon
Indiana	Pennsylvania
Kansas	Utah
Kentucky	Vermont
Louisiana	Virginia
Maryland	Washington
Massachusetts	West Virginia
Minnesota	Wyoming (wholesale only)
Mississippi (retail only)	
Missouri	
Nebraska	
Nevada	
New Jersey	
New Mexico	
New York	
North Dakota	
Oklahoma	
Rhode Island	
South Carolina	
South Dakota	
Tennessee	
Texas	
Wisconsin	
Wyoming (retail only)	
District of Columbia	

is, the buyer orders merchandise, it is delivered by the distributor, and the bill is paid at a later date. Even in open states, though, there are some credit restrictions. The most common is a requirement that bills must be paid within thirty days. Failure to do so would result in a blacklisting of the establishment, which then would not be able to purchase additional beverages.

Because a competitive market exists, the alcoholic beverage purveyors have to be responsive to consumer demands. This generally means that wholesalers compete on prices, delivery, and other supplier services, as well as the range of brands offered. There is not, however, the full and open price competition that one might suppose. There are two reasons for this. One is that some distributors have what are known as exclusive distribution rights; they are the only source of a particular brand. The other is that some brands are so popular that all on- and off-premise establishments must stock them.

Local

In addition to the federal and state regulations, there is a bewildering variety of local laws and regulations to contend with. Some of these are known as *local option laws;* the state allows local communities to decide whether alcoholic beverages can be sold and, if so, how. This means that there could be one or more dry communities in a state, regardless of whether it is a control or licensed state. There are also many zoning ordinances, health codes, building codes, and fire codes that specifically or indirectly affect the operation of an alcoholic beverage establishment.

AREAS SUBJECT TO REGULATION

As pointed out, many, if not most, areas subject to regulation are controlled by state and local agencies; the main involvement of the federal government is to establish and collect taxes and to provide the broad structure for alcoholic beverage control. To understand the wide variety of laws and regulations, one has to have an understanding of the history of Prohibition in this country. Americans have always had an ambivalent attitude toward alcoholic beverages, an attitude that led, in 1920, to the Eighteenth Amendment to the U.S. Constitution: the National Prohibition Amendment, prohibiting the manufacture, sale, or transportation of alcohol for use in beverages. This law was clearly unenforceable and cost the government billions of dollars both in attempts to control it and in lost revenue. Estimates are that some $36 billion was spent on illegal liquor during Prohibition, expenditures for which the government received not a penny in taxes. When the Twenty-first Amendment repealed Prohibition, in 1933, each of the states was given wide latitude to establish regulations of its own. The only requirement was that each had to meet all federal standards; however, it could establish stricter ones if it wished. Because the temperance movement still had great strength in many areas, many restrictive practices continued. This is why there is such a patchwork quilt character to alcoholic beverage regulations across the country.

The Right to Conduct Business

Due to the local option laws, the sale of alcoholic beverages may not even be permitted in a particular area. In just about any other business, if someone has the necessary resources, he or she can set up shop. It does not matter whether it is a good decision or not; a person has the freedom to establish a business if that person wishes to do so. With alcoholic beverages, this is not the case.

Even if alcoholic beverage sales are permitted in a particular locality, the seller must be licensed. In some areas licenses are limited to a percentage of the population; unless there is growth, no additional licenses are available. There could even be only a fixed number regardless of population growth. In both these cases, they only way to get a license would be to purchase an existing business that has one. This may not be possible, but even when it is, it places many more operating constraints on entrepreneurs than they would have if they started their own business. There is also the problem of obtaining licensing approval. One could purchase an existing license and still not be approved.

Location of the Business

Local zoning ordinances can play an important role. If a desired location is zoned for residential purposes only, it will not be possible to operate a beverage establishment there. This type of restriction is not unique to the alcoholic beverage business, but there is another that is: in some areas the sales of alcoholic beverages are prohibited even if the area is zoned for commercial purposes. It is also common to have stipulations that alcoholic beverages cannot be sold near churches and schools; the regulation may even state a specific distance from one, less than which alcohol cannot be sold.

The Source of Products

In the case of control states, the source of alcoholic beverages is simple: all purchases are from the state; there is absolutely no choice in the matter. Even in open states, though, only licensed wholesalers can be used. Although there are certainly restrictions in supplier selection with other products, they are restrictions imposed by the marketplace, not by government agencies.

The Availability of Products

Relatively few brands are equally available across the country; this is due partly to marketing realities and partly to governmental decree.

Bottle Sizes

Metric sizes are required by the federal government, which also stipulates the specific bottle sizes that may be used. The full range of these bottles may not be available in all states, due to state regulations. These mainly deal with extremes in size, both large and small.

Days of Operation

It is not uncommon to find areas where alcoholic beverage sales are not permitted on Sundays. A variation prohibits the sale of distilled spirits but allows beer and wine to be sold. Sometimes, only sales of 3.2 percent beer are permitted on Sundays. In the latter case, the operator must decide whether a dual inventory — 3.2 percent and regular-strength beer — is justified. In such a case, the operator may well decide not to offer any alcoholic beverages at all on Sundays. Similar prohibitions are often present on holidays and, very commonly, on election days.

Hours of Operation

Each locality regulates the hours of operation. In some areas, bars may have to close at midnight, in others at 1:00 or 2:00 A.M., while in still others they may be permitted to stay open until 4:00 or 6:00 A.M. In Las Vegas, a twenty-four-hour city, bars may operate continuously around the clock.

Atlantic City, in contrast to Las Vegas, is not a twenty-four-hour city and has to close the casinos and bars for a period of several hours each day. Along with closing hours, there are often regulations controlling when establishments may begin to sell alcoholic beverages.

Age of Consumers

All states have regulations prohibiting the sale of alcoholic beverages to minors. Where they do not agree is what age constitutes a minor. The most common traditionally has been twenty-one, but there have been many examples of legal drinking ages eighteen, nineteen, or twenty. In recent years, due to concern over driving after drinking, two developments have taken place. One has been a fluctuation in the drinking age as a state passes a law changing the age, then passes another law a year or two later changing it again as one group or another exerts pressure. In addition, the groundswell of popular opinion against alcohol abuse finally gained such strength in the early 1980s that the federal government decreed a uniform age of twenty-one across the country, then threatened to withhold federal highway funds from any states that did not comply. It is interesting to note that the federal government has no jurisdiction over the drinking age and cannot legally require a uniform drinking age. However, it can exert sufficient pressure to force compliance. There is not much doubt that at the time it was done, this was a popular and well-supported move on the part of the federal government. As a result, there is now, for the first time, a uniform United States drinking age—21.

In the past, one could even find a sexual basis for deciding who could or could not consume alcoholic beverages. In Chicago in the 1950s, the drinking age was twenty-one for males, eighteen for females. Whatever the reasoning behind such a law, it was clearly sexual discrimination and long ago passed into history.

Age of Alcoholic Beverage Service Personnel

There are also restrictions on the age of service personnel, and usually, but not always, they are uniform with the drinking-age requirements. In some cases, this could increase the difficulty of locating and hiring service personnel.

Advertising Practices

There are federal and many state provisions on what kinds of advertising can be done. The federal government is interested in the prevention of misleading, false, and offensive product advertising. There are regulations providing for what type of advertising is permitted. Distilled spirits cannot be advertised on television, while beer and wine can. There is an implication here that beers and wines are somehow safer than spirits and less dangerous to the public welfare. Spirits manufacturers naturally object to this attitude, but it is a fact of life. It shows up not only in advertising practices, but in taxation as well. Spirits are taxed at a higher rate than beers or wines, and in 1985, when the federal excise taxes were increased for the first time since 1951, only distilled spirits taxes were affected.

Marketing Practices

Regulation of marketing practices is a fairly recent phenomenon. Beverage operators traditionally have been reasonably free to decide how to market and price their products, but with the increasing concern over alcohol abuse, more and more restrictions are being imposed on hotels, restaurants, and bars. Specifically, it is now illegal in some areas to have so-called happy hours, when drinks are sold at below normal prices. Other restrictions of this nature include bans on two-for-one promotions and or free drinks for women on ladies nights. These have always been regarded as legitimate traffic- and sales-building strategies, but they undeniably encourage overconsumption, and that is becoming increasingly intolerable, if not legally, then from a moral standpoint. As a result, even in locations where they are not required to eliminate or modify such marketing practices, many beverage operators are doing so anyway.

The Prices of Products

In the control states, pricing is established by regulation, not market conditions. This is not altogether bad, because small, independent bar operators pay the same prices as do large, corporate buyers and are not at a competitive disadvantage. Quantity buyers, of course, look at this situation rather differently. It is also easier and less time-consuming to manage in a control state, because less time and effort go into discussing prices with suppliers and evaluating all the deals and discounts that are typically available in licensed states. At any rate, it is a fact that, due to price regulation, prices are higher in control states.

Types of Products Served

State and local regulations sometimes proscribe the specific types of products that can be sold. There are examples of limitations on spirit proofs. In such instances the maximum allowed is 100 proof. This makes it impossible, for example, to mix an authentic zombie drink—no 151-proof rum is available—nor can 101-proof Wild Turkey bourbon or 110-proof green Chartreuse be stocked on the bar. The percentage of alcohol in beer is another area of legislation, as is the strength of malt liquors. National breweries, therefore, are forced to prepare different products for various markets.

Alcoholic beverage sales licenses are also restrictive in that they stipulate the types of products that may be sold. Thus, there may be what is known as a full license, or one permitting the sale of only beer and wine. Regulations in general are quite different for distilled spirits compared to beers and wines.

Record Keeping

Both the federal and the state governments have requirements about what kinds of records must be maintained and for how long they have to be made available. The federal government requires receiving records for all wines, spirits, and beers. These include such information as the quantities received, who the sellers were, the dates of sales, and records of payment. With state governments, sales tax collection responsibilities require a great deal of record keeping.

Bill Payments

In control states, payment of bills is simple: the buyer pays when he or she obtains the products, either in cash or by certified check. Licensed states allow credit, but put a time limit on how long the bill may remain outstanding. In some states there are various restrictions on consumer credit, although most allow customers to charge to hotel rooms and private club accounts and to pay by credit card.

Liquor Service with or without Food

There are some bizarre regulations about alcohol and food. In some localities a person cannot serve alcoholic beverages unless he or she also has food available. In others, the person cannot serve them if food is available. The latter is uncommon, but the former is not and may become more widespread, considering the changes in attitude toward the consumption of alcoholic beverages.

Parking Requirements

It is common to require having a specific number of parking spaces available, based on the number of seats or square feet of public space.

Liquor Liability Insurance Requirements

The entire aspect of liquor liability is discussed in detail later in this chapter.

Entertainment and Dancing

Entertainment and dancing may be prohibited in some locations where alcoholic beverages are sold.

Relationships between Suppliers and Beverage Operators

No wholesalers may have a financial or legal relationship with any establishment serving alcoholic beverages. This includes any interests in the business itself, the equipment, and the premises. Distributors may not provide equipment or fixtures to beverage retailers. There are limitations on the type and value of promotional materials that may be made available to on- and off-premise retailers. Consignment sales are expressly prohibited; this is where a distributor would provide products under an agreement that they would be paid for only if sold, while unsold products could be returned to the distributor. Discounts must be equally available to all buyers. Wholesalers can establish a wide range of discount policies, but they cannot discriminate as to who can receive such discounts. Most of these types of regulations are federal ones.

Product Standards

The federal Standards of Identity for the various types of alcoholic beverages were established by the federal government following the repeal of Prohibition in 1933, because of the widespread availability during that era of some terrible, even lethal, products. One of the three primary objectives of the BATF is the protection of the public, and the Standards of Identity are intended to meet that responsibility.

Labeling Standards

The BATF must approve all alcoholic beverage container labels. The specific requirements are type of product (as described in the Standards of Identity), bottle contents in milliliters or liters, alcoholic content or proof (except for beer), and the name of the bottler, manufacturer, or importer. With wines of 14 percent alcohol or less, the alcoholic content need not be on the label, but the type of wine must be. For example, wines containing from 10 to 14 percent alcohol are legally identified as table wines, and wines of less than 10 percent alcohol are called light wines. Therefore, the wine type implies a specific alcohol level. Also, with distilled spirits, the percentage and source of neutral spirits must be stated on the label, except for cordials and specialties.

Bottle Usage and Handling

It is illegal to reuse a liquor bottle for anything. This includes using it on the bar for a Bloody Mary mix, water, or anything else. It is also illegal to add anything to a bottle, even the same brand. This regulation is in place specifically to protect the consumer from products that are watered, adulterated, or mixed with cheaper brands. Some state and local regulations require bottles to be broken when emptied.

TAX STRUCTURES

One of the primary areas of interest to the regulatory agencies is the imposition of taxes and the collection of revenue. With the federal government, this is achieved through federal excise taxes (FET) and custom duties on imported alcoholic beverages (Tables 8–2 and 8–3).

Federal Excise Taxes

With wines, the federal excise taxes vary according to the alcoholic content and the type of wine. With the exception of sparkling and carbonated wines, the tax rates have been unchanged since 1951. Sparkling and carbonated wine rates were increased in 1955 to the present ones. Wines of over 24 percent alcohol are taxed as distilled spirits.

Beer has been taxed at the rate of $9.00 per thirty-one-gallon barrel since 1951. The FET on distilled spirits was $10.50 per proof gallon from 1951 to

Table 8–2 Federal Excise Taxes

Type of Product	Tax
Wine (per wine gallon)	
0 to 14 percent alcohol	$ .17
14 to 21 percent alcohol	.67
21 to 24 percent alcohol	2.25
Carbonated	2.40
Sparkling	3.40
Beer (per thirty one-gallon barrel)	$ 9.00
Distilled spirits (per proof gallon)	$12.50

Table 8–3 Federal Customs Duties

Type of Product	Duty
Wine (per wine gallon)	
0 to 14 percent (one gallon or less)	$ .375
0 to 14 percent (over one gallon)	.625
Over 14 percent (depending on the type and container size)	.315 to 1.00
Sparkling	1.17
Carbonated	1.17
Beer (per gallon)	$ .06
Distilled spirits (per proof gallon)	
Brandy (varies depending on the value of the brandy and the size of the container). For containers of one gallon or less, the duty rate ranges from $.62 to $5.00. For larger containers, it is $.50 to $5.00.	
Cordials and liqueurs	.50
Gin	.50
Rum	1.75
Scotch whisky, Irish whiskey	.51
Canadian whisky	.62
Tequila	1.25
Duties for Communist countries	
Table wines (per wine gallon)	$1.25
Sparkling and carbonated wines (per wine gallon)	$6.00
Beer (per gallon)	$ .50
Distilled spirits (per proof gallon)	$5.00

1985 but was raised to $12.50 per proof gallon on October 1, 1985. The term *proof gallon* refers to one gallon of 100-proof spirits.

Even though the FET on distilled spirits was increased in 1985 for the first time in nearly thirty-five years, indications are that the government will continue its attempts to gain additional revenue from the alcoholic beverage industries. In 1986 the Senate Finance Committee considered a proposal that would have eliminated all FET payments as a tax deduction. Additional proposals were to raise the FET on wines, which escaped the 1985 increase, and to tie future taxes to the inflation rate. The trade association DISCUS (Distilled Spirits Council of the United States) conducted a study and estimated that the change in the tax deduction alone was equivalent to an FET increase on all alcoholic beverages of over 50 percent. With wine, because the proposal also would calculate the tax differently, the effect would be to raise the wine FET from seventeen cents to eighty-seven cents, an increase of over 400 percent.

Customs Duties

Customs duties on imported alcoholic beverages depend on the type of beverage and the country of origin.

Countries the President declares to be under Communist control are required to pay a duty premium. The rates are those in effect when Prohibition was repealed: sparkling and carbonated wines, $6.00 per wine gallon; all other wines, $1.25 per wine gallon; beer, $.50 per gallon; distilled spirits, $5.00 per proof gallon. Communist nations that are exempt due to their most-favored-nation status are Poland, Romania, and Yugoslavia.

A strip stamp is affixed to each bottle of spirits at the time of bottling, and the taxes are paid at that time. Aside from its role in revenue production, the strip stamps are important in prevention of illegal sales and in assurance of product quality. Green strip stamps are used for 100-proof bonded bourbon, and red stamps are used for all other spirits. When the bottle cap is removed and the strip stamp broken, the bottom portion must be left on the bottle. It is a violation of federal law to have bottles on the bar without the strip stamp; federal law provides for fines of up to $10,000 and/or imprisonment of up to five years. There may also be state tax stamps on bottles.

State and Local Taxes

In addition to the federal excise taxes and custom duties, there are many state and local taxes. In 1980, the federal government collected $4 billion from excise taxes, while state and local governments collected nearly $3 billion more. Because the excise tax on distilled spirits has been increased 19 percent, it can be expected that government revenues will increase even with reduced shipments of distilled spirits.

DRAMSHOP LAWS AND LIABILITY

One of the most serious problems ever to confront the alcoholic beverage industry—and, by extension, all sectors of the hospitality industry that serve alcoholic beverages—is the rapid evolvement of dramshop laws in the United States. Dramshop laws were developed from tort law, which was established to protect people from the negligence of others. Any wrongful damage, act, or injury for which financial damages can be sought is a tort.

When dramshop laws were first enacted, they were intended to prevent minors, drunken persons, and habitual drunkards from having access to alcoholic beverages. The evolution of tort law from the 1960s to the early 1980s resulted in a change of the standard of negligence to strict liability and then to absolute liability. This meant that, regarding negligence—the failure to exercise reasonable care and so forth—individuals and organizations could be strictly liable regardless of whether they exercised reasonable care or were unable to foresee injury-causing circumstances. The concept of absolute liability implies compensation regardless of who is actually responsible.

In particular, it is third-party liability legislation that has caused the major problems. This is known in some quarters as the "deep pockets" syndrome: why sue some drunken individual who probably has little money when one can sue a business backed by hundreds of thousands, perhaps millions, of dollars of insurance? Some states have statutory laws that hold servers of alcoholic beverages accountable for the actions of the consumers. Other states have case law that establishes liability. Only a few states, by late 1986, had no dramshop liability. Liability is no longer limited to owners or servers of alcoholic beverages in commercial establishments; recent court rulings have extended dramshop legislation to include social hosts. The New Jersey Supreme Court ruled in 1984 that the host or hostess of a private party could be held liable if an inebriated guest became involved in a drunken-driving accident after leaving the party.

The combination of looser interpretations as to who is liable and the changing thrust of tort law has been devastating to the alcoholic beverage industry. There has been a significant increase in liquor liability suits brought against foodservice operators, and huge claims and settlements have become common. The International Risk Management Institute and the Insurance Information Institute reported that there had been a 300 percent increase in such suits in 1985. Multimillion-dollar liquor liability awards have been made with increasing frequency. The head of the North Carolina Restaurant Association was quoted in early 1986 as saying that his state had the "dubious distinction" of having the first $50 million liability suit on file. One insurance industry executive has said that "the tort system has gone haywire" and compared collecting from insurance companies as an equivalent pastime to winning the New York State lottery. The result of all this is that liquor liability insurance in the mid-1980s became simultaneously unaffordable and unavailable.

PUBLIC CONCERN OVER ALCOHOL ABUSE

Because there is a highly positive correlation between alcohol consumption and driving accidents, public concern with the problem finally has led to aggressive and militant commitment. Many groups organized to develop alcohol education programs. The first was Mothers Against Drunk Driving (MADD), and it was followed by such other citizen activist groups as Students Against Driving Drunk (SADD) and Remove Intoxicated Drivers (RID). There have even been groups formed by industry members in recognition of the seriousness of the problem. One such is Beverage Retailers Against Drunk Driving (BRADD), composed of such companies and organizations as S&A Restaurant Corp., General Mills Restaurant Group, Chili's, Miller Brewing Company, Howard Johnson, the National Association of Convenience Stores, and many others.

Partly because of the actions of such groups, and partly because of the general feeling that something had to be done, in particular in the case of alcohol-related driving accidents and fatalities, significant changes have been made in legal interpretations and laws. Public attitudes toward drinking also have changed substantially, and the American people generally have radically altered their beverage consumption habits. The percentage of the population that abstains completely from alcoholic beverages increased in 1985 to 35 percent. The highest percentage previously reported was 29 percent, in 1969. As has been pointed out in the consumption trends and patterns sections at the end of each chapter on products, Americans are not only drinking less, but also are drinking different kinds of alcoholic beverages. They are consuming a lot less distilled spirits and much more wine, although even the latter seems to be dropping off. Wine and beer are generally perceived as being alcoholic beverages of moderation. This perception may not be based on fact, but nonetheless it exists, and the spirits industry has had to take steps to counter it.

COSTS ASSOCIATED WITH ALCOHOLIC BEVERAGE SERVICE
Liability Insurance

The problem of liquor liability insurance is another one with potentially disastrous consequences for the foodservice industry. The costs of such insurance have escalated so rapidly in recent years that they often cannot be economically justified from a beverage operator's standpoint. The National Restaurant Association (NRA) sponsored a Gallup poll in 1985, which showed that, although 92 percent of the respondents had never been named in a liquor liability suit, their average premiums had gone up by 110 percent. The survey further established that the average premium paid by these operators was $39,500. Looking at it from another angle, an operation doing $800,000 per year in food-and-beverage business would be spending 5 percent on liquor liability insurance. Relatively few food-and-beverage units do this much business, and even if they did, spending 5 percent for insurance typically would erode profits dangerously and, in many cases, eliminate them completely. These types of insurance costs have traditionally been well under 2 percent of sales, and it is difficult, sometimes impossible, to pass on the increased costs to the customers. To illustrate the latter point, the New Hampshire Hospitality Association planned a bizarre promotion in February 1986. It was called the "Great New Hampshire Unhappy Hour," and drink prices were to be based on liability insurance percentage increases. Because some operators claimed increases of 1,000 to 2,000 percent, selling prices of $11.88 for a Seagram's Seven and $14.07 for a Budweiser were proposed. Needless to say, the event never took place.

Isolated examples of insurance costs are even more dramatic. NRA members reported specific increases of from $185 to $26,500, $6,700 to $30,520, and $25,000 to $92,000. An equal, if not worse, problem is that insurance is often not obtainable at any price. The legal counsel of the American Hotel and Motel Association stated at the International Hotel/Motel & Restaurant Show in 1985 that in certain instances you could not get insurance at all in New Jersey, even though rates in that state had gone up by some six times what they had formerly been.

On the other hand, because of rising and unpredictable settlements, the insurance companies are in a position where they do not want to be in the liability business. They have a unique business problem: their costs may not be known until many years after the policies have been issued. This puts them in a position of being unable to predict future costs accurately. According to an insurance company executive, the companies "are not able to calculate with reasonable accuracy the amounts for which their clients will be held liable, and they will not offer coverage."

From a business standpoint, their position is sensible, especially because the property and casualty insurance industry reported operating losses of nearly $4 billion in 1984 and over $5 billion in 1985. These losses were incurred even though their premium income—the profit they made from loaning their premiums—was up over 9 percent in 1984 and over 20 percent in 1985.

Many establishments, unable either to afford or to obtain liability insurance, simply began operating without it. The phrase used to describe this practice is *going bare*, and some estimates are that as many as 25 percent of independent operators have been doing so. The obvious danger they face is that one lawsuit could put them out of business. There is also the disturbing question of whether they are avoiding a moral responsibility to protect the public.

Other Legal Aspects

Laws concerning drinking and driving have been broadened and tightened at the same time. They range from tougher laws dealing with driving under the influence (DUI) and driving while intoxicated (DWI) to several proposals made by the New York State Division of Alcoholism and Alcohol Abuse. These would have placed a moratorium on new retail alcoholic beverage licenses, given the state control over the location of new retail outlets, increased the state excise taxes on alcoholic beverages and changed the manner in which they would be calculated, and, most extreme of all, lowered the blood alcohol content, which defines legal intoxication, from 0.10 percent to 0.05 percent. Most states at present use 0.10 percent; none use less than 0.08 percent. It is quite possible that two or three beers or glasses of wine consumed in an hour could produce levels of 0.05 percent, although individuals and drinking circumstances vary so widely that it may not be possible to make a definitive statement.

With the National Highway Traffic Safety Administration estimating over 22,000 alcohol-related deaths a year, and with the increase in public activism over alcohol abuse, most states are actively pursuing more and more laws on drunken driving. Forty-four states considered 874 laws in 1984, and thirty-five of them passed 108 laws. In 1985, the legal activity increased as forty-three states enacted 207 new laws. There have been positive results regarding highway safety. The 22,000 deaths in 1984 were 13.6 percent less than the 25,000 in 1980, despite an increased number of drivers and miles driven. Other factors contributed to the decrease, of course. Examples include increasingly safer automobiles and highway speed restrictions.

In addition to broadening liability, these legislative changes include stiffer fines, more severe driver's license suspension and revocation penalties, increasing reliance on jail sentences, use of police roadblocks to check drivers' sobriety, and provision that a blood alcohol count of 0.10 percent constitutes proof of being legally drunk. Others are administrative per se laws that allow an arresting officer to revoke, on the spot, the license of any drivers who refuse to take, or fail, an alcohol breath test, and presumptive laws that allow the arresting officer's self-administered tests to provide proof of guilt. Some states prohibit drinking while driving and make it illegal to have open containers of alcohol in vehicles. Happy hours are being limited or reduced, and hours of operation are being cut back. Even warning labels on alcoholic beverage containers are being considered. In several states, the increased fines are being returned to the counties where the arrests are made, to help pay for increased law enforcement, public education programs, prosecution, and treatment.

There have been proposals to eliminate beer and wine advertising from television, as has been done with cigarettes. The broadcast industry understandably reacted vigorously to this; in 1984, the beer industry alone spent $533 million on spot and network television advertising, and wine advertising added another $125 million. For beer, this was 70 percent of total advertising expenditures; for wine, 68 percent. By way of contrast, none of the $346.2 million spent for distilled spirits in 1984 found its way into television, because spirits producers are already prohibited from advertising there.

Training of Service Personnel

The training of alcoholic beverage service personnel has become a very high priority at all levels of the foodservice industry. Chain operators, independent operators, trade associations, citizens, even governmental agencies are getting involved. The reason is that neither the industry nor society can risk doing business as usual. It is too expensive financially for the industry and emotionally for society.

COPING WITH CHANGING LAWS AND PUBLIC ATTITUDES
Manufacturers of Alcoholic Beverages

Many spirits producers have promoted an *equivalency campaign*. This is aimed specifically at the concept that wine and beer are the alcoholic beverages of moderation and are somehow less dangerous than distilled spirits. This issue has deeply divided the industry. Basically, what the producers have proposed is publicizing that there are similar amounts of ethyl alcohol in a shot of spirits (1.25 ounces of 80-proof spirits), one bottle of beer (12 ounces), and one glass of wine (4 ounces). This fact is incontestable. There are 0.5 ounces of alcohol in 1.25 ounces of 80-proof (40 percent alcohol) spirits, in 12 ounces of 4.2 percent beer, and in 4 ounces of 12 percent wine.

The beer and wine producers have countered with two arguments. One is that wine and beer contain buffers that slow the absorption of alcohol, thereby delaying the increase in blood alcohol concentration (BAC). The other is that beer and wine are consumed under different conditions than are spirits; specifically, that they are often, if not mainly, consumed with food, which also slows the absorption of alcohol.

As regards the claim that the alcohol in wines is absorbed more slowly, the National Institute on Alcoholism and Alcohol Abuse (NIAAA) has evaluated studies that the wine industry submitted to the BATF as definitive. The BATF is the regulatory agency, while the NIAAA is the government agency with scientific expertise in the field of alcohol studies. It found that the studies were scientifically flawed because of inadequate control of variables. One of the problems is that individual absorption and elimination rates vary widely, due partly to metabolic rates for alcohol. Data have established wide individual variability, with the rate differing over a threefold range. There are many other variables, enough that definitive statements about alcohol absorption cannot be made at this time. The other contention, that food slows alcohol metabolism, is perfectly true, but the source of the alcohol does not appear to matter. When food is consumed, the rate of absorption of alcohol from beer, wine, or spirits is reduced by a significant margin.

The equivalency campaign has been successful from the standpoint of public perception of the actual alcoholic content of the various types of beverages. The distilled spirits trade association DISCUS had the Gallup organization conduct polls to ascertain how many people knew that there was no difference in the total alcoholic content of a bottle of beer, a glass of wine, or a shot of liquor. In 1982 only 17 percent knew it, but in 1985 35 percent were aware of it. The spirits industry has not been alone in promoting equivalency, nor did it even invent the concept. Many of the citizen groups mentioned earlier, as well as the NIAAA, have been saying the same thing. Their position seems to be that it is important, from a public health perspective, that people be aware of how much alcohol they are actually consuming.

The alcoholic beverage producers have also joined with on-premise retailers in lobbying for changes in the tort system, which, because it ultimately reduces the consumption of alcoholic beverages, is as harmful for them as it is for the retailers. These efforts have also had some success. At the annual National Restaurant Association Show in Chicago in 1986, the outgoing president spoke of a broad trend toward making dramshop laws more equitable and civil suits more predictable.

The beverage producers and manufacturers have also worked with concerned public and private groups and organizations in promoting moderation and responsible drinking. They have participated in the preparation of educational and server-training materials, both of which were sorely needed by the food and beverage industry.

On-Premise Retailers

The major hospitality industry trade associations—the National Restaurant Association, the state restaurant associations, and the American Hotel and Motel Association—all made legislative reform their top priority in the mid-1980s. They were specifically interested in liability and tort law reform. The types of changes they called for include placing limitations on awards for "pain and suffering" and other noneconomic damages, restricting joint and multiple liability, spreading insurance payment awards over several years, reducing the time period for filing a lawsuit under the statute of limitations, requiring advance notice of a suit, limiting the contingency fees that lawyers can collect, and imposing dollar caps on defendants' liability.

In order to offer the possibility of liability insurance to those unable to obtain any, some state restaurant associations are supporting the concept of insurance offered by the state. Massachusetts was the first state to begin a Joint Underwriting Association (JUA). Starting in January 1986, the state offered liquor liability insurance at 5 percent of an operator's total liquor volume. For those establishments selling only alcoholic beverages, this is quite expensive, but it was an improvement over the previous situation, whereby insurance was unobtainable. With restaurants selling both food and beverages, the cost was easier to justify. A typical ratio of food to beverage sales in the industry is 75 percent to 25 percent, and on this basis, the liquor liability cost would drop to 1.25 percent of total sales. Massachusetts also came up with an innovative approach to providing insurance for caterers. They were offered the opportunity to purchase insurance by the day at one dollar per guest served. New York and North Carolina were also reported to be forming JUAs for the purpose of providing liquor liability insurance.

In a related matter, the Health Education Foundation of Washington, D.C., has developed a program designed to alert beverage servers to the signs of consumer intoxication. It is called TIPS, or Training for Intervention Procedures by Servers (of alcohol). Because of insurance premium discounts for companies taking part in such programs, they have received support from the hospitality industry. With the TIPS program, for example, the president of Ramada Inns has noted that a major insurance carrier provided such discounts to policyholders who enroll a minimum of 75 percent of their servers in the course. Virtually all chain organizations and many independents have actively pursued server education programs, with the objectives of showing the insurance carriers that they were not an unacceptable risk, demonstrating public responsibility, and protecting their businesses. It is recognized that a knowledgeable staff is one of the best defenses a bar or restaurant has against patron drunkenness. In Nevada, Clark County (Las Vegas) has passed an ordinance requiring *all* sources of alcoholic beverages to have completed a four-hour course on alcohol awareness.

Although there are few locations where drink promotions are being legally curtailed, most operators are voluntarily cutting back on such activities. Included are happy hours, ladies nights, two-for-one and all-you-can-drink promotions, and the like. Aside from the possible public perception of irresponsibility regarding alcohol service, these types of marketing activities run a real risk of promoting overconsumption, and beverage establishments simply cannot chance that. These types of promotions were developed to maintain a competitive position and increase sales. When everyone eliminates them, there is no competitive disadvantage, though the lost sales remain a problem. But as one restaurant owner has said, although you can make a lot of money selling alcoholic beverages, you can also lose a lot of money from being sued.

In recognition of the fact that drinking and driving are a dangerous combination, many establishments that sell alcoholic beverages are attempting to keep drinkers from driving, by adopting *designated driver programs*. The basic idea is that one member of a group is designated as the driver, and that individual does not consume alcoholic beverages. Instead, he or she is provided with free nonalcoholic drinks and/or a rain check for alcoholic drinks at a later date. Designated drivers sometimes are given a card or button to indicate their status. Several hotels and restaurants have had success with this policy. Other strategies designed to keep drivers off the road include complimentary taxicabs and hotel or motel rooms.

New Year's Eve parties present particular problems, and there have been many reports of restaurants and bars arranging rooms for their guests in advance. Hotels and motels have an advantage here in that they can readily provide rooms.

All of these programs encourage safety and responsible drinking habits, without discouraging consumption of alcoholic beverages.

SUGGESTED READINGS

Alva, M. "N.Y. Group Fights Drinking Changes." *Nation's Restaurant News*, December 9, 1985.

———. "Operators Demand Liability Law Reform." *Nation's Restaurant News*, February 10, 1986.

————. "Operators Stage 'Unhappy Hour.' " *Nation's Restaurant News*, February 17, 1986.

————. "State Legislatures to Consider 80 Dramshop Bills." *Nation's Restaurant News*, March 3, 1986.

————. "State Offers Liquor Liability Insurance." *Nation's Restaurant News*, April 14, 1986.

Brown, A. "Equivalency: A Raging Debate in the Alcoholic Beverage Industry." *Market Watch* 5 (December 1985).

"Designated-Driver Programs Gain Greater Acceptance." *Nation's Restaurant News*, March 24, 1986.

Edwards, J. "Independents Eye Steps to Combat Liquor Decline." *Nation's Restaurant News*, March 3, 1986.

————. "Liability Insurance Crisis Grows Despite State Reform Attempts." *Nation's Restaurant News*, June 2, 1986.

"First Line of Defense." *Nation's Restaurant News*, March 24, 1986.

Frydman, K. "Operators Rethink Strategies as Liquor Sales Drop." *Nation's Restaurant News*, February 24, 1986.

Greenberg, M. R. "Inside the Liability Crisis." *Nation's Restaurant News*, April 28, 1986.

Grossman, H. J. *Grossman's Guide to Wines, Beers & Spirits*. 6th rev. ed., rev. H. Lembeck. New York: Charles Scribner's Sons, 1977.

Gutman, R. Y., and A. J. Kaufman. "Stretching Liquor Liability." *Nation's Restaurant News*, January 13, 1986.

"The Happy Hour Legacy." *Nation's Restaurant News*, March 24, 1986.

The Impact American Beer Market Review and Forecast. New York: M. Shanken Communications, Inc., 1985.

The Impact American Distilled Spirits Market Review and Forecast. New York: M. Shanken Communications, Inc., 1985.

The Impact American Wine Market Review and Forecast. New York: M. Shanken Communications, Inc., 1985.

"Industry Unites to Battle Packwood Proposal." *Impact* 16 (April 15, 1986).

Katsigris, C., and M. Porter. *The Bar & Beverage Book*. New York: J. Wiley & Sons, 1983.

Lee, J. R. "An Attitude Adjustment." *Nation's Restaurant News*, February 17, 1986.

"Liquor Liability and the Underage Drinker." *Nation's Restaurant News*, March 24, 1986.

"NRA Warns of Rising Premiums." *Nation's Restaurant News*, March 10, 1986.

"Ramada's Program Fights Drunk Driving." *Nation's Restaurant News*, January 20, 1986.

Rella, S. "America Toughens its DWI Penalties." *Market Watch* 5 (December 1985).

Schoifet, M. "Chains, Beverage Retailers Fighting Drunk Driving." *Nation's Restaurant News*, October 7, 1985.

Scoggin, D. R. " 'Happy Hour' in Sober Spot." *Nation's Restaurant News*, November 4, 1985.

Zaccarelli, H. E. "Hospitality and Alcoholic Beverages: Facing the Future With Responsibility." *Food Executive Newsletter* 2 (May 1986).

THE REGIONS
& DOC WINES
OF ITALY

Region	DOC Wines[1]	Type of Wine	Grape(s)
ABRUZZI	Montepulciano d'Abruzzo	Red, Rosé	Montepulciano d'Abruzzo; Sangiovese (up to 15%)
	Trebbiano d'Abruzzo	White	Trebbiano d'Abruzzo and/or Trebbiano Toscano; Malvasia Toscana, Coccociola, Passerina permitted up to 15% total
APULIA	Aleatico di Puglia	Red	Aleatico di Puglia (85%); Negroamaro, Malvasia Nera, Primitivo (15%)
	Alezio	Red	Negroamaro and Malvasia Rossa
	Cacc'e Mmitte di Lucera	Red	Uva di Troia (35 to 65%); Montepulciano, Sangiovese, Malvasia Nera (25 to 35%)
	Castel del Monte	Red	Uva di Troia (70%); Bombino Nero, Montepulciano, Sangiovese (35%)
		Rosé	Bombino Nero; Uva di Troia and Montepulciano (up to 35%)
		White	Pampanuto
	Copertino	Red, Rosé	Negroamaro
	Gravina	White	Verdeca
	Leverano	Red, Rosé	Negroamaro; others up to 35%
		White	Malvasia Bianco; others up to 35%
	Locorotondo	White	Verdeca (50 to 65%); Bianco di Alessano (35 to 50%); Fiano, Bombino, Malvasia Toscana (5%)

Martina Franca	White	Same as Locorotondo
Matino	Red, Rosé	Negroamaro (70%); Sangiovese, Malvasia Nera (30%)
Moscato di Trani	White, sweet	Moscato Reale (Moscato Bianco); other Muscats up to 15%
Ostuni Bianco	White	Impigno (50 to 85%); Francavilla (15 to 50%); Bianco di Alessandro, Verdeca (10%)
Ostuni Ottavianello	Red	Ottavianello
Primitivo di Manduria	Red	Primitivo
Rosso Barletta	Red	Uva di Troia; others up to 30%
Rosso Canosa	Red	Uva di Troia (65%)
Rosso di Cerignola	Red	Uva di Troia (55%); Negroamaro (15 to 30%); Sangiovese, Barbera, Montepulciano, Malbec, Trebbiano Toscano (15%)
Salice Salentino	Red, Rosé	Negroamaro; others up to 20%
San Severo	Red, Rosé	Montepulciano di Abruzzo (70 to 100%); Sangiovese (up to 30%)
	White	Bombino Bianco, Trebbiano Toscano (40 to 60%) Malvasia Bianca, Verdeca (up to 20%)
Squinzano	Red, Rosé	Negroamaro; others up to 30%
Torre Quarto (2)	Red	Malbec, Uva di Troia, Negroamaro
BASILICATA		
Aglianico dei Colli Lucani (2)	Red	Aglianico
Aglianico del Vulture	Red	Aglianico

(continued)

[1]This list includes DOCG wines as well (1), plus non-DOC wines worth noting (2).

Appendix A (*Continued*)

Region	DOC Wines	Type of Wine	Grape(s)
CALABRIA	Cirò	Red, Rosé	Gaglioppo; Greco Bianco, Trebbiano Toscano (10%)
		White	Greco Bianco
	Donnici	Red	Gaglioppo (50%); Greco Nero (10 to 20%); Malvasia Bianca, Mantonico Bianco, Percorella (20%)
	Greco di Bianco or Greco di Gerace	White, sweet	Greco Bianco
	Lamezia	Red	Nerello Mascalese and/or Nerello Cappuccio (up to 30 to 50%); Gaglioppo (Magliocco) (25 to 35%); Greco Nero (Marsigliana (25 to 35%)
	Melissa	Red	Gaglioppo (75 to 95%). Other grapes are: Greco Nero, Greco Bianco, Trebbiano Toscano, Malvasia Bianca
		White	Greco Bianco (80 to 95%); Trebbiano Toscano, Malvasia Bianca (5 to 20%)
	Pollino	Red	Gaglioppo (60%); Greco Nero, Malvasia Bianca, Montonico Bianco, Guarnaccia Bianca
	Sant'Anna di Isola Capo Rizzuto	Red	Gaglioppo (40 to 60%)
	Savuto	Red, Rosé	Gaglioppo (35 to 45%) Greco Nero, Nerello, Cappuccio, Magliocco Canino, Sangiovese (30 to 40%)

Region	Wine	Color	Grape composition
CAMPANIA	Capri	Red	Piedirosso; others up to 20%
		White	Falanghina; Greco Bianco; others up to 20%
	Falerno (2)	Red	Aglianico
	Fiano di Avellino	White	Fiano; others up to 15%
	Greco di Tufo	White	Greco Bianco (80 to 100%); Coda di Volpe Bianco (20%)
	Ischia	Red	Guarnaccia (50%); Per é Palummo (Piedirosso) (40%); Barbera (10%)
		White	Forastera (65%); Biancolella (20%); others (up to 15%)
		White (Bianco Superiore)	Forastera (50%); Biancolella (40%); San Lunardo (10%)
	Lacryma Christi del Vesuvio (2)	Red, Rosé	Olivella, Piedirosso, Aglianico
		White	Greco del Vesuvio, Coda di Volpe, Falanghina, Others
	Solopaca	Red	Sangiovese (45 to 50%); Aglianico (10 to 20%); Piedirosso (20 to 25%); Sciascinoso (10%)
		White	Trebbiano Toscano (50 to 70%); Malvasia di Candia (20 to 40%); Malvasia Toscano, Coda di Volpe (10%)
	Taurasi	Red	Aglianico; Piedirosso, Sangiovese, Barbera (up to a maximum of 30%)
EMILIA-ROMAGNA	Albana di Romagna	White	Albana
	Bianco di Scandiano	White	Sauvignon Blanc (up to 85%); Malvasia di Candia, Trebbiano Romagnolo (up to 15%)

(continued)

Appendix A (*Continued*)

Region	DOC Wines	Type of Wine	Grape(s)
EMILIA-ROMAGNA	Cabernet Sauvignon dei Colli Bolognesi (2)	Red	Cabernet Sauvignon
	Colli Bolognesi Barbera	Red	Barbera; Sangiovese (15%)
	Colli Bolognesi Bianco	White	Albana (60 to 80%); Trebbiano Romagnolo (20 to 40%)
	Colli Bolognesi Merlot	Red	Merlot (minimum of 85%)
	Colli Bolognesi Pinot Bianco	White	Pinot Bianco (minimum of 85%)
	Colli Bolognesi Riesling Italico or Pignoletto	White	Riesling Italico or a local clone called Pignoletto (minimum of 85%)
	Colli Bolognesi Sauvignon	White	Sauvignon Blanc (minimum of 85%)
	Colli di Parma	Red	Barbera (60 to 75%); Bonarda, Croatina (up to 40%)
	Malvasia	White	Malvasia di Candia (85 to 100%); Moscato Bianco (up to 15%)
	Sauvignon	White	Sauvignon Blanc
	Colli Piacentini (new DOC as of 1983) replaces 3 DOCS; see Gutturnio dei Colli Piacentini, Monterosso Val d'Arda, Trebbianino Val Trebbia		
	Gutturnio dei Colli Piacentini (DOC until 1983)	Red	Barbera (60%); Bonarda (40%)
	Lambrusco Grasparossa di Castelvetro	Red	Lambrusco Grasparossa (85%); other Lambrusco, Uva d'Oro (15%)

Lambrusco Reggiano	Red	Lambrusco Marani, Salamino, Monterico, and Maestri, either individually or together; Ancellotta (up to 20%)
Lambrusco Salamino di Santa Croce	Red	Lambrusco Salamino (90%); other Lambrusco and Uva d'Oro (10%)
Lambrusco di Sorbara	Red	Lambrusco di Sorbara (minimum 60%) and others
Monterosso Val d'Arda (DOC until 1983)	White	Malvasia di Candia (30 to 50%); Moscato Bianco (10 to 30%); Trebbiano Romagnolo, Ortrugo (20 to 30%)
Rosso Armentano (2)	Red	Cabernet Franc, Sangiovese di Romagna, Pinot Nero
Sangiovese di Romagna	Red	Sangiovese Romagna
Trebbiano di Romagna	White	Trebbiano di Romagna
Trebbianino Val Trebbia (DOC until 1983)	White	Ortrugo (35 to 50%); Malvasia di Candia (10 to 30%); Trebbiano Romagnolo (15 to 30%); Moscato Bianco, Sauvignon Blanc (15%)
FRIULI-VENEZIA GIULIA		
Aquilea:		
Cabernet	Red	Cabernet Franc or Cabernet Sauvignon
Merlot	Red	Merlot
Pinot Bianco	White	Pinot Bianco
Pinot Grigio	White	Pinot Grigio
Refosco	Red	Refosco del Peduncolo Rosso

(continued)

Appendix A (*Continued*)

Region	DOC Wines	Type of Wine	Grape(s)
FRIULI-VENEZIA GIULIA	Riesling Renano	White	Riesling Renano
	Tocai Friulano	White	Tocai Friulano
	Carso	Red	Terrano (85%); Pinot Nero, Piccola Nera
		White	Malvasia Istriana (85%)
	Collio Goriziano or Collio:		
	Cabernet Franc	Red	Cabernet Franc
	Collio	White	Ribolla Malvasia Tocai
	Malvasia	White	Malvasia
	Merlot	Red	Merlot
	Pinot Bianco	White	Pinot Bianco
	Pinot Grigio	White	Pinot Grigio
	Pinot Nero	Red	Pinot Nero
	Ribolla	White	Ribolla
	Riesling Italico	White	Riesling Italico
	Sauvignon	White	Sauvignon
	Tocai Friulano	White	Tocai Friulano
	Traminer	White	Traminer
	Colli Orientali del Friuli:		
	Cabernet	Red	Cabernet Sauvignon or Cabernet Franc
	Merlot	Red	Merlot
	Picolit	White, semisweet or sweet	Picolit (90%)
	Pinot Bianco	White	Pinot Bianco
	Pinot Grigio	White	Pinot Grigio

Pinot Nero	Red
Refosco	Red
Ribolla	White
Riesling Renano	White
Sauvignon	White
Tocai Friulano	White
Verduzzo (Ramandolo)	White, dry or semisweet

Grave del Friuli:

Cabernet	Red
Merlot	Red
Pinot Bianco	White
Pinot Grigio	White
Refosco	Red
Tocai	White
Verduzzo	White

Isonzo:

Cabernet	Red
Malvasia Istriana	White
Merlot	Red
Pinot Bianco	White
Pinot Grigio	White
Riesling Renano	White
Sauvignon	White
Tocai	White
Traminer Aromatico	White
Verduzzo Friulano	White

Pinot Nero	Red
Refosco	Red
Ribolla	White
White Riesling	White
Sauvignon Blanc	White
Tocai Friulano	White
Verduzzo	White, dry or semisweet

Cabernet Franc	Red
Merlot	Red
Pinot Bianco	White
Pinot Grigio	White
Refosco	Red
Tocai	White
Verduzzo	White

Cabernet Sauvignon or Cabernet Franc	Red
Malvasia Istriana	White
Merlot	Red
Pinot Bianco	White
Pinot Grigio	White
Riesling Renano	White
Sauvignon	White
Tocai	White
Traminer Aromatico	White
Verduzzo Friulano	White

(continued)

Appendix A (*Continued*)

Region	DOC Wines	Type of Wine	Grape(s)
FRIULI–VENEZIA GIULIA	Latisana:		
	Cabernet	Red	Cabernet Sauvignon or Cabernet Franc
	Merlot	Red	Merlot
	Pinot Bianco	White	Pinot Bianco
	Pinot Grigio	White	Pinot Grigio
	Refosco	Red	Refosco
	Tocai Friulano	White	Tocai Friulano
	Verduzzo Friulano	White	Verduzzo Friulano
	Picolit (2)	White, dessert	Picolit
LATIUM	Aleatico di Gradoli	Red	Aleatico
	Aprilia:		
	Merlot	Red	Merlot (95% minimum)
	Sangiovese	Red	Sangiovese (95%)
	Trebbiano	White	Trebbiano (95%)
	Bianco Capena	White	Malvasia (di Candia, del Lazio, Toscana) (55%); Trebbiano (Toscano, Romagnolo, Giallo) (25%); Bellone and Bombino (up to 20%)
	Cerveteri	Red	Sangiovese and Montepulciano (60%); Cesanese Comune (25%); Canaiolo Nero, Carignano, Barbera (30%)
		White	Trebbiano (Toscano, Romagnolo, Giallo) (50%); Malvasia (35%); Verdicchio, Tocai, Bellone, Bombino (15% maximum)

Cesanese del Piglio	Red	Cesanese
Cesanese di Affile	Red	Cesanese
Cesanese di Olevano Romano	Red	Cesanese
Colli Albani	White	Malvasia Rossa or Malvasia Bianca di Candia (60%); Trebbiano (Toscano, Verde, Giallo) (25 to 50%); Malvasia del Lazio (15 to 40%)
Colli Lanuvini	White	Malvasia Bianca di Candia (70%); Trebbiano (Toscano, Verde, Bianco) (30%); Bellone and Bonvino (10%)
Cori	Red	Montepulciano (40 to 60%); Nero Buono di Cori (20 to 40%); Cesanese (10 to 30%)
Cori	White	Malvasia di Candia (40 to 60%); Bellone (20 to 30%); Trebbiano Toscano (15 to 25%); Trebbiano Giallo (5 to 10%)
Est! Est!! Est!!! di Montefiascone	White	Trebbiano Toscano (65%); Malvasia Bianca Toscana (20%); Rossetto (15%)
Falerno (2)	Red	Aglianico, Barbera
Fiorano (2)	Red	Cabernet Sauvignon or Cabernet Franc
Frascati	White	Malvasia di Candia, Sémillon
Marino	White	Malvasia, Trebbiano, and other grapes
	White	Malvasia Rossa (60%); Trebbiano and other grapes
Montecompatri Colonna	White	Malvasia (70%); Trebbiano and other grapes

(continued)

Appendix A (*Continued*)

Region	DOC Wines	Type of Wine	Grape(s)
LATIUM	Orvieto	White	Trebbiano, Verdello, Grechetto, Malvasia and other grapes
	Torre Ercolana (2)	Red	Cesanese, Cabernet Sauvignon or Cabernet Franc, Merlot
	Velletri	Red	Sangiovese (20 to 35%); Montepulciano (20 to 35%); Cesanese Comune (30%); Bombino Nero, Merlot, Ciliegiolo (10%)
		White	Malvasia (70%); Trebbiano (30%); Bellone and Bonvino (10%)
	Zagarolo	White	Malvasia (70%); Trebbiano (30%); Bellone and Bonvino (10%)
LIGURIA	Cinqueterre	White	Bosco (60%); Albarola and/or Vermentino (40%)
	Rossese di Dolceacqua or Dolceacqua	Red	Rossese
LOMBARDY	Botticino	Red	Barbera (30 to 40%); Schiava Gentile (20 to 30%); Marzemino (15 to 25%); Sangiovese (10 to 20%)
	Capriano del Colle	Red	Sangiovese (40 to 50%); Marzemino (35 to 45%); Barbera (3 to 10%)
	Capriano del Colle–Trebbiano	White	Trebbiano di Soave
	Cellatica	Red	Schiava Gentile (35 to 45%); Barbera (25 to 30%); Marzemino (20 to 30%); Incrocio Terzi (Barbera + Cabernet Franc) (10 to 15%)
	Clastidium (2)	White	Pinot Nero, Pinot Grigio

Name	Type	Grapes
Colli Morenici Mantovani del Garda	Red, Rosé	Rossanella (30 to 60%); Rondinella (20 to 50%); Negrara Trentina (10 to 30%)
	White	Garganega (20 to 25%); Trebbiano Giallo (20 to 25%); Trebbiano Nostrano (10 to 40%)
Franciacorta: Pinot	White	Pinot Bianco
	Sparkling	Pinot Bianco
	Rosé	Pinot Nero, Pinot Bianco, Pinot Grigio
Rosso	Red	Cabernet Franc (40 to 50%); Barbera (20 to 30%); Nebbiolo (15 to 25%); Merlot (10 to 15%)
Lugana	White	Trebbiano di Lugano
Oltrepò Pavese:		
Barbacarlo	Red	Barbera, Croatina, Uva Rara, Ughetta
Barbera	Red	Barbera
Bonarda	Red	Bonarda
Buttafuoco	Red	Barbera, Croatina, Uva Rara, Ughetta
Cortese	White	Cortese
Moscato	White, sweet	Moscato
Pinot	Red	Pinot Nero
	White	Pinot Grigio
	Sparkling	Pinot Grigio, Pinot Nero
Riesling	White	Riesling Renano and/or Riesling Italico
Rosso	Red	Barbera, Croatina, Uva Rara, Ughetta
Sangue di Giuda	Red	Croatina and other grapes

(continued)

Appendix A (*Continued*)

Region	DOC Wines	Type of Wine	Grape(s)
LOMBARDY	Riviera del Garda Bresciano	Red, Rosé	Groppello (50 to 60%); Sangiovese (10 to 25%); Barbera (10 to 20%); Marzemino (5 to 15%)
	Rosso di Bellagio	Red	Cabernet Franc, Merlot, Pinot Nero
	Tocai di San Martino della Battaglia	White	Tocai Friulano
	Valtellina:		
	Rosso	Red	Nebbiolo, here called Chiavennasca (minimum of 70%)
	Sfursat	Red	Same as above
	Valtellina Superiore:		
	Grumello	Red	Nebbiolo (minimum of 95%)
	Inferno	Red	Same
	Sassella	Red	Same
	Valgella	Red	Same
THE MARCHES	Bianchello del Metauro	White	Bianchello (95%); Malvasia (5%)
	Bianco dei Colli Maceratesi	White	Trebbiano Toscano (50%); Maceratino (30 to 50%); to Malvasia Toscano and Verdicchio (15%)
	Falerio dei Colli Ascolani	White	Trebbiano Toscano (80%); Passerina, Verdicchio, Malvasia Toscano, Pinot Bianco, Pecorino (20%)
	Rosso Cònero	Red	Montepulciano (85%); Sangiovese (15%)
	Rosso Piceno	Red	Sangiovese (60%); Montepulciano (40%)

Sangiovese dei Colli Pesaresi	Red	Sangiovese Romagna (85%); Montepulciano and/or Ciliegiolo (15%)
Verdicchio dei Castelli di Jesi	White	Verdicchio; Trebbiano and/or Malvasia (up to 20%)
Verdicchio di Matelica	White	Verdicchio, Trebbiano Toscano, Malvasia
Vernaccia di Serrapetrona	Red	Vernaccia di Serrapetrona
MOLISE		No DOC Wines
PIEDMONT		
Barbaresco (1)	Red	Nebbiolo
Barbera d'Alba	Red	Barbera
Barbera d'Asti	Red	Barbera
Barbera del Monferrato	Red	Barbera (75 to 90%); Freisa, Grignolino, Dolcetto (up to 15%)
Barolo (1)	Red	Nebbiolo
Boca	Red	Nebbiolo (Spanna) (45 to 70%); Vespolina (20 to 40%); Bonarda Novarese (20%)
Brachetto d'Acqui	Red, sparkling	Brachetto
Bramatera	Red	Nebbiolo (Spanna) (50 to 70%); Croatina (20 to 30%); Bonarda and Vespolina (10 to 20%)
Carema	Red	Nebbiolo (Picotener or Pugnet)
Colli Tortonesi:		
Barbera	Red	Barbera (minimum of 85%); Freisa, Bonarda, Dolcetto (up to 15%)
Cortese	White	Cortese
Cortese di Gavi or Gavi	White	Cortese

(continued)

Region	DOC Wines	Type of Wine	Grape(s)
PIEDMONT	Dolcetto d'Acqui	Red	Dolcetto
	Dolcetto d'Alba	Red	Dolcetto
	Dolcetto d'Asti	Red	Dolcetto
	Dolcetto delle Langhe Monregalesi	Red	Dolcetto
	Dolcetto di Diano d'Alba	Red	Dolcetto
	Dolcetto di Dogliani	Red	Dolcetto
	Dolcetto di Ovada	Red	Dolcetto
	Erbaluce di Caluso:		
	Bianco	White	Erbaluce
	Passito	Amber, sweet	Erbaluce
	Fara	Red	Nebbiolo (30 to 50%); Vespolina (10 to 30%); Bonarda Novarese (up to 40%)
	Freisa d'Asti	Red	Freisa
	Freisa di Chieri	Red	Freisa
	Gabiano	Red	Barbera
	Gattinara	Red	Nebbiolo (Spanna); Bonarda (up to 10%)
	Ghemme	Red	Nebbiolo (60 to 85%); Vespolina and Bonarda (15 to 40%)
	Grignolino d'Asti	Red	Grignolino; Freisa (up to 10%)
	Grignolino del Monferrato Casalese	Red	Grignolino; Freisa (up to 10%)
	Lessona	Red	Nebbiolo (Spanna); Vespolina and Bonarda (up to 25%)
	Malvasia di Casorzo d'Asti	Red	Malvasia di Casorzo; Freisa, Grignolino, Barbera (up to 10%)

Malvasia di Castelnuovo Don Bosco	Red	Malvasia di Schierano; Freisa (up to 15%)
Moscato d'Asti–Moscato d'Asti Spumante	White, sparkling	Moscato Bianco
Nebbiolo d'Alba	Red	Nebbiolo
Nebbiolo delle Langhe (2)	Red	Nebbiolo
Rubino di Cantavenna	Red	Barbera (75 to 90%); Grignolino and/or Freisa (10 to 25%)
Sizzano	Red	Nebbiolo (40 to 60%); Vespolina (15 to 40%); Bonarda Novarese (up to 25%)
Spanna (2)	Red	Spanna (Nebbiolo)
Vinòt (2)	Red (Beaujolais-*nouveau* style wine prepared by using carbonic maceration)	Nebbiolo
SARDINIA		
Campidano di Terralba, or Terralba	Red	Bovale; others up to 20%
Cannonau di Sardegna	Red, Rosé, some sweet	Cannonau; Bovale Grande Carignano, Pascale di Cagliari, Monica, and Vernaccia di S. Gimignano (up to 10% total)
Carignano del Sulcis	Red, Rosé	Carignano; Monica, Pascale, Alicante-Bouschet (up to 15% total)
Girò di Cagliari	Red, generally sweet	Girò
Malvasia di Bosa	White, dessert	Malvasia di Sardegna

(continued)

Region	DOC Wines	Type of Wine	Grape(s)
SARDINIA	Malvasia di Cagliari	White, dry and sweet	Malvasia di Sardegna
	Mandrolisai	Red, Rose	Bovale Sardo, Cannonou, Monica
	Monica di Cagliari	Red, generally sweet	Monica
	Monica di Sardegna	Red	Monica; Pascale di Cagliari, Carignano, Bovale Grande, Bovale Sardo (up to 15%)
	Moscato di Cagliari	White, dessert	Moscato Bianco
	Moscato di Sardegna	White, sparkling	Moscato Bianco and 10% others
	Moscato di Sorso-Sennori	White, sweet	Moscato Bianco
	Nasco di Cagliari	White, dry, semi-sweet, and sweet	Nasco
	Nuragus di Cagliari	White	Nuragus (85 to 95%); Trebbiano Toscano and Romagnolo, Vermentino, Clairette, Semidano (up to 15%)
	Vermentino di Gallura	White	Vermentino
	Vernaccia di Oristano	White, dry, similar to sherry	Vernaccia di Oristano
SICILY	Alcamo, or Bianco Alcamo	White	Catarratto Bianco; Damaschino, Grecanico, Trebbiano Toscano (up to 20% total)
	Cerasuolo di Vittoria	Red	Calabrese (up to 60%); Frappato (40%); Grosso Nero and Nerello Mascalese (up to 10% total)

282

Corvo (2)	Red	Nerello Mascalese, Perricone, Nero d'Avola
	White, sparkling	Inzolia, Trebbiano, Catarratto
Corvo Stravecchio di Sicilia	Fortified	Inzolia, Catarratto, Grillo
Etna	Red, Rosé	Nerello Mascalese (80%); Nerello Mantellato (20%); others (up to 10%)
	White	Carricante (60%); Catarrato Bianco (40%); Trebbiano and Minella Bianca (15%)
Faro	Red	Nerello Mascalese (45 to 60%); Nerello Cappuccio (15 to 20%); Nocera (5 to 10%); others (up to 15%)
Malvasia delle Lipari	White, dessert	Malvasia di Lipari (95%); Corinto Nero (8 to 9% maximum)
Marsala	White (amber), dry and fortified sweet	Catarratto and/or Grillo; Inzolia (up to 15% maximum)
Moscato di Noto	White, semisweet, sparkling, and dessert	Moscato Bianco
Moscato di Pantelleria	White, semisweet, sparkling, and dessert	Zibibbo (large Moscato) or Moscatellone

TRENTINO–ALTO ADIGE

Alto Adige (Südtirol):		
Cabernet	Red	Cabernet Sauvignon or Cabernet Franc
Lagrein Rosato (Lagrien Kretzer)	Rosé	Lagrein

(continued)

Appendix A *(Continued)*

Region	DOC Wines	Type of Wine	Grape(s)
TRENTINO–ALTO ADIGE	Lagrein Scuro (Lagrein Dunkel)	Red	Lagrein
	Malvasia (Malvasier)	Red	Malvasia Nera
	Merlot	Red	Merlot
	Moscato Giallo (Goldenmuska-teller)	White, sweet	Moscato Giallo
	Moscato Rosa (Rosenmusca-teller)	Rosé, semisweet	Moscato Rosa
	Müller-Thurgau	White	Müller-Thurgau
	Pinot Bianco (Weissburgunder)	White	Pinot Bianco; some Chardonnay
	Pinot Grigio (Rülander)	White	Pinot Grigio
	Pinot Nero (Blauburgunder)	Red	Pinot Nero
	Riesling Italico (Welschriesling)	White	Riesling Italico
	Riesling Renano (Rheinriesling)	White	White Riesling
	Sauvignon	White	Sauvignon Blanc
	Schiava (Vernatsch)	Red	Schiava
	Sylvaner	White	Sylvaner
	Traminer Aromatico (Gewürz-traminer)	White	Gewürztraminer
	Caldaro or Lago di Caldaro (Kal-terersee)	Red	Schiava Grossa (85 to 100%); Pinot Nero and Lagrein (15% maximum)
	Castel San Michele (2)	Red	Cabernet Sauvignon or Cabernet Franc, Merlot
	Casteller	Red, Rosé	Schiava (minimum of 30%); Lambrusco (up to 40%); Merlot (up to 20%)

Name	Type	Grapes
Colli di Bolzano (Bozner Leiten)	Red	Schiava (90%); Lagrein and Pinot Nero (up to 10%)
Meranese di Collina (Meraner Hügel)	Red	Schiava, Tschaggeler
Santa Maddalena (St. Magdalener)	Red	Schiava, Tschaggeler
Sorni	Red	Schiava (70%); Teroldego (20 to 30%); Lagrein (up to 10%)
	White	Nosiolo (70%); others (up to 30%)
Terlano (Terlaner):		
Müller-Thurgau	White	Müller-Thurgau
Pinot Bianco (Weissburgunder)	White	Pinot Bianco, some Chardonnay
Riesling Italico (Welschriesling)	White	Riesling Italico
Riesling Renano (Rheinriesling)	White	White Riesling
Sauvignon	White	Sauvignon Blanc
Sylvaner	White	Sylvaner
Terlano (Terlaner)	White	Pinot Bianco (at least half), with other varieties
Teroldego Rotaliano	Red	Teroldego; Lagrein or Pinot Nero (up to 10%)
Trentino:		
Cabernet	Red	Cabernet Sauvignon or Cabernet Franc
Lagrein	Red, Rosé	Lagrein
Marzemino	Red	Marzemino
Merlot	Red	Merlot
Moscato	White, semisweet, sweet	Moscato Bianco, Giallo
Pinot Bianco	White	Pinot Bianco, Chardonnay, Pinot Grigio (permitted up to 50%)

(continued)

Appendix A (*Continued*)

Region	DOC Wines	Type of Wine	Grape(s)
TRENTINO–ALTO ADIGE	Pinot Nero	Red	Pinot Nero
	Riesling	White	Riesling Renano (White Riesling), Riesling Italico, or Müller-Thurgau
	Traminer Aromatico	White	Traminer Aromatico (Gewürztraminer)
	Vino Santo	White (amber), sweet	Nosiola, Pinot Bianco
	Valdadige (Etschtaler):		
	Rosso	Red, Rosé	Various combinations of Lambrusco, Schiava, Merlot, Pinot Nero, Lagrein, Teroldego, Negrara
	Bianco	White	Many grapes are permitted: Pinot Bianco, Pinot Grigio, Riesling Italico, Müller-Thurgau, Bianchetta Trevigiana, Trebbiano Toscano, Nosiola, Vernaccia, Sylvaner, Veltliner. Grapes can be used alone or in combinations.
	Valle Isacro (Eisacktaler):		
	Müller-Thurgau	White	Müller-Thurgau
	Pinot Grigio (Rülander)	White	Pinot Grigio
	Sylvaner	White	Sylvaner
	Traminer Aromatico (Gewürztraminer)	White	Gewürztraminer
	Veltliner	White	Veltliner

TUSCANY		
Bianco della Valdinievole	White	Trebbiano
Bianco di Pitigliano	White	Trebbiano Toscano (65 to 70%); Greceto (30 to 35%); Malvasia Bianca Toscana and Verdello (up to 15%)
Bianco Pisano di San Torpé	White	Trebbiano Toscano (75%); Canaiolo Bianco, Malvasia Toscano
Bianco Vergine della Valdichiana	White	Trebbiano Toscano (70 to 85%); Malvasia del Chianti (10 to 20%); others (up to 5 to 10%)
Brunello di Montalcino (1)	Red	Brunello (Sangiovese Grosso)
Candia dei Colli Apuani	White	Vermentino Bianco (70 to 80%); Albarola (10 to 20%)
Carmignano	Red	Sangiovese (45 to 65%); Canaiolo Nero (10 to 20%); Cabernet Sauvignon (6 to 10%); Trebbiano Toscano, Canaiolo Bianco, Malvasia del Chianti (10 to 20%); Mammolo, Colorino, Occhio di Pernice (up to 5%)
Chianti (1): Chianti Classico Chianti Colli Fiorentini Chianti Colli Senesi Chianti Colli Pisane Chianti Montalbano Chianti Rufina	Red	Sangiovese (50 to 80%); Canaiolo Nero (10 to 30%); Trebbiano Toscano and Malvasia del Chianti (10 to 30%)

(continued)

Appendix A (*Continued*)

Region	DOC Wines	Type of Wine	Grape(s)
TUSCANY	Elba		
	Rosso	Red	Sangiovese (90%); Canaiolo, Trebbiano Toscano, Biancone (up to 25%)
	Bianco	White	Procanico (Trebbiano Toscano)
	Galestro (2)	White	Trebbiano Toscano
	Monte Antico	Red	Similar to Chianti
	Montecarlo	White	Trebbiano Toscano (60 to 70%); Sémillon, Pinot Bianco, Pinot Grigio, Vermentino, Sauvignon Blanc, Roussanne (30 to 40%)
	Montescudaio:		
	Rosso	Red	Sangiovese (65 to 85%); Trebbiano Toscano, Malvasia (up to 25%)
	Bianco	White	Trebbiano Toscano (70 to 85%); Malvasia del Chianti, Vermentino (up to 30%)
	Morellino di Scansano	Red	Sangiovese; other red grapes (up to 15%)
	Parrina:		
	Rosso	Red	Sangiovese (80%); Canaiolo Nero, Montepulciano, Colorino (20%)
	Bianco	White	Procanico (Trebbiano) (80%); Ansonica and/or Malvasia del Chianti (up to 20%)

Pomino:		
Rosso	Red	Sangiovese (60 to 75%); Canaiolo and/or Cabernet Sauvignon or Cabernet Franc (15 to 25%); Merlot (10 to 20%)
Bianco	White	Pinot Bianco and/or Chardonnay (60 to 80%); Trebbiano (up to 30%)
Rosso delle Colline Lucchesi	Red	Sangiovese (45 to 60%); Canaiolo (8 to 15%); Ciliegiolo and Colorino (5 to 15%); Trebbiano Toscano (10 to 15%); Vermentino, Malvasia Toscana (5 to 10%)
Rosso di Montalcino	Red	Brunello (Sangiovese)
Sassicaia (2)	Red	Cabernet Sauvignon
Tignanello	Red	Similar to Chianti, with 10% Cabernet Sauvignon
Val d'Arbia	White	Trebbiano Toscano, Malvasia, others such as Riesling, Chardonnay, Pinot Bianco
Vernaccia di San Gimignano	White	Vernaccia di San Gimignano
Vino Nobile di Montepulciano (1)	Red	Prugnolo Gentile (Sangiovese Grosso) (50 to 70%); Canaiolo (10 to 20%); Malvasia del Chianti, Trebbiano Toscano (10 to 20%)
UMBRIA		
Colli Altotiberini:		
Rosso, Rosato	Red, Rosé	Sangiovese (55 to 70%); Merlot (10 to 20%); Trebbiano, Malvasia (10%)

(continued)

Appendix A (*Continued*)

Region	DOC Wines	Type of Wine	Grape(s)
UMBRIA	Bianco	White	Trebbiano Toscano (75 to 90%); Malvasia (up to 10%); others (up to 15%)
	Colli Perugini:		
	Rosso, Rosato	Red, Rosé	Sangiovese (65 to 85%); Montepulciano, Ciliegiolo, Barbera and/or Merlot (15 to 35% but no more than 10% Merlot)
	Bianco	White	Trebbiano Toscano (65 to 85%); Greceto, Verdicchio, Garganega and/or Malvasia del Chianti (15 to 35% but no more than 10% Malvasia)
	Colli del Trasimeno:		
	Rosso	Red	Sangiovese (60 to 80%); Gamay, Ciliegiolo, or white grapes (up to 40%)
	Bianco	White	Trebbiano Toscano (up to 70%); Malvasia del Chianti, Verdicchio Bianco, Verdello and Greceto (up to 40%)
	Grechetto, or Greco (2)	White	Greceto
	Montefalco:		
	Montefalco Rosso	Red	Sangiovese (65 to 75%); Trebbiano Toscano (15 to 25%); Sagrantino (5 to 10%)

	Type	Grapes
Sagrantino di Montefalco	Red, dry and dessert	Sagrantino (100% – or with up to 5% Trebbiano Toscano)
Orvieto	White	Trebbiano Toscano (50 to 65%); Verdello (15 to 25%); Greceto, Drupeggio, Malvasia Toscana (20 to 30%)
Torgiano: Rubesco	Red	Sangiovese (50 to 70%); Canaiolo (15 to 30%); Ciliegiolo and/or Montepulciano (10%)
Torre di Giano	White	Trebbiano (50 to 70%); Greceto (15 to 35%); Malvasia or Verdello (up to 15%)
VALLE d'AOSTA		
Donnaz	Red	Nebbiolo
Enfer d'Arvier	Red	Petit Rouge
THE VENETO		
Bardolino	Red, Rosé	Corvina Veronese (50 to 65%); Rondinella (10 to 30%); Molinara (10 to 20%); Negrara, Rossignola, Barbera, Sangiovese (10%)
Bianco di Custoza	White	Trebbiano Toscano (5 to 15%); Garganega (20 to 30%); Tocai Friulano (5 to 15%); Cortese (20 to 30%)
Breganze: Bianco	White	Tocai Friulano
Carbernet	Red	Cabernet Sauvignon or Cabernet Franc

(continued)

291

Region	DOC Wines	Type of Wine	Grape(s)
THE VENETO	Pinot Bianco	White	Pinot Bianco
	Pinot Grigio	White	Pinot Grigio
	Pinot Nero	Red	Pinot Nero
	Rosso	Red	Merlot
	Vespaiolo	White	Vespaiolo
	Colli Berici:		
	Cabernet	Red	Cabernet Franc; some Cabernet Sauvignon
	Garganega	White	Garganega
	Merlot	Red	Merlot
	Pinot Bianco	White	Pinot Bianco
	Sauvignon	White	Sauvignon Blanc
	Tocai Italico	White	Tocai Italico
	Tocai Rosso	Red	Tocai Rosso
	Colli Euganei:		
	Bianco	White, dry, some semisweet and sparkling	Garganega (30 to 50%); Serprina (20 to 40%); Tocai and/or Sauvignon (20 to 30%); Pinella, Pinot Bianco, Riesling Italico (up to 30% total)
	Moscato	White, semisweet, sweet, sparkling	Moscato Bianco
	Rosso	Red, dry, some semisweet and sparkling	Merlot (60 to 80%); Cabernet Franc, Cabernet Sauvignon, Barbera, Raboso Veronese (20 to 40%)

Gambellara:		
Gambellara Bianco	White	Garganega (80 to 90%); Trebbiano di Soave (5 to 20%)
Recioto di Gambellara	White, sweet	Same as above
Vin Santo di Gambellara	White (amber), sweet	Same as above
Montello and Colli Asolani:		
Cabernet	Red	Cabernet Sauvignon or Cabernet Franc; other grapes may be blended (up to 15%)
Merlot	Red	Merlot; other grapes may be blended (up to 15%)
Prosecco	White, dry, semi-sweet, sparkling	Prosecco
Piave:		
Cabernet del Piave	Red	Cabernet Sauvignon or Cabernet Franc
Merlot del Piave	Red	Merlot
Tocai del Piave	White	Tocai
Verduzzo del Piave	White	Verduzzo
Pramaggiore:		
Cabernet di Pramaggiore	Red	Cabernet Sauvignon or Cabernet Franc; Merlot (up to 10%)
Merlot di Pramaggiore	Red	Merlot; Cabernet (up to 10%)

(continued)

Appendix A (*Continued*)

Region	DOC Wines	Type of Wine	Grape(s)
THE VENETO	Prosecco di Conegliano–Valdobbia-dene	White, dry, semi-sweet, sweet, sparkling	Prosecco; Verdiso (up to 10%)
	Soave	White	Garganega (70 to 90%); Trebbiano di Soave (10 to 30%)
	Recioto di Soave	White, dessert	
	Tocai di Lison	White	Tocai Friulano (95%); other white grapes (5%)
	Valpolicella:	Red	Corvina Veronese (55 to 70%); Rondinella (25 to 30%); Molinara (5 to 15%); Rossignola, Negrara, Barbera, Sangiovese (up to 10%)
	Recioto della Valpolicella	Red, semisweet, sweet	Same as Valpolicella
	Recioto della Valpolicella Amarone, or Amarone	Red, very dry	Same as Valpolicella

BASIC DRINK RECIPES

DEFINITIONS OF MIXING INSTRUCTIONS
Build

Drinks are mixed by adding the ingredients, in the order listed, in the glass in which the drink is to be served. The types of drinks that are built are highballs, fruit-juice drinks, and hot drinks. Some drinks call for one or more ingredients to be floated on top of others. These drinks also are built.

Stir and Strain

Two or more ingredients are stirred together in a mixing glass with ice and then strained into a chilled glass, typically a cocktail glass. The procedure has two objectives: to chill the ingredients and to obtain the proper dilution ratio.

Shake/Blend and Strain

A drink is shaken either by hand or with a mechanical mixer or shake mixer. A blended drink is made using an electric blender. If the ingredients contain no solid foods or ice, either can be used. Solids, however, must be blended. Following the mixing, the drink is strained into a chillled glass.

ACAPULCO

Light rum or tequila	1.0 ounce
Sugar	0.5 teaspoon
Lime juice	1.0 ounce
Triple sec	0.5 ounce
Pineapple juice (optional)	Dash

Mixing Method: Shake/blend and strain into a cocktail glass (no ice).

AGGRAVATION

Scotch	1.0 ounce
Kahlua	0.5 ounce
Milk	To fill

Mixing Method: Build in a highball glass (three-quarters filled with ice cubes).

BRANDY ALEXANDER

Brandy	0.75 ounce
Crème de cacao (dark)	0.75 ounce
Cream	1.0 ounce

Mixing Method: Shake/blend and strain into a cocktail glass (no ice).

BACARDI

Bacardi Rum	1.5 ounces
Lime juice	1.5 ounces
Grenadine	0.50 ounce

Mixing Method: Shake/blend and strain into a cocktail glass (no ice).

BANSHEE (also called WHITE MONKEY)

A Grasshopper made with crème
   de banana instead of green
   créme de menthe
(See GRASSHOPPER)

Mixing Method: Shake/blend and strain into a cocktail glass (no ice).

BETWEEN THE SHEETS

Rum	0.75 ounce
Brandy	0.75 ounce
Lemon juice	0.75 ounce
Triple sec	0.75 ounce

Mixing Method: Shake/blend and strain into a cocktail glass (no ice).

BLACK RUSSIAN

Vodka	1.5 ounces
Kahlua	0.75 ounce

Mixing Method: Build in a rocks glass (filled with ice cubes).

BLACK VELVET

Guiness Stout (bitter stout)	One part
Champagne (or other sparkling wine)	One part

Mixing Method: Build in a collins, cooler, or zombie glass (no ice). Pour simultaneously into the glass without stirring.

BLACK WATCH

Scotch	1.5 ounces
Kahlua	0.75 ounce
Lemon twist	1 each

Mixing Method: Build in a rocks glass (filled with ice cubes).

BLOODY MARY

Vodka	1.5 ounces
Tomato juice*	3.0 ounces
Lemon juice*	0.5 ounce
Worcestershire sauce*	2 to 3 dashes
Tabasco sauce*	2 drops
Salt, pepper, or celery salt*	To taste
Or replace all items marked* with Bloody Mary Mix.	Fill glass

Garnish with celery stick or a lemon or lime wedge.
Bloody Bull: Replace half of tomato juice with beef bouillon.
Bloody Maria: Replace vodka with tequila.

Mixing Method: Build in a highball or collins glass rimmed with salt (half-filled with ice cubes).

BLUE-TAIL FLY

Blue Curaçao	0.75 ounce
White crème de cacao	0.75 ounce
Cream	1.5 ounces

Mixing Method: Shake/blend and strain into a cocktail glass (no ice).

BUCK

Liquor of choice	1.5 ounces
Ginger ale	To fill
Lemon wedge, squeezed	1 each

Mixing Method: Build in a highball glass (three-quarters filled with ice cubes).

CAPE CODDER

Vodka	1.5 ounces
Cranberry juice	To fill
Lime wedge	1 each

Mixing Method: Build in a highball glass (half-filled with ice cubes).

CHAMPAGNE COCKTAIL

Sugar cube	1 each
Or sugar	1 teaspoon
Or simple syrup	0.25 ounce
Angostura bitters	Dash
Champagne or other sparkling wine	To fill
Lemon twist	1 each

Mixing Method: Build in a Champagne glass (no ice).

COBRA (HAMMER, SLOE SCREW)

Sloe gin	1.5 ounces
Orange juice	To fill

Mixing Method: Build in a highball glass (half-filled with ice cubes).

COLLINS (TOM, JOHN, VODKA, RUM)

Gin (or bourbon, vodka, or rum)	1.5 ounces
Sweet-and-Sour Mix	2.0 ounces
Soda	Top after straining

Garnish with cherry and orange slice

Mixing Method: Shake/blend and strain into a collins glass (filled with ice cubes).

COMFORTABLE SCREW

Southern Comfort	1.5 ounces
Orange juice	To fill

Mixing Method: Build in a highball glass (half-filled with ice cubes).

CUBA LIBRE

Rum	1.5 ounces
Cola	To fill
Lime wedge, squeezed	1 each

Mixing Method: Build in a highball glass (three-quarters filled with ice cubes).

DAIQUIRI

Light rum	1.5 ounces
Lime juice*	2.0 ounces
Sugar*	1 teaspoon
*Or Sweet-and-Sour Mix	2.0 ounces

Mixing Method: Shake/blend and strain into a cocktail glass (no ice).

DRY MANHATTAN

Bourbon or blended whisky	2.0 ounces
Dry vermouth	0.5 ounce
Lemon twist	1 each

Mixing Method: Stir and strain into a cocktail glass (no ice).

FOG HORN

Lime juice	0.5 lime; retain lime
Gin	1.5 ounces
Ginger ale	To fill

Mixing Method: Build in a highball glass (three-quarters filled with ice cubes).

FRAPPÉ

Liqueur of choice	Pour evenly over ice
Short straws	

Mixing Method: Build in a cocktail glass (filled with crushed ice).

FREDDY FUDPUCKER

Tequila	1.5 ounces
Orange juice	To fill
Galliano (float on top)	0.75 ounce

Mixing Method: Build in a highball glass (half-filled with ice cubes).

FRENCH CONNECTION

Brandy	1.5 ounces
Amaretto	0.75 ounce

Mixing Method: Build in a rocks glass (filled with ice cubes).

GALLIANO STINGER

Brandy	1.5 ounces
Galliano	0.75 ounce

Mixing Method: Build in a rocks glass (filled with ice cubes).

GIBSON

Gin	2.0 ounces
Dry vermouth	0.25 ounce
Cocktail onion (This is what distinguishes a Gibson from a Martini)	1 each

Mixing Method: Stir and strain into a rocks glass (filled with ice cubes).

GIMLET

Gin or vodka	1.5 ounces
Gimlet lime juice (Rose's)	1.0 ounce
Lime wedge, squeezed	1 each

Mixing Method: Shake/blend and strain into a cocktail glass (no ice).

GIN AND TONIC

Gin	1.5 ounces
Tonic	To fill
Lime wedge, squeezed	1 each

Mixing Method: Build in a highball glass (three-quarters filled with ice cubes).

GODFATHER (GODMOTHER*)

Scotch	1.5 ounces
Amaretto	0.75 ounce

*Godmother: substitute vodka
   for Scotch

Mixing Method: Build in a rocks glass (filled with ice cubes).

GOLDEN CADILLAC

Galliano	0.75 ounce
White crème de cacao	0.75 ounce
Cream	1.5 ounces

Mixing Method: Shake/blend and strain into a cocktail glass (no ice).

GOLDEN DREAM

Galliano	1.0 ounce
Triple sec	0.5 ounce
Orange juice	0.5 ounce
Cream	1.0 ounce

Mixing Method: Shake/blend and strain into a cocktail glass (no ice).

GRASSHOPPER

White crème de cacao	0.75 ounce
Green crème de menthe	0.75 ounce
Cream	1.5 ounces

Mixing Method: Shake/blend and strain into a cocktail glass (no ice).

GREYHOUND

Vodka	1.5 ounces
Grapefruit juice	To fill
(This is a Salty Dog without the salt.)	

Mixing Method: Build in a highball glass (half-filled with ice cubes).

HARVEY WALLBANGER

Vodka	1.5 ounces
Orange juice	4.0 ounces
Galliano (float on top)	0.5 ounce

Mixing Method: Build in a highball glass (half-filled with ice cubes).

IRISH COFFEE

Irish whiskey	1.5 ounces
Sugar	1 teaspoon
Coffee, hot	To fill
Whipped cream	Top

Mixing Method: Build in a cup, mug, or wine glass (no ice).

KIR

Crème de cassis	0.5 ounce
White wine, chilled	5.0 ounces
Lemon twist (optional)	1 each

Mixing Method: Build in a wine glass (no ice).

KIR ROYALE

Crème de cassis	0.5 ounces
Champagne or other sparkling wine	5.0 ounces
Lemon twist (optional)	1 each

Mixing Method: Build in a sparkling wine glass—tulip or flute, not a saucer (no ice).

LONG ISLAND TEA

Vodka	0.33 ounce
Rum	0.33 ounce
Triple sec	0.33 ounce
Gin	0.25 ounce
Tequila	0.25 ounce
Sweet-and-Sour Mix	1.5 ounces
7-Up	1.5 ounces
Cola (to approximate the color of iced tea)	About 0.5 ounce
Lime wedge, squeezed	1 each

Mixing Method: Build in a 10-12-ounce collins glass (filled with iced cubes).

MAI TAI

Light rum	1.5 ounces
Mai Tai Mix	Fill to three-quarters of the glass
Jamaica rum (pour on top, stir)	0.75 ounce

Garnish: cherry, orange slice, or pineapple spear

Mixing Method: Shake/blend and strain into a double old-fashioned glass (with crushed or shaved ice).

MANHATTAN

Bourbon or blended whisky	2.0 ounces
Sweet vermouth	0.5 ounce (change according to taste)

Garnish: stemmed cherry

Mixing Method: Stir and strain into a cocktail glass (no ice).

PERFECT MANHATTAN

Bourbon or blended whisky	2.0 ounces
Dry vermouth	0.25 ounce
Sweet vermouth	0.25 ounce (adjust the vermouth according to taste)
Garnish: lemon twist	1 each

Mixing Method: Stir and strain into a cocktail glass (no ice).

MARGARITA

Tequila	1.5 ounces
Lime juice	0.5 ounce
Triple sec	0.5 ounce

Mixing Method: Shake/blend and strain into a cocktail or margarita glass rimmed with salt (no ice).

MARTINI

Gin	2.0 ounces
Dry vermouth	0.25 ounce (vary according to taste)

Garnish: olive

Mixing Method: Stir and strain into a cocktail glass (no ice).

PERFECT MARTINI

Gin	2.0 ounces
Dry vermouth	0.25 ounce
Sweet vermouth	0.25 ounce (vary according to taste)
Garnish: lemon twist	1 each

Mixing Method: Stir and strain in a cocktail glass (no ice).

MIMOSA

Champagne or other sparkling wine	one-half
Orange juice	one-half

Mixing Method: Build in a wine or sparkling wine glass, not a saucer (no ice).

MINT JULEP

Mint leaves (fresh, bruised)	10 to 12 each
Sugar	1 teaspoon
Soda	Splash
Muddle the mint, sugar, and soda	
Crushed ice	One-half glass
Bourbon	1.5 ounces
Crushed Ice	To fill
Bourbon	1.5 ounces

Stir up and down until glass frosts, then add long straws and garnish with mint sprigs.

Mixing Method: Build in a 16-ounce glass.

MOSCOW MULE

Vodka	1.5 ounces
Ginger beer	To fill
Lime half, squeezed	1 each

Mixing Method: Build in a copper mug (three-quarters filled with ice cubes).

OLD-FASHIONED

Sugar	1 to 2 teaspoons
Angostura bitters	1 to 3 dashes
Cubed ice	Fill glass
Bourbon or blended whisky	2.0 ounces
Soda (or water)	To fill

Garnish: cherry, orange slice, or lemon twist

Mixing Method: Build in an old-fashioned glass.

PIÑA COLADA

Light rum	1.0 ounce
Jamaica rum	0.5 ounce
Piña colada Mix	3.0 ounces

Mixing Method: Shake/blend and strain into a wine glass or glass mug (no ice).

PINK LADY

Sweet-and-Sour Mix	1.0 ounce
Cream	1.0 ounce
Grenadine	0.5 ounce
Gin	1.5 ounces

Mixing Method: Shake/blend and strain into a cocktail glass (no ice).

PINK SQUIRREL

Créme de Noyaux (almond)	0.75 ounce
White crème de cacao	0.75 ounce
Cream	1.5 ounces

Mixing Method: Shake/blend and strain into a cocktail glass (no ice).

PLANTER'S PUNCH

Light rum	1.0 ounce
Jamaica rum	0.5 ounce
Sweet-and-Sour Mix	1.0 ounce
Orange juice	1.0 ounce
Grenadine	0.5 ounce

Garnish: cherry, orange slice, pineapple spear, straws

Mixing Method: Shake/blend and strain into a collins glass (three-quarters filled with ice cubes).

ROB ROY

Scotch	2.0 ounces
Sweet vermouth	0.5 ounce
Bitters (Angostura or Orange)	Dash

Garnish: stemmed cherry

Mixing Method: Stir and strain into a cocktail glass (no ice).

RUSSIAN BEAR (VODKA ALEXANDER)

Vodka	1.0 ounce
White crème de cacao	1.0 ounce
Cream	1.5 ounces

Mixing Method: Shake/blend and strain into a cocktail glass (no ice).

RUSTY NAIL

Scotch	1.5 ounces
Drambuie	0.75 ounce

Mixing Method: Build in a rocks glass (filled with ice cubes).

SALTY DOG

Vodka	1.5 ounces
Grapefruit juice	To fill

Mixing Method: Build in a salt-rimmed collins glass (half-filled with ice cubes).

SAZARAC

Pernod: Place a splash in the glass, roll it around to coat the glass, then discard excess.	
Peychaud's Bitters	2 dashes
Simple syrup	1 teaspoon
Rye or bourbon whisky	2.0 ounces
Ice cubes, large	1 to 2 each

Garnish: lemon twist or cherry

Mixing Method: Build in an old-fashioned glass.

SCORPION

Rum	1.5 ounces
Brandy	1.5 ounces
Orange juice	3.0 ounces
Lemon juice	1.5 ounces
Orgeat (flavoring syrup)	1.5 ounces
151-proof rum	Float on top

Mixing Method: Shake/blend and strain into a collins glass (three-quarters filled with crushed ice cubes).

SCREWDRIVER

Vodka	1.5 ounces
Orange juice	To fill

Mixing Method: Build in a highball glass (half-filled with ice cubes).

SEVEN AND SEVEN

7-Crown Whisky	1.5 ounces
7-Up	To fill

Mixing Method: Build in a highball glass (three-quarters filled with ice cubes).

SIDE CAR

Brandy	1.5 ounces
Lemon juice	1.5 ounces
Triple sec	1.5 ounces

Mixing Method: Shake/blend and strain into a cocktail glass (no ice).

SINGAPORE SLING

Sweet-and-Sour Mix	1.5 ounces
Gin	1.0 ounce
Grenadine	0.5 ounce
Cherry-flavored brandy	0.5 ounce
Soda	Top glass

Garnish: cherry and orange slice

Mixing Method: Shake/blend and strain into a collins glass (half-filled with ice cubes).

STINGER

Brandy	1.5 ounces
White crème de menthe	0.75 ounce

Mixing Method: Build in a rocks glass (filled with ice cubes).

STRIP AND GO NAKED

Sweet-and-Sour Mix	1.0 ounce
Gin	1.0 ounce
Grenadine	0.5 ounce
Beer	To fill

Mixing Method: Build in a highball glass (half-filled with ice cubes).

SLOE GIN FIZZ

Sweet-and-Sour Mix	1.5 ounces
Sloe gin	1.0 ounce
Soda	Fill glass

Mixing Method: Shake/blend and strain into a highball glass (half-filled with ice cubes).

TEQUILA SUNRISE

Tequila	1.5 ounces
Orange juice	To fill
Grenadine	0.5 ounce (do not stir)

Mixing Method: Build in a highball glass (half-filled with ice cubes).

VELVET HAMMER (SILVER FOX)

White crème de cacao	0.75 ounce
Triple sec	0.75 ounce
Cream	1.5 ounces

Mixing Method: Shake/blend and strain into a cocktail glass (no ice).

VODKA MARTINI

Vodka	2.0 ounces
Dry vermouth	0.25 ounce

Garnish: olive

Mixing Method: Stir and strain into a cocktail glass (no ice).

WHITE RUSSIAN

Vodka	1.5 ounces
Kahlua	0.5 ounce
Milk (or half-and-half)	Fill to three-quarters

Mixing Method: Build in a highball glass (filled with ice cubes).

ZOMBIE

Sweet-and-Sour Mix	1.0 ounce
Orange juice	1.0 ounce
Grenadine	0.5 ounce
Light rum	1.0 ounce
Amber rum	0.5 ounce
Jamaica rum	0.5 ounce
Cherry-flavored brandy	Dash
151-proof rum	0.75 ounce (Top drink, do not stir)

Garnish: green and red cherry, orange slice, and straws

Mixing Method: Shake/blend and strain into a collins glass (half-filled with ice cubes).

READING
WINE LABELS

This appendix contains 25 largely fictitious sample labels for typical French, German, and Italian wines, along with explanatory text describing how to read, interpret, and understand the various label elements.

Except for the label shown on page 317, all the Bordeaux labels are fictitious; if they resemble an actual property or proprieter, it is merely coincidental. None of the Burgundy labels represent actual owners of specific properties, although the regions and vineyards named are authentic. The German regions and vineyards are actual, but the corresponding proprietors are fictitious. And the Italian labels represent only actual regions, not owners or wine forms.

READING FRENCH WINE LABELS—1

☐ 1982
☐ BORDEAUX BLANC
☐ APPELLATION   BORDEAUX   CONTRÔLÉE

—————— Bottled and Shipped by: ——————

☐   Pierre LaBreque
Negociant A Bordeaux (Gironde) France

---

1. *1982:* The vintage year. Regulations require a minimum of 95%. The 5% is allowed for "topping up" the barrels during maturation.

2. *Bordeaux Blanc:* Simply means "white wine from Bordeaux."

3. *Appellation Bordeaux Contrôlée:* This is the key phrase on the label. It indicates that the wine is an Appellation Contrôlée wine, but that the wine can come from grapes grown anywhere in Bordeaux. The less specific the location, the less stringent are the regulations and the less the buyer knows about what is in the bottle.

4. *Bottled and Shipped by Pierre LaBreque, Negociant A Bordeaux (Gironde) France:* Pierre LaBreque bought and bottled the wine. He is a marketer of wine as opposed to a maker. He is in business in Bordeaux. Gironde is the French Department in which Bordeaux is located.

READING FRENCH WINE LABELS—2

---

① 1982

② BORDEAUX SUPÉRIEUR

③ APPELLATION BORDEAUX SUPÉRIEUR CONTRÔLÉE

Bottled and Shipped by:

④ **Pierre LaBreque**

Negociant A Bordeaux (Gironde) France

---

1. *1982:* The vintage year. Regulations require a minimum of 95%.

2. *Bordeaux Supérieur:* The name of the wine.

3. *Appellation Bordeaux Supérieur Contrôlée:* This wine has slightly more stringent requirements than does a wine labeled with an AC of Bordeaux.

4. *Bottled and Shipped by Pierre LaBreque, Negociant A Bordeaux (Gironde) France:* Pierre LaBreque bought and bottled the wine.

READING FRENCH WINE LABELS—3

1️⃣ **SAINT - ÉMILION**

2️⃣ **Appellation Contrôlée**

3️⃣
1982

4️⃣ Produced and Bottled by

Georges Ducasse & Fils — Bordeaux

1. *Saint-Émilion:* A regional wine. The grapes came from one of the most prestigious regions in Bordeaux—St. Émilion.

2. *Appellation Contrôlée:* This phrase, when it appears under the region has the same meaning as when it brackets the region. For example: Appellation Saint-Émilion Contrôlée. This is a more meaningful label for two reasons: the region is highly regarded, and the geographical designation is more specific than simply Bordeaux. The buyer knows more about the type and style of wine.

3. *1982:* The vintage year.

4. *Produced and Bottled by Georges Ducasse & Fils—Bordeaux:* The firm of Georges Ducasse and Sons (Fils) both made and bottled the wine. They are located in Bordeaux.

READING FRENCH WINE LABELS–4

1 CHÂTEAU BRUNÉT
2 APPELLATION MÉDOC CONTRÔLÉE
3 1985

4 *Mis en Boutilles au Château*
5 C. Mileau
Propriétaire A Médoc (Gironde)

1. *Château Brunét:* A vineyard or property. In Bordeaux, Château is legally used in this sense regardless of whether or not there is a castle or grand house on the property.

2. *Appellation Médoc Contrôlée:* The vineyard is located somewhere in the Médoc. It may even be in one of the communes (towns/villages) in the Médoc, but it does not meet the more stringent regulations required for those appellations.

3. *1985:* The vintage year.

4. *Mis en Boutilles au Château:* This is the official Bordeaux term for estate bottled wine. The grapes were grown on the named property, vinified into wine there, and bottled there. This phrase is often interpreted as a guarantee of quality, but it is a guarantee only of authenticity of origin. If the property happens to be a great one, the term does indeed connote quality, but with an inferior vineyard it is meaningless and, with an unknown one, it does not provide much information.

5. *C. Mileau, Propriétaire A Médoc (Gironde):* The owner and location.

READING FRENCH WINE LABELS–5

1 **CHÂTEAU GASPARDIN**
2 **Appellation Haut Médoc Contrôlée**
3 **1985**

4 *Mis en Boutilles au Château*
5 **Jean Lautrec**
Propriétaire A Médoc (Gironde)

1. *Château Gaspardin:* The property.

2. *Appellation Haut Médoc Contrôlée:* This is a more specific *appellation* than Médoc. The Haut Médoc is the better portion of the Médoc. Consequently, this is a more meaningful *appellation* than the previous one.

3. *1985:* The vintage year.

4. *Mis en Boutilles au Château:* Château (estate) bottled.

5. *Jean Lautrec, Propriétaire A Médoc (Gironde):* The owner and location.

READING FRENCH WINE LABELS–6

1️⃣ **CHÂTEAU LE BLANC**
2️⃣ **ST. JULIEN**
Appellation Contrôlée
3️⃣1985

4️⃣ **Francis Peyron**
Propriétaire A St. Julien (Gironde)
5️⃣ *Mis en Boutilles au Château*

1. *Château Le Blanc:* The property.

2. *St. Julien—Appellation Contrôlée:* This is a more specific *appellation* than Médoc or Haut Médoc. St. Julien is a commune in Haut Médoc, one of the four most famous and highest classified ones. There are many officially rated properties in Saint-Julien, but this is not one of them. It could still be a fine wine, however, since it has to meet the production requirements of Saint-Julien, which are more stringent than those of the Médoc or Haut Médoc. The most delimited *appellation* that can be used in Bordeaux is the commune; vineyards, unlike in some other regions in France, are not entitled to their own AC.

3. *1985:* Vintage year.

4. *Francis Peyron—Propriétaire A St. Julien (Gironde):* Owner and location.

5. *Mis en Boutilles au Château:* Estate bottled.

READING FRENCH WINE LABELS—7

[1]

[2]

[3]

[4]

[5]

[6]

[7]

> GRAND CRU CLASSÉ EN 1855
>
> CHÂTEAU
> # BRANE-CANTENAC
> MARGAUX
> ## 1970
> APPELLATION MARGAUX CONTRÔLÉE

L. LURTON, PROPRIÉTAIRE A CANTENAC—GIRONDE

MIS EN BOUTILLES AU CHÂTEAU

1. *Grand Cru Classé en 1855:* This is a legal phrase indicating a wine that was officially classified in 1855 when sixty-one properties, out of thousands in the Médoc, were ranked in five growths. One vineyard in the Graves region, Château Haut-Brion, was included simply because it was too highly regarded to omit. Brane-Cantenac was ranked as a second growth.

2. *Château Brane-Cantenac:* The name of the vineyard.

3. *Margaux:* The name of the commune or town that Château Brane-Cantenac is located in. Margaux is the southernmost of the four great Médoc Communes: Saint-Estéphe, Pauillac, Saint-Julien, and Margaux. This is the most delimited *appellation* that can be used in Bordeaux.

4. *1970:* The vintage year.

5. *Appellation Margaux Contrôlée:* The AC.

6. *L. Lurton, Propriétaire A Cantenac—Gironde:* L. Lurton is the owner of Brane-Cantenac. He is located in Cantenac, which is part of Margaux.

7. *Mis en Boutilles au Château:* Brane-Cantenac is estate bottled.

READING FRENCH WINE LABELS—8

1	# BOURGOGNE ROUGE
2	### Appellation Contrôlée
3	## 1986
4	### *JEAN DUPRÉ*
	Négociant A Nuits-St-Georges (Cote-D'or)

1. *Bourgogne Rouge:* Red wine from Burgundy. It must be from the Pinot Noir grape, but the restrictions on yield and minimum alcohol requirements are not stringent.

2. *Appellation Contrôlée:* The AC.

3. *1986:* The vintage year.

4. *Jean Dupré, Négociant A Nuits-St-Georges (Côte-D'Or):* Jean Dupré bought and bottled the wine. His business is located in Nuits-St-Georges, a commune in the Côte d'Or region of Burgundy.

READING FRENCH WINE LABELS—9

1
2
3
4

COTE DE NUITS - VILLAGES

Appellation Contrôlée

1985

JEAN DUPRÉ

Négociant A Nuits-St-Georges (Cote-D'or)

1. *Côte de Nuits—Villages:* This is a more specific *appellation* than the previous one (Bourgogne Rouge). The grapes must have been grown in the villages (towns) of the Côte de Nuits, the northern portion of the prestigious Côte d'Or section of Burgundy. The allowable yield is reduced relative to the previous wine, and the alcohol requirement is increased.

2. *Appellation Côntrolée:* The AC.

3. *1985:* The vintage year.

4. *Jean Dupré, Négociant A Nuits-St-Georges (Côte D'Or):* Bottler and location.

READING FRENCH WINE LABELS—10

1 | **GEVREY - CHAMBERTIN**

2 | **Appellation Contrôlée**

3 | **1985**

4 | *JEAN DUPRÉ*

Négociant A Nuits-St-Georges (Côte-D'or)

1. *Gevrey-Chambertin:* More specific than Côte de Nuits—Villages. Gevrey-Chambertin is a commune, or village, in the Côte de Nuits. It is, along with Vosne-Romanée, the most highly regarded of the red Burgundy villages. The regulations regarding yield and alcohol remain the same as with the previous "Villages" wine, but the more restricted growing area provides additional information about the wine—along with increased prestige and price.

2. *Appellation Côntrôlée:* The AC.

3. *1985:* The vintage year.

4. *Jean Dupré, Négociant A Nuits-St-Georges (Côte D'Or):* Bottler and location.

READING FRENCH WINE LABELS—11

```
┌──────────────────────────────────────────────────┐
│  1  │  VOSNE - ROMANÉE 1ᵉʳ CRU                    │
│  2  │  Appellation Contrôlée                       │
│  3  │  1985                                        │
│  4  │  Mise du Domaine                             │
│  5  │  Domaine CLAUDE ROCHAT                       │
│  6  │  Propriétaire A Vosne-Romanée, Côte D'Or    │
└──────────────────────────────────────────────────┘
```

1. *Vosne-Romanée 1er Cru:* This indicates not only that the wine is from one commune, as in the previous example, but that all the grapes were grown in vineyards officially classified as *premier cru* vineyards. This is the second-highest ranking in Burgundy. Because it is common for Burgundian owners to fragment their holdings, a vintner may not own enough of any one vineyard to make sufficient wine for commercial purposes. In that case, vintners can combine the wine made from grapes grown in several vineyards. If they are all *premier cru* vineyards, they are entitled to the *premier cru* appellation.

2. *Appellation Contrôlée:* The AC. It can be below the phrase "Vosne-Romanée," as here, or it could bracket it (Appellation Vosne-Romanée Premier Cru Contrôlée).

3. *1985:* The vintage year.

4. *Mise du Domaine:* This is the equivalent of "mis en boutilles au château" in Bordeaux. Mise du Domaine, outside of Bordeaux, is the phrase most generally used with French wines to indicate estate bottling.

5. *Domaine Claude Rochat:* The owner of the vineyard plots.

6. *Propriétaire A Vosne-Romanée, Côte D'Or:* Location.

READING FRENCH WINE LABELS—12

1	
	## NUIT-SAINT-GEORGES CLOS DE L'ARLOT
2	**Appellation Nuits-St-Georges Contrôlée**
3	## 1985
4	**Mise du Domaine**
5	***Domaine BERNARD GROS***
6	Propriétaire A Nuits-St-Georges, Côte D'Or

1. *Nuits-Saint-Georges, Clos de l'Arlot:* This wine is from a single *premier cru* vineyard—the Clos de l'Arlot. The commune name must appear with the vineyard, although the vineyard type size is permitted to be the same as that of the commune.

2. *Appellation Nuits-St-Georges Contrôlée:* The commune AC is the most delimited allowed to a *premier cru* property.

3. *1985:* The vintage year.

4. *Mise du Domaine:* Estate bottled.

5. *Domaine Bernard Gros:* The owner of a portion of the Clos de l'Arlot vineyard. One of the many differences between Burgundy and Bordeaux is that vineyard ownership in Burgundy is fragmented, whereas in Bordeaux, the entire vineyard is owned by one individual or firm.

6. *Propriétaire A Nuits-St-Georges, Côte D'Or:* Indicates that Bernard Gros is an owner whose business is located in Nuits-St-Georges in the Côte D'Or.

READING FRENCH WINE LABELS—13

1	**CHAMBERTIN**
2	APPELLATION CÔNTROLÉE
3	**1984**
4	***DOMAINE JACQUES CLARET*** Propriétaire A Gevrey-Chambertin, Côte D'Or
5	**Mise du Domaine**

1. *Chambertin:* This is a *grand cru* vineyard, the top rank in the Burgundian system of classifying vineyards. *Grand cru* properties are given their own Appellation Contrôlée; they do not have to list the name of the commune on the label. What makes this confusing is that many of the communes have added the name of the most famous vineyard to the commune name. Thus, we have the villages of Gevrey-Chambertin, Vosne-Romanée, Puligny-Montrachet, Chassagne-Montrachet (both share the legendary Le Montrachet), Aloxe-Corton, and so forth. In the case of Chambertin, the labeling is even more confusing, because several other *grand cru* vineyards in Gevrey-Chambertin have added Chambertin to their own names (Chapelle-Chambertin, Charmes-Chambertin, Griotte-Chambertin, Latriciéres Chambertin, Mazis-Chambertin, Mazoyéres-Chambertin, and Ruchottes-Chambertin; all *grand cru* vine-yards, but considered a little below Le Chambertin).

2. *Appellation Contrôlée:* The AC.

3. *1984:* Vintage year.

4. *Domaine Jacques Claret, Propriétaire A Gevrey-Chambertin, Côte D'Or:* Owner and location.

5. *Mise du Domaine:* Estate bottled.

READING GERMAN WINE LABELS—1

DEUTSCHER
TAFELWEIN

MOSEL

1987

BEREICHE BERNKASTEL

BOTTLED AND SHIPPED BY

ULLMANN WEINKELLEREI, GRAACH

1. *Deutscher Tafelwein:* The wine must be made from 100 percent German grapes.

2. *Mosel:* One of the five Tafelwein regions. Wine of this quality level cannot use one of the eleven quality wine region names (Gebiete).

3. *1987:* At least 85 percent of the wine must have come from the 1987 harvest.

4. *Bereiche Bernkastel:* At this quality level, neither the Grosslage nor the Einzellage (if the wine even comes from a specific Grosslage or Einzellage) can be named.

5. *Ullmann Weinkellerei Graach:* The bottler must be named. Graach is the town where Ullmann is located.

READING GERMAN WINE LABELS—2

1 QUALITÄTSWEIN

A.P.Nr. 2 602 034 05 87
2

3
𝔐𝔒𝔖𝔈𝔏-
𝔖𝔞𝔞𝔯-
𝔯𝔲𝔴𝔢𝔯

4 1986
5 GRAACHER HIMMELREICH
6 RIESLING
7 BOTTLED AND SHIPPED BY
ULLMANN WEINKELLEREI, GRAACH

1. *Qualitätswein:* Wine thus labeled (or as Qualitätswein b.a.) must conform to the restrictions and come from one of the eleven Anbaugebiete.

2. *A.P. Number:* This is the control number given by the government following testing.

3. *Mosel-Saar-Ruwer:* One of the eleven Anbaugebiete.

4. *1986:* A minimum of 85 percent of the grapes have to be from the 1986 vintage.

5. *Graacher Himmelreich:* The village or town comes first (with an *er* on the end) followed either by the Grosslage or Einzellage. In this case, the wine is from the Himmelreich vineyard (Einzellage) located in the town of Graach.

6. *Riesling:* A minimum of 85 percent of the wine must be from the Riesling grape.

7. *Ullmann Weinkellerei, Graach:* The bottler must be named. Graach is the town where Ullmann is located.

READING GERMAN WINE LABELS—3

[3] MOSEL-SAAR-RUWER

[1] QUALITÄTSWEIN
A.P. Nr. 2 602 034 05 87
[2]

[4] 1986

[5] GRAACHER MÜNZLAY

[6] RIESLING

[7] BOTTLED AND SHIPPED BY
ULLMANN WEINKELLEREI, GRAACH

1. *Qualitätswein:* Wine thus labeled (or as Qualitätswein b.a.) must conform to the restrictions and come from one of the eleven Anbaugebiete.

2. *A.P. Number:* This is the control number given by the government following testing.

3. *Mosel-Saar-Ruwer:* One of the eleven Anbaugebiete.

4. *1986:* A minimum of 85 percent of the grapes have to be from the 1986 vintage.

5. *Graacher Münzlay:* The village or town comes first (with an *er* on the end) followed either by the Grosslage or Einzellage. In this case, the wine is from the Münzlay Grosslage located in the town of Graach.

6. *Riesling:* A minimum of 85 percent of the wine must be from the Riesling grape.

7. *Ullmann Weinkellerei, Graach:* The bottler must be named. Graach is the town where Ullmann is located.

READING GERMAN WINE LABELS—4

1. *Qualitätswein:* Wine thus labeled (or as Qualitätswein b.a.) must conform to the restrictions and come from one of the eleven Anbaugebiete.

2. *A.P. Number:* This is the control number given by the government following testing.

3. *Mosel-Saar-Ruwer:* One of the eleven Anbaugebiete.

4. *1986:* A minimum of 85 percent of the grapes have to be from the 1986 vintage.

5. *Ürziger Würzgarten:* The village or town comes first (with an *er* on the end) followed either by the Grosslage or Einzellage. In this case, the wine is from the Würzgarten vineyard (Einzellage) located in the town of Ürzig.

6. *Riesling:* A minimum of 85 percent of the wine must be from the Riesling grape.

7. *Ullmann Weinkellerei, Graach:* The bottler must be named. Graach is the town where Ullmann is located.

READING GERMAN WINE LABELS—5

[3] **MOSEL-SAAR-RUWER**

[1] **QUALITÄTSWEIN**
A.P. Nr. 2 602 034 05 87
[2]

[4] **1986**
[5] **ÜRZIGER SCHWARZLAY**
[6] **RIESLING**
[7] **BOTTLED AND SHIPPED BY**
ULLMANN WEINKELLEREI, GRAACH

1. *Qualitätswein:* Wine thus labeled (or as Qualitätswein b.a.) must conform to the restrictions and come from one of the eleven Anbaugebiete.

2. *A.P. Number:* This is the control number given by the government following testing.

3. *Mosel-Saar-Ruwer:* One of the eleven Anbaugebiete.

4. *1986:* A minimum of 85 percent of the grapes have to be from the 1986 vintage.

5. *Ürziger Schwarzlay:* The village or town comes first (with an *er* on the end) followed either by the Grosslage or Einzellage. In this case, the wine is from the Schwarzlay Grosslagen located in the town of Ürzig.

6. *Riesling:* A minimum of 85 percent of the wine must be from the Riesling grape.

7. *Ullmann Weinkellerei, Graach:* The bottler must be named. Graach is the town where Ullmann is located.

READING GERMAN WINE LABELS—6

RHEINGAU [3]   [1]QUALITÄTSWEIN MIT PRÄDIKAT

A.P. Nr. 2 602 034 05 87 [2]

[4]**1986er**

[5]HOCHHEIMER HÖLLE

[6] *RIESLING KABINETT*

[7]**ERZEUGERABFÜLLUNG**

[8]**GRAF VON ERLICHE, JOANNISBERG**

1. *Qualitätswein mit Prädikat:* The highest quality level; never sugared.

2. *A.P. Number:* Control number; all quality wine must have it.

3. *Rheingau:* One of the eleven Anbaugebiete.

4. *1986er:* At least 85 percent of the grapes must be from the named harvest. It is not uncommon to place an *er* on the vintage year.

5. *Hochheimer Hölle:* The grapes are from the Hölle vineyard in the town of Hochheim.

6. *Riesling Kabinett:* The grape variety and the Prädikat. They are often together.

7. *Erzeugerabfüllung:* The German term for estate bottled.

8. *Graf Von Erliche, Johannisberg:* The bottler and location.

READING GERMAN WINE LABELS—7

[3] RHEINGAU

[1] QUALITÄTSWEIN MIT PRÄDIKAT

A.P. Nr. 2 602 034 05 87
[2]

[4] 1986er
[5] ERBACHER MARCOBRUNN
[6] RIESLING BEERENAUSLESE
[7] ERZEUGERABFÜLLUNG
[8] GRAF VON ERLICHE, JOANNISBERG

1. *Qualitätswein mit Prädikat:* The highest quality level; never sugared.

2. *A.P. Number:* Control number.

3. *Rheingau:* One of the eleven Anbaugebiete.

4. *1986er:* At least 85 percent of the grapes must be from the named harvest.

5. *Erbacher Marcobrunn:* The grapes are from the Marcobrunn vineyard in the town of Erbach.

6. *Riesling Beerenauslese:* The grape variety and the Prädikat.

7. *Erzeugerabfüllung:* Estate bottled. The producer grew the grapes and made and bottled the wine.

8. *Graf von Erliche, Johannisberg:* Producer or bottler and location.

READING ITALIAN WINE LABELS—1

[1] # VALPOLICELLA
[2] **DENOMINAZIONE D'ORIGINE CONTROLLATA**

[3] Annata **1987**

[4]   —————— CASA VINICOLA ——————
[5]   **FRATELLI BOSCA**
    —————— **VERONA** ——————

1. *Valpolicella:* Name of wine. Italian wines can be named for an area, as in this case, for the grape from which they were made, or for a proprietary name.

2. *Denominazione d'Origine Controllata:* The basic regulatory system for the traditional Italian wines. There are very specific rules established as to the grape varieties permitted, the alcoholic content, the yield, and the wine-making practices.

3. *Annata 1987:* The vintage year.

4. *Casa Vinicola:* A wine company; generally one that makes wine from grapes it has purchased.

5. *Fratelli Bosca, Verona:* Producer and location.

READING ITALIAN WINE LABELS—2

[1] **SOAVE**
[2] **CLASSICO**
[3] **DENOMINAZIONE D'ORIGINE CONTROLLATA**

[4] **Annata 1987**

[5] ——— CASA VINICOLA ———
[6] **FRATELLI BOSCA**
——— VERONA ———

1. *Soave:* The name of the wine. Soave has legally defined geographical boundaries.

2. *Classico:* The heart, or most favored sector, of the region.

3. *Denominazione d'Origine Controllata:* The DOC.

4. *Annata 1987:* The vintage year.

5. *Casa Vinicola:* A wine company.

6. *Fratelli Bosca, Verona:* Producer and location.

READING ITALIAN WINE LABELS—3

① SOAVE
② CLASSICO SUPERIORE
③ DENOMINAZIONE D'ORIGINE CONTROLLATA

④ Annata 1987

⑤ ┌─────── CASA VINICOLA ───────┐
⑥ │   **FRATELLI BOSCA**   │
     └─────────── VERONA ───────────┘

1. *Soave:* The name of the wine. Soave has legally defined geographical boundaries.

2. *Classico Superiore:* The wine not only comes from the most desirable section of the Soave region, but also is designated as superior under DOC rules. It typically has a higher alcohol requirement.

3. *Denominazione d'Origine Controllata:* The DOC.

4. *Annata 1987:* The vintage year.

5. *Casa Vinicola:* A wine company.

6. *Fratelli Bosca, Verona:* Producer and location.

READING ITALIAN WINE LABELS—4

⒈CHIANTI CLASSICO
⒉RISERVA
⒊DENOMINAZIONE D'ORIGINE CONTROLLATA GARANTITA

⒋ VILLA BELLINI
⒌1987

⒍ **Imbottigliato dal**
Produttore all'Origine

⒎**SERGIO ALBANI**
Firenze

---

1. *Chianti Classico:* The wine is from the Classico region of Chianti.

2. *Riserva:* The wine has been given additional aging. The specific amount is regulated by the DOC.

3. *Denominazione d'Origine Controllata Garantita:* The wine is a DOCG, the most prestigious classification for Italian wines. Only five wines are in this category.

4. *Villa Bellini:* The name of the winery.

5. *1987:* The vintage year.

6. *Imbottigliato dal Produttore all'Origine:* The preferred term for estate-bottled wines.

7. *Sergio Albani, Firenze:* Name of the owner and location of the firm.

READING ITALIAN WINE LABELS—5

[1]VENEGAZZÚ

[2] PINOT BIANCO

1985 [3]

**[4] IMBOTTIGLIATO DAL
PRODUTTORE ALL'ORIGINE**

[5]

Vino da
Tabola

[6] GIORGIO VASPARINI
Venegazzú Del Montello

1. *Venegazzú:* The name of the wine.

2. *Pinot Bianco:* The wine was made from the white Pinot (Pinot Blanc in France).

3. *1985:* The vintage year.

4. *Imbottigliato dal Produttore all'Origine:* Estate bottled.

5. *Vino da Tabola:* This is not a DOC wine; it translates simply as "table wine." DOC can be viewed as representing the traditional wines of Italy. Wines made in nontraditional areas or with nonregulated grapes cannot be DOC and must be declassified to Vino da Tavola. Many fine wines and a few extraordinary ones are labeled only as table wines.

6. *Giorgio Vasparini, Venegazzú Del Montello:* Producer and location.

INDEX